ROBERT SOUTHEY

ROBERT SOUTHEY

ENTIRE MAN OF LETTERS

W. A. SPECK

YALE UNIVERSITY PRESS
NEW HAVEN AND LONDON

For information about this and other Yale University Press publications, please contact:
U.S. Office: sales.press@yale.edu   yalebooks.com
Europe Office: sales@yaleup.co.uk   www.yalebooks.co.uk

Set in Garamond by J&L Composition, Filey, North Yorkshire
Printed in Great Britain by St Edmundsbury Press Ltd, Bury St Edmunds

Library of Congress Cataloging-in-Publication Data
Speck, W. A. (William Arthur), 1938–
  Robert Southey: entire man of letters/W. A. Speck.
    p.cm.
  Includes bibliographical references and index.
  ISBN 0–300–11681–0 (cl.: alk. paper)
  1. Southey, Robert, 1774–1843. 2. Authors, English—19th century—Biography. 1. Title.
PR5466.S67 2006
821'.7—dc22
                                                                    2006002193

A catalogue record for this book is available from the British Library

10 9 8 7 6 5 4 3 2 1

Published with assistance from the Annie Burr Lewis Fund.

For Mary,
And to the Memory of Robert Woof

Contents

List of Illustrations ix
Family Tree xi
Preface xiii
Acknowledgements xvii

Part I: 'A morning of ardour and of hope'

1. Schoolboy (1774–1792) 3
2. Student (1792–1794) 24
3. Pantisocrat (1794–1795) 42
4. 'Jacobin' (1795–1800) 62
5. 'Shuttlecock of Fortune' (1800–1803) 83

Part II: 'A day of clouds and storms'

6. Laker (1803–1807) 101
7. Lake Poet (1807–1809) 119
8. 'Historiographer to Mr Ballantyne' (1809–1813) 136
9. Poet Laureate (1813–1816) 154
10. 'Apostate' (1817–1822) 169
11. 'The most powerful literary supporter of the Tories' (1822–1829) 189
12. 'The Doctor' (1829–1834) 208

Part III: 'An evening of gloom closed in by premature darkness'

13. Widower (1834–1837) 229
14. Old Man (1837–1839) 240
15. Epilogue 251

Abbreviations 257
Notes 259
Bibliographical Note 291
Index 295

Illustrations

1. John James Masquerier, *Robert Southey* (*c.* 1798). By permission of Historical Portraits Ltd.

2. John Downman, *Edith Southey* (1812). From the frontispiece of the second volume of C. C. Southey (ed.), *The Life and Correspondence of Robert Southey* (2 volumes, London, 1850).

3. James Sharples, *Robert Southey* (1795). By permission of Bristol's Museums, Galleries and Archives.

4. Southey's bookplate. By permission of Devon Library and Information Services.

5. James Gillray, *New Morality* (1798), detail. By permission of the National Portrait Gallery, London.

6. William Henry Egleton, engraving after John Opie, *Robert Southey* (1806). By permission of the Wordsworth Trust.

7. John Downman, *Robert Southey* (1812). By permission of the Wordsworth Trust.

8. Samuel Lane, *Robert Southey* (1824). By permission of Balliol College, Oxford.

9. Sir Thomas Lawrence, *Samuel Taylor Coleridge* (1828). By permission of the South African National Gallery, Cape Town.

10. Portrait after James Northcote, *Robert Southey* (1804). By permission of the Wordsworth Trust.

11. Henry Edridge, *William Wordsworth* (1806). By permission of the Wordsworth Trust.

12. John Hoppner, *William Gifford* (*c.* 1800). By permission of the National Portrait Gallery, London.

13. William Fisher, *Walter Savage Landor* (1839). By permission of the National Portrait Gallery, London.

14. William Owen, *John Wilson Croker* (*c.* 1812). By permission of the National Portrait Gallery, London.

15. Robert Hancock, *Joseph Cottle* (1800). By permission of the National Portrait Gallery, London.

16. Miss Turner, *John Rickman* (1831), after Samuel Lane. By permission of the National Portrait Gallery, London.

17. William James Ward, *Charles Watkin Williams Wynn* (1835), after Sir Martin Archer Shee. By permission of the National Portrait Gallery, London.

18. Caroline Bowles, *Self-Portrait* (undated). By permission of the Wordsworth Trust.

19. Caroline Bowles, *South Window of Study, Greta Hall* (1841). By permission of the Wordsworth Trust.

20. W. J. Wheeler, *The 'Cottonian Library'* (1926), from sketches made by Hannah Felloby in 1838. By permission of the Wordsworth Trust.

21. Caroline Bowles, *Greta Hall* (undated). By permission of the Wordsworth Trust.

22. John Graham Lough, Effigy of Robert Southey, Crosthwaite Parish Church. Photograph by Ian C. Mason.

23. Edward Nash, *Robert Southey, 'reartraiture'*. From the frontispiece of Robert Southey, *The Doctor*, edited by John Wood Warter (London, 1848).

Family Tree

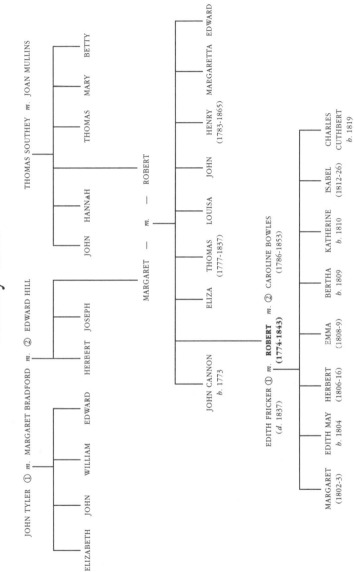

Preface

I began to write this Preface sitting at a desk in Robert Southey's study in Greta Hall. The view from the window where he himself sat, even though Keswick has grown since he lived in the house so that the lake is now scarcely visible, is still stunning. Castle Head, 'the very nose in the face in the prospect' as he described it, is directly ahead, with the dramatic backdrop of the mountains that surround Derwentwater.[1] He conjured up the scene as he gazed at it when the news of George III's death reached him in 1820.[2]

> Pensive, though not in thought, I stood at the window, beholding
> Mountain and lake and vale; the valley disrobed of its verdure;
> Derwent retaining yet from eve a glassy reflection
> Where his expanded breast, then still and smooth as a mirror,
> Under the woods reposed; the hills that, calm and majestic,
> Lifted their heads in the silent sky, from far Glaramara
> Bleacrag, and Maidenmawr, to Grizedal and westermost Withop.
> Dark and distinct they rose.

Southey was surveying the view 'at that sober hour when the light of day is receding'. He remarked how, with the twilight

> from surrounding things the hues wherewith day has adorn'd them
> Fade, like the hopes of youth.

At forty-six the Poet Laureate, executing his duties with an obituary poem to the dead king, was himself no longer young. Indeed his own youthful hopes had faded long ago.

In a review of Barré Charles Roberts' *Letters and Miscellaneous Papers* published in 1815, Southey observed 'A morning of ardour and of hope; a day of clouds and storms; an evening of gloom closed in by premature darkness: such is the melancholy sum the biography of a man of letters almost uniformly presents.'[3] This was an uncanny premonition of the stages of his own career, which I have used to mark out the key periods in his life. His 'morning of ardour and of hope' extended from his birth in Bristol in 1774 to his arrival at Greta Hall on 7 September 1803; the 'day of clouds and storms' lasted until his wife Edith succumbed to dementia in 1834; the 'evening of gloom' began with her illness and death, and was briefly brightened by his marriage to his second wife Caroline Bowles in 1839; but 'premature darkness' closed in shortly after they returned from their honeymoon to Greta Hall, when he slipped into senility.

Southey would have denied that the time he spent in Keswick with his first wife Edith Fricker was equivalent to a stormy day. On the contrary, he assured his friend John May in July 1820 that 'I have lived in the sunshine, and am still looking forward with hope.'[4] This claim, which he repeated to others, was in the first of a series of autobiographical letters that he wrote to May. Southey's voluminous correspondence is the main evidence the biographer has available for his career – yet it would be hazardous to rely on his word alone for it. He was quite capable of inventing versions of himself for his correspondents, and even for himself. As we shall see in the account he gave of his boyhood to May, which is the sole source for much of the information about his early years, his letters could be very misleading. He might even have deceived himself into believing that he had led a charmed life. There is often an air of him whistling in the dark, or laughing to keep from crying. And there was plenty to cry about. 'Death has so often entered my doors', he confessed in 1816 when his only son Herbert died at the age of nine, 'that he and I have long been familiar. The loss of five brothers and sisters (four of whom I remember well) of my father and mother, of a female cousin who grew up with me, of two daughters before this last and severest affliction.'[5] He never got over the death of Herbert. The loss of another daughter, Isabel, in 1826 affected his wife more than himself, deepening the depression she had suffered all her life, though Edith's melancholia and her lack of humour certainly darkened the day of clouds and storms. Superficially, Southey was a simple scholarly man, contented with his lot. But underneath there was a great deal of suppressed rage against his fate: 'The truth is', he himself acknowledged, 'that though some persons, whose knowledge of me is scarcely skin-deep, suppose I have no nerves, because I have great self-control as far as regards the surface; if it were not for great self-management, and what may be called a strict intellectual regimen, I should very soon be in a deplorable state of what is called nervous disease.'[6]

Thomas Carlyle saw beneath the surface when he met Southey in February 1835. His first impression was of a man 'with very much of the militant in his aspect – in the eyes especially was visible a mixture of sorrow and of anger, or of angry contempt, as if his indignant fight with the world had not yet ended in victory, but also never should in defeat.' On a second acquaintance a few days later he deliberately introduced the subject of Thomas De Quincey into the conversation, aware that it was sensitive to Southey, who disliked the man. But Carlyle was not prepared for the violence of his reaction. 'Southey's face, as I looked at it, was become of slate colour, the eyes glancing, the attitude rigid, the figure altogether a picture of Rhadamanthine rage – that is, rage conscious to itself of being just.' Southey felt that De Quincey's exposure in print of Coleridge's opium habit was a treacherous betrayal of the hospitality he had received from the Lake Poets. Carlyle was taken aback by the rapidity with which Southey's features could move from an 'amiable red blush, beautiful like a young girl's, when you touched genially the pleasant theme' to a 'serpent-like flash of blue or black blush . . . when you struck upon the opposite'. He asked himself, 'How has this man contrived, with such a nervous system, to keep alive for nearly sixty years? Now blushing under his grey hairs, rosy like a maiden of fifteen; now slaty almost, like a rattle-snake or fiery serpent? How has he not been torn to pieces long since, under such furious pulling this way and that?' He suspected that the answer lay partly in the strict regimen that Southey imposed upon himself. It was as if he had told himself: 'You are capable of running mad, if you don't take care. Acquire habitudes; stick firm as adamant to them at all times, and work, continually work!'[7]

Certainly he had a clockwork routine that many visitors to Greta Hall observed. De Quincey himself noted that 'a certain task he prescribed to himself every morning before breakfast . . . from breakfast to a latish dinner (about half after five or six) was his main period of literary toil, after dinner . . . being dedicated to his correspondence.'[8] One of the tasks Southey gave himself before breakfast was writing verse, 'at which time nine tenths of Thalaba, Madoc, Kehama and Roderick were written'.[9] 'Imagine me in this great study of mine', he wrote a few months after his arrival in Keswick, 'from breakfast till dinner till tea, and from tea till supper, in my old black cravat and my corduroys alternately with my long worsted pantaloons . . . sitting at my desk, and you have my picture and my history.'[10] He would work on his poems for a set number of hours, then turn to history and biography, then to his reviewing and finally to his correspondence.

His poetry included *Joan of Arc, Thalaba the Destroyer, Madoc, The Curse of Kehama* and *Roderick the last of the Goths*. After *Roderick* appeared in 1814, apart from writing poems in fulfilment of his duties as Poet Laureate, his poetic output was slight in relation to his historical works. Thus his *History of Brazil* was published in three volumes between 1810 and 1819, and his

History of the Peninsular War, also in three volumes, came out between 1823 and 1832. Southey's *Book of the Church* (1824) was a contribution to ecclesiastical history, as well as a polemic to justify the Church of England, while *Sir Thomas More, or Colloquies on the progress and prospects of Society* (1829) used historical parallels to justify his own pessimistic view of social trends. He also wrote biographies, of which the most celebrated were his *Life of Nelson* (1813) and the *Life of Wesley and the Rise and Progress of Methodism* (1820). Southey's creative and scholarly writings were, however, dwarfed by his journalism. In addition to his essays for the *Quarterly Review* he wrote much of the *Edinburgh Annual Register*, a chronicle of the years 1808 to 1811. He even produced a long, rambling novel, *The Doctor*, in the style of Laurence Sterne's *Tristram Shandy*. This was published in seven volumes between 1834 and 1847, the last two appearing posthumously. Finally, his voluminous private letters must be considered along with his other writings. In Thackeray's view they 'are worth piles of epics'.[11]

It was the sheer range of his writing that made him stand out among his contemporaries. Byron, no admirer of Southey, conceded that he was 'the only existing entire man of letters'.[12]

If Southey's contemporaries recognised his prominent place in literature, later generations failed to do so. His stock slumped as the Victorians came to regard Romanticism as the dominant influence of his era. Since Southey did not conform to their vision of a Romantic genius he was dropped from the canon, and this neglect has lasted until relatively recent times. Of late, however, his reputation has risen as students of literature have called the canon into question. His interest in oriental themes, for instance, is more central to current concerns now that orientalism and the 'other' are firmly on the literary agenda. Historians and political scientists have also rescued him from oblivion, seeing Southey as a missing link in the development of English Conservatism between Burke and Disraeli. As an 'entire man of letters', therefore, he again occupies a central place in the literary and political worlds of the early nineteenth century.

Acknowledgements

I owed the pleasure of writing the opening paragraphs of the Preface in Southey's study on 7 September 2003, the two hundredth anniversary of his own arrival there, to the hospitality of Scott Ligertwood, the present owner of Greta Hall. Southey would have been delighted to know that, after a long period when it had been a school, it has again become a family home, ringing with the joyful laughter of children, and a guest house accommodating 'Lakers'. Scott has been extremely generous in support of my work, for which I am very grateful.

There are many others whom I must thank for their help in my research. The idea of writing about Southey occurred to me while teaching a course on 'English literature and society in the long eighteenth century' at Leeds University before I took early retirement from the Chair of Modern History there in 1997. The students who attended that course, and especially those in the evening class of the part-time BA, made it the most rewarding teaching experience of my career. I became aware that Southey's reputation had suffered by contrast with his fellow 'Lake Poets' Coleridge and Wordsworth. Until Lynda Pratt published her superb *Robert Southey: Poetical Works, 1793–1810* in 2004 there were hardly any scholarly editions of his works, whereas theirs have appeared with fine critical apparatus. Again, biographies of him are few and far between compared with the many that have appeared of his better-known contemporaries. Geoffrey Carnall is one of the few scholars who have sustained a long interest in Southey, and I much appreciated exchanging views with him, and his sending me copies of his articles on Southey and Walter Savage Landor in advance of their publication in the *Oxford History of National Biography*. Otherwise Southey has been relatively neglected. I came to feel that this neglect was undue and that he deserved more attention. Others had come to the same conclusion before me, and there are signs of a revival of interest in his life and work. Two scholars who have contributed to this revival, David Eastwood and Lynda Pratt, have given a newcomer to the field friendly advice and encouragement. Lynda loaned me a copy of her Oxford D.Phil. thesis 'The Literary Career of Robert Southey 1794–1800', which was indispensable for his early years.

Southey's manuscripts lie scattered to the four winds in repositories on both sides of the Atlantic. Their locations are listed by the National Registry of Archives, an invaluable resource for scholars embarking on a new research project. Without the prompt and professional responses to my enquiries about them from archivists and librarians, mine could not have been completed. Many saved me time and expense by kindly sending me photocopies of manuscripts in their care. I am grateful to those who did so, and particularly to Alison Girling, reference librarian at the E. J. Pratt library of Victoria University in the University of Toronto; Richard Virr, Curator of Manuscripts at McGill University, Montreal; and Tara Wenger, reference librarian at the Harry Ransom Humanities Research Center at the University of Texas at Austin. Direct access to other archives was made possible thanks to an Emeritus Fellowship from the Leverhulme Trust, a Douglas W. Bryant/ASECS Fellowship from Harvard University, and a Fellowship at the Huntington Library. In 1998 I visited the Huntington, and wish to thank those there, especially Kent Clark, Carol Pearson, Roy Ritchie and Mary Robertson, who made my month in that scholarly haven – Kent would call it heaven – profitable as well as pleasant. I am also grateful to Andy and Sarah Ingersoll for their kind hospitality when I stayed with them while I was in California. A sojourn in the Bodleian Library, Oxford, in Michaelmas term 1999 was particularly pleasurable thanks to Peter Thompson and his colleagues at St Cross College, who awarded me a visiting fellowship, and John Stevenson and his colleagues at Worcester College, who provided me with a flat in Oxford. Helen Williams let me stay in her flat when I visited Edinburgh, and gave helpful advice on writing a biography. My visits to other repositories in Britain, including the British Library, Keswick Museum and the National Library of Wales, which hold major Southey collections, were facilitated by their archivists and librarians, whose assistance I gratefully acknowledge. I took up the fellowship at Harvard in the summer of 2000, and spent a delightful month working in the Houghton library. It also enabled me to visit other holdings in the United States, where again I met with courteous and friendly help, particularly from Isaac Gewirtz and Stephen S. Wagner, curators respectively of the Berg and Pforzheimer collections in New York Public Library, and Mary Huth at the University of Rochester. I wish to thank Woody Holton and his brother Dwight for providing accommodation and friendly company while I was working in libraries in New York City, and my nephew Jeffrey and his wife Karen (and my great nephew and niece Christopher and Kate), for putting me up – and up with me – in Hopkinton, Massachusetts, while I was at Harvard.

My initial forays into the archives were made before I decided to write a biography. This decision required me to revisit libraries in North America in 2004, and I again appreciated the help I received, particularly from Eric Frasier in Boston Public Library, Vanessa Pintado and Christine Nelson at the Pierpont Morgan library, and Stephen Crook, librarian of the Berg collection in New York Public Library. I also went for the first time to consult the Bertram R. Davis 'Robert Southey' collection at the University of Waterloo, Ontario. I made my pilgrimage to Waterloo in a bitterly cold week in January 2004. Susan Saunders Bellingham, head of the Special Collections Department of the library, and Warren Ober, who was instrumental in getting the valuable Davis collection housed in it, gave me a very warm welcome, which I much appreciated. I must also record my appreciation of the reception I received from the archivist of the John Murray Archive, Virginia Murray, when I visited it in Albermarle Street, London. Southey addressed about 130 letters there from Greta Hall to the first John Murray, most of them unused by previous investigators. It was particularly rewarding to read them in the house to which they had been posted.

In the summer of the year 2000 I decided to relocate from the West Riding of Yorkshire to Cumbria. The relocation was made easier when Robin Smith, then head of the Carlisle Campus of the University of Northumbria, kindly undertook to recommend me for a visiting professor-ship, which the University conferred. I am grateful to colleagues in Carlisle for the support they have given me. A problem that Southey faced when he moved to Keswick is one that I have also encountered in Carlisle – the lack of a research library in the town. The Wordsworth Library in Grasmere, however, more than compensates for the deficiency, with its unrivalled collection of printed and manuscript sources for the British Romantic period, now housed in the superb Jerwood Centre. Robert Woof, director of the Wordsworth Trust, the librarian Jeffrey Cowton and their colleagues made me very welcome there. There are some books that a Southey scholar needs to have immediately available, but are very hard to come by. Not having them to hand would have made my task extremely difficult if my old friend Geoffrey Forster, who is the librarian of Leeds Library, had not come to my aid. Leeds Library was founded in the eighteenth century – Joseph Priestley was one of Geoffrey's predecessors as librarian. I was admitted as an associate reader, which gave me the privilege of borrowing books. Geoffrey cannot be thanked enough for enabling me to put editions of works by and about Southey – some long out of print, and which rarely come on the market – on the shelves in my study.

Thanks are due to the reader of the manuscript for Yale University Press, whose thorough report made many valuable suggestions and saved me from numerous errors. If any remain they are entirely my responsibility. I also wish to thank Robert Baldock, Managing Director at Yale University Press, London, for his warm encouragement of my efforts.

Ian Mason was a great help when it came to putting the finishing touches to the book. He took photographs of Southey's effigy in Crosthwaite parish church to provide an illustration and checked proofs with me.

Throughout the research and writing I received constant support from Mary Geiter, who urged me to try to do full justice to Southey's memory. If I have come anywhere near to succeeding it is in great part due to her encouragement and suggestions. The book is dedicated to Mary in acknowledgement of, and gratitude for, all her endeavours on my behalf.

After writing these acknowledgements I learned the sad news of the death of Robert Woof. Robert used to tease me about my enthusiasm for Southey, which he did not share. He would have been amused by my dedication of this life of Southey to him too.

PART I

'A morning of ardour and of hope'

CHAPTER ONE

Schoolboy (1774–1792)

When Robert Southey was born on 12 August 1774 his mother asked the nurse if her baby was a boy. 'Ay, a great ugly boy' was the reply. 'When I saw what a great red creature it was, covered with rolls of fat', his mother was to tell him, 'I thought I should never be able to love him.'[1] Despite this inauspicious start to their relationship she became very fond of her son, and he of her. She fretted over him when at the age of two he was inoculated against smallpox. Though the inoculation was successful, preparations for it led to his changing from being 'plump and fat' into 'the lean, lank, greyhound-like creature that I have ever since continued'. Of his mother Southey observed that 'never was any human being blessed with a sweeter temper or a happier disposition. She had an excellent understanding, and a readiness of apprehension which I have rarely known surpassed. In quickness of capacity, in the kindness of her nature, and in that kind of moral magnetism which wins the affections of all within her sphere, I never knew her equal. To strangers she must have appeared much disfigured by the small pox.'

Her disfigurement had not put off Robert's father from marrying her two years earlier when she was twenty years old. While Southey tells us much about his mother, he rarely mentions his father, and consequently relatively little is known about Robert Southey senior, not even his date of birth. He was probably born in 1745 and spent his boyhood on a farm in Somerset. After serving an apprenticeship with a London grocer he returned to the West Country when his master died and for the next twelve or fourteen years was an assistant to a draper in Bristol. He then went into business with his brother Thomas, opening a draper's shop in Wine Street. Their sign was a hare, which Southey recalled fondly since his father had been reduced to tears on seeing one being carried by a porter in the streets of London. It reminded him of the countryside, which Robert considered to be more his father's element than the city. Robert senior put up a series of four prints representing hare hunting in his bedchamber in his house in Bristol.[2] Southey often thought of having a hare 'cut upon a seal, in remembrance of him and of the old shop'.

Southey's father was introduced to his mother, Margaret Hill, after getting to know her family through a business connection. She lived at Bedminster, about an hour's walk from Bristol. Robert senior began to visit the Hills at weekends, and eventually this resulted in his marriage to Margaret. Her family was to play a more important part in Southey's life than his father's. Margaret's mother had married twice, the first time to John Tyler, and after his death to Edward Hill. Margaret's half-sister, Elizabeth Tyler, and her brother Herbert Hill were to exert considerable influence on Robert's progress, his aunt in his early childhood, his uncle in his prime. He noted of his grandmother's second marriage that it was not a happy one, adding 'but I am too nearly concerned in the consequences to call it an unfortunate one', in an ironic reference to his own existence being dependent on the consequence of his mother's.[3]

Robert was not his parents' first child. An elder brother, John Cannon, was born in August 1773, just a year before his own birth. The baby was remembered by his mother as being 'singularly beautiful', which is why, in Southey's view, her reaction to his own appearance was so disparaging. By 22 October 1773, however, John Cannon was dead and buried.[4] Curiously, Robert was to recollect that his brother had lived to be nine or ten months old, 'and died (I believe) at nurse, where he had been sent because he was not strong enough to be weaned, and my mother could not nurse him. She had received serious injury from a blow on one of her breasts and I was coming . . . The woman who nursed him . . . lived at Bedminster and was so trusty and respectable a woman that I hope my poor brother suffered no real injury or sensible privation on my account.'[5] There was in fact no way his dead sibling could have so suffered, since he died before Robert was even conceived. Southey's memory was clearly faulty on this point, which raises the question of the reliability of other recollections of his boyhood. As we shall see, in the autobiographical letters he wrote to John May, which are the principal source for his childhood, his father played a lesser role, and his mother and her relations played a greater part in his upbringing than appears to have been the case.

'The blow which my mother had received on the breast', Southey observed, 'was attended with serious consequences. She underwent several operations, and the functions of that breast were destroyed. She was able to nurse her younger children with the other, but it was my lot to be consigned to a foster-mother', a servant employed by his grandmother at Bedminster.[6] While in her care, before he was three years old, Robert went 'for a few hours morning and evening' to a school run by a Madam Powell. On his very first day there he took exception to her 'ugly eyes', and demanded to be taken back to his foster-mother. '"Take me to Pat – I don't like ye"', he remembered saying, 'and this was accompanied by an angry jig or stamping which I inherited, and which my maternal relations called the Southey jig.'[7] Although the request was denied, Southey was clearly proud of this incident, which he insisted displayed traits of character that were to become ingrained. 'When, for the first time in my life, I saw nothing but strange faces about me, and no one to whom I could look for kindness or protection, I gave good proof of a sense of physiognomy which never misled me yet, of honesty in speaking my opinion, and of a temerity in doing it by which my after life has often been characterised.'

While he was at this dame school, Southey also spent considerable time with his maiden aunt Elizabeth in Bath. As a result he was rarely at home, and so had imperfect recollections of his sisters Eliza ('my earliest playmate') and Louisa ('a beautiful creature'), both of whom died in early childhood. One memory of Eliza he did recall vividly was that her thumb had been bitten through by a rat while she was asleep in their father's house.[8] Louisa's death was due to hydrocephalus, which Southey believed might have been induced by the cold bath that her parents made her take each day. She was put into a tub placed directly under a pump, from which it was filled with the coldest spring water. 'This was done from an old notion of strengthening her: the shock was dreadful; the poor child's horror of it, every morning, when taken out of bed, still more so. I cannot remember having seen it without horror.'

Why he spent so much of his time between the ages of two and six in his aunt's house in Bath Southey does not tell us. It could have been that his sickly mother needed help to bring up children. Or his relatively well-off aunt might have taken him off his parents' hands to ease her brother-in-law's fragile finances, for the elder Robert Southey's drapery business did not prosper and ended, in his son's words, in 'the household wreck of bankruptcy'. Then again it could simply have been that the house in busy Wine Street, which Robert senior shared with his brother Thomas, was not suitable to raise a growing family. This seems to be the most likely explanation, as Robert's brother Henry was taken in by their aunt at the age of five following the birth of their sister Margaretta. Whatever the reason, Southey's father seems to have resented the arrangements made for Robert to stay with Miss Tyler in Bath. 'My father once when he came to see me found me pale and thin', he reminisced. 'He returned home in a rage – swore my Aunt would kill "the boy" and in consequence I was transported to Bristol.'[9]

Elizabeth Tyler was a formidable lady, with a 'violent temper'. Southey was in awe of her as a small child, but was scathing about her when he reached maturity. She was born in 1739 and 'passed the earlier part of her life' in the household of William Bradford, her maternal uncle and Southey's great uncle. Bradford, a curate of Shobdon, Herefordshire, was a clergyman of independent means, owning an estate in Radnorshire. When his wife died he was 'too confirmed in celibate habits to think of marrying again'. Upon this, Miss Tyler became his housekeeper, and when Bradford himself died he left all his property to her 'except £50 to my mother and a small provision' for her brother William.

Southey was very critical of her decision to devote her inheritance entirely to herself.

> My grandmother was wholly overlooked in his will and the pain which she felt at this unkindness was not mitigated by the use which her daughter made of this accession of fortune. The use which she ought to have made of it was obvious. She should have made Bedminster her home as long as she might remain single. . . . Instead of this, finding herself mistress of £1500 in money from Mr Bradford's effects, besides the estate, and her personal portion of £600, she began to live at large, and to frequent watering places.[10]

At one of these resorts she struck up with John Armstrong, a Scottish physician and poet notorious for a salacious poem 'The Economy of Love'. Since she was only thirty-four while he was sixty-five, it seems unlikely that there was any love lost between them, economical or otherwise, though he did recommend her to go to Lisbon, advice which she followed. 'And thus, before you and I were born', Southey pointed out to John May, whom he had met in Portugal, 'did Armstrong prepare the way for our friendship, as well as the great literary labors of my life.' The latter were to be encouraged and facilitated by his uncle Herbert Hill, Miss Tyler's half-brother. Bradford had taken care of Hill's education at Oxford University, where he had recently been ordained. Thanks to Elizabeth's efforts in Portugal on his behalf, he was to become chaplain at Oporto and later of the English factory in Lisbon, which led to Southey's visits to Portugal in 1795 and 1800.

On Elizabeth's return from Portugal she moved into a house in Bath, where, Southey noted, 'my earliest recollections begin, great part of my earliest childhood having been passed there'. Although this was undoubtedly true, the impression he gives in his autobiographical letters to John May that his aunt virtually brought him up for the next four years is misleading. While he was at the school near Bedminster he lived in his grandmother's house. Indeed, he was to claim in 1793 that 'I past the greatest part of my infancy' with her.[11] He even occasionally spent time in what he significantly called 'my father's house' in Wine Street, Bristol. His feelings about the three homes were very different. 'My father's house was in one of the busiest and noisiest streets in Bristol and of course had no outlets. At Bath I was under perpetual restraint. But here (Bedminster) I had all wholesome enjoyments; and the delight which I there learned to take in rural sights and sounds has grown up with me, and continues unabated to this day.'[12]

The restraints he endured when he stayed with his aunt made the days seem interminable, which is perhaps why they left him with the impression that they lasted longer than they did in reality. One was not being allowed to play outside, since it might make him dirty, his aunt having an obsessive aversion to dirt and a phobia about dust. She even put a curtain over her own portrait, by Gainsborough, to keep off flies. Something of her obsession rubbed off on Southey, for he was fastidious about cleanliness all his life. His confinement to the house, however, ruled out contact with any other children. Another restraint was to be kept up late at night, when he should have been in bed. Given the choice, Southey always went to bed early. 'When she went out to an evening visit', he recalled, 'I was at 8 o clock put into the maids, and then removed when she returned, a hideous transportation!'[13] Yet another was that he slept with his aunt, who insisted that she should not be disturbed until she awoke naturally. The poor child, usually waking as early as six o'clock, had to lie stock still alongside her until she woke up at nine, ten or even eleven o'clock in the morning. He was clearly bored to tears during these 'tedious hours of compulsory idleness', during which he was reduced to staring at the green squares of the check curtains and at the light coming through the shutters. 'These were, indeed, early and severe lessons in patience.'

The late nights were due to Miss Tyler's hectic social life, visiting or entertaining her society friends and frequenting the theatre. These diversions had their compensations for keeping Southey up past his bed time, since he was a precocious child and benefited mentally if not physically. One of his aunt's friends was Francis Newberry, the publisher of children's stories such as *Goody Two Shoes*. 'Mr. Newberry presented me with a whole set of these books, more than twenty in number', Southey recollected. 'This was a rich present, and may have been more instrumental than I am aware of in giving me that love of books, and that decided determination to literature, as the one thing desirable, which manifested itself from my childhood.'

Another of Southey's aunt's acquaintances was a Miss Palmer, who obtained for her free admission to the theatre at Bath. Miss Tyler took him along with her, for the first time when he was only four years old. Initially he could not take in the idea of acting, and thought that the action on the stage was real. In one play he heard that a character was to have his head cut off, upon which Robert buried his head in the lap of one of his aunt's female friends, 'and could not be persuaded to look up until the dreaded scene was

over.' However, it was not long before he 'acquired a keen relish for the stage'.
As soon as he could read he went through Shakespeare's plays. His favourite
at first was *Titus Andronicus*, a recent production of which by the Royal
Shakespeare Company warned that it was not suitable for 'people under 14
years of age'! Southey, though, was not perturbed by the horrifying scenes on
stage, since 'tales of horror make a deep impression upon children . . . they
excite astonishment rather than pity.' In taking him to the theatre at so
tender an age Miss Tyler treated Southey as a small adult and not as a child.
In otherwise confining him to her house she acted as a jailor, treating him as
a prisoner.

Southey's visits to his grandmother's house in Bedminster released him
from this prison to 'the very Paradise of my childhood'.[14] Whereas he was not
allowed out in Bath, here his 'chief amusement was in the garden'. He studied
flowers and insects so much that, had a botanist or an entomologist been
around, he would have found him a keen student. 'If I had fallen in with one,
I might, perhaps, at this very day have been classifying mosses, and writing
upon the natural history of snails or cock-chafers, instead of recording the
events of the Peninsula War.'

The years when he travelled between Bath and Bedminster came to an
end in 1780. At the age of six he was sent to a school in Bristol run by a Mr
Foot, a Baptist minister. Southey claimed that this was of no concern either
to himself or to his parents. Yet this seems odd, as his family were all
Anglicans. There was a family pew in their local church, Christ Church, in
Bristol, where Southey was baptised, and his father served as churchwarden.
Moreover his grandmother never missed going to church unless the weather
was bad. His aunt took him to church in Bath, and he recalled how one
Sunday, returning from morning service, he innocently described the congre-
gation in terms he had learned in the theatre as 'a full house', for which he
was severely reprimanded. It could be that his father had no scruples about
sending his son to be taught by a nonconformist who 'had passed into a sort
of low Arianism, if indeed he were not a Socinian'. Robert senior had radical
political tracts of the 1760s among a meagre collection of books. He also
cherished a sword worn by an ancestor, who had taken part in Monmouth's
rebellion against James II in 1685, and was almost certainly a dissenter.
Indeed, Southey's father seems to have been more of a rebel himself than his
wife and her relations.

Despite its being regarded as the best school in Bristol, in Southey's
opinion it did not deserve that reputation. The discipline was severe. Indeed,
he remembered it as the one school in which he was ever caned, which is an
interesting recollection in view of his later criticism of corporal punishment
when he attended Westminster. He was also bullied, and was glad he was not

a boarder, but went home in the evenings, presumably to his parents' house in Wine Street.

When Foot died in 1781, Southey's father took him out of the school, even though the boy liked the new master, 'a Socinian minister'. It seems that Robert senior had taken a grip on his son's education, for he placed him in another school at Corston, a village between Bristol and Bath, where for the first time he was a boarder, causing his mother to burst into tears when he left home. The sight of her crying made a lasting impression on him. In 1794 he wrote a poem which noted how

> Years intervening have not worn away
> The deep remembrance of that distant day,
> Effac'd the vestige of my earliest fears
> A mother's fondness, and a mother's tears;
> When close she prest me to her sorrowing heart,
> As loath as even myself to part . . .[15]

His father, notwithstanding his wife's distress, took the boy to Corston and left him at the school. 'Sadly at night', he recorded in another poem,

> I sat me down beside a stranger's hearth;
> And when the lingering hour of rest was come,
> First wet with tears my pillow.[16]

'Here one year of my life was passed', he wrote to John May, 'with little profit and with a good deal of suffering.' The school's headmaster, Thomas Flower, preferred mathematical calculations to 'teaching a set of stupid boys, year after year, the rudiments of arithmetic'. As far as he could he left the teaching to his son Charley. A few of the boys, including Southey, were taught Latin by a French teacher who visited the school twice a week. Robert was then in turn made to teach the language to other boys. He was clearly regarded as a star pupil, being chosen for a spelling competition in which he showed his ability to spell 'crystallisation' and 'coterie'. This made him, as he put it to May, 'one of the most effective persons in the contest', adding with typical vanity, 'which might easily be'. The school was better in one respect than Mr Foot's had been, for there was no corporal punishment. The food was generally foul, though Robert looked forward to one meal a week when they ate no meat but were treated to cake and cheese. Moreover, he was at an age when he could enjoy boyish games, such as 'conquerors', or conkers, in which they used snails instead of horse chestnuts.

Southey came to feel sorry for Flower, whose wife took to drink and neglected her household duties. As a result the domestic servants became so negligent that hygiene suffered. Robert's mop of black curly hair became infested with lice, for which his head was lathered in soap, 'and in that condition I was sent home, with such sores in consequence of long neglect that my mother wept at seeing them.' The lack of cleanliness led to a report that scabies had been contracted by some of the boys, which determined many parents, including Southey's, to withdraw their sons, to his great joy.

Southey immediately went to stay with his aunt Elizabeth who, following his grandmother's death in 1782, had moved into her house at Bedminster until it was sold. His father sent him there while he searched for yet another school. Robert remembered a visit that Miss Palmer made to Bedminster to make up after a quarrel with Miss Tyler. For some reason Miss Palmer had reacted to their bickering by placing an apron over her head, which the eight-year-old boy solemnly warned her was bad for her eyesight, since 'every thing gets out of order if it is not used. A book, if it is not opened, will become damp and moldy; and a key, if it is never turned in the lock will get rusty.' Just then Miss Tyler joined them, and Miss Palmer complained that her nephew had compared her eyes to a rusty key and a mouldy book.

Southey's father found a school that was run by a Welsh master, William Williams. He was presumably an Anglican, for he insisted that the boys learned the Catechism punctiliously. Southey considered it a better school than Corston and indeed the four years or so he spent there were the happiest of his schooldays. Latin was taught every day instead of three times a week and he apparently acquired some French as well. German lessons, too, were provided, for Robert came to admire the black letter that he later used on title pages, claiming that he set the fashion for doing so. The only lessons he disliked were those provided by the dancing master, for he lacked the coordination required to dance elegantly, for which he was hit about the head with a fiddle stick.

His handwriting was considered to be so bad that Williams made him start all over again on his letters. This Southey blamed on a diversion he had resorted to in order to alleviate the boredom at his aunt's. She had hundreds of play bills, which he perforated with a pin around the titles of the plays, so that they were highlighted when held up to a window. Holding the pin to puncture them, he insisted, had made him incapable of handling a pen properly. Even at home, where Southey went after school, being what he called 'a day boarder', his father and uncle Thomas 'used to shake their heads at me, and pronounce that I would never write with a decent hand'. In fact his handwriting was to become neat and generally clear, though it can occasionally pose problems for the reader of his letters, particularly with the Us and Ns that Williams made him practise 'with absurd and wearisome perseverance'. On the other hand, Southey was much better at writing numbers than letters. Indeed, his ciphering book, in which he used to do his sums, was held up as a model of neatness. Each page appeared orderly. 'I found the advantage of this when I came to be concerned with proof-sheets', he informed May. 'The method which I used in my ciphering book led me to teach the printers how to print verses of irregular length upon a regular principle.'

Williams would occasionally spring a task on the boys, one of which was to write a letter. Southey, who was to become a prolific letter writer, had never composed one before, and 'actually cried for perplexity and vexation'. The master managed to coax him into completing one, in which he described Stonehenge. Williams praised it inordinately, which aroused envy in some pupils. Six of them accosted Southey one morning when he arrived at the school, and asked him, since he was so clever, to tell them the meaning of the letters 'i.e.' Not wishing to show his ignorance he guessed that they stood for John the Evangelist. The derision that this answer met with taught him 'never again to be ashamed of acknowledging myself ignorant of what I really did not know'.

Southey went back and forth to his father's house in term-time. In his account of the life of the poet John Frederick Bryant, he recorded how he passed Bryant's workshop in Christmas Street 'for several years . . . morning and evening, with a satchel in my hand, or across my shoulder, on my way to and from school'.[17] During the school holidays he still stayed with his aunt, who had moved into lodgings in Bath. Apparently she usually spent Easter with a friend, Mrs Dolignon, who lived in Cheshunt with her sisters. Southey remembered 'a moss walk under a long avenue of elms' that was in her garden. 'Often & often', he recalled, 'have I walked there in the Easter holydays which I always spent with those good women.'[18] In 1783 he spent the summer vacation with Miss Tyler and Mrs Dolignon, and was struck by his first view of the sea, the sight of which from the shore impressed him ever afterwards more than any other except that of the stars. 'If I could live over any hours of my boyhood again', he confessed, 'it should be those which I then spent upon the beach at Weymouth.'

Mrs Dolignon, a widow whom he remembered with 'the utmost reverence and affection', as one who 'had been to me almost as a mother', gave him the first book he acquired since Mr Newberry's gift.[19] His father, though he read nothing but a Bristol newspaper, had a modest collection of books, which he kept in a cupboard with his wine glasses. It included three bound volumes of very miscellaneous works, along with the *Spectator* and some pamphlets of the 1760s and 1770s, some with engravings. Robert, along with his brother Tom, daubed the prints with paint, and picked up 'some knowledge of the political wit, warfare and scandal of those days'. Among them was the *Town and Country Magazine* for 1777 from which Southey cut out 'The Old Bachelor', a poem he thought so highly of that he was to publish it in the *Annual Anthology* for 1800. To this collection his mother added the *Guardian* and Elizabeth Rowe's *Letters*.[20] In them he came across translations of Torquato Tasso's *Gerusalemme Liberata*, an epic poem about the first crusade, and wanted to read it. Naively he thought that, since it dealt with Jerusalem, the original must be in Hebrew, an error that nobody in his immediate family could correct. Then, shortly before going to Weymouth, his mother took him to a circulating library and he saw John Hoole's translation of 1763, *Jerusalem Delivered*. While on holiday he mentioned this to Mrs Dolignon, who bought a copy for him that he treasured all his life. She was also presumably the 'lady whom I must ever gratefully and affectionately remember as the kindest friend of my boyhood' who gave him a copy of William Hayward Roberts' *Judah Restored*, a poem in six books of blank verse published in 1774. 'I read it often then, and can still recur to it with satisfaction', Southey observed in 1836, adding 'and perhaps I owe something to the plain dignity of its style, which is suited to the subject, and every where bears the stamp of good sense and careful erudition.'[21]

The circulating library substantially widened his access to books. On one visit he stumbled across Spenser. 'No young lady of the present generation falls to a new novel of Sir Walter Scott with keener relish', he wrote in 1823, 'than I did that morning to the Faery Queen.' It was probably his discovery of Spenser, whom he rated as one of the finest English poets, that led him to preserve 'The Old Bachelor' for posterity, as it was written in Spenserian style. He was given an edition of Milton's *Paradise Lost*, which he also came to value as a crowning poetic achievement, by a Mrs Wraxall, a pious widow who invited him to tea one day. She startled him when, after tea, she knelt down and got him to kneel with her, and prayed for him 'by the hour'. When she told him she was leaving Bristol he retailed this to his aunt, who was seeking a house in order to settle down. In 1784 she bought Mrs Wraxall's house, and since it was nearer to school than his father's, he again moved in with her. Although it was only ten minutes away from Wine Street, so that Southey visited his family as often as he could, these visits were discouraged by his aunt. She had fallen out with his uncle Thomas to the point where they cordially hated each other. She would not step into the house, and Southey 'was seldom allowed to dine or pass the evening there'.

Miss Tyler invited her brother William to join them in her new home. Robert was very fond of his uncle William, a simple soul whom the family called 'the Squire'. He was so eccentric and unpredictable that he needed to be looked after, a role which his sister now took on. 'He was what we call in this country "half-saved" – that is not an Idiot but something like it', Southey informed a friend in 1803. 'Of course the man was fit for nothing. He spent his life in chewing tobacco and getting drunk.'[22] William's stock of anecdotes and stories was prodigious. Southey remembered many of them, and was to use one of his sayings, 'curses are like chickens, they always come home to roost', as the motto on the title page of *The Curse of Kehama*. Now in sad decline, and drinking beer for breakfast, William spent his days staring at passers-by from a bay window. One day, when Robert had gone home for dinner, he found his uncle in the summer house recovering from a seizure. The following day he had another and died.

Robert enjoyed being able to go to his aunt's house between noon and two o'clock, which made these the most pleasant of his schooldays. They were to come to an abrupt end, however, when one day while he was reading aloud to Williams, the master criticised him, asking who had taught him to read. When Robert replied that it was his aunt, Williams bade him to inform her that 'my old horse, that has been dead twenty years, could have taught you as well'. Robert did as he was bid, and Miss Tyler, not surprisingly, was shocked and angry. 'It was never forgotten or forgiven', Southey recalled, 'and perhaps it accelerated the very proper resolution of removing me.'

The decision to take him out of the school, however, was instigated not by his aunt Elizabeth but by his uncle, Herbert Hill. Herbert wanted his nephew to go to Christ Church, Oxford, the best opportunity for which lay in his going to Westminster School. 'But as I was in feeble health', Southey recollected, 'and moreover had been hitherto very ill taught, it was deemed advisable that I should be placed under a clergyman competent to prepare me for public school.' His aunt had her say in the choice of a suitable clerical tutor, a Mr Lewis who lodged with two sisters of her acquaintance. One of them was a widow whose son, Jem Thomas, was being instructed by Lewis, who was prepared to take on other pupils. Jem was the same age as Robert, though two others, Cooper and Rawlins, who also attended the lessons, were older. Southey nicknamed Cooper Caliban, saying he resembled a cross between a pig and a baboon; Rawlins, the son of a Bristol surgeon, he thought vain and conceited; while he did not like the look of Jem Thomas's face.

It would be fascinating to know what they made of him. He surely struck them as a rather strange boy. At the age of twelve, Southey had lived in various houses and been to four schools. His upbringing by his domineering aunt, not to mention the influence of her eccentric brother, was unconventional. He had grown up surrounded mainly by women – his aunt, his mother, his grandmother and their female friends. His fellow pupils probably regarded him as being somewhat effeminate. He himself acknowledged 'the effeminating and debilitating tendency of the habits to which my aunt's peculiarities subjected me'. These were only offset by the friendship of her maid's brother Shadrach Weeks. He and 'Shad', as he called him, enjoyed flying kites they had made and running around the rocks and woods on the banks of the river Avon.

The disrupted schooling he had received made the year he spent under Lewis's tuition less improving than was expected. He would have preferred spending it at a good school, for his tutor was ill equipped to rectify the bad teaching he had previously endured. Lewis did encourage him in composition until, as Southey put it, 'when I had learned that it was not more difficult to write in prose than in verse, the ink dribbled as daintily from my pen as ever it did from John Bunyan's.' Left to his own devices, however, Southey made great strides in poetry, so much so that looking back in the 1820s he could not think of any other period in his life when he was so aware of intellectual development as he was in the eighteen months before he went to Westminster. He began a dramatic poem on the Trojan War, wrote three books of another on the Anglo-Saxons, then abandoned them both, finding the task of devising an overall plan for an epic more difficult than the actual writing. He worked on this, telling May that he could trace distinctly 'the progress of my own mind towards attaining it', adding the disclaimer 'so far as I may be thought to have attained it'.

In February 1788 Southey left the West Country for the first time in his life, never having been more than a mile east of Bath before. Now he was taken to London by his aunt, and Miss Tyler made the most of the opportunity for extravagance that this journey afforded, taking expensive lodgings in fashionable Pall Mall. She soon spent the £30 that Southey's father had given her to cover their expenses. The trip to town took up about six weeks before Robert finally entered the gate of Westminster School.

Southey informed John May that he arrived by carriage in the Dean's Yard at Westminster on 1 April 1788, adding 'of all ominous days that could be chosen'.[23] He had not been an April Fool, however, for he was in fact admitted to the school on the 2nd.[24] Again his memory was playing tricks with him.

Southey was placed in a boarding house known as Ottley's, run by a Mrs Farren. There he shared a first-floor room with Robert Sparrow, who bullied him so much that he came to the conclusion that his fellow boarder, who had an uncontrollable temper, was not entirely sane. Sparrow 'was not without some noble seeds in his nature', Southey later conceded, 'but of ungovernable passions, which he had never been taught to regulate or control'.[25] He used to pour water into Robert's ear while he slept. On one occasion he tried to hang him out of a window by the leg, which had he succeeded might have proved fatal. Southey asked to be moved to another room. Even there he was not safe from his tormentor, for Sparrow visited him late one night wearing a sheet to scare him into thinking the room was haunted. Southey woke and grappled with Sparrow, making enough noise to attract the attention of the usher of the house, Samuel Hayes. Hayes made Sparrow promise never to molest Robert again. He probably would have left him alone anyway after the manhandling he had received from his intended victim. Southey may have been bullied, but he was never afraid to stand up to a bully who accosted him, either physically or in print.

The usher was also second master in the school, known to the boys as 'Botch Hayes' from his efforts at improving their verses. Pupils were encouraged to write them with rewards of silver coins. The poet William Cowper recalled receiving a groat for one of his exercises. Southey, commenting on this achievement, noted that 'my first literary profits were thus obtained, and, like Cowper, I remember the pleasure with which I received them. But there was this difference, that his rewards were probably for Latin verse, in which he excelled, and mine were always for English composition.'[26] Because he could not compose verses in Latin when he arrived at Westminster he was placed in the under fourth form.

There, in accordance with the school's custom, he was initially assigned 'for a week . . . under the direction of one in the same remove, who is called his substance, the newcomer being the shadow'. The form master, Edward Smedley, placed Southey under George Strachey, a day boy who lived in Queen Anne Street. Robert never forgot 'his very many very excellent qualities, nor the deep and uneffaced prepossession in his favour which I felt the very first day I ever saw him, when I was placed under him as a shadow'.[27] Strachey was destined to become chief secretary to the East India Company's administration of Indian affairs in Madras. On his departure to take part in the government of the sub-continent in 1798, Southey wrote a sonnet for him with the opening lines

Fair be thy fortunes in the distant land,
Companion of my earlier years, and Friend . . .[28]

Acquaintance with such companions as Strachey at Westminster made the school ideal for what today would be called 'networking'. Southey was aware that his time there created opportunities for forging relationships that no other experience would equal: 'after-life seldom or never affords another opportunity of knowing so many persons so well.' Among those he struck up an intimate acquaintance with were William Bean and John Dolignon.

William Bean was a day boy who lived in Camberwell; Southey remembered his cockney accent. Bean's father, an apothecary, had sent him to

Westminster hoping he would get into either Christ Church, Oxford, or Trinity College, Cambridge, where the school usually sent those scholars who progressed to university. Unfortunately Bean failed the school examination known as 'standing out', which led his father to withdraw him to follow his own profession. Southey regarded this as unfair, since Bean in his view had the intellect to do well at university, but as a day boy was not adequately coached for the examination. After Bean's removal he continued to visit him in Camberwell as long as he was at Westminster himself.[29]

Southey remembered John Dolignon as 'one of my earliest playmates. . . . I used to shoot with him, fish with him, and lay snares for rabbits.' He also recalled that 'while I was at Westminster his mother's house was my home every Saturday and Sunday.'[30] Mrs Dolignon was an acquaintance of Southey's aunt Elizabeth. Her house where he spent his weekends during term time was at Cheshunt.

Other acquaintances at the school with whom Southey kept up after he left were Charles Collins, Peter Elmsley and Thomas Davis Lamb. His relations with some of them did not last long after leaving Westminster. Collins was to take offence at Southey's mocking of him for adopting airs and graces at Oxford. Southey knew Lamb's family well enough to spend a holiday with them at Hampstead in Kent in 1791. There they witnessed a trencher man devour huge piles of meat. While Mr and Mrs Lamb averted their gaze, 'Tom and I with school-boys' privilege kept our eyes rivetted on him.'[31] Southey got on well enough with Tom's father, Thomas Philips Lamb, to write gossipy letters to him. While he seems to have lost touch with the Lambs when he left Oxford, with other former school friends he kept up a longer acquaintance. Thus in 1824 he was to dedicate his *Book of the Church* to Elmsley, who had become Camden Professor of Ancient History. After his death in 1825 Southey acknowledged to another old Westminster friend 'his social and moral qualities as well as his intellectual worth . . . and the wisdom of his heart, for in the heart it is that true wisdom has its seat.'[32]

Two friendships he made at Westminster were to last his own lifetime. These were with Grosvenor Charles Bedford and Charles Watkin Williams Wynn. 'When I was a school-boy at Westminster', he reminisced, 'I frequented the house of a school-fellow [which] was so near Dean's Yard that it was hardly considered as being out of my prescribed bounds; and I had free access to the library':[33] the school fellow was Grosvenor Charles Bedford, whose parents owned the house. Among the authors Southey read there were Gibbon, Rousseau, Voltaire and Goethe. One work which he came across that particularly influenced his poetic development was Bernard Picart's *Religious Ceremonies. The Ceremonies and Religious Customs of the various Nations of the known World* (1733).[34] 'I got at Picart when I was about fifteen', he recalled in 1812. 'This led me to consider a design of rendering every mythology which had ever extended itself widely, and powerfully influenced the human mind, the basis of a narrative poem.'[35] The seeds of his epics *Thalaba*, *Kehama* and *Madoc* were thus sown at Westminster, not in his formal lessons, but in his extensive private reading. Bedford was to become a civil servant, rising through the ranks in the Exchequer from clerk to chief clerk in the Auditor's office. His younger brother Horace was also at Westminster, and Southey kept up a correspondence with him, too, for a year or so after he left the school. His letters to Grosvenor Bedford and Charles Wynn, however, were to continue as long as he was able to write. Wynn, though the son of a Welsh baronet, had no social scruples about establishing a firm friendship with Southey: in 1796 he generously settled an annuity of £160 on his impecunious friend. Wynn's connection on his mother's side with the politically influential Grenville family and his own political career, which culminated in his becoming president of the Board of Control from 1822 to 1828, and secretary at war from 1830 to 1831, were also to be beneficial to Southey. 'Chance brought us together as schoolboys', Southey noted about his relationship with Wynn and Elmsley on the latter's death:

> choice, founded upon esteem and liking, had united us through life, and no difference in pursuits, opinions, or station ever in the slightest degree influenced the friendship which had thus been formed; neither time nor separation affected it; the heart remained unchanged, and the attachment of youth acquired strength and maturity from years. Now, therefore, when one of the cords has been cut, I would not let pass this occasion for expressing a wish that death may not divide our names.[36]

His close friendship with Wynn inspired him to write an epic on the Welsh prince Madoc, who had reputedly discovered America centuries before Columbus. Robert began to write it in 1789 when he was a schoolboy at Westminster, though it was then in prose rather than blank verse.

Another of Southey's contemporaries at Westminster was Matthew Lewis, who was to achieve notoriety as the author of the most lurid Gothic novel, *The Monk*. Southey knew 'Monk Lewis', as he became known, well enough to dream many years later after his death that they were back at school together, and when he asked him if he were dead Lewis replied that he was. This did not upset Southey as much as an identical dream involving Thomas Davis Lamb, as he had never had any affection for Lewis.[37] Nevertheless, he was familiar enough with him to contribute poems to a collection *Tales of Wonder* that Lewis edited in 1800. Lewis presumably was aware of Southey's interest in the Gothic that inspired him to write a poem 'To Horror' as early as 1791. The schoolboy poet summoned up the Genius of Horror from its retreat

> On some old sepulchre's moss-cankered seat
> Beneath the Abbey's ivied wall.

Horror leads him to survey horrific scenes, from a shipwrecked mariner facing the Arctic cold and polar bears on Greenland to 'that accursed shore, where on the stake the Negro writhes'.[38]

Southey also wrote a Gothic novel that summer, *Harold, or the Castle of Morford*.[39] Although it is usually called a prose romance, *Harold*, an adaptation of the traditional story of Robin Hood, contains several Gothic passages. These were clearly inspired by Southey's obsession with Malory's *Le Morte D'Arthur* and Spenser's *Faerie Queene*. 'When I was a schoolboy', he recalled in an introduction to Malory's work, 'I possessed a wretchedly imperfect copy, and there was no book, except the Faery Queen, which I perused so often or with such deep contentment.'[40] One of the more striking echoes of these in the work of a precocious adolescent is a ballad sung by Robin Hood's minstrel. This relates how a knight, Sir Lancelot, becomes lost in a forest at night and hears groans from the trees. It turns out that the wood is made up of men who were turned into trees by a witch who seduced them in the guise of a fair maiden. She attempts to lure Sir Lancelot by similar wiles, but is twice thwarted because of his love for Guenever. Some passages in which Southey depicts the attempted seduction reveal not only his familiarity with Spenser, but also the sexual fantasies of an adolescent schoolboy. In the witch's first attempt she bathes naked in a pool to entice the knight:

> A lovely damsel wanton played
> Within the crystal tide
> And oft beneath the glassy wave
> Her dainty limbs would hide.
> And oft above the waves appear'd
> Her gently heaving breast.
> That charm alone exposed to view
> For waves obscured the rest.
> 'Come Lancelot' the nymph exclaim'd
> ''Tis now the time for love
> For silent is the midnight hour
> And pleasant is the grove.'
> With that she leap'd from out the waves
> Exposing all her charms

'Come Lancelot' again she cried
'Come riot in my arms'.[41]

There is very little explicit political comment in the novel, which betrays a preference for the Middle Ages over his own time that was to stay with Southey all his life: 'in those days luxury had not so inverted the order of nature as to turn the day into night and the night into day. . . . But those days are passed, and like the wind which bends down the yellow harvest, they have scarcely left a trace behind them. If we compare them with the present age, I fear we shall not gain by the comparison.'[42] Yet his only overt comment on the contrast between the late twelfth and eighteenth centuries is curious. 'Coeur de Lion was a Prince whose name must ever be mentioned with veneration by the English nation', he asserted. 'Misled by the vain superstition of the time he expended his treasure in the Holy Land. Yet even then he acquired Eternal Glory. How differently has the wealth of England been expended since in preparations which only serve to blast the British laurels. Her flag insulted, her sons treated with barbarity by her foes, and laden with oppressive taxes, too well may she wish for a king like Coeur de Lion.' Although the complaint about oppressive taxes was to become a refrain of Southey's throughout the 1790s, his comments on foreign affairs are hardly in keeping with the anti-war stance he was to adopt soon after he made them.

What seems to have radicalised the young Southey was the harsh treatment he received for his contributions to a new school magazine, *The Flagellant*. This was the brainchild of Grosvenor Bedford, George Strachey and Charles Wynn as well as of Southey himself. They planned to produce one on similar lines to *The Microcosm*, which was produced at Eton. There had been an earlier Westminster periodical, *The Trifler*, which had also sought to emulate the Eton paper, but this had folded after forty numbers had appeared. Southey himself had tried to publish an elegy in it upon the death of his sister, Margaretta. She had been taken ill with consumption shortly before he left home to attend the school, and had died soon after. 'This was the first death that I had ever apprehended and dreaded', he was to tell John May, 'and it affected me deeply.' His grief found expression in what he admitted were very bad verses, which, perhaps fortunately for his reputation, were rejected by the editors of *The Trifler*.

Announcing the forthcoming publication of *The Flagellant* to his friend Charles Collins, Southey claimed that 'Old Westminsters at Oxford and Cambridge will be glad to see some sparks of genius from their old habitation. Should it fail it cannot well be worse than the Trifler, should it succeed it will retrieve the reputation of the school and establish our own. Allow me to say I do not much doubt of success.' After outlining proposals from other potential contributors he boasted of his own. 'If I thought my verses only equal to those in that paper', he observed, referring to *The Trifler*, 'I would burn every line. Remember what Rough said the other day and allow my vanity not half so bad as if I affected modesty.'[43]

Before the first number of *The Flagellant* appeared, Strachey and Wynn had left Westminster and so it was produced by Bedford and Southey. They brought out nine weekly numbers, Bedford being responsible for the first and Southey for the second. Thereafter they shared the work between them, Bedford writing numbers three, four, six and eight, Southey numbers five and seven, while the ninth and last, which announced that the magazine 'has not succeeded', was a joint effort.[44]

In the second number Southey, signing himself 'Basil', developed the conceit of the Flagellants being a monastic order. Basil described his discovery of their monastery, where a rod above the door was the 'insignia of domestic cruelty'. He and three other 'Westminster boys', presumably Bedford, Strachey and Wynn, had entered the building and formed themselves into a band of brothers, 'resolved to pursue their observations aloof from mankind'. This and Bedford's contributions to numbers three and four were little more than essays in schoolboy humour, which did little to prepare the readers of the magazine for Southey's diatribe against flogging in the fifth, which appeared on 29 March 1792. Why he felt so strongly about it, especially since by his own admission he himself was never caned at Westminster, is puzzling.

It opens with a letter signed 'Thwackee', a pupil at a school whose headmaster Thwackum, the namesake of the tutor in Henry Fielding's *Tom Jones*, had discovered him reading *The Flagellant*. He had confiscated the magazine, 'exclaiming "Pretty times indeed if boys are allowed to think for themselves!"' Thwackee urged the Flagellants 'to let the lash of your displeasure fall upon tyranny; expose it in its proper colours, the brutality and absurdity of flogging.' Southey, adopting the pseudonym Gualbertus, responded by investigating the history of corporal punishment and concluding that it should be abolished. He traced the history of the practice to the influence of the devil. 'Satan cannot be driven out of his stronghold', he maintained, since 'he has sheltered himself behind the unrelenting beasts of the disciplinarians, and in the pleasure of exercising the rod, the impiety is forgotten.' He singled out clergymen, particularly of the Church of England 'as most schoolmasters are', for special condemnation for employing 'so beastly and idolatrous a custom'. Southey concluded his essay by 'commanding all doctors, reverends, and plain masters, to cease, without delay or repining, from the beastly and idolatrous custom of flogging . . . ANATHEMA. ANATHEMA.'

The headmaster, William Vincent, had taken over the headship of the school shortly after Southey's arrival in 1788. He took umbrage at this accusation that he was doing the devil's work by chastising errant schoolboys, and might even have been particularly incensed by the implication that he enjoyed sadistic pleasure from it. Southey seems to have been amazed by the headmaster's reaction. As he naively put it years later, 'Heaven knows I thought as little of giving offence by it as of causing an eclipse or an earthquake.'[45] Vincent was so outraged that he sought out the author, apparently immediately suspecting Southey. Why he should have aroused suspicion can only be conjectured. Vincent might have been aware that Southey was reputed by his fellow schoolboys to have been prominent in an attack on the statue of Major Andre in Westminster Abbey. Indeed, he was alleged to have broken the nose off it. Then again the headmaster had possibly marked Southey down as a rebel when Robert wrote an essay criticising Edmund Burke, which Vincent criticised in turn. Burke's *Reflections on the Revolution in France*, published in 1790, had made a considerable stir. Burke had acquired the reputation of being a friend to liberty and an opponent of arbitrary power in his previous writings, particularly those that defended the American colonists in their stance against the British government. However, with his *Reflections* he seemed to have done an about turn, attacking the French revolutionaries for their overturning of the country's institutions and their threat to its social fabric. Ironically in view of the charges that were to be made that he had apostatised from his own youthful political principles, Southey criticised Burke on the same grounds. 'Is it possible you can join Justice and Burke in one sentence?' he asked Grosvenor Bedford in December 1792. 'Oh how fallen how changed from him who foremost stood in freedom's cause . . . . Seriously speaking I do not know any one man whom I so despise and execrate.'[46] If he expressed such sentiments in his essay then it is not hard to see why Vincent took exception to it. Although Westminster had shaken off its earlier Tory and even Jacobite reputation, the headmaster himself came from a Tory family. The turbulent events that occurred across the Channel in 1789 left their mark on the school, for the Epilogue written for the annual Latin play that year was on the theme of the fall of the Bastille.[47] A sermon Vincent delivered in St Margaret's Westminster in 1792 was to be published by the reactionary Association for the Defence of Liberty and Property against Republicans and Levellers. Southey himself was later to claim that the headmaster 'never used me well – because I was the son of a country tradesman'.[48]

Whatever aroused Vincent's suspicions that Southey had written the offending essay, he obliged him to withdraw from the school until the identity of the author was established, and Robert found refuge at the home of Mrs Dolignon. On 9 April, eleven days after the appearance of the fifth issue of *The Flagellant*, Vincent wrote to her explaining that 'Southey is supposed to be the author of a Publication reflecting very indecently upon public education, and the characters of those who conduct it. As I have commenced a prosecution against the publisher, I should wish that you would keep Southey under your protection, until I see the effect of the steps I have taken.'[49] Vincent approached the printer of the fifth number, Egerton, threatening to prosecute for libel if he did not reveal the name of the author of it. Although Isaac Reed, a friend of the Bedfords, tried to persuade him not to divulge it, Egerton informed Vincent that Southey was responsible.

Meanwhile, there are signs of an attempt to conceal the identity of the author of the fifth number of *The Flagellant*. One of the editors, presumably Bedford, persuaded another publisher, Jeffrey, to print a sixth issue. In it the death of Gualbertus was announced 'on Thursday last', i.e. 29 March, the day of the publication of number five. Gualbertus was alleged to have died 'of a disorder in the pericranium, which shewed itself early in the morning, by strong delirious symptoms and some wandering language. Something very offensive issued from his head.' This appears to be an oblique apology for the fifth number, attributing it to a fit of insanity on the part of the author. Southey even dared to appear as 'Basil' in the seventh number, on 12 April, when he claimed that Gualbertus was merely asleep. If all this was intended to throw Vincent off the scent it did not succeed, for when Egerton disclosed Southey's name to him he had him expelled from the school.

Southey was at first defiant. He was prepared to keep up the publication of *The Flagellant* and even to counter the headmaster's suit for libel by suing Vincent for damages: 'For expulsion is a bitter pill and will not go down unless I sweeten it over, but for every pill I swallow Vincent shall have a bolus.'[50] Bedford, however, accepted that the game was up, and persuaded Southey to drop the magazine. 'I am obliged to discontinue the Flagellant', he informed Thomas Davis Lamb on 26 April.[51] Although he was 'not conscious of having acted wrong', Southey accepted that Bedford's letter had 'waked me from a pleasant dream'.[52] This changed his mood from defiance to attrition – though not contrition – for he wrote a letter apologising to Vincent for his authorship of the offending article, then immediately regretted it. 'I deserve to be despised', he abjectly told Bedford: 'I am despicable in my own eyes and criminal in those of my friends.'[53] Despite his apology, Vincent took his vendetta against Southey as far as getting him barred from entering Christ Church, Oxford. Robert was outraged. 'I cannot help hoping one day to tell him that he has behaved to me in a manner equally ungenerous and unjust', he expostulated on learning the news. 'Before I wrote that letter (for which I must reproach myself as expressing contrition I did not feel and apologizing for an action which I thought needed no apology) before I was persuaded to write he had engaged his honour never to mention the circumstance. As Queen Bess once said God forgive him but I never can.'[54]

Southey felt deeply that he had been a victim of tyranny. 'I am not quite eighteen', he wrote to Bedford in May, 'and few men of eighty have been more persecuted.'[55] At the end of the year he observed '1792 is now expiring – good god how many events have transpired – from the fall of Gualbertus to that of Louis! From my libel upon rod to Paine's upon sceptres.'[56] This drew a direct parallel between the views he had expressed in *The Flagellant* and those Paine expounded in *Rights of Man*. The first part of Paine's polemic had appeared in 1791 in direct response to Burke's *Reflections*. It attacked the hereditary principle and upheld the proceedings of the French revolutionaries. Southey's expulsion from Westminster for expressing objections to corporal punishment in print was apparently instrumental in forming his own radical political views.[57]

CHAPTER TWO

Student (1792–1794)

Southey suspected early in 1792 that he might not go to the university after all. 'Should I be rejected at Oxford the grave is always open', he wrote on 16 April, adding 'there at least I shall not be molested.'[1] However, he did not find out for certain that he had been refused a place at Christ Church until late September that year. 'I am at length enabled to answer you with respect to my future situation at Oxford', he informed Thomas Philips Lamb around the 30th of that month. 'I am rejected at Christ Church.' Yet in the same letter he was able to add that he was going up to Balliol instead.[2] How this came about is not entirely clear, as the series of autobiographical letters to John May, the main source for his childhood and early youth, unfortunately came to an end when he had reached the age of fifteen.[3] 'Many years ago I began to write my own Life and Recollections in letters to an old and dear friend', he recalled when he was sixty-three, 'till it became inconvenient to afford time for proceeding, – and to confess the truth my heart began to fail. This, no doubt, is the reason why so many autobiographies proceed little beyond the stage of boyhood. So far all our recollections are delightful as well as vivid; but when the cares and the griefs of life are to be raised up, it becomes too painful to live over the past again.'[4] Apparently the memories of his career after his expulsion from Westminster were so unbearable that he could not bring himself to narrate them.

Southey was ambivalent about the influence of public schools on the formation of character. On the one hand he told May that they were 'nurseries . . . for tyranny and brutality'. On the other hand he acknowledged that 'good is to be acquired there, which can be attained in no other course of education'. Looking back on his own experiences, he was similarly ambivalent about his time at Westminster. Thus he could bid farewell to 'the seat of Pedantry and Pride', yet he could also confess that

still my soul
Parts with reluctance from the scene belov'd
Where every bliss of social joy I prov'd.[5]

'Yet severely as I really reprobate them', Southey observed of public schools, 'many, many happy hours have I passed in Dean's Yard, & shall ever look back to the two last years without experiencing any unpleasing sensation from the retrospect.' Westminster was to provoke unpleasant feelings in his sleep, for memories of his days there were to haunt his dreams long after he left. In his 'dream book' he recorded that 'Westminster often makes a part of my dreams, which are always uncomfortable. Either I have lost my books, or have Bible exercise to do, and feel that I have lost the knack, or am conscious that it is not befitting me to continue at school, and so determine to leave it by my own will.'[6]

The recurrent dream perhaps signified wish-fulfilment, for in reality Southey left the school not by his own free will but through expulsion. Immediately after that event he took refuge with Mrs Dolignon at Cheshunt, before spending some time with the family of Thomas Philips Lamb, whose son, Thomas Davis Lamb, had been a schoolfriend at Westminster. His sojourn at Mountsfield Lodge, their house in Sussex, buoyed him up after the depression he had experienced once the reality of being expelled from school had finally sunk in. 'The sunniest days of my youth', he was to tell his daughter, 'were those which I passed at Mountsfield.'[7] After two days' hard drinking in Brighton he set to reading Sterne's *Tristram Shandy*, a novel that was to become a favourite over the years, which is perhaps surprising of one who has been accused of priggishness. For Sterne's long shaggy dog story frequently indulges in prurient passages, which led F. R. Leavis, the English literary critic, to dismiss him as 'a nasty trifler'. Yet Shandean humour was later to inform Southey's own attempt to become a novelist in his rambling novel *The Doctor*. He still anticipated going up to Christ Church, for he mentioned that in addition to practising imitations of the verse of poets such as William Shenstone, Edmund Spenser and Isaac Watts, he was reading Richard Watson's *Chemical Essays* (1781), as he hoped 'to practice a little chemistry at Oxford when I get there'.[8]

While he was at Mountsfield, he attended church, where he was 'pestered . . . with the Athanasian creed and a sermon in defence of incomprehensibility. . . . Believe me I lost all patience and tho' the sermon pronounced damnation to me if I doubted the Trinity I still must doubt and deny.' His radical views had hardened, for he now thought that both Church and State were 'rotten at the heart and . . . should be hewn down and cast into the fire'. His attitude was stiffened by recent events at home and abroad.

A 'Church and King' mob had attacked dissenters in Nottingham that spring. Southey denounced the attack, claiming that the government had raised the mob. He also objected to the attempts by Austria and its allies to crush the French Revolution. What was needed was 'a good flaming libel', 'a good hot inflammatory piece of treason', but he was wary of publishing one. 'The whole bench of Bishops and every Schoolmaster in the Kingdom are my avowed enemies and so I must take warning.'[9] He even 'planned a week's amusement in France and actually embarked twice from Rye'. Ten years later he informed a friend that 'the wind prevented my voyage and this is one of the very few circumstances in my life which I remember with regret.'[10]

When he returned to the West Country from Sussex in June, he appears to have resigned himself to the possibility of not going to university. 'If I could get an appointment to the East Indies I should like it', he informed Bedford, but the prospect scarcely filled him with enthusiasm. 'This is a damned world and the sooner I quit it the better', he complained. 'God gave me the happiest disposition ever mortal was blest with, had he not I must have sunk long ago.'[11] Southey's characteristic assertion of having been blessed with the happiest disposition, as is often the case, has an air of desperation about it. Yet he was still not without hopes of getting a studentship at Christ Church, which a Dr Randolph, 'from the friendship which he professed for my uncle', had virtually promised him.[12] At the end of June or early in July he wrote to tell Thomas Philips Lamb that 'every day I expect to hear from Dr Randolph when I am to set off for Oxford, which will certainly be in the course of a fortnight.'[13]

While he waited in vain for the summons to Oxford, Southey spent the summer at his aunt's house, taking walks over the familiar countryside between Bristol and Bath. One of these was with a friend whose only identity we have is the name Euryalus, Robert assuming that of Nilus. They discovered a cave above the river Avon at Clifton, which they visited on several occasions, spending their time in writing verses.

Southey's hopes of going to Christ Church were finally crushed 'by Dr Vincent's arts'. His former headmaster had apprised the dean of that college, Cyril Jackson, of his contribution to *The Flagellant*. That, Southey informed Bedford on 29 September, 'shut me out of Christ Church'. Yet he could add, 'I fancy I shall enter at Balliol'.[14] An application to Balliol College was presumably made by his uncle Herbert Hill, who had undertaken to pay for his university education. It was in a letter that his uncle sent to him from Portugal that he learned that he had been rejected at Christ Church.[15] Southey must have been concerned about his uncle's views on the unfortunate contribution to the *The Flagellant* that had cost him his place there. He was clearly relieved when, subsequent to his matriculation at Balliol, he received a letter from his uncle in Lisbon, 'chiefly upon a subject which I have been much employed upon since March 1. It is such as I expected from one who has been to me more than a parent; without asperity, without reproaches.'[16]

Because of his late admission to Balliol, Southey could not go up to Oxford for the Michaelmas term of 1792. Instead he was to commence his college career in January 1793. Meanwhile he prepared himself for his studies with some reluctance. 'I have four years and a half to spend poring over Euclid and the fathers, and in laying out plans for the future which probably will never be put in execution', he confided to Thomas Philips Lamb. 'I have been attempting Euclid but without a master I could make no progress. Perhaps disgust at the dry study contributed but I did not want perseverance. My brain was so confused with parallels, horizontals, triangles, parallelograms and all the jargon of mathematical precision that after a fortnight's hard study I fairly laid it on the shelf, and took up my constant study Spenser.'[17] Poetry was always to have a stronger appeal to him than abstract speculation.

'Is it not rather disgraceful', Southey asked Bedford, 'at the moment when Europe is on fire with freedom – when man and monarch are contending – to sit and study Euclid?'[18] Like many students during times of international upheaval, Southey felt that the momentous events unfolding in Europe made his studies seem trivial. Nevertheless, he kept abreast of them throughout the period between leaving school and arriving at university. The French Revolution became more radical socially that summer with the appearance of the so called 'sans-culottes', or those without knee breeches, that is not wearing the genteel clothes of their social superiors. On 20 June, with the apparent connivance of Pétion, the mayor of Paris, they invaded the Tuileries, the Parisian residence of the royal family, where they confronted the king. The episode rather cooled Southey's enthusiasm for the Revolution. 'Time has justified all your prophecies with regard to my French friends', he admitted to Thomas Davis Lamb. 'The sans culottes the Jacobines [sic] and the fishwomen carry every thing before them that is respectable. Every barrier that is sacred is swept away by the ungovernable torrent. The people have changed tyrants and for the mild irresolute Louis bow to the savage the unrelenting Pethion. . . . These horrid barbarities have rendered me totally indifferent to the fate of France.'[19] Southey's indifference was short-lived, however, for he took heart at the meeting of the convention in September when it proclaimed a republic. 'If France models a republic and enjoys tranquillity', he observed to Bedford, 'who knows but Europe may become one great republic and Man be free of the whole? You see I use Paine's words, but politics must not make us quarrel.'[20]

Before he went up to Oxford Southey had to cope with problems at home. His father's business, never financially healthy, now ran him into bankruptcy, and Robert Southey senior found himself in jail for debt. Southey tried desperately to get him out of his difficulties. He even went cap in hand to his uncle John, his father's elder brother, a lawyer reputedly worth £100,000. But he returned empty handed. Fortunately his aunt Elizabeth, doubtless aghast that she had a close relative in a debtor's prison, bailed his father out. The experience, however, seems to have been detrimental to Robert senior's health. Following the collapse of his business he moved to Bath where Southey's mother opened a boarding house, and when their son visited him there on his way to matriculate at Oxford in November he found his father ill in bed. 'He prest my hand with affection', he recalled, 'and for the only time in his life blest me.' Southey had a premonition that he would never see him alive again. His relationship with his father was problematic because of the latter's difficulties in showing affection. Southey himself was to ensure that his own children were aware how much he loved them. His father died in December and the funeral was held a week before Christmas. 'The melancholy silence of sorrow', observed Southey, 'wears away with me that season appropriated to festivity.'[21] Later he recollected his emotions at the funeral in 'The Retrospect'.[22]

> I knew not even the comfort of a tear
> O'er a beloved father's timeless bier;
> His clay-cold limbs I saw the grave inclose,
> And blest that fate which snatch'd him from his woes.

Southey went up to Oxford in the middle of January 1793. He was not exactly looking forward to it, partly because he suspected he would meet with 'pedantry, prejudice and aristocracy, from all of which good Lord deliver poor Robert Southey'.[23] He was particularly apprehensive of what awaited him at Balliol since he knew nobody there, all his Westminster friends who went to the university being at Christ Church. However, he soon made new acquaintances in the college. Three – George Burnett, Nicholas Lightfoot and Edmund Seward – became close companions. Burnett, the son of a Somerset farmer, was not to fulfil the promise he seemed to show at Balliol, where, as we shall see, he became one of the most enthusiastic advocates of Pantisocracy. Lightfoot was also a West Country man, from Devon, where he returned after taking orders at Oxford to be master of the grammar school at Crediton. Southey recalled how he and Lightfoot 'literally lived together at College, for we breakfasted together every morning, read together, and passed every evening together'.[24]

The fellow student who made the biggest impression on Southey, however, was Edmund Seward. Seward, indeed, had as great an influence upon him as any of his school fellows. He had been at Balliol since 1789, being three years older than Southey. He became a father figure to Southey, who confessed: 'I loved him with my whole heart and shall remember him with gratitude and affection as one who was my moral father.' This was an extraordinary claim for Southey to make, implying as it does that his own father had not been a good role model for him as far as morality was concerned. But what Southey seems to have had in mind was that Seward tested his moral philosophy, found it wanting and put it right. He 'led me right, when it might have been easy to have led me wrong. I used to call him *Talus* for his unbending morals and iron rectitude, and his strength of body also justified the name.'[25] 'He was stay and staff of my moral being, a sort of second conscience whose reproof I could not have borne.'[26]

Seward seems to have tamed some of the rebelliousness that Southey had exhibited when he first arrived in Oxford. He had objected to Balliol's prohibition of the wearing of boots, and had ostentatiously refused to have his hair cut and powdered by the college barber. The insistence on appearing in public with unpowdered hair was the sign of a radical, since it demonstrated that one was opposed to the tax that the prime minister Pitt had laid on hair powder in 1786. After he had come under Seward's influence Southey seems to have regretted this gesture, observing that philosophy 'is not wearing the hair undressed, in opposition to custom perhaps (this I feel the severity of, and blush for)'.[27] Seward also set an example of sobriety, while other students in Southey's view drank to excess. Where two years earlier he had drunk wine, when Southey met Seward he was drinking only water. Again, where previously at breakfast he had sweetened his tea and buttered his bread, now he breakfasted on tea without sugar and ate dry bread. Southey took to such asceticism with enthusiasm, rising at five o'clock in the morning to start his studies, albeit not eschewing luxuries altogether for his breakfast. Although this strict regimen does not seem to have lasted long, he came to appreciate that Seward practised self-restraint not because he was deliberately resisting temptation, but because he positively enjoyed it. Thus when Southey observed that 'if our tutors would but make our studies interesting we should pursue them with pleasure'. Seward replied, 'I feel a pleasure in studying them because I know it is my duty.' The reply, which others might have taken as sanctimonious, deeply impressed Southey. 'This I take to be true philosophy', he remarked, 'of that species which tends to make mankind happy, because it first makes them good.'[28]

'He it was who taught me to lay aside Rousseau for Epictetus', Southey informed Seward's namesake Anna.[29] He acquired a copy of *All the works of Epictetus* translated from the original Greek by Elizabeth Carter, and carried it in his pocket for twelve years 'until my very heart was ingrained with it'.

The works, and especially the *Enchiridon*, taught how to make virtues of necessities. Epictetus's precepts, distilled through Seward's example, were to become maxims for Southey, such as 'duty and happiness are inseparable'. He was to maintain for the rest of his life that the practice of self-restraint was more conducive to contentment than self-indulgence.

Epictetus began to wean Southey off the diet of Enlightenment philosophy he had imbibed at Westminster. His ill-fated contribution to *The Flagellant* had been inspired by reading Gibbon and Voltaire. Their influence was relatively short-lived, for he came to detest their anti-Christian views. Rousseau's impact on his adolescent ideology was much deeper and longer lasting. His notions that man in a state of nature was a noble savage, and that the effect of civilisation was detrimental to his well-being, informed Southey's basically pessimistic interpretation of history. They can also be detected behind his detestation of cities, especially London, and his preference for simple country life. Rousseau had been generally denounced as anti-Christian too, for he placed organised religion among the institutions that corrupted man's natural benevolence. Yet Southey denied this. While conceding Rousseau's anti-clericalism, he insisted that the 'profession of faith of the Savoyard curate' in his *Emile* was 'the creed of rational Christianity'.[30] This was Southey's own creed in his Oxford days. He rightly refuted later suggestions that his early radicalism shared the atheism as well as the republicanism of continental revolutionaries. He objected to Hume and Voltaire precisely because 'the man who destroys religion deprives us of the only substantial happiness'.[31] His conversion to Epictetus was probably facilitated by the insistence in the Introduction to Elizabeth Carter's edition that his philosophy was compatible with Christianity.

What Southey was reading by way of formal study while at college he scarcely mentions. Later in life he used to say that he learned only two things at Oxford – to row and to swim. Though this was rather too dismissive, he does not appear to have followed a regular course of instruction. His tutor, Thomas Howe, once told him that 'you won't learn any thing by my lectures Sir, so if you have any studies of your own you had better pursue them', an offer Southey 'thankfully accepted'.[32] He was to spend relatively little time in college, residing at Balliol from January to June in 1793 and again in 1794. There seems to have been no problem about Southey absenting himself for the whole of Michaelmas term in 1793, or in going down without taking any examinations, let alone a degree, at the end of his second year.

Though Southey kept up the acquaintance of Westminster friends like Collins and Wynn, he was not sorry he had not joined them at Christ Church. He convinced himself that 'Christ Church would not have suited me. I should have been a grave owl amongst a set of chattering jays – here at

Balliol I am as happy as I ever can be at Oxford.'[33] His first terms there were dominated by his relationship with Seward, with whom he spent a part of every day from 30 January to 31 May. During the Easter vacation they went on a ramble from Oxford to Worcestershire, which Southey recalled as 'my first journey afoot'.[34] The first day they walked to Moreton in the Marsh, which Southey described as 'a vile, unhealthy, horrible town', where they spent the night. 'Early the next morning we rose after a curious division of the bed, for we slept together. He took all the bed and I took all the cloathes; but we did not need rocking.'[35] He presumably meant by this that they were so tired they did not need to be rocked to sleep. It may strike some modern readers as odd that they shared a bed, but it was quite normal with travellers of the same sex in those days, and had no homosexual overtones to it.

The following day they proceeded to Evesham, whose abbey inspired Southey to extol its Gothic simplicity.[36] At Worcester they had breakfast with one Miller, a clergyman from whom Southey 'learnt much of the Glasgow mode of education, & all I learnt but served the more to disgust me with Oxonian stupidity'.[37] He particularly disliked being in all male company in Oxford. 'A company of all men is at all times bad,' he observed to Thomas Philips Lamb. 'There it is abominable.'[38] They visited Seward's family home at Sapey, near Clifton in Worcestershire, where they spent six days snowed in before returning to Oxford. 'I put my Stoicism to a trial which might have cost me dearly when walking from Worcestershire to Oxford,' he recalled over forty years later. 'I sprained my ankle violently, and, tho' a stage coach passed me presently afterwards, persevered in walking the nineteen miles that remained of our journey. Edmund Seward was my companion, and he I knew would have done the same if the accident had befallen him. But we both took warning by the result, for I was laid up on the sofa for some weeks in consequence.'[39]

Long walks nevertheless appealed to Southey, who began to call himself a peripatetic philosopher. In the summer term he walked from Oxford to Cambridge and back, covering 183 miles in twelve days. He went with Seward, apparently to visit the latter's brother who was at St John's College. Like a true Oxonian Southey was not impressed by the countryside around the rival university, which he thought 'without exception the ugliest I ever beheld. Flat and open with scarce a tree to break the amplitude of space. The town itself I do not think any way equal to Oxford', though he did concede that 'King's College chapel is far superior to any building there'.[40]

While in Cambridge Southey attended the trial of William Frend, a fellow of Jesus College, who had been an Anglican minister until he was deprived of his church living on becoming a Unitarian. In February 1793 he published *Peace and Union recommended to the associated bodies of Republicans and anti-Republicans.* The tract was designed to reconcile the political extremes by proposing a programme of moderate reform of English institutions, upon which Frend felt that all sides could agree. These included parliament, the law and the Church. It was his advocacy of measures aimed at reforming the Church of England that aroused hostile criticism from the Anglican clergy of Cambridge University. They objected to his assertion that the Book of Common Prayer was 'a composition derived from the mass book of Rome'.[41] They also took exception to his advocacy of Unitarianism and his anti-clericalism.

The master and fellows of Jesus College drew the tract to the attention of the vice-chancellor of Cambridge University, who set up a committee to investigate it. As a result Frend was arraigned before the vice-chancellor's court to answer the charge that in his pamphlet 'religion as established by public authority within this realm, and also all ecclesiastical ranks and dignities are impugned.' Even before the trial began he was stripped of his fellowship. The hearing of the case against him took up five meetings of the court between 24 April and 17 May. Then on 24 May Frend was heard in his own defence. Southey was present in the Senate house when he made his speech, which he thought was 'a most capital piece of oratory'.[42] In it Frend made the point that, while he had welcomed the initial outbreak of the French Revolution, he had been disillusioned by 'the dreadful outrages to which that country has been exposed', a conclusion that Southey himself had not yet come to, but was moving towards.[43] He must have been aware of the vociferous support being made for the accused by undergraduates in the public gallery. The ringleader of these 'noisy and tumultuous irregularities of conduct' was none other than Samuel Taylor Coleridge.[44] Though he and Southey were not to meet for another year, it is hard to believe that, after they became acquainted, they did not get round to discussing their earlier presence together in the same room at Cambridge in the summer term of 1793.

At the end of May Seward took his degree and left Oxford, and Southey and Burnett accompanied him as far as Hopcroft Heath. For Southey the parting with a man who had become a father figure had been very emotional, and he had gone back to Oxford with Burnett in a day dream.

Seward wrote to him from the house of a clergyman friend with whom he stayed, recounting a sermon he had delivered on the difficulty facing sinners immediately after they repented. They missed their sins but had not acquired spiritual peace of mind to replace them, and were vulnerable to apostasy. Perhaps Seward was sending his own convert a reassuring message. He also informed him of Frend's expulsion from Cambridge University after saying that he would sooner have his hand cut off than recant. Seward had learned that Frend had preached at the house of the Unitarian Joseph Priestley, and the vice-chancellor and his supporters 'were not pleased with his conduct in professing doctrines quite different to the established church and yet holding its emoluments. Orthodoxy! Orthodoxy! Orthodoxy! What a door hast thou opened for perjury, falsehood, strife hatred and persecution. But I am now getting on a subject which has a very close connexion with politics.'[45] It could be that Seward's information sowed the first seeds of doubt in Southey's mind about Frend's integrity, which became full grown soon after.

The most remarkable event of Trinity term 1793 in Oxford was the installation of the duke of Portland as chancellor of the university. Southey had invited several of his friends to witness the ceremony, which lasted three days in June, since 'such sights do not chance every day'.[46] When Bedford responded to his invitation by enquiring where he could stable a horse Southey advised him that it would be difficult, and that he should consider walking to Oxford 'in all the pride of humility and for once feel that total independence upon foreign aid which Peripatetics must feel'.[47] However, it seems that Bedford did not share Southey's new-found enthusiasm for hiking, for nearer the time, when Southey wrote to inform him of the arrangements, he warned him with a characteristic pun that 'installation will be difficult to procure' for a horse. Southey undertook to be Bedford's host, and Collins that of his brother Horace, while 'if any of your friends like to come we can quarter a whole regiment upon young Wynn.'[48] How many of Southey's acquaintances were present in the event is not known, though three weeks after it he remarked 'what a party we were'.

Much of the installation was taken up with laudatory verses congratulating the duke on his election. Southey did not contribute one. As he put it in a facetious poem 'to a college cat, written soon after the installation at Oxford',

> For three whole days I heard an old Fur Gown
> Beprais'd, that made a Duke a Chancellor:
> Trust me, tho' I can sing most pleasantly
> Upon thy well-streak'd coat, to that said Fur
> I was not guilty of a single rhyme![49]

He presumably did not join in the chorus of praise because he disapproved of Portland's politics. The duke had been regarded as the leader of the Whig opposition to the government after William Pitt was appointed prime minister in 1783. However, though he welcomed the French Revolution in 1789, he came to share many of the misgivings that Burke expressed in his *Reflections*. By 1793 he was thoroughly alarmed, and supported the Pitt ministry after war was declared on France in February. The chancellorship of Oxford University was regarded as a reward for his changing political position, which was to be sealed the following year when he became home secretary. Of his behaviour in that office Southey was to observe in 1803 that 'there was a cruelty in the old administration which seems to have proceeded more from the Duke of Portland than any one else.'[50] Ten years earlier he had still to earn that reputation, but already Southey was sufficiently suspicious of the duke's politics to praise that 'most Democratic beast', the college cat.

> I like thine independence! treat thee well,
> Thou art as playful as young Innocence;
> But if we play the Governor, and break
> The social compact, God has given thee claws,
> And thou hast sense to use them. Oh! that man
> Would copy this thy wisdom! spaniel fool
> He crouches down and licks his tyrant's hand
> And courts oppression.

At the start of the summer vacation Southey went home to his mother's boarding house in Bath. He did not look forward to it, telling Bedford that it was 'far from being for me the comfortable retreat you enjoy. I have been so long enured to misery there that the idea of it when it comes across happier scenes clouds them. Keen as my relish is for the pleasures of domestic life, I have experienced them but little.'[51] Such sentiments informed much of his early poetry, which has been read as 'a quest for home'.[52] He did not find it in Bath, where he did not stay long, for by mid-July he was staying with his aunt in Bristol. Here too he had hardly experienced domestic bliss, and before the end of the month Southey went to Herefordshire to see his uncle, who was visiting a living he held in that county. As his uncle Herbert Hill was now responsible for his education, having undertaken to pay his college expenses, this must have been a traumatic meeting for Southey. He was aware that Herbert wished him to follow in his footsteps by becoming an Anglican clergyman. Being unable to subscribe to the Thirty-Nine Articles of the Church of England, the very first of which enjoined belief in the Trinity, Southey could not contemplate a clerical career. On his way to meet his uncle his religious scruples exercised Southey's mind. 'As I rode along now fast now slow now wet now dry before I joined my uncle', he informed Bedford, 'I ran over your thoughts upon religion etc a thousand times.'[53] Previously he had only seen his uncle 'a few days at long intervals in childhood'. Now he spent 'a ten days journey on horseback with him'.[54] What they discussed on their journey is not known, but Southey can hardly have failed to bring up his objections to becoming a clergyman. This could account for his failure to return to Oxford for the Michaelmas term.

His decision to stay at home has been ascribed to his becoming involved with his future wife, Edith Fricker. Her father had tried his hand at several occupations, including tavern-keeper and owner of a coal wharf in Bath, but had gone bankrupt before his death in 1786. His widow had tried to make a living by opening a school and then a dress shop in Bristol. Edith and her sisters Eliza, Mary, Martha and Sara undertook needlework to help towards their mother's income. Byron was to refer to them as 'milliners of Bath', the innuendo that they were whores being as inaccurate as the location he ascribed to them. Southey's mother gave them employment, and the two families came to know each other while he was a boy. The Fricker sisters were by all accounts attractive girls. Sara, the eldest, was impulsive and sensual and Southey was apparently attracted to her initially. Edith, more repressed than her sister, was to be described as 'the most beautiful creature I had ever seen' by somebody who met her in 1800.[55] There has been some speculation as to when Southey's friendship ripened into affection, and some accounts place it at about this time.

Certainly Southey's thoughts did turn to marriage that summer as he considered the outcome of the trial of William Frend, who was found guilty and sentenced to banishment from Cambridge University. Although Southey execrated the conduct of his 'persecutors', he now despised that of Frend too, having apparently read some of the proceedings in the case, though not the offending tract itself. 'The little I know of his pamphlet is too contemptible to deserve notice' he informed Bedford on 31 July.[56] What little he knew could be derived from the articles exhibited against Frend, which quoted the critical passages. One, which Southey seems to have found particularly objectionable, gave rise to the sixth article against Frend. This quoted a section from *Peace and Union* in which Frend had accused the clergy of affecting a superiority over the laity, who 'like brute beasts sit tamely under this usurpation: a man . . . cannot pledge his faith to a lovely woman without the interference of the priest.' Southey took this to be an attack upon marriage itself. This seems to have incensed him more than anything else Frend had written, for the only explanation of his contempt for *Peace and Union* that he gave to Bedford was 'marriage is a sacred institution and the man who would lessen the reverence due to it is a villain.'[57] Although he no doubt still approved much of what the pamphlet proposed by way of reform, especially of the law and parliament, it is significant that he took exception to its cavalier treatment of marriage. Already he had made the firm commitment to it which was to be so momentous in his future life, not least in his relationship with Coleridge.

However, if there was an immediate prospect of marriage concentrating his mind on the subject at this time, it was not to Edith Fricker. On the contrary, when he visited Seward at Sapey in April 1793, he fell for Augusta Roberts, who lived in the same house. He was smitten enough to write to her in the summer, apparently proposing marriage, but enclosed the letter in one to Seward so that he could read it too. Seward, taken aback by its contents, replied that his brother John was bespoken for her. 'What remained for me?' Southey asked. 'At the expense of my happiness I preserved that of two persons more deserving. I directed him to burn my letter, desired him to forget it and promised what never can be performed, to forget Augusta.' The thoughts on marriage inspired by the fate of Frend were probably due to his feelings for Miss Roberts. Certainly, he had no romantic interest in Edith at that time, for when he returned home he complained that 'the only society that could please me here is that of some women, sisters, with whom I was partly educated and whose histories are as melancholy as my own', referring to the Frickers. Unfortunately 'the ill-grounded fears of my Aunt forbid it.'[58] Miss Tyler looked down on the Fricker girls, and did not want him to become attached to any of them, a possibility that Southey clearly ruled out at this stage. His aunt's fears might have been aroused by the fact that he had found a new friend, Robert Lovell, a son of staunch Quakers who also lived in Bristol. More to the point, as far as his aunt was concerned, Lovell had become engaged to one of the Fricker sisters, Mary, who as an actress was even more undesirable than a milliner. Apropos of Mary, Southey admitted: 'nor could I entertain a sincerer affection for a sister'.[59] It was, however, only brotherly affection he felt for any of the Fricker girls at the end of 1793 – he was still in love with Augusta Roberts.

Southey wrote the letter to Augusta, and got the devastating reply from Seward, while he was staying with the Bedfords that summer. On 8 August he had left Bristol to take up an invitation from his friend Grosvenor Bedford to spend a few weeks with his family at Brixton. When they were together in Oxford early in July they had discussed Joan of Arc, and it occurred to Southey that her story was ideal for an epic poem. He had gathered materials for it, sketched out a plan, and even written about three hundred lines, before he went to Brixton. There on 13 August, the day after his nineteenth birthday, he sat down to write in earnest 'the original poem in twelve books, finished in six weeks from that time', as he unfortunately put it in the Preface to the first edition.[60] The remark was a hostage to fortune to critics who claimed that the epic was too hastily written. In fact it was to change significantly between the manuscript he completed in Brixton and the published version that appeared in 1796.[61]

What immediately inspired Southey to set his poem in France, albeit in the Middle Ages, was the opportunity this gave him to express his opposition to the war with the French revolutionaries that had broken out in February

1793. His pacific views had been strengthened by the sight of soldiers in Bristol. 'Oh Bedford the red robes of slaughter militate very strongly against my ideas', he had written to his friend. 'When I see men at least negatively good and certainly useful, taken from the plough to learn the trade of murder I wonder where the thunder sleeps.'

Southey was not enamoured of the Jacobins who, led by Robespierre, had seized power in the Convention by purging it of the Girondins that summer. 'I soon hope to hear of the fall of Marat Robespierre Thuriot and David', he went on to inform Bedford. 'Vive la Republique! My Joan is a great democrat or rather will be.'[62] After his return to Bristol from Brixton in mid-October, news reached England that the French queen, Marie Antoinette, had been executed on the 16th. Bedford wrote to question whether Southey's republicanism condoned this outrage. 'To suppose that I felt otherwise than grieved and indignant at the fate of the unfortunate Queen of France was supposing me a brute', he protested in his reply. 'I can condemn the crimes of the French and yet be a republican.'[63] The subsequent execution of Brissot, the leader of the Girondins, particularly depressed him. 'I am sick of this world and with everyone in it', he wrote to Bedford on 8 November upon hearing the news.

> The murder of Brissot has completely harrowed up my faculties and I begin to believe that virtue can only aspire to content in obscurity, for happiness is out of the question. I look around the world and every where find the same mournful spectacle. The strong tyrannise over the weak – man and beast. The same depravity pervades the whole creation. Oppression is triumphant every where and the only difference is that it acts in Turkey thro' the organ of a Grand Signior, in France of a Revolutionary Tribunal and in England of a prime minister.[64]

Within a week Southey made an exception of the United States of America, which had adopted a republican constitution in 1789. 'It was the favourite intention of Cowley to retire to a cottage in America and seek happiness in solitude which he could not find in society', he observed in another letter to Bedford. 'I should be pleased to reside in a country where mere abilities would ensure respect, where society was upon a proper footing and man was considered as more valuable than money, and where I could till the earth and provide by honest industry the meal which my wife would dress with pleasing care.'[65] Family ties at that time seemed to 'chain me to England', as he informed Bedford's brother, 'otherwise the first vessel that sails to America should bear with it one more emigrant'.[66]

Southey was engrossed in philosophical speculations during the autumn of 1793. He joined the Bristol library on his return from Brixton, and the very first book he borrowed was William Enfield's *History of Philosophy*. He was particularly intrigued by the history of Gallienus, who contemplated a platonic utopia in Campania. Southey imagined himself creating a similar city state, which he called 'Southeyopolis'.[67] His imaginary utopias even included the United States. 'Fancy me in America', he invited Bedford.

> Imagine my ground uncultivated since the Creation and see me wielding the axe to cut down the tree and now the snakes that nestled in it. Then see me grubbing up the roots and building a nice snug little dairy with them. Three rooms in my cottage and my only companions some poor negros whom I have bought on purpose to emancipate. After a hard day's toil see me asleep upon rushes . . . so thus your friend will realise the romance of Cowley and even outdo the seclusion of Rousseau till at last comes an ill-looking Indian with a tomahawk and scalps me – a most melancholy proof that society is very bad and that I shall have done very little to improve it . . . poor Southey will either be cooked for a Cherokee or oysterised by a tyger![68]

Thus months before he met Coleridge he was engaged in visionary schemes for a utopian community, and even contemplating emigration to America – ideas that were to find fuller expression through Pantisocracy.

On 25 November Southey borrowed William Godwin's *Enquiry Concerning Political Justice* from the Bristol library, and was completely converted to the theories expounded in it. Godwin advocated that the test of the utility of any institution should be its rationality. Monarchy and aristocracy exposed to rational inquiry were demonstrably absurd. In their place he proposed democracy, exercised in small communities, in which anti-social behaviour could be eradicated by the application of reason. *Political Justice* continued Southey's gradual conversion from Enlightenment philosophers. 'Five years ago', he wrote in 1799, 'I counteracted Rousseau by dieting upon Godwin and Epictetus.'[69] Although he never completely renounced the French philosopher, he was offsetting his Romanticism with a kind of utilitarian stoicism.

Southey told his friend Charles Collins, who was at Christ Church, that the Bristol library kept him as well employed as he would have been at Oxford, 'at least in my own opinion, & you know, to me that is the most material'. He admitted that 'I may not form a taste here but I can increase a stock of useful knowledge, and you know the prettiest nosegays are formed of various flowers. Oxford would have been very dull this term as none of my Balliol friends reside, & it is with them that I mostly live. We shall meet again in January & college will have something of novelty to recommend it.'[70]

Southey had decided to return to Oxford, having resolved his problems about pursuing a clerical career by studying medicine instead. 'I purpose studying physic', he informed Grosvenor Bedford. 'This resolution has relieved me from a weight that hung heavy upon my mind and embittered many hours.'[71] His relief is palpable in a verse letter he wrote to his close friend Nicholas Lightfoot anticipating the forthcoming term when 'with pleasure I once again my friends shall view'.[72] After they met, Lightfoot argued with him that a minister was more useful to society than a doctor. 'Suppose you and I, Lightfoot, resided in the same village as priest and apothecary', Southey riposted in defence of his decision. 'A labouring man with a wife and family is dangerously ill. Who renders him the most essential service – you in talking of heaven and closing his eyes in peace, or I in restoring him to the world and giving him time to prepare for death?'[73] Such bold assertions were all well and good as long as he stuck to his resolution. Unfortunately he was not destined to fulfil the programme he outlined to Bedford, 'to perfect myself in anatomy – attend the clinical lectures and then commence – Doctor Southey!!!'[74] Scanty evidence makes it difficult to determine when and why he dropped medicine, though he apparently kept up the study for the whole of Hilary term. His son attributed his failure to continue with it to his dislike of anatomy, but he does not appear to have been squeamish about dissecting corpses. On the contrary, he boasted that he was 'waiting eagerly to cut up human flesh' when he arrived back at Balliol in February.[75] And he retailed with ghoulish relish a rumour that Dr Christopher Pegge, a reader in anatomy, fed a dog on the pickings from the anatomy school, so that 'his room may be smelt at Woodstock whiffing the accumulated stinks of the dead bodies, the Dog and the Doctor himself.'[76] It was what occurred in the Easter vacation when he went to Bristol from mid-April to mid-May 1794, however, that changed his mind.

Before this, Southey appears to have spent his most enjoyable term in Oxford. Away from his studies he relaxed and sang discordantly to the music produced by his friends Burnett and Lightfoot on a harpsichord, a piano and a flute. When a senior member of Balliol fell ill and could not say grace at dinner, he wrote a light-hearted letter satirising the failure to find a substitute among the students. 'Jeremiah the scout grew more fearful and the chief priests and elders more impatient; then spake he to Southey – go thou and say grace, but Southey knew it not, and the chief priests and elders departed in wrath.'[77] He engaged in earnest political discourse with Robert Allen, an undergraduate at University College whom he met in the anatomy school. Recognising a man of extraordinary ability, Southey introduced himself and found Allen to be 'an excellent republican'. He was also a fellow poet, and Southey presumably showed him the 'Botany Bay Eclogues', which he had begun to compose and which versified some of the political concerns that they discussed. Thus the first empathised with 'Elinor', a whore, 'the hireling prey of brutal appetite', 'the mercenary tool of savage lust'.[78] She finds redemption in Australia,

> The reign of Nature! for, as yet unknown
> The crimes and comforts of luxurious life,
> Nature benignly gives to all enough,
> Denies to all a superfluity.

Looking back on the discussions he had engaged Allen in, Southey concluded: 'we democratised gloriously, nor did I quit Oxford without feeling something like regret.'[79]

By the time Southey returned to Oxford after a month in Bristol, his whole outlook on life had altered. He was no longer interested in pursuing a medical qualification. On the contrary he was desperate to raise money immediately and to get a job as soon as possible. He vainly tried to capitalise on the reversion to property he thought he would inherit when his uncle, John Southey, died, though he might have realised from John's refusal to help out his bankrupt father that there was not much to be hoped from that quarter. He then asked Bedford to try to get him a post in the Exchequer, but this, too, came to naught when his friend Charles Wynn politely pointed out that Southey's radical politics scarcely qualified him for a position in the civil service. 'I am a Republican', he admitted, 'and did wrong in even thinking of the situation.'[80]

The reason Southey gave for pursuing these objectives was that he was committed to a young woman. Of the reversion he said that: 'had I a sufficiency in independence, I have every reason to expect happiness. The most pleasing visions of domestic life would be realised.' Again of the government post he wrote: 'in case of success I shall joyfully bid adieu to Oxford, settle myself in some economical way of life, and when I know my situation, unite myself to a woman whom I have long esteemed as a sister, and for whom I now indulge a warmer sentiment.'[81] Although he did not give her name, it was clearly Edith Fricker. In May 1799 he was to remind her that 'it is five years ago since you and I first became intimate, five years ago at this season did you and I play with the lilac blossom in the Old Market.'[82] It seems that while Southey was in Bristol he had proposed to her and she had accepted. There was no way an impecunious student could support a wife – hence Southey's desperate attempts to secure an income.

When these attempts failed Southey was resigned to spending another two years at Oxford. He was determined not to be in residence during the forthcoming Michaelmas term, and 'if possible never to reside again', he told Bedford on 25 June, 'but I am doomed to take orders and little less than a miracle can rescue me.'[83] In fact the miracle had already occurred in Southey's fateful meeting with S. T. Coleridge, and the prospects opened up by Pantisocracy.

CHAPTER THREE

Pantisocrat (1794–1795)

In the middle of June 1794 Samuel Taylor Coleridge set out from Cambridge on a walking tour to Wales accompanied by another undergraduate, Joseph Hucks. When they arrived in Oxford Coleridge went to see his former school friend Robert Allen, with whom Southey had recently become acquainted. Allen recognised that Coleridge and Southey had similar views on politics and religion, and shared his own love of poetry. He therefore took his visitor round to Balliol College to introduce them to each other. 'Coleridge was brought to my rooms', Southey recollected in 1811, 'and that meeting fixed the future fortunes of us both.'[1]

Although their outlooks might have had much in common, they were in fact temperamentally and intellectually very different. Coleridge was notoriously an elemental force of nature, like a hurricane or volcano, bowling over all who met him by the sheer force of his personality. His mind was in a constant ferment with philosophical ideas, which he communicated with a zeal and a flow of eloquence that left his hearers spellbound. He came to be widely regarded as the greatest genius of the age. Southey, though gifted, was no genius. He confessed that his cast of mind could not cope well with abstract ideas, and approached life's problems empirically. Coleridge was an unstable, erratic character, whose lack of will power was to lead to opium addiction and to incapacitate him from prolonged application. Southey by contrast was stable, controlling violent emotions with an iron will, and applying himself to a rigid discipline of hard work and productivity.

While these differences were to lead eventually to a cooling of their relationship, they hit it off immediately. Coleridge, Southey reported soon after their first meeting, 'is of most uncommon merit – of the strongest genius, the clearest judgement, the best heart'.[2] For his part Coleridge was sufficiently impressed by Southey to extend his visit to Oxford for three or four weeks, during which they met apparently every day. Southey presumably told Coleridge about his engagement to Edith Fricker, his need for money, his objections to becoming a clergyman and his thoughts of emigrating. It was Coleridge who came up with a solution to all these problems in the establishment of a utopian commune. 'We planned a utopia of our own', Southey reminisced years later, 'upon the basis of common property – with liberty for all – a Pantisocracy – a republic of reason and virtue.'[3] At the time, the conversations that resulted in this outcome were probably more practical on Southey's side, more philosophical on Coleridge's. Coleridge was 'one whom I very much esteem and admire', Southey observed, 'tho two thirds of our conversation be spent in disputing metaphysical subjects.'[4] The 'tho' is significant. One did not dispute with Coleridge, certainly not on metaphysics, on which he was an expert, and on which Southey was on a less sure footing. One listened. It was not so much a conversation as a monologue. Southey would be exposed to a brilliant exposition of philosophers such as Godwin, whom he had recently read, and David Hartley, whose works he was not familiar with.[5] Godwin provided the political theory behind Pantisocracy, Hartley the psychological concepts. In a face-to-face society, such as that envisaged as the ideal in *Political Justice*, individuals could be educated to realise that allowing their passions rather than their reason to rule them was destructive to self as well as to social fulfilment. The few who refused to curb their irrational impulses would have their behaviour controlled by the majority. Coleridge was inspired more by David Hartley than by Godwin, having been convinced by his *Observations on Man* that the key to a harmonious society was to induce in children a love and respect for their parents, from which would develop love for family, then neighbours and ultimately for society in general. This is what made the 'second generation' crucial to Coleridge's contribution to the project that he dubbed 'Pantisocracy'. Fired with enthusiasm by Southey's bare suggestions, he developed it into a fullblown system in which the Pantisocrats were to practise 'aspheterism', another term he invented. Where Pantisocracy involved the government of all, aspheterism meant that property would be held communally rather than individually.

To realise these utopian aspirations required a group of like-minded people to join them. Coleridge and Southey began recruiting such a body at Oxford among their friends. Allen and Burnett were early recruits to it. The meeting at which Coleridge coined the term 'Pantisocracy' was held in the rooms of Matthew Bloxam, an undergraduate at Worcester College. At this stage, according to Burnett, there 'were the mere outlines of the plan'.[6]

If Coleridge's philosophical scheme of things needed to be hammered into shape, so did the practical arrangements for getting the commune established. This fell to Southey's lot. His first concern was how to raise the money necessary for the voyage and settlement. The only way he could think of was by writing. Over the summer of 1794 he tried to get *Joan of Arc* accepted for publication by subscription, wrote *The Fall of Robespierre* with Coleridge, finished a volume of his own poems together with some by his brother-in-law Robert Lovell, and composed a verse tragedy on Wat Tyler in a week, all with a view to making money. Even before he left Oxford the thought occurred to him of getting his 'Botany Bay Eclogues' published there, but he decided that it was too near the summer vacation.

Botany Bay was much on Southey's mind during his last weeks at Balliol. He had been moved by the fate earlier in the year of Joseph Gerrald, Thomas Muir, Thomas Fyshe Palmer and Maurice Margarot, who had all been sentenced to transportation for seditious activities in Scotland. Gerrald, Muir and Margarot had attended a so-called 'British Convention' in Edinburgh that was suppressed in December 1793 by the authorities, who accused the delegates of modelling its proceedings on those of the French national Convention. They, along with William Skirving, the leading light in the British Convention, were tried for treason before the notorious Judge Braxfield, found guilty and sentenced to fourteen years in Botany Bay. Palmer, who was accused of seditious libel, was sentenced to seven years. Margarot, Muir and Palmer were all shipped out to Australia on the *Surprise* at the end of April 1794. Gerrald, whom Southey was to visit in prison in January 1795, did not sail until the following May.

Their sentences inspired Southey to write verses 'To the Exiled Patriots'. Introducing them to Bedford he noted that 'I must take my own advice to my brothers Muir Palmer etc.'

> So shall your great examples fire each soul
> So in each freeborn heart for ever dwell
> Til Man shall rise above the unjust controul
> Stand where ye stood – and triumph where ye fell.

'You will like the poetry better than the sentiment', Southey admitted, referring to Bedford's conservative sympathies, 'but the man who wrote and felt those lines must never be guilty of silence.'[7] Before the end of the year he had completed the poem in sixteen verses, and signed it 'Caius Gracchus Southey'.[8] Caius Gracchus was a reforming Roman tribune of the second century BC whose name was also adopted by the French revolutionary Babeuf. Southey was at his most radical in the heady months when he was planning the Pantisocracy project.

Early in July Coleridge and Hucks resumed their journey to Wales. Southey and Burnett accompanied them along the western road through Witney as far as Northleach, where they went their separate ways, the Cambridge men carrying on towards Wales while the Oxonians headed down to Bath. As Southey and Burnett walked along they discussed 'no other subject but that of Pantisocracy'.[9] Where at Oxford, according to Southey, it had been 'talked of, but by no means determined on', now 'it was . . . talked into shape by Burnet and myself'.[10] They agreed that it could only be feasible in America, and hoped that Coleridge would join them there. Burnett was more taken with the theoretical aspects of the scheme than his companion, observing that 'our grand object then was the Abolition of Property, at least of individual property. Conceiving the present unequal distribution of property to be the source of by far the greater part of the moral evil that prevails in the world.'[11]

No sooner had Southey arrived in Bath than he applied himself to the practical problems of the projected commune, which he now decided should be located in Kentucky. He set himself up as the chief recruiter of potential Pantisocrats. Southey was at first doubtful whether his brother-in-law Robert Lovell would accompany him to America, but confident that his own brother Tom and his friend Edmund Seward would join them. By 1 August he was able to inform Horace Bedford that he had six lined up, now including Lovell, and his own mother, even though it would probably be another year before they could set sail. He was not without hopes of persuading the Bedfords to sign up too.

Southey also set about the problem of raising money from publications in earnest. Two volumes of poems by himself and Lovell were in progress. On 19 July he went to see Richard Cruttwell, a printer in Bath, with a view to publishing a subscription edition of *Joan of Arc*, hoping to get fifty subscribers at a guinea each. As he informed Bedford, 'should the publication be any ways successful it will carry me over and get me some few acres a spade and a plough'.[12] Bedford replied to recommend that it should be placed in the hands of a London publisher, William Nicol. This had never occurred to Southey, who responded to the suggestion with cautious enthusiasm: 'if he or any bookseller will give me a hundred guineas for the copy right, when I have secured subscribers enough to indemnify publication, I shall be glad to rid myself of the poem. You know it breathes freedom, but a piece ending with a coronation can hardly be stiled republican.' As the 'argument' to the tenth book of *Joan* indicates, 'the poem concludes with the coronation of Charles at Rheims'.[13] He anticipated that he could 'write enough to clear 200 pounds before March and more would not be wanted'.[14] When they learned of the execution of Robespierre, which took place on 28 July, Coleridge, Lovell and Southey cobbled together a verse play on it, contributing an act each. *The Fall of Robespierre* was written hastily, in two days, with a view to raising money. In the event Lovell's contribution was deemed to be inferior, and Southey rewrote it, so that the finished play consisted of two acts by him and only one, the first, by Coleridge. In the third act Southey put a speech into the mouth of Barrere that expressed the same sentiments he developed at large in *Joan of Arc* about the war with revolutionary France.

> Never, never,
> Shall this regenerated country wear
> The despot yoke. Though myriads round assail
> And with worse fury urge this new crusade
> Than savages have known; though all the leagued despots
> Depopulate all Europe, so to pour
> The accumulated mass upon our coasts,
> Sublime amid the storm shall France arise
> And like the rock amid surrounding waves
> Repel the rushing ocean. – She shall wield
> The thunder-bolt of vengeance – She shall blast
> The despot's pride, and liberate the world.

Again, his attitude towards Robespierre's execution reveals the extent of his radicalism in 1794. He was alleged to have said, 'I had rather have heard of the death of my own father', which if he did was a bit pointless since his father was already dead.[15] More to the point, he told Horace Bedford 'that Robespierre was the benefactor of mankind and that we should lament his death as the greatest misfortune Europe could have sustained'.[16]

Coleridge was able to collaborate with Lovell and Southey as he had walked from Wales to Bristol early in August. Shortly after his arrival he was introduced to the Fricker family and quickly became infatuated with Sara. Southey was surprised by this since he had been led to believe that Coleridge was in love with a Mary Evans. He nevertheless encouraged the relationship, seeing that it fitted in perfectly with his scheme to include the Frickers in the proposed colony on the Susquehanna River. He even hoped that George Burnett would marry Martha, one of the sisters, but she prudently turned down Burnett's proposal. As Coleridge's biographer has suggested, 'the entire Fricker family was also caught up in the Pantisocratic whirlwind, and as Coleridge later observed mournfully, it was easy to mistake "the ebullience of schematism for affection, which a moment's reflection might have told me, is not a plant of so mushroom a growth".'[17] Things certainly developed rapidly, for by 5 September Southey could inform Horace Bedford that by the time they went to America 'I shall then call Coleridge my brother in the real sense of the word'.[18]

Southey had got to know his future brother-in-law quite well in the month since he had arrived in Bristol. On 14 August they set off on a week's walking tour of Somerset, accompanied only by Southey's dog Rover. They stayed at a 'pothouse' in Cheddar, where they were put up in a garret. Rover was consigned by the landlady to the stable, which Southey disliked as the dog used to sleep either on his bed or his mother's. During the night Rover slipped his halter and finished up in the garret after all. Southey, who clearly did not object to sharing his bed with a dog, did not enjoy sharing one with Coleridge, whom he found 'a vile bedfellow'.[19] On their walk they visited George Burnett at Huntspill and Thomas Poole, an acquaintance of Coleridge who lived at Nether Stowey. Poole heard from them the latest version of Pantisocracy, which they had presumably thrashed out as they made their way across Somerset.

> Twelve gentlemen of good education and liberal principles are to embark with twelve ladies in April next . . . each man should labour two or three hours a day, the produce of which labour would, they imagine, be more than sufficient to support the colony. As Adam Smith observes that there is not above one productive man in twenty, they argue that if each laboured the twentieth part of time, it would produce enough to satisfy their wants. The produce of their industry is to be laid up in common for the use of all; and a good library of books is to be collected, and their leisure hours to be spent in study, liberal discussion and the education of their children. . . . They calculate that each gentleman providing £125 will be sufficient to carry the scheme into execution.[20]

They had not yet decided whether the marriage contract could be dissolved if one or both partners agreed. This reflected the divergent views of Coleridge, whose libertine proclivities toyed with the idea of free love in the colony, and Southey, whose strict views on marriage required the couples to marry before they set sail, in James McKusick's words, 'like Noachic animals, two and two, in connubial bliss aboard the American ark'.[21] Southey was critical of Coleridge's loose morals, while Coleridge commented ruefully on Southey's 'strength of mind and confirmed habits of strict morality'.[22]

Poole's assessment of the relative merits of the two Pantisocrats was perceptive. Coleridge he considered to be 'the Principal in the undertaking. . . . His aberrations from prudence, to use his own expression, have been great; but he now promises to be as sober and rational as his most sober friends could wish' – how often was he to make that vow? – 'In religion he is a Unitarian, if not a Deist; in politics a Democrat, to the utmost extent of the word.' Poole was less impressed by Southey, 'a younger man, without the splendid abilities of Coleridge, though possessing much information, particularly metaphysical, and is more violent in his principles than even Coleridge himself. In Religion, shocking to say in a mere Boy as he is, I fear he wavers between Deism and Atheism.' The two must have come across as the wildest radicals when they arrived in Nether Stowey, for Poole's cousin recorded that 'each of them was shamefully hot with Democratic Rage as regards politics, and both Infidel as to religion'.[23] The reality was rather different. As disciples of Godwin, both Pantisocrats were more disposed towards meritocracy than strict democracy. Coleridge was indeed a Unitarian at this time, while Southey was never an atheist. He was later to claim that Coleridge had 'disposed me towards Christianity by showing me that none of the arguments which had led me to renounce it was applicable against the Socinian scheme.'[24]

Their journey consolidated their partnership in Pantisocracy. Shortly after returning home, Southey wrote that 'should the resolution of others fail, Coleridge and I will go together, and either find repose in an Indian wig-wam – or from an Indian tomahawk. . . . When Coleridge and I are sawing down a tree we shall discuss metaphysics; criticise poetry when hunting a buffalo, and write sonnets while following the plough.' He was nevertheless confident that others would join them. 'We go at least twelve men with women and children', he wrote on 22 August. 'By this day twelvemonths the Pantisocratic society of Aspheterists will be settled on the banks of the Susquehanna.'[25] Switching their destination from Kentucky to Pennsylvania has been attributed to the Pantisocrats coming to prefer the promotional literature of a group associated with the Unitarian Joseph Priestley, who had settled in Northumberland at the forks of the Susquehanna, over that of Gilbert Imlay, the American lover of Mary Wollstonecraft, who sang the praises of Kentucky.[26] Coleridge was to study these and other accounts of settlements in the United States, and even to consult with acquaintances and agents of Priestley, when he returned to Cambridge for the autumn term. The change had been made before then, however, some time in August, probably while Southey and Coleridge were tramping through Somerset. They told Poole where they planned to settle when they met him in Nether Stowey – unfortunately he could 'not recollect the place, but somewhere in a delightful part of the new back settlements!'[27]

When Coleridge left for London on 2 September Southey felt that 'it was like the losing a limb to part with him'.[28] By then, according to Burnett, 'our scheme was brought to such maturity as to be almost ripe for execution'.[29] Coleridge took with him the text of *The Fall of Robespierre* and Southey's 'Botany Bay Eclogues', which they hoped would raise money for the expedi-tion. When he reached Cambridge he managed to place the play with a publisher there, Benjamin Flower, who printed five hundred copies. When it appeared early in October, however, the title page announced that it was the work of just one author, Samuel Taylor Coleridge of Jesus College. Coleridge explained this to Southey, saying that it would sell at least a hundred copies in Cambridge; but he never completely explained it away, and when recrim-inations broke out later for the failure of Pantisocracy, this incident added to the bitterness between them.[30] Perhaps as a sop to Southey's authorial pride Coleridge placed two of his poems, including 'Elinor', the first of the 'Botany Bay Eclogues', in the *Morning Chronicle* for 17 and 18 September. Southey was unaware of this gesture. His mother told him that when she was travel-ling from Bristol to Bath a stranger in the coach had insisted on reading out a poem that appeared in the paper. When she recalled it he recognised it as 'Elinor', and was delighted that his mother had liked it. 'Perhaps no praise that I ever obtained in after life', he observed years later, 'gave me so much pleasure'.[31] Coleridge also gave the manuscript of all the eclogues to Joseph Johnson, a London publisher, 'for purchase if he chuses to give 15 guineas for them'.[32]

Meanwhile, another hopeful venture – the volume of poems that Southey had written with Lovell – was emerging from Cruttwell's press in Bath. Horace Bedford was promised a copy when it was published. He had sent some of his own verses to Southey, who praised them but recommended that Horace 'buy Bowles poems and study them well. They will teach you to write better, and give you infinite pleasure.' Southey had followed his own advice. One of his favourite books of poetry was W. L. Bowles's *Fourteen Sonnets written chiefly on Picturesque Spots during a Journey* (1789), which served as a model for his own early poems such as 'The Retrospect', which he consid-ered to be 'certainly the best piece I have ever written'.[33] Indeed, it was to be the first in the volume of poems by himself and Lovell, which was published in December.[34] Prefaced by a quotation from Bowles, it begins with a plea to Memory to

> Let thy vivid pencil call to view
> Each distant scene, each long-past hour anew,
> Ere yet my bosom knew the touch of grief,
> Ere yet my bosom lov'd the lyre's relief.

The chief memory recalled is that of Southey's schooldays at Corston. He had been reminded of them while returning home from Oxford at Easter 1794, when he had visited the brook that went through the grounds of the school 'in which every morning I washed my hands and face'.[35] This brook features in the poem when Southey remembers the years

When one small acre bounded all my fears:
And even now with pleasure I recall
The tapestry'd school, the bright-brown boarded hall;
The murmuring brook, that every morning saw
The due observance of the cleanly law.

While the leading Pantisocrats were hopeful of raising money for the voyage to America from their publications, they were also recruiting followers to go with them. Coleridge preached Pantisocracy and aspheterism to the dons of Cambridge, and Southey drummed up support in the West Country. In mid-October he assured his brother Tom that there were 'now twenty seven adventurers'. His enthusiasm was boundless. 'This Pantisocratic system has given me new life new hope new energy. All the faculties of my mind are dilated. I am weeding out the few lurking prejudices of habit and looking forward to happiness.'[36]

There were, however, ominous signs of scepticism and downright disapproval that might have curbed his optimism. Edmund Seward had had second thoughts about the venture and withdrawn from it. Southey was mortified, seeing his friend's decision 'as a dereliction of Christianity itself'. Seward was relieved to learn 'that his disappointment at my declaring off has not amounted to anger, but contrariwise he supposed me to act upon laudable motives'.[37] He was nevertheless very uneasy about his decision to abandon the scheme, wishing that he had earlier tried to dissuade Southey from 'so rash an enterprise . . . an arduous if not a calamitous and ruinous adventure, from which I might at first perhaps have diverted him'. 'Southey's offending his aunt too', he informed Lightfoot, 'was no trifling occasion of sorrow to me.'[38]

Seward was referring to the extreme reaction of Miss Tyler when she learned about Southey's plans to marry Edith Fricker and go to America. She flung him unceremoniously out of her house on 17 October, vowing never to see him again, or even to open a letter with his handwriting on it. She was as good as her word. Why she behaved so harshly after being so involved in his upbringing is hard to explain. The faded gentility in which she lived may well have led her to look down on the more humble Frickers, and to wish that her nephew could find a more socially acceptable wife. She also no doubt thought that he was acting irresponsibly and throwing his future away on a hare-brained scheme. That these considerations should lead her to cut him off for ever shows how much he had offended her sense of propriety. Southey, 'the Apostle of Pantisocracy', made his way through 'the pelting of the pityless storm' to his mother's house in Bath. On the road he met up with an old man 'most royally drunk' who needed his assistance, so he 'dragged this foul animal thro the dirt wind and rain' for nine miles.[39] 'Poor Shadrack is left there in the burning fiery furnace of her displeasure', Southey told his brother Tom; 'he saw me depart with astonishment – "why, Sir, you be'nt going to Bath at this time of night, and in this weather!"'[40]

Aunt Elizabeth's servant Shadrach Weeks was to be the cause of an even more ominous development. Southey had recommended that he accompany the Pantisocrats to America. Coleridge at first welcomed him as a brother, but when he learned that Southey intended him to go in the capacity of a servant he was outraged. On 21 October he wrote to remind Southey of the principles of Pantisocracy, which treated all as equals. He took exception to the suggestion that there should be servants in utopia. 'Let them dine with us and be treated with as much equality as they would wish', Robert had suggested, 'but perform that part of labour for which their education has fitted them.' 'Southey should not have written this sentence', Coleridge objected; 'is every family to possess one of these unequal equals, these Helots Egalites?'[41] Coleridge also objected to other Pantisocrats whom Southey had recruited, particularly not wanting Mrs Southey or Mrs Fricker to be among them. 'I wish, Southey, in the stern severity of judgement, that the two mothers were not to go', he complained. '*That* Mrs Fricker – we shall have her teaching the infants *Christianity*, – I mean – that mongrel whelp that goes under its name – teaching them by stealth in some ague fit of superstition.'[42]

Despite these setbacks Southey could still write to his brother on 6 November that 'our American scheme goes on right well ... [Gerr]ald, Holcroft and Godwin – the first men in England, perhaps in the world – highly approve our plan'. It was a curious triumvirate to praise so highly. Godwin, as a leading philosopher, possibly deserved it. But Joseph Gerrald, the radical convicted for his part in the British Convention, and Thomas Holcroft, a minor dramatist who got caught up in the English treason trials of 1794, would scarcely have been similarly praised by most contemporaries. Southey was also 'writing a tragedy on my uncle Wat Tyler, who knocks out a tax gatherers brains, then rose in rebellion. Our toast today was: May there never be wanting a Wat Tyler whilst there is a Tax-gatherer.'[43] It is ironic in view of his aunt's treatment of him that Southey wrote a verse play about Wat Tyler, for he always claimed that the rebel, with whom she shared a surname, was a remote relative of hers, hence the reference to him as 'my uncle'. Nevertheless 'in the course of three mornings' he completed it. Where none of the poems he published, in the collection with Lovell, was overtly political, this was a work so radical that the publisher to whom he sent it, James Ridgeway, held on to it for fear of prosecution. In Act One Tyler, a blacksmith, bemoans the incidence of a tax that would take away the six groats he possessed. His neighbour Hob sympathises:

> Curse on these taxes – one succeeds another –
> Our ministers, panders of a king's will,
> Drain all our wealth away, waste it in revels,
> And lure, or force away our boys, who should be
> The props of our old age, to fill their armies,
> And feed the crows of France.[44]

Indeed, this had as much relevance to the year 1794 as it did to 1381, when the real Wat Tyler led the Peasants' Revolt. Tyler murders a tax collector who attempts to ravish his fifteen-year-old daughter, then joins those who rise up against the state with cries of 'Liberty, Liberty! No Poll-tax! No War!' They release from jail the priest John Ball, who addresses them in 'the cause of freedom'. The king defuses the situation temporarily by promising to relieve his subjects of the hated tax, but reneges on his promise when he gets the upper hand of the rebels. Ball is then put on trial, accused

> of preaching up strange notions
> Heretical and treasonous; such as saying
> That kings have not a right from Heaven to govern;
> That all mankind are equal; and that rank,
> And the distinctions of society,
> Ay, and the sacred rights of property,
> Are evil and oppressive.

Southey is surely here alluding to the treason trials of 1794 involving Thomas Hardy, John Horne Tooke and his friend John Thelwall.[45] Had *Wat Tyler* appeared that year he might well have found himself in the dock alongside the accused. Where they were acquitted, Ball in his verse drama is found guilty and sentenced to death.

At the end of the volume of *Poems* by Lovell and Southey appeared an advertisement for 'publishing by subscription Joan of Arc, an epic poem by Robert Southey of Balliol College, Oxford, to be handsomely printed in one volume quarto, price one guinea, to be paid on delivery. Subscriptions will be received by Mr C. Dilly, Poultry, London; by the booksellers of Oxford, Cambridge and Bath.' Unfortunately this edition never materialised, for Southey failed to find the fifty subscribers needed to make it viable. About 22 November, he announced to Bedford that he was to sell the copyright for fifty guineas and fifty copies.[46] Though he did not name the publisher this had to be Joseph Cottle, who recalled in his reminiscences that he had made exactly that proposal to the young Southey, who accepted it 'without a moment's hesitation'.[47] Lovell, who knew that Southey was having difficulties finding a publisher for *Joan*, had introduced them. 'Never will the impression be effaced, produced on me by this young man', Cottle remarked. 'Tall, dignified, possessing great suavity of manners; an eye piercing, with a countenance full of genius, kindliness, and intelligence.'[48] Despite Cottle's generosity, the amount of money raised from royalties on publications came miserably short of the sum required to finance the expedition to America. This stark reality led Southey to consider establishing the utopian settlement in Wales. The idea perhaps occurred to him as he had taken up the Welsh epic *Madoc*, which he had started at Westminster and subsequently abandoned. In 1794 he began writing it again in verse, completing a book and a half. Coleridge initially rejected out of hand relocating their utopia from America to Wales: 'As to the Welsh scheme', he wrote, 'pardon me – it is nonsense – We must go to America if we can get money enough.'[49] Coleridge's relations with Southey were strained at the end of 1794, not just over disagreements concerning Pantisocracy, but also regarding his own intentions towards Sara Fricker. He clearly had cold feet over the proposed marriage once he got away from Bristol, even hankering after Mary Evans until she declared that she was engaged to another. Still he did not return to Bristol when the Cambridge term ended in December, but went instead to London. Coleridge was staying in the capital at the Salutation and Cat Inn when Southey wrote to express his concerns over his engagement to Sara. His 'rectitude', as Coleridge called it, led him to impress upon his friend that marriage to Sara was his 'duty'. Coleridge reluctantly undertook to visit her, even appointing a day when he would arrive in Bristol. Southey waited for him in Bath, where he planned to join the coach and proceed to the Fricker household with his friend. He went out to await the arrival of each coach, but there was 'no Coleridge!' He wrote to Sara that 'I believe I should be angry were it not for the hope that he has written to Bristol. Your sister [Edith] desired me to let you know when he would arrive . . . this vile expectation unhinges me so lamentably. They laugh at my punctuality . . . why it is the very prominent feature in my character . . . why will he ever fix a day if he cannot abide by it?'[50]

Coleridge succumbed to Southey's pressure to the point of undertaking to leave London by waggon and be in Bath on 3 January 1795. Instead of waiting for the waggon to arrive, Southey and Lovell set off to meet it at Marlborough, only to find that Coleridge was not on it. In sheer exasperation Southey continued to London to try to track Coleridge down. His first port of call was the Salutation and Cat, which Southey called 'a most foul stye', but Coleridge had adjourned to the Angel Inn in Newgate Street, where he was eventually tracked down. 'My heart was very heavy', Southey wrote to Edith Fricker. 'Coleridge objected to Wales and thought it best to find some situation in London till we could prosecute our original plan. He talks of a tutorage – a public office – a newspaper one for me. I went to bed in dirty sheets – and tost and turned, cold weary and heart sick till seven in the morning.'

Southey's despondency was so profound that he reached out to Edith for security. 'Love me, my dear Edith, or there will be no comfort for me.' For the first time genuine doubts about the feasibility of establishing a utopian commune began to assail him. 'I lean strongly to Wales in spite of his strong arguments', he confided to her, 'but if it be not practicable will get a place in some public office of 80 or 100 per year which with some 50 more by writing for reviews etc we can live with frugality and happiness.' The dawning realisation that Pantisocracy was a pipe dream woke him up to reality, where he had to face up to his future prospects and responsibilities. He had invested so much of his emotional and mental energies in pursuit of what now seemed to be a chimera that it left him exhausted and desperate. 'Do not forget me', he beseeched Edith, 'do not believe that any circumstances can ever make me unhappy while secure of your affection.'[51]

Despite his misgivings over Southey's plans for Pantisocracy and the Fricker sisters, Coleridge was persuaded to return to Bristol. About the middle of January 1795, he and George Burnett rented rooms at 25 College Street from a Mrs Saviers, and Southey moved in with them before the end of the month. For the next seven months the three leading Pantisocrats lived together, not in the wide open spaces of America, but in cramped lodgings in Bristol. 'America is still the place to which our ultimate views tend', Southey informed Bedford, 'but it will be years before we can go. As for Wales, it is not practicable.'[52] Instead of engaging in philosophical discussions while sawing down a tree, therefore, Southey and Coleridge discussed poetry and politics sitting together at the same table. They planned a journal to be called the *Provincial Magazine* in which they would publish their poems. Though nothing came of this, they did compose verses during their weeks together. They even collaborated on one poem which was to become notorious, 'The Soldier's Wife'. It was an essay in dactylics, probably influenced by Southey's favourite contemporary poet, Frank Sayers, 'whose *Disquisitions Metaphysical and Literary* . . . had argued for the introduction of classical metre into English verse'.[53] When the *Anti-Jacobin* was launched in November 1797 against radicals in general, and 'Jacobin' poets in particular, this poem was singled out for its scorn.

More serious than their collaboration on 'The Soldier's Wife' was the contribution of Coleridge to Southey's *Joan of Arc*. When Cottle finally published it in 1796 they had quarrelled bitterly, and Southey gave Coleridge the barest acknowledgement in the Preface. 'The 450 lines at the beginning of the second book', he explained, 'were written by S. T. COLERIDGE. But from this part must be excepted the lines 141, 142, 143; and the whole intermediate passage from 148 to 222. The lines from 266 to 272 are likewise mine, and the lines from 286 to 291.'[54] This was a very grudging, even ungracious, indication of the help he had received from his fellow lodger in College Street.

'If Coleridge and I can get 150 pounds a year between us', Southey wrote at the time they lived together, 'we purpose marrying, and retiring into the country, as our literary business can be carried on there . . . till we can raise money for America – still the grand object in view.'[55] It is curious and significant that, even when all prospects of emigration had faded, they did indeed live off their writings, marry sisters and retire into the Lake District to write.

In addition to raising funds by writing, they also arranged to give a series of public lectures each, for which they charged one shilling a lecture for admission. Despite the price they were well attended, and a group of prominent Bristolians undertook to be patrons. These included John Prior Estlin, a Unitarian minister whose views were sympathetic to those of the lecturers. Coleridge started the series by lecturing on moral and political subjects. Southey followed him from 14 March to 24 April with twelve talks on history. They were advertised as being 'unconnected with the politics of the day', though Southey confided to his brother Tom that he was 'teaching what is right by showing what is wrong'.[56] When they were over he boasted that he had 'said bolder truths than any other Man in this country has ever ventured. Speaking of my friend Tom I cried O Paine! Hireless Priest of Liberty! Unbought teacher of the poor! Chearing to me is the reflection that my heart ever acknowledged – that my tongue hath proudly proclaimed – the truth and Divinity of thy Doctrines!'[57]

Beginning with 'The Origin and Progress of Society', the lectures ranged over the history of Europe from Ancient Greece to the War of American Independence. Southey admitted that preparation for them had taken up almost all of his time so that there was little left for any other writing. Some of the reading he did for them can be ascertained through his borrowings from Bristol Library. W. Mitford's *History of Greece*, borrowed on 5 March, was no doubt useful for the lectures he gave on 'Legislations of Solon and Lyrcugus' and 'State of Greece from the Persian War to the Dissolution of the Achaean League'. A. Ferguson, *The History of the Progress and Termination of the Roman Republic*, taken out on 23 March, despite its three volumes must have been intended to provide information for a lecture on 'The Rise, Progress and Decline of the Roman Government' he planned to give on the following day. Coleridge, however, who later claimed to have provided half of the materials for Southey's lectures, insisted on giving this one himself. Southey reluctantly stood down and announced at the end of his third lecture that the next would be given by Coleridge. On 24 March an audience duly assembled at the card room of the Assembly Coffee House in Prince's Street. Seven o'clock, the time for the lecture to start, arrived; but Coleridge failed to appear. Again, where this was to become characteristic behaviour on Coleridge's part, it took the punctilious Southey aback. He delivered his own lecture on the subject on 27 March, adding an extra date to the schedule to complete the series.

The range and scope of the lectures was an astonishing feat for the twenty-year-old Southey, one which he was never to repeat. He found the whole experience unnerving, and his confidence cannot have been bolstered by a review of his performance in a Bristol paper, the *Observer*.[58] Although the anonymous writer praised Southey and the subjects of his talks as 'the language of Truth ... the language of Liberty', he went on to criticise 'his gesticulation and attitude when he is speaking in Public ... his body is always too stiff, his features are apt to be distorted'. Despite the review insisting that these 'are faults which he can easily obviate', and that if he did he could 'possess Demosthenian or Ciceronian abilities', Southey never again lectured in public, except in his dreams – 'the only time in which I can play the Orator'.[59]

What could only have undermined his confidence further was Coleridge's impact as a lecturer. He was a born public speaker, spellbinding his audiences with his impassioned rhetoric. Coleridge confidently published his lectures, whereas Southey resisted any urge to publish his 'as they are only splendid declamation'.[60] Jealousy of Coleridge's oratorical skills might partly explain Southey's reaction to his friend's offer to give, and failure to deliver, the fourth lecture in his own series. The day after the fiasco they set out to visit Tintern Abbey accompanied by their fiancées and Joseph Cottle. The party dined at the Beaufort Arms in Chepstow, and Cottle recorded that 'after dinner an unpleasant altercation occurred between – no other than the two Pantisocritans!' Southey remonstrated with Coleridge over his failure to give a lecture he had specifically requested, pointing out that he should never have asked to deliver it 'unless he had determined punctually to fulfill his voluntary engagement'. Coleridge shrugged off his failure to appear as a matter of no great moment. When an argument ensued Cottle tried to intervene but could not stop the quarrel. The paradox of the leading lights of Pantisocracy, committed to subdue all anti-social passions by the exercise of reason, quarrelling in public struck him as a demonstration 'even to themselves, [of] the rope of sand to which they had confided their destinies'.[61]

It was about this time – after they had commenced their lectures – that Coleridge dated Southey's reneging on 'those broad principles in which Pantisocracy originated', even accusing him of having 'long laid a Plot of separation' from the scheme'.[62] Their disagreement at Chepstow renewed his suspicion, and he was 'greatly agitated even to many tears'. It could well have been the case that Coleridge's cavalier behaviour gave the conscientious Southey considerable pause about committing his destiny further to such an irresponsible and unreliable partner. Cottle's efforts to reconcile them during the subsequent excursion to Tintern Abbey helped to patch up their differences. His amusing account of how they left Chepstow so late that they nearly lost their way in the gathering dusk conveys an impression of forced mirth during an outing soured by the altercation at the inn. Shortly afterwards, however, Southey reassured Coleridge that he was still a Pantisocrat. By that stage Coleridge had come to terms with a trial period in Wales prior to going to America, and Southey convinced him that he, too, was committed to the Welsh experiment. Throughout May and early June they appear to have worked in harmony again. Coleridge wrote and delivered six more lectures on 'revealed religion', and together they completed *Joan* while Southey made progress with *Madoc*. Some time in the summer, however, the day after a strawberry party, Southey revealed to Burnett that he was not prepared to share his own resources with the others, but that they were to remain his private property. Charles Wynn had generously offered to award Southey an annuity of £160 when he came of age the following year, and Burnett was convinced that this had caused Southey to change his mind about becoming an unpropertied Pantisocrat. It could have done, for Southey was already grumbling that he had contributed four times more to the common stock in College Street than Burnett and Coleridge. The thought of keeping them indefinitely on his own resources might well have given him pause about their joint endeavour. Coleridge was not surprisingly beside himself with fury when Burnett repeated the conversation to him. 'It scorched my throat', he told Southey. 'Your private resources were to remain your individual property, and every thing to be separate except on five or six acres. In short we were to commence Partners in a petty Farming Trade. This was the Mouse of which the Mountain Pantisocracy was at last safely delivered! I received the account with Indignation & Loathings of unutterable Contempt.' Coleridge was right to feel that Southey had badly let down the Pantisocrats, particularly Burnett. But he was wrong to conclude that he had plotted to leave them in the lurch. Rather an accumulation of pressures, in themselves separate, combined to make him abandon Pantisocracy. The zeal of 1794 was bound to cool when the sheer logistics of realising the enterprise were brought home to him. He later objected that he had been left with the hard work of organising the settlement. 'I had devoted myself to the establishment of a system which I still believe to be the panacea of all human calamities', he complained. 'But in the ardent perception of the end I glanced rapidly over the means . . . for the founders of such a system fortune, ability, energy and virtue were indispensable. The first we were all deficient in – of the second there was a quantum. Energy was confined to me alone.'[63] There was some truth in that. Coleridge had been the inspired philosopher of Pantisocracy, but Southey had been the main entrepreneur, and his energy was slowly drained during the course of 1795. A psychological blow was the death in June of Seward, a mentor whose change of mind about the scheme might also have influenced him more than he was prepared to admit. 'He purified and strengthened my heart', he observed on hearing of his death, 'and he has left a vacancy there which will not easily be supplied.'[64] A philosophical setback was his disillusion with Godwin, whom 'I read and all but worshipped', he told Bedford, though 'I have since seen his fundamental error, – that he theorises for another state, not for the rule of conduct in the present.'[65]

Perhaps the most important single influence on Southey's decisions was the view that his uncle Herbert took towards his abandonment of his studies and preoccupation with Pantisocracy. Southey had announced these intentions to him in a letter he wrote on 7 November 1794, when he also revealed that he had been forced to leave his aunt's house. Herbert's reply, written from Lisbon on 24 January 1795, was devastating: 'I was more concern'd than surprized at your letter', he began.

> I knew what your politics were and therefore had reason to suspect what your religion might be. I have no reason to be angry with you on account of the resolution you have taken, for as you never consulted me on the subject you have spared me the mortification of having my advice slighted. I have still less reason to be so on account of your not taking Orders – for I never, that I recollect, proposed it to you or in the least hinted that the education given you was with that view – if you have been taught, as you say you have been, to look upon that Church as your future destination – it must have been by some of your friends, who perceived that in that line you had an establishment ready for you, and that in that line you could immediately have been of assistance to me and contributed to the support and comfort of your family. At present perhaps those friends may think you desert both. – But you say your Plan is fixed. – If however any circumstance should occur to induce you to give up this plan you would do well I think to make some excuse to your Tutor for your absence – put yourself on board a packet and come for a short time to Lisbon till you and your Aunt can be reconciled.[66]

It is not known when Southey received this letter, though its icily calculated reproof must have hurt him even more than Coleridge's heated outburst.

When his nephew did not book a passage to Portugal, Herbert went to England to insist that he determined on a career. Southey was convinced that he meant him to take holy orders, and seems seriously to have considered it, despite his objections to the Thirty-Nine Articles. After he had talked it over with Coleridge and gone to bed, his fellow lodger wrote him a letter, which he gave him the next morning, hoping that it would steel Southey's resolve against entering the ministry by stressing that 'the point is whether or no you can perjure yourself?'[67] That day they walked to Bath, and again Coleridge tried to dissuade Southey from acquiescing in his uncle's desires. He pointed out that he could scarcely conceal his views for two years until he was ordained, as they would be proclaimed to the world when *Joan of Arc* was published. Southey replied flippantly that he was 'pretty well up to their Jargon and shall answer them accordingly'. Coleridge attributed his ultimate decision not to pursue a clerical career to 'the weight of infamy which you perceived coming towards you like the Rush of Waters'.

In fact Southey's flippancy concealed his grave reservations about becoming an Anglican priest. Coleridge's arguments had registered with him, for in a letter to Bedford he used the very idea put to him in the nocturnal letter. 'My uncle urges me to enter the church', he wrote, 'but the gate is perjury, and I am little disposed to pay so heavy a fine at the turnpike of orthodoxy.'[68] He had decided instead to become a lawyer, which meant studying in London, where he hoped to find lodgings near his friend in Brixton. In the event his uncle did not insist that he became a minister, and accepted his proposal to study law instead. Coleridge saw little difference between a clerical and a legal career, and reproached Southey for settling for the latter. He determined that Southey should be relegated from the status of friend to that of mere acquaintance. Robert felt his coldness towards him, and on 1 September moved out of College Street. Thereafter he divided his time between his mother's house in Bath and Cottle's in Bristol, spending more nights in the latter so as to be nearer Edith. The two leading Pantisocrats parted with mutual recriminations, even cutting each other when passing in the street. Southey complained that Coleridge 'has behaved wickedly towards me'.[69] For his part Coleridge wrote a scathing letter to Southey, sanctimoniously repudiating him with the words: 'You are lost to me, because you are lost to Virtue'. Since he considered that it was probably the last letter he would write to his former friend he added another three thousand words for good measure, tracing 'the History of our connection'. It was a virtuoso display of studied superiority, ending with 'farewell!'

Ironically, just as their relationship was breaking down, they met for the first time the man who was to be for ever linked with them in the expression 'the Lake Poets'. William Wordsworth visited Bristol some time during the late summer and sought them out. He was impressed by them both, remarking that Coleridge's talent seemed 'very great', while he had 'every reason to think very highly of [Southey's] powers of mind'.[70] He read the manuscript of *Joan of Arc* while Southey furnished some lines for one of his poems. Their paths did not cross again for many months, however, whereas Wordsworth and Coleridge were to form a friendship which would result in *Lyrical Ballads* three years later.

Coleridge and Southey might well never have seen or spoken to each other again but for the fact that they became brothers-in-law when Coleridge married Sara Fricker on 4 October, and Southey married her sister Edith on 14 November. Southey was in fact about to embark with his uncle for Portugal in order to spend time there before he began his study of the law. Herbert had hoped that getting him away from England would cool his ardour for Edith too, but Southey insisted on marrying her before they sailed, thwarting his uncle by keeping his wedding secret. The ceremony, as recorded in the register of St Mary's Redcliff, took place 'with the utmost privacy'.[71] It was witnessed by Joseph Cottle, who had given Southey the money for a wedding ring and the Church fees, and by Cottle's sister Sara. Only the groom himself, his young bride, the two witnesses and the presiding clergyman, George Campbell, were present. The couple pressed hands and then parted, Edith, who kept her maiden name, going home while Southey stayed with Cottle. It seems they did not so much as consummate their union before he left Bristol the following day, though Southey's extreme anxiety about Edith's reputation arose perhaps because they had anticipated their nuptials, and he was concerned that she might have become pregnant. One of the explanations for marrying Edith he gave to Bedford was that he did not wish her to be the subject of gossip: 'if the tongue of malice should whisper that I have forsaken her (and Calumny has been busy with me) there is now an answer that will make it dumb.'[72] He went to Falmouth to board the ship that was to take him to Corunna. Before he sailed he learned that his marriage was public knowledge in Bristol, and wrote to Cottle to tell him that he was unconcerned by it, adding characteristically 'I have done my duty'.[73]

The circumstances of Southey's departure were very bleak. Not only had he left his bride behind, which caused him to 'burst into tears', but he also received the blistering letter from Coleridge ending their relationship. Southey suffered bouts of melancholy and frustration as he went with his uncle to stay with a Cornish clergyman prior to their sailing. Not surprisingly perhaps, he had a jaundiced view of Cornwall, which he described as 'a foul country; the tinmen inhabit the most agreeable part, for they live underground. Above it is most dreary; desolate.' The dreariness and desolation must have been as much in his mind as in his eye, and his uncle did little to help, confessing to their host that he had not read his nephew's published poems. 'Never had man so many relatives so little calculated to inspire confidence', Southey complained.[74] His letters convey a gallows humour as he waited impatiently for the packet to sail. Although he was relieved when they finally departed at the beginning of December, he seems to have been genuinely apprehensive of death by drowning. He assured Bedford, to whom he entrusted his will, that if he were drowned he would certainly contrive to visit him as a ghost. On the eve of his departure he half shuddered 'to think that a plank only will divide the husband of Edith from the unfathomed ocean!'[75]

CHAPTER FOUR

'Jacobin' (1795–1800)

Southey set sail from Falmouth on the *Lauzarotte* on Tuesday 8 December 1795, and arrived at Corunna on the 13th, after a very rough passage through the Bay of Biscay, which left him 'in momentary expectation of death'.[1] He spent five days there, staying with Alexander Jardine, the British consul, 'the only place I met with the society I wished'.[2] Then he and his uncle made their way to Madrid by coach before going to Lisbon, where they arrived on 27 January.

Frustration at being wrenched from the side of his beloved Edith found relief in Southey's *Letters written during a short residence in Spain and Portugal*, which were ostensibly to her.[3] He was particularly affected by having to spend Christmas Day in Spain rather than with his wife, which inspired him to express his own home thoughts from abroad.

> How many a heart is happy at this hour
> In England! brightly o'er the cheerful hall
> Beams the heaped hearth, and friends and kindred meet.

Southey recalled the festive seasons of his childhood, and contrasted them with his comfortless Christmas in Spain. 'I will not wish thee not to weep', he told Edith.

> There is a strange pleasure in Affection's tears
> And he who knows not what it is to wake
> And weep at midnight, is an instrument
> Of Nature's common work.[4]

His thoughts about women in general, as well as Edith in particular, developed during his time abroad. Before he left England he told Bedford that 'her virtues are of the domestic order . . . I hate your daffydown-dilly women'.[5] While he was in Spain and Portugal he reflected on woman's role in society. Clearly influenced by Mary Wollstonecraft, he observed that 'a man of well cultivated mind will seldom find a woman equal to him while the present execrable system of female education prevails; however if he does not find equality he can make it; woman is a more teachable animal than man.'[6] Hopes of converting Edith from a helpmate devoted to domesticity into an intellectual companion, even if she had wished to make the change, were doomed to disappointment. When on his next visit to Portugal Southey found a woman who was his intellectual equal, Mary Barker, he was to become infatuated with her to the point that Edith felt threatened by their relationship.[7] On his first sojourn in the Iberian peninsula, however, he still pined for his beloved bride.

Southey's separation from Edith seems to have coloured his view of Spain and Portugal, which struck him as being characterised by filth and fleas, vermin and bigotry. Even when he conceded that, as they journeyed towards Madrid, they passed through 'a lovely country, a paradise of nature', he observed that 'the inhabitants are kept in ignorance and poverty by the double despotism of their church and State'.[8] His reaction to Roman Catholicism was typical of that of most Protestant English travellers in the late eighteenth century. He himself commented that 'here in the words of Mary Wollstonecraft "the serious folly of superstition stares every man of sense in the face".'[9] In Southey's case, however, the reaction was more extreme and more intolerant. The expulsion of the Moslems struck him as being almost regrettable, since 'a tolerant and cleanly superstition has been exchanged for the filth and ferocity of Monks'.[10] His own experience of Catholic countries confirmed a deeply held distrust and even detestation of Catholicism, which never left him.

Witnessing 'Popery' at first hand reinforced Southey's radicalism. 'I looked on with – I trust the prophetic eye of Hope, to the promised Brotherhood of Mankind', he observed, 'when Oppression and Commerce shall no longer render them miserable by making them vicious.' These sentiments were echoed by Henry V in *Joan of Arc*, which had appeared in December, just before he went abroad. The king anticipates the day when men would see

the genuine blackness of our deeds
And warn'd by them, till the whole human race,
Equalling in bliss the aggregate we caus'd
Of wretchedness, shall form ONE BROTHERHOOD
ONE UNIVERSAL FAMILY OF LOVE.[11]

Southey's political opponents dubbed these ideas 'Jacobin', identifying him with the extreme democrats of the French Revolution associated with Robespierre. Yet he himself sympathised more with the Girondins, the moderate revolutionaries whom the Jacobins supplanted, and whose leaders, like Brissot, they executed. Looking back on them years later he conceded to another sympathiser that he 'thought as highly of the Girondistes as you . . . but was too young and too ignorant to see their errors. . . . I entered, therefore, warmly into their views; and no public event ever caused me so much pain as the fate of Brissot and his associates.' Similar sympathies were also expressed in *Joan of Arc*, where he compared Chinon, the royal capital in her time, with Paris in 1796:

> . . . one day doom'd to know the damning guilt
> Of *Brissot* murder'd, and the blameless wife
> Of *Roland*! – Martyr'd patriots – spirits pure,
> Wept by the good ye fell!

Joan of Arc was written 'in a republican spirit'. The epic story of the Maid of Orleans who led a French patriotic resistance against the English, despite being set in the Middle Ages, was subversive stuff at a time when England was at war with revolutionary France. In the Preface Southey went out of his way to defend this position. 'It has been established as a necessary rule for the Epic', he wrote, 'that the subject be national. To this rule I have acted in direct opposition, and chosen for the subject of my poem the defeat of my country. If among my readers there be one who can wish success to injustice, because his countrymen supported it, I desire not that man's approbation.'[12]

The initial critical response was, on the whole, favourable. One of the first notices, John Aikin's in the *Monthly Review*, appeared while Southey was in Lisbon. Like most other reviewers he criticised Southey for the impression he gave in the Preface that the epic had been written in a mere six weeks. Nevertheless Aikin praised the poetical powers displayed in it as being 'of a very superior kind'. As for the politics of the work, he noted that 'in many parts a strong illusion to later characters and events is manifest; and we know not where the ingenuity of a crown lawyer would stop, were he employed to make out a list of innuendos.'[13]

'Of what advantage has this journey been to me?' Southey asked shortly after his arrival in Lisbon. 'Why I have learnt to thank God that I am an Englishman, for though things are not quite so well there as in El Dorado, they are better than anywhere else.'[14] This again was a typical reaction of English visitors abroad in the eighteenth century – Southey even headed a letter he wrote 'Lisbon, from which God grant me a speedy deliverance'.[15] He considered that 'an English pigsty is cleaner than the metropolis of Portugal', yet the longer he stayed and grew accustomed to Portuguese culture and society, the less typically English his attitude became. He studied Spanish and Portuguese poetry during his visit, and wrote an essay on them that he published in his *Letters written during a short residence in Spain and Portugal*. He began to study the history of the Iberian peninsula, which was to become an absorbing and abiding interest. Above all he went to Sintra, where his uncle had a house, and was stunned by the setting of that idyllic summer retreat of the kings of Portugal. 'I know not how to describe to you the strange beauties of Cintra', he wrote. 'It is, perhaps, more beautiful than sublime, more grotesque than beautiful, yet I never beheld scenery more calculated to fill the beholder with admiration and delight.' His uncle's house, set amongst orchards of lemon and orange trees, enchanted him: 'I shall always love to think of that lonely house and the stream that runs beside it, whose murmurs were the last sounds I heard at night, and the first that awoke my attention in the morning.' Years later he was to experience similar sounds from the Greta, which reminded him of the nights he spent in what Byron was to call 'that glorious Eden'.[16] When the time came to leave Portugal he could observe that, although he was eager to return to England, 'my heart will be very heavy when I look back upon Lisbon for the last time'.[17]

Southey sailed from Lisbon on 5 May on an American ship bound for Hull, which docked at Portsmouth late on the 14th. From there he made his way to Bristol, arriving two days later to an emotional reunion with Edith. One of the first things she told him was that their brother-in-law Robert Lovell had died while he was away. The news shocked Southey: 'the tidings of his death was the most sudden check I ever experienced. I learnt it on my return to England when I expected to pass that very evening in his company.'[18]

Southey and Edith rented accommodation in Kingsdown for several months, until the time came when he had to go to London to start his legal studies. 'I shall live a secluded life in London, probably without ever making another friend', he predicted. 'The repellent coldness of my manners will protect me from any acquaintance for I cover the milk of human kindness with as rough an outside as a cocoa nut.'[19] This was a very revealing comparison, indicating an awareness that he could be off-putting to people who saw the husk and not the contents.

Towards the end of September Southey sought out Coleridge with a view to reconciliation. Coleridge loftily acknowledged that he was prepared to reinstate him to the status of acquaintance, but not yet to that of friend. 'In the close of 1796 we were so far reconciled as to resume the common intercourse of acquaintance', Southey recollected. 'Something was owing to the interference of common friends, more to our connection by marriage, and probably what influenced me was the habit of mind which induces us rather to remember the good qualities of a lost friend than his faults, and to select for remembrance chiefly what is pleasurable to recollect.'[20] Coleridge invited Southey to breakfast on 13 November, where they were joined by Thomas Beddoes, Charles Lloyd and James Losh. This was Southey's first meeting with Losh, a North Country man who, like Wordsworth, had left Cambridge to go to France during the Revolution. Southey took immediately to Losh's radical views, telling Bedford that he 'carries with him one of the most open democratic faces I ever saw'.[21] They met several times before Southey set off for London in February.[22]

On 7 February 1797 Southey entered Gray's Inn, where he committed himself to a rigorous routine, rising early in the morning to devote nine hours to his legal studies, and spending his evenings learning German and writing *Madoc*. 'This morning I began the study of the law' – he recorded on 22 February – 'this evening I began Madoc'.[23] He also somehow found time to translate the second volume of Jacques Necker's book *On the French Revolution*.[24] This was a commission he obtained from the publishers Cadell and Davies, who paid him twenty-five guineas. He translated 480 pages at the rate of sixteen pages a day. 'It is an employment from which neither pleasure or credit can be derived,' he admitted, 'nothing but mere money'.[25]

The volume of poems he published in December 1796 (it bore the imprint 1797) was greeted favourably by fellow radicals. John Thelwall, the radical reformer, told Henry Crabb Robinson that 'there were luminaries rising above the Horizon who bid fair to eclipse the dazzling splendour of Mr Burke's orb'. Robinson understood 'that Coleridge and Southey were the *Starlets* he alluded to – indeed they have both Genius. . . . Southey's poems contain most exquisite morsels.'[26] The volume was dedicated to Mary Wollstonecraft. Southey had confided his esteem for her to Horace Bedford, extolling her as 'an excellent woman, of mild feminine and unassuming manners and whose character calumny cannot blacken'.[27] His admiration was made public not only with the verse dedicatory to her but also with the poem 'The Triumph of Woman'. Southey got to meet Mary Wollstonecraft, among other 'lions of literati', while he was in London early in 1797. He described her as having 'an expression indicating superiority; not haughtiness, not sarcasm . . . but still it is unpleasant . . . but her manners are the most pleasing I ever witnessed, they display warm feeling, and strong understanding; and the knowledge she has acquired of men and manners, ornaments, not disguises, her own character.'[28] Notwithstanding finding her expression unpleasant, the twenty-three-year-old Southey was clearly smitten by the thirty-eight-year-old Mary Wollstonecraft. Byron was to claim many years later that 'Mary was a former love of Southey's' and that 'he did his best to get [her] and could not'.[29] This accusation seems highly unlikely. Although Southey was undoubtedly infatuated by Mary Wollstonecraft, his feelings for her were almost certainly platonic. Indeed, he was what used to be called a ladies' man, confessing to 'like the women better than the men'.[30] When Southey's friend George Dyer took it upon himself to introduce him to writers on the London literary scene, he warmed to women like the poet Ann Christal and the novelist Mary Hays more than to men. The women no doubt found him handsome and charming, while he was so vain about his own appearance at this time that he could even facetiously suggest a revolutionary tribunal, which would judge men by their physiognomy, and sentence all men who were not good looking to transportation. He obviously thought there was no danger of his being condemned by the 'Physiognomical Tribune', doubtless reassured by the response he got from flirting with the women writers he met. Yet he showed no inclination whatsoever to graduate from intellectual to physical intimacy with any of them.

On the contrary, Southey was living with his wife Edith at the time in lodgings at 20 Prospect Place, Newington Butts, having persuaded her to join him in London because he was missing her. So far from seeking companionship, he had declined to take up the membership of a literary society to which he had been elected. 'Surely a man does not do his duty who leaves his wife to evenings of solitude', he maintained, 'and I feel duty and happiness to be inseparable. I am happier at home than any other society can possibly make me.'[31] Mary Wollstonecraft was already pregnant with Godwin's child, on which account she married him that April. On 3 May the Godwins invited the Southeys to dinner. It was possibly on this occasion that Mary Wollstonecraft expressed her opinion of François Noël Babeuf, the French Jacobin whose trial (which concluded with his execution at the end of May) was then in the news. 'Babeuf was a great man', Southey asserted later, 'Mary Wollstonecraft told me he was the most extraordinary one she had ever seen and in the orgasm of the Revolution the system of total equalisation would have been wise.'[32] Before the end of the month Southey left London for Hampshire, and, apart from a brief visit in June, did not return until 6 October. Wollstonecraft had been buried nearly a month before, having slowly died of septicaemia and loss of blood due to retaining the placenta following the birth of her daughter Mary.

Robert and Edith left London as soon as he had fulfilled the residency requirements at Gray's Inn, apart from the obligation to attend a dinner towards the end of June. They both disliked the capital intensely and wished to get out into the country. Edith was also unwell. Her illness detained them in Southampton for an 'unpleasant' week, after which they moved to Burton, near Christchurch, where they rented a cottage for six months. 'I am in a place I like', Southey observed there, 'and the acquaintance I have made here pleasant.'[33] One of the acquaintances he had made was John Rickman, whom he described as 'a sensible young man, of rough, but mild manners, and very seditious'.[34] Rickman, who was largely responsible for organising the first British census in 1801, was to become Southey's life-long friend. Another friend he made was Charles Biddlecombe, who also lived in the neighbourhood. Shortly after moving into the cottage Southey had to go up to London to dine in Gray's Inn, leaving Edith behind in Burton. While in town he wrote to her to express his 'vexation' at their being apart. 'You know Edith with what reluctance I ever absent myself one hour from you', he assured her, though he added: 'we are more the masters of our feelings than we are willing to confess.' He stayed with Anthony Carlisle, a surgeon at Westminster Hospital who moved in the same radical circles as his own. Robert wrote to Edith from Carlisle's, joking that 'he has the worst pens in the world, and they [are] like our Constitution – too bad to be mended, and like the barren fig tree and our ministers fit only to be hewn down and cast into the fire.' He saw Charles Wynn, who gave him a deed spelling out the financial terms of the annuity he had settled on Southey: '£160 for life, payable quarterly on the 20 of January, April, July and October.'[35]

An unwritten condition of the payments was that Southey should study law. He had written to Wynn to clarify his obligations, telling him: 'with regard to what branch of the law I must follow, I would say something. You spoke of the common law as a high road to eminence, I think; of Chancery as equally advantageous. But is it not probable that, in practising common law, I may be called upon in criminal cases to plead against the life of a man? If so, I should decidedly prefer Chancery. . . . Were I to be instrumental in bringing a murderer to the gallows, I should ever after feel that I had become a murderer myself.'[36] Wynn probably regarded such squeamishness as stemming from Southey's misplaced radicalism. He himself was about to enter parliament and took a more conservative view. When they met in London they discussed the naval mutiny then raging at Spithead. Southey informed Edith that 'Wynn wants to hang the sailors. I and Carlisle want to hang their betrayers and judges, and there are probably people in London who would like to hang us.'[37]

Southey was relieved to retreat from London back to Edith in Hampshire. Joseph Cottle and his brother Amos visited in July, when they discussed publishing an edition of the poems of Thomas Chatterton, with a view to helping the poet's impoverished sister, Mrs Newton. In mid-August Charles Lamb and Charles Lloyd, whose poems had just appeared in a volume along with Coleridge's, descended on Burton. While Lamb stayed only two days before returning to London, Lloyd not only spent longer with Southey, but persuaded him to accompany him to Birmingham in pursuit of a Miss Sophia Pemberton, with whom he hoped to elope to Scotland. (Although this mission was not accomplished, Lloyd did eventually get married to Miss Pemberton in 1799.) During their abortive journey he and Robert apparently discussed Coleridge, with whom Lloyd had been staying prior to his journey to Burton. They had parted on bad terms, and Lloyd's account of their quarrel included some criticisms of Southey that he alleged Coleridge had made, and so this exchange led to a fresh cooling of Southey's relationship with Coleridge. 'It is not possible to think too highly of Coleridge's abilities', he wrote to John May, 'or too despicably of him in every other character.'[38] He called off a visit to Nether Stowey to see Coleridge and Wordsworth, who were staying in Somerset that summer, even though it meant that Edith would not see her sister.

While at Burton Southey worked on the second edition of *Joan of Arc*, cutting out all the lines that Coleridge had contributed to the first and the ninth books, which he proposed to publish as a separate work. He also hoped to continue to write *Madoc*, but found himself frustrated in this, despite his fondness for isolation, because of his distance from a library that held the rare books he required. The frustration of not having access to books proved too much for him, and on 15 September he and Edith, together with his mother, Tom and Charles Lloyd, all of whom had come to stay with them, moved out of the cottage to go to Bath, so that he would be able to use the libraries there and in Bristol.

Southey stayed with Edith at his mother's lodging house in Bath. Coleridge, apparently oblivious of any coolness Southey felt for him following his conversations with Lloyd, called on them there. He read a play of his own, *Osorio*, to Southey, who thought it 'uncommonly fine'. He also brought a copy of a tragedy of Wordsworth's, *The Borderers*, which Robert considered 'equal to any dramatic pieces' he had ever seen.[39] Amos Cottle's translation of the Icelandic poem *Edda* appeared in November, with introductory verses by Southey, which he hoped would 'perhaps sell some half-dozen copies among my friends'.[40] In them he expressed his loathing 'of the commerce of this wretched world', and his preference for 'the unfrequented field'.[41] These feelings intensified as he prepared to return to his legal studies in London. 'Almost could I prefer a snow proof hovel in Siberia', he confided to Bedford. 'Nothing suits me in that foul city.'[42]

The reception that awaited him in the capital from the government press doubtless deepened his depression. When George Canning and John Hookham Frere launched the *Anti-Jacobin* in November 1797, Southey's *Poems* were singled out for its censure.[43] A parody of Southey's 'The Widow' took the form of a dialogue between 'The Friend of Humanity and the

Knife-Grinder'. Southey had used the expression 'friends of humanity' in his introduction to the poems on the slave trade, where he had castigated those of them who had temporarily stopped buying sugar in order to hit the economic interests of the West Indian planters but had then given up 'this sacrifice (I prostitute the word, but they thought it a sacrifice)'. They justified themselves by claiming 'that Parliament would do all, and that individual efforts were no longer necessary'.[44] It is noteworthy that the *Anti-Jacobin*, while it picked up the expression to ridicule Southey, steered clear of attacking his anti-slavery poems. Instead, along with 'The Widow', it savaged two others: 'Inscription for the apartment in Chepstow Castle, where Henry Marten, the regicide, was imprisoned thirty years' and 'The Soldier's Wife'. The 'Inscription' first fell under its lash. Marten was imprisoned in Chepstow Castle for having 'rebell'd against the King and sat in judgement on him'. Southey extenuated this crime because

>   his ardent mind
> Shaped goodliest plans of happiness on earth
> And peace and liberty. Wild dreams! But such
> As Plato lov'd; such as with holy zeal
> Our Milton worshipp'd. Blessed hopes! A while
> From man with-held, even to the latter days
> When Christ shall come, and all things be fulfill'd![45]

A pastiche of the poem, apparently composed by Canning and Frere, appeared in the first number of the *Anti-Jacobin* on 20 November 1797.[46] It was given the title 'Inscription for the door of the cell in Newgate, where Mrs Brownrigg, the 'Prentice-cide, was confined previous to her execution'. Her crime was that 'she whipp'd two female 'prentices to death'. In 'extenuation' the parody of Southey's poem claimed that she

> Shaped strictest plans of discipline. Sage schemes!
> Such as Lycurgus taught, when at the shrine
> Of the Orthyan goddess he bade flog
> The little Spartans; such as erst chastised
> Our Milton, when at college. For this act
> Did Brownrigg swing. Harsh laws! But time shall come
> When France shall reign, and laws be all repeal'd!

The *Anti-Jacobin* resumed its campaign against Southey in its fifth issue on 11 December 1797 with an attack on 'The Soldier's Wife'. It had ridiculed the metre of 'The Widow' and now poured scorn on 'the present effusion' for its 'Dactylics'.[47] The *Anti-Jacobin* made a final sally against Southey's metre in 'The Soldier's Wife' in its issue number six for 18 December 1797, when it dismissed him as a 'wearisome Sonnetteer, feeble and querulous'.

Not only was Southey burlesqued in the *Anti-Jacobin* but he also suspected Coleridge of imitating him in 'Sonnets attempted in the manner of contemporary writers', which appeared in the *Monthly Magazine* for November. Coleridge claimed that he was merely parodying modern poets, such as himself and Charles Lamb, in these verses, which he wrote 'to excite a good natured laugh' and signed 'Nehemiah Higginbottom'.[48] Southey complained that one, 'To Simplicity', was aimed at him. Although Coleridge wrote to reassure him that he had not intended to ridicule him, the episode added to the negative feelings he felt for Coleridge as well as to his depressed mood. His relationship with the unstable Charles Lloyd also deteriorated, which can only have deepened his depression. Lloyd lodged with Robert and Edith until after Christmas, when they moved to 12 Lamb's Conduit Street, and he went into separate lodgings. 'Our living together was unpleasant', Southey admitted, 'and we separated at his proposal.'[49]

To add to Southey's miseries at this time he was desperately short of money. On 9 December he was reduced to asking Cottle to lend him ten pounds, explaining that 'my expenses this quarter have exceeded my income'.[50] He was so hard up that he took on a prodigious amount of literary work, reviewing for the *Critical Review* and publishing poems in the *Morning Post*. The *Critical Review* paid him 'at the low rate of three guineas a sheet', though he admitted that 'my work was not worth more. It brought me from £50 to £100 yearly, a very acceptable addition to my straitened income.'[51] 'In 1798 [Daniel] Stuart offered me a guinea a week to supply verses for the *Morning Post*', he was to recall many years later: 'that offer was very acceptable & all the pieces which bear date from that time to 1800, when I went for the second time to Portugal, were written under that engagement. About 60 lines a week I thought a fair discharge.'[52] All this writing was on top of his revisions for the second edition of *Joan of Arc*, which involved research in Dr Williams' library, and the legal work he was engaged on, which occupied him from ten in the morning to eight at night. His hours were so taken up that he complained to his brother Tom about 'the swarms of acquaintances who buzz about me and sadly waste my time'.[53]

Yet on the very same day he urged Charles Biddlecombe to visit him in London, since 'the chance of seeing friends who live far away is among the few advantages this detestable city offers.'[54] Among Robert and Edith's visitors at this time were William Wordsworth and his sister Dorothy, who dined with them three times during December. In January Southey's mother arrived with a friend, Mrs Cookman, and stayed for two nights. They all went to Drury Lane theatre on the first and Covent Garden theatre on the second. On 27 January their visitors returned home to Bath. Robert and Edith, who was again unwell, followed them a few weeks later. Southey stayed in the West Country until 18 May, when he was due to fulfil the residence requirement at Gray's Inn by dining there.

In the spring of 1798 the gloomy outlook for radical politics in England led Southey to contemplate emigration. 'As for this country', he wrote to his brother Tom on 12 March 1798, 'I think its liberties are destroyed, & hope one day to chuse a better. To take away the liberty of the press was the last stroke.'[55] James Losh recorded in his diary an exchange he had with Southey on 3 April 1798. 'Our conversation turned principally upon the invasion of liberty. I stated the probability of a stop being put to Southey's Joan of Arc, in that case he declared his intention of leaving this country.'[56] The second edition of *Joan of Arc* appeared early in May. There were significant changes from the first edition. Coleridge's lines had been excised, along with the ninth book which was to reappear as 'The Vision of the Maid of Orleans'. Southey also seems to have shifted his own religious position in the interval between the two editions. In Book Three of the first edition Joan is interrogated by doctors of theology to establish whether she is a sound Catholic or a heretic. They are very dubious when she ascribes her faith not to the rituals of the Church but to her observation of nature. When asked how nature could reveal that St Peter held the keys of heaven she replies

> 'Tis true my youth,
> Conceal'd in forest gloom, knew not the sound
> Of mass high-chaunted, nor with trembling lips
> I touch'd the mystic wafer; yet the Bird
> That to the matin ray prelusive pour'd
> His joyous song, methought did warble forth
> Sweeter thanksgiving to Religion's ear
> In his wild melody of happiness
> Than ever rung along the high-arch'd roofs
> Of man.[57]

Southey abandoned Socinianism, however, when he came to feel that more was needed for religious belief than historical evidence, such as 'an operation of Grace, a manifestation of the Spirit, an inward revelation, a recognition of revealed truth'. The change is apparent in the second edition of *Joan* published in 1798. Where in the first edition the 'missioned maid' was entirely ignorant of revealed religion in her early childhood, in the second her reply to the doctors makes clear that she was exposed to the ceremonies of the Church as a child.

> The forms of worship in mine earlier years
> Waked my young mind to artificial awe
> And made me fear my GOD.[58]

Most of the 153 poems Southey contributed to the *Morning Post* in 1798 were dashed off to fulfil his agreement with the editor Daniel Stuart. Thus not a few were translations from French, Italian, Portuguese and Spanish poets. Some were to arouse accusations that he had plagiarised other poets, including Coleridge and Wordsworth. Only eighteen were deemed by their author to be of sufficient merit to appear in other editions of his poems.[59] Among them was 'History', which has been read as a response to the criticisms of the *Anti-Jacobin*.[60] In the opening lines Southey declares his intention to eschew history for poetry, since the past was a 'chronicle of crimes', including the 'polluted scenes' of the Court, 'dungeon horrors' and 'fields of war'. Clio, the Muse of History, rebukes him for this escapism, and shames him into engaging with history, asking

> Was it for this I waken'd thy young mind?
> Was it for this I made thy swelling heart
> Throb at the deeds of Greece, and thy boy's eye
> So kindle when that glorious Spartan died?
> Boy! Boy! Deceive me not! . . . What if the tale
> Of murder'd millions strike a chilling pang . . .
> Hast thou not risen
> With nobler feelings, . . . with a deeper love
> For freedom?

Towards the end of May Southey went to Great Yarmouth to see Burnett, who was a Unitarian minister there. He was also acting as tutor to Henry Taylor, the younger brother of William Taylor, one of the foremost Germanists of his day, who lived in Norwich. Burnett introduced Robert to William, and their mutual interests led them to forge a long-lasting friendship. Taylor introduced Southey to the Odes of Friedrich Gottlieb Klopstock 'by translating them for me till I heard these I knew nothing of lyric poetry. All that I had previously seen were the efforts of imagination. These are the burst of feeling.'[61]

While he was in Norwich Southey wrote a verse letter to his wife:

Edith it ever was thy husband's wish
To find some little home, some low retreat,
Where the vain uproar of the worthless world
Might never reach his ear.[62]

For the first time in his life he was to find such a haven at Westbury on Trim, now a suburb of Bristol, where he rented a house for a year. On 25 June he moved in with Edith, his mother (who had sold her house in Bath) and his cousin Margaret, whom the family called Peggy. They had called their new abode Martin Hall, from the birds that nested in its eaves, after toying with 'the appropriate names of Rat Hall, Mouse Mansion, Vermin Villa, Cockroach Castle, Cobweb Cottage, and Spider Lodge'. A sure sign that he was intent on settling down into domesticity there was he had 'bespoke a cat, a great carroty cat'.[63] And after fixing up the place, which had been an old ale house and needed a lot of work, he did settle, looking back on the year at Westbury as one of the happiest in his life. There he produced a prodigious amount of poetry, including his most famous poem, 'The Battle of Blenheim'. Such lines as

It was the English, Kaspar cried
That put the French to rout;
But what they kill'd each other for
I could not well make out;
But every body said, quoth he
That 'twas a famous Victory[64]

are among the more celebrated of anti-war sentiments in English poetry. Southey also worked on his epic *Madoc*, getting into a routine of rising at a quarter-past five to write it.

If Southey was hoping to be left undisturbed by the world in this retreat, he was soon to be disabused of the idea. The second edition of *Joan of Arc* was given a savage review that August in the first number of the *Anti-Jacobin Review and Magazine*, which had succeeded Canning's *Anti-Jacobin* when its run ended in the summer. Another attack from the new journal exposed Southey even more to public scrutiny than had the old. For it took the form of an elaborate engraving by Gillray, in the centre of which appears a 'cornu-copia of ignorance' pouring out radical publications. Conspicuously kneeling to receive them is Southey with the ears of an ass and holding *Southey's Sapphics*, a reference to his *Poems* (1797), while *Joan of Arc* is sticking out of his pocket. He tried to laugh it off. 'Do you know that I have been carica-tured in the Anti-Jacobin magazine?' he wrote to his brother Tom. 'The fellow has not however libelled my likeness, because he does not know it, so he has clapt an asses head on my shoulders.'[65] But he was unnerved by the experience. 'The conductors of the Anti-Jacobine will have much to answer for in thus inflaming the animosities of this country', he complained. 'The old systems of government must fall; but in this country the immediate danger is on the other hand – from an unconstitutional and unlimited power.'[66]

Early in September Southey received *Lyrical Ballads* by Coleridge and Wordsworth for review in the *Critical Review*. His initial reaction was dismis-sive of their style and subjects, as being like the writing of a child or an old woman, and 'of very unequal merit'.[67] The review, when it appeared in October, was not calculated to please the authors of the poems. Of 'The Idiot Boy', which Southey considered the most important of the experimental poems, he observed: 'no tale less deserved the labour that appears to have been bestowed upon it. It resembles a Flemish picture in the worthlessness of its design and the excellence of its execution.' He poured scorn on 'The Thorn': 'The advertisement says it is not told in the person of the author but in that of some loquacious narrator. The author should have recollected that he who personates tiresome loquacity becomes tiresome himself.' But he reserved his most scathing remarks for 'The Rime of the Ancient Mariner', which he dismissed as 'a Dutch attempt at German sublimity'. Because *Lyrical Ballads* was published anonymously Southey reviewed it as though it had been written by one author. Insofar as he discriminated between the two he knew to have written them, he seems to have been more severe on Coleridge than he was on Wordsworth. Thus he went out of his way to praise 'Tintern Abbey': 'In the whole range of English poetry', he noted of lines 65 to 112, 'we scarcely recollect any thing superior.' Neither author welcomed, however, his conclusion that the 'experiment' announced in the advertisement 'has failed, not because the language of conversation is little adapted to "the purposes of poetic pleasure" but because it has been tried on uninteresting subjects.' Yet he ended the review by conceding that 'every piece discovers genius; and, ill as the author has employed his talents, they certainly rank him with the best of living poets.'[68]

The review went against the grain of others that appeared at the time, and is obviously almost completely at odds with the critical reputation that *Lyrical Ballads* has enjoyed ever since. This demands an explanation of why Southey was so disparaging of his former partner and new acquaintance. It could be put down to petty personal dislike of Coleridge after the breakdown of their relationship and its fragile repair. But Wordsworth was equally offended, if not more so, complaining to Cottle that Southey knew they needed to make money from the publication, and should have declined to review it if he could not conscientiously praise it. They needed the money to finance a visit to Germany, where both were when the review appeared. That Coleridge had left his wife and children to go with the Wordsworths abroad probably added to Southey's disapproval, and possibly influenced his negative view of their poems. But, though he could be petty, the episode cannot just be put down to personal feelings. His criticism was genuine too. Many of his own early poems dealt with similar themes to those in *Lyrical Ballads*. Indeed, he has been criticised for borrowing from them to the point of plagiarism.[69] In fact, the three poets borrowed from each other. Southey must have been hurt by the claims of novelty made in the advertisement to *Lyrical Ballads*, which overlooked his own contributions to the ballad form, such as his popular 'Mary the Maid of the Inn'. He wrote three ballads in the weeks following his arrival at Westbury.

Despite his later insistence that his year at Westbury was one of the happiest he ever spent, at the time Southey was not well. He seems to have been suffering from acute anxiety, which left him restless and eager to go on long walks for the sake of his health. In October he took off for nearly three weeks touring Wales with his friend Charles Danvers. The expedition into the remoter parts of Breconshire helped him in the composition of the epic about his Welsh hero Madoc. After his return to Westbury he left again to spend the second half of November in London. Early in December he wrote to Nicholas Lightfoot that he was living in Westbury 'with no children of my own, but a ready made family of relations. Sedentary habits, always my choice and of late rendered necessary, have injured my health something. This I am endeavouring to remedy by a little medicine and much exercise.'[70] The onset of a severe winter obliged him to take his daily walks 'wrapped up in my great coat, almost like a dancing bear in hirsute appearance'. Despite the regimen his condition grew worse. 'My heart is affected', he informed William Taylor at the end of December; 'this at first alarmed me, because I could not understand it; however, I am scientifically satisfied it is only a nervous affection.'[71] The curious assertion that the diagnosis was scientific possibly came from the doctor who was treating him – Thomas Beddoes, a prominent Bristol chemist and physician. 'I am driven again to my nightly dose of ether, sorely against my will, for it is very unpleasant to accustom myself to such a stimulus', Southey wrote to Wynn a month later. 'I am told that without great and daily exercise, there is danger of its [his illness] troubling me thro life.'[72] The remark throws light on a poem he contributed to the *Morning Post* on 17 January 1799 – 'The old man's comforts and how he procured them'. With its opening line 'You are old father William the young

man cried', this is now chiefly remembered for the parody of it by the
Victorian writer Charles Dodgson, better known as Lewis Carroll. Although
it almost asked to be parodied, some of its sentiments were close to the bone
given Southey's concern about his health at the time.

You are hale, father William, a hearty old man,
   Now tell me the reason I pray.

In the days of my youth, Father William replied,
   I remember'd that youth would fly fast
And abused not my health and my vigour at first,
   That I never might need them at last.[73]

Southey felt too ill to undergo a journey to London in the wintry conditions
of early February. The nervous aspect of his disability led his friend William
Taylor to suggest that he had 'a mimosa sensibility', i.e. one that recoiled
when touched. 'Once indeed I had a mimosa sensibility, but it has long ago
been rooted out', he replied. 'I have a dislike to all strong emotion, and avoid
whatever could excite it.'[74]

It was just as well that he stayed at home, for he was called upon by his
sister-in-law Sara to help her cope with the death of her infant son Berkeley,
whose father, Coleridge, was away in Germany. Southey proved a tower of
strength for her at the time of this bereavement. He made the arrangements
for the funeral: as Sara herself put it, he 'has undertaken the business of my
babe's internment'.[75] He also invited Sara and her surviving son Hartley to
move into the house at Westbury.

Despite his ill health, Southey completed the second volume of his *Poems*,
which was published in February, along with a first volume containing those
of 1797. Among other works Southey was engaged with were contributions
to the first *Annual Anthology*. Taylor himself had suggested the idea to him,
wondering why British poets did not do what their French and German
counterparts did: publish annual anthologies of minor poems. Southey
thought about it, and on 3 December wrote to inform Taylor that he had
decided to edit such a volume. It would serve as a means of perpetuating
some otherwise ephemeral poems he had published in the *Morning Post*
together with contributions from his 'more intimate friends'.[76] When it
finally appeared in September no fewer than 62 of the 104 poems that were
published in it were by Southey. They included many that had first seen
the light of day in the *Morning Post*. Besides his there were contributions
from twelve other poets, including Taylor, Bedford, Joseph Cottle, Thomas
Beddoes and Humphry Davy. Beddoes and Davy were associates at the

Bristol Pneumatic Institute, which opened in the spring of 1799. There, among other experiments, they conducted research with nitrous oxide, which Southey was to inhale for medicinal purposes, with beneficial, if hilarious, results.

His symptoms of acute anxiety, however, were not relieved for long. Financial difficulties caused further concerns, especially when Pitt introduced an income tax that, though Southey approved of it in principle, he thought was very unfair in practice. It provoked him to contribute a poem to the *Morning Post* of 10 April on 'the tax repealed, or, an historical ballad of King Edward the Confessor'. 'We are growling at the income bill here and wondering what will be the next measure', he wrote, summarising the poem. 'Edward the Confessor returned a tax to the people because he saw the Devil dancing on the money raised by it. I wish he would make his appearance in the Treasury now!'[77]

Early in May Southey went to London to keep term at Gray's Inn. Meanwhile Edith went with her sister and nephew Hartley to their cottage in Nether Stowey. Southey wrote to his wife regularly while he was away, and his letters to her throw an interesting light on their relationship.[78] They are affectionate, and he clearly missed her very much. At the same time, compared with letters to his male friends, they are gossipy and trivial, as though he were talking down to her. He summed them up when he told her, 'Here Edith do I write to you where I have been, where I am going, all the idle business of yesterday today and tomorrow, and all the nonsense that comes from mine own heart.' He saw Wynn, who recommended him to be called to the bar, which could be done at Christmas 1801. This plan suited Southey since he was 'told that tho my name must be on the Inn books five years before I can be called to the bar, it will be only necessary to keep terms for three. If this be the case I will keep no more till we come up to reside, for it is a miserable thing to be from home.'[79] He also kept up his radical credentials by visiting Benjamin Flower and Gilbert Wakefield, both of whom had been imprisoned for seditious libel, and by having breakfast with the prominent reformer Major John Cartwright. 'There is no man whom I could more have wished to see', he informed Edith, 'when the Pantheon of British Liberty shall be erected no man whose name will more deserve to be inscribed on the columns of glory.'[80] Towards the end of his stay in town he spent an evening with some Quaker friends of Bedford's, though he confessed to Edith, 'I do not like the Quakers, they are so plaguey civil that they must be insincere.'[81]

Southey returned to Westbury at the end of May. The lease of the house expired in June, and another home had to be found. Charles Biddlecombe came to the rescue by offering to sub-let to them one in Burton, which he had leased for five years, though it would not become available for them until October. For a few weeks at the beginning of the summer, therefore, Southey stayed with Charles Danvers in Bristol, where he finished *Madoc* and began work on *Thalaba*. Then late in July Southey went with Edith to Somerset on their way to Devon, where they intended to spend the time until the Burton house became available. Unfortunately, when they reached Minehead Edith felt too unwell to continue. This was, however, close enough to Nether Stowey for Sara Coleridge to go there to look after her sister. Edith went back with her to Stowey, while Robert took himself off on a walk along the north coast of Somerset and into Devon as far as Lynmouth, which he compared with his beloved Sintra. Sara persuaded her husband, who had just got back from Germany, to write a conciliatory letter to Southey, inviting him to stay with them in Stowey. The invitation was accepted, and Southey and Edith stayed with the Coleridges for a fortnight. On 20 August Southey wrote to tell Charles Danvers that he was at Stowey 'and at the same table with Coleridge. This will surprise you. . . . However here I am, and have been some days wholly immersed in conversation. In one point of view Coleridge and I are bad companions for each other. Without being talkative I am conversational, and the hours slip away and the ink dries upon the pen in my hand.'[82] One can almost see the two poets sitting side by side, Southey trying to get on with writing but unable to do so since Coleridge was holding forth as usual.

On 27 August they all left together for Devon. After a visit to Coleridge's birth place at Ottery St Mary, they pressed on to Exeter. Coleridge and Southey left Edith in Exeter to go on a walking tour that took them to Torbay. On their return to Exeter Coleridge stayed until the last week in September before going back to Stowey with Sara. Altogether Southey and Coleridge were in each other's company for about six weeks. The coldness in their recent relationship, which had both contributed to and been aggravated by Southey's critical review of *Lyrical Ballads*, was somehow thawed out. They conveniently blamed it on Charles Lloyd's malicious gossip, accusing him of treachery and even insanity. Although they did not quite recapture the rapport they enjoyed at the height of their enthusiasm for Pantisocracy, they nevertheless were able to collaborate again. Thus together they composed 'The Devil's Thoughts', a 'Siamese production' that was expanded over the years into 'The Devil's Walk'.

Other signs of their close collaboration in the summer of 1799 appear in Coleridge's 'Kubla Khan', the genesis of which has been hotly disputed. Coleridge claimed that it had occurred to him in a drug-induced dream while staying in a cottage near Porlock in the summer of 1797. Most commentators accept the dating, if not Coleridge's version of events, though others have opted for early 1798. Yet it was not published until 1816, so he had plenty of opportunity to add to it. That he did so while collaborating with Southey in 1799 has been convincingly demonstrated by comparisons between lines in 'Kubla Khan' and some of the sources for *Thalaba*.[83] Southey was working on that epic, which he then called 'The Destruction of Dom Daniel', while he was close to Coleridge that summer.

Among contemporary works that were grist to the mill for *Thalaba*, none struck Southey more forcibly than *Gebir*, a poem in seven books by Walter Savage Landor. What fascinated Southey were its epic aspects, which like his own *Joan of Arc* included a visit to the underworld, and the sensuousness of the blank verse.

Southey and Edith went to take up their 'palace', as he called it, in Burton, but found that Biddlecombe had bungled the lease, so they had to rent another place until the sitting tenants moved out at the end of the month. During his stay in Burton Southey was able to make progress with *Thalaba*, as he had finally decided to call his 'Romance'. He also kept up his contributions to the *Morning Post*. These included 'God's Judgement on a Bishop', which recounted the crime and punishment of Bishop Hatto of Mentz during the famine of AD 914. When the poor flocked to his barn, hoping to relieve their hunger, he shut them in and set fire to it. God punished him by sending a plague of rats that not only consumed his corn, but forced him to flee to a tower on the Rhine. However, there was no refuge there, for the army of rats followed and attacked him.

> They gnaw'd the flesh from every limb
> For they were sent to do judgment on him.[84]

Although it is set safely back in the tenth century, it also warns the rich and powerful of 1799 that a judgement awaits them, if they exploit their power to oppress the poor.

Southey had hoped to settle down in Burton, but he and Edith only occupied their new home during November, for he was taken ill again. This time the nervous symptoms were very disturbing, especially 'a sudden stoppage of the heart, followed by quick pulsations which were hardly less alarming'.[85] 'I often wish myself at Bristol', Southey wrote to Humphry Davy, telling him of his fears that 'as I have more and more reason to apprehend, a constitution debilitated by the worst possible management in childhood, the most ruinous system of coercion from all things proper, should for ever incapacitate me from the labour and confinement of professional studies.'[86] Whatever he meant by this outspoken criticism of the way he had been brought up, he does seem to have been apprehensive that the acute anxiety from which he was suffering might end in mental derangement. On 1 December he moved to Bristol to be near the medical attentions of Beddoes and Davy. Their prescriptions included gaseous oxide, upon which, and other stimulants, including port wine, Southey became so dependent that he confessed he was 'unable to do without them'.[87]

When Southey's condition did not improve, Beddoes advised him to go abroad to recover his health. Southey had announced his intention of writing a 'History of Portugal' to his uncle, who tried to persuade him that it could only properly be undertaken after another visit to that country. Robert did not need much persuading to go, as he thought it would be necessary for his health. Another powerful motive for leaving was that it would give him a good reason for abandoning his legal studies, at least temporarily. 'I never believed myself qualified for the profession', he confessed to John May at the end of December. 'My powers are only vigorous in solitude or in the society that imposes no restraint. I am easily confounded.'[88]

Southey also expressed to May concern about the continued attacks of the *Anti-Jacobin* on Coleridge, Charles Lamb and himself. It must have made him even more anxious to leave the country. The paper had exposed him as the leading Jacobin poet, which had led him to modify his radicalism in print, partly to avoid its censure. His political position was undergoing a readjustment anyway in response to events taking place in France. Until the end of 1799 he still felt that the French Revolution, for all its excesses, had been a salutary event. When earlier in the year Coleridge had indicated a loss of faith in that idea in his 'Ode upon France', Southey had been critical of his 'recantation'. 'Mary Hays asked me if I too had changed my principles', he told Edith. 'Had she known more of me I should have been hurt at the question.'[89] 'I see evil produced by existing establishments', he maintained in October, 'and know that it might be better, and am with all the ardour and sincerity of my soul a Republican.'[90] The coup of 18 Brumaire that November, which brought Napoleon to power, shook his faith in France. 'The Corsican has offended me', he wrote in January 1800. 'Once I had hopes – the Jacobines might have done much – but the base of morality was wanting. . . . Buonaparte has made me anti-Gallican.'[91] Although, as he put it to Coleridge, 'the Corsican [had] trod upon my Jacobine corns', he still gave the benefit of the doubt to Napoleon against the British government's aggressive policy towards him.[92] 'I do not justify his assumption of power', he told his brother Tom, 'let the use he makes of it, do that, but in reviewing his past conduct . . . I do not hesitate in pronouncing him the greatest man that events have called into action since Alexander of Macedon.'[93] He blamed the ministers for blackening Bonaparte's name by handing over letters of his that they had intercepted, and others that they had forged, to William Gifford, the editor of the *Anti-Jacobin*. On the eve of Southey's departure for Portugal, therefore, his politics were still sufficiently 'Jacobin' for him to feel vulnerable to another attack from that ministerial organ.

CHAPTER FIVE

'Shuttlecock of Fortune' (1800–1803)

Southey left Bristol on his second journey to Portugal on 14 April 1800. This time he took Edith with him, though she was 'not much pleased with the prospect of a journey to Falmouth, a voyage afterwards, and then a land of strangers'.[1] Her dislike of the journey was heightened by her lacking a fellow traveller of her own sex, on which Southey commented rather tetchily to Coleridge that 'she must learn to be contented without one'.[2] Before they left Southey made arrangements for his financial and literary affairs to be entrusted to his friends. He wrote to his chief benefactor Wynn to explain his expenditure and debts, and to ask for a loan. Wynn arranged to meet him in Gloucester on 13 March, where they discussed Southey's poem 'The Old Woman of Berkeley', and doubtless the more pressing matter of his finances. John May undertook to manage these, including the annuity of £160 from Wynn, while Robert was abroad. Southey pointed out to May that his ceasing to review for the *Morning Post* entailed a loss of £100 a year. On the other hand Peter Elmsley had cushioned him against that by giving him £100 towards the expenses of his voyage. He also expected between £10 and £20 from the *Critical Review*, to which could be added payment for reviews of Spanish and Portuguese literature, which he hoped to contribute while he was away. A further £100 he anticipated from the publication of *Thalaba*, which he would send from Portugal when he had finished it. He arranged for May and Coleridge to take care of the subscriptions to the edition of Chatterton's poems, and its publication if enough subscribers were found during his absence. The collection of materials for a third *Annual Anthology* he entrusted to Humphry Davy and Charles Danvers; in fact it never materialised.

Robert and Edith made their way from Bristol to Falmouth. At Ivybridge Southey's brother Tom unexpectedly joined them to say farewell. They arrived in Falmouth on 18 April, only to find that their departure for Lisbon was delayed by contrary winds, obliging them to cool their heels in port until they became favourable. Meanwhile Southey continued to work on *Thalaba* and probably perused two works he had taken along to read on the voyage, Landor's *Gebir* and, despite his review of the first, the second edition of *Lyrical Ballads*. At last on 24 April the captain announced that the packet was to sail. Although the sea was smooth much of the way, they were both seasick. There was one remarkable event for Southey to report, when a cutter crossed their path and it was feared it was French. Edith hid in the cockpit 'half dead with fear', while he armed himself with a musket. Fortunately it turned out to be a false alarm, as the boat was English.[3] 'God knows I think nothing worth fighting for, and my little luggage was insured', he wrote to John May, 'I who have [not] fired a gun these seven years and never intend to fire one again.'[4] They were both glad to reach Lisbon on 30 April.

Southey was to stay in Portugal until June 1801. While he was there his literary efforts were devoted to finishing *Thalaba*, polishing *Madoc*, and above all to starting his 'History of Portugal'. He hoped to complete *Thalaba* before he and Edith moved away from the heat of Lisbon in June 1800 to the cool retreat of his uncle's house at Sintra. There he intended to work on *Madoc*, and then return to the capital to take advantage of its libraries to start the research on his 'History of Portugal'. He had declared his intention of commencing it to his brother Tom before setting out, describing it as 'a long and arduous and interesting and important undertaking which I think I can do as it ought to be done'.[5] 'My plan is this', he wrote to Coleridge after his arrival, 'immediately to go through all the chronicles in order, and then make a skeleton of the narrative; the timbers put together, the house may be furnished at leisure. It will be a great work, and worthy of all labour.'[6]

In fact he did not complete all twelve books of *Thalaba* until 23 July. Even then he worked on correcting it before sending it to England. Towards the end of August he had to admit that it had monopolised his time, as he had spent more on it than he had anticipated. It was not until the beginning of October that he felt sufficiently happy with the text to inform Wynn that 'now Thalaba is off my hands compleatly; corrected – transcribed – annotated – and ready to be shipped off to market.'[7] His agent was to be John Rickman, to whom he sent instructions 'to make the best bargain you can, and on no terms to sell the copyright'.[8] If Longman, who had acquired the copyright of *Joan of Arc* from Cottle, did not offer a good deal, Rickman should approach J. and A. Arch, to whom Cottle had sold the copyright of *Lyrical Ballads*.

One reason why Southey did not make as much progress on *Thalaba* as he had expected was that there were too many distractions. At first there were many letters to write to his friends in England, and visits to make to officials and acquaintances in Lisbon. By 23 May he was already aware that time was passing and that he 'must set at Thalaba in good earnest to get it out of the way'.[9] Then the heat of summer arrived early, making him lazy. They had proposed to go to Sintra in July, but were so overcome by the temperature and the humidity that they decided to go earlier. 'At Cintra we shall be cool', Southey informed Tom, 'we wait only for the processions of the Body of God, and St Anthony, the 12th and 13th of June, and the Heart of Jesus on the 28th, and the first bull-fight, which will be about that time.'[10] In fact they went to the bull fight on 22 June, and were sickened by the spectacle. He noted that no English spectators went to a bull ring twice. The sight of a bull aware that it is facing death is indeed enough to put anybody off, unless they have been brought up in a culture where it is acceptable. Southey drew on it for a line in *Thalaba* describing a deer being pursued by dogs: 'and now the death-sweat darkens his dun hide'.

Robert and Edith arrived in Sintra on 26 June. As before, Southey was enchanted by the summer residence of the Portuguese kings. 'Cintra is too good a place for the Portuguese', he declared. 'It is only fit for us Goths – for Germans or English.'[11] There, too, Southey found himself distracted from his writing by the social life. One person in particular attracted his attention, Mary Barker, 'who is here with a convalescent aunt', he informed May. 'She is a very clever girl, all good humour, and a head brimful of brains.'[12] Mary accompanied Robert and Edith on a ramble around Sintra. Then about the middle of July she unexpectedly left for England, and Southey was devastated. 'I feel a heavier depression of spirits at losing her than I have known since Tom left me at Liskard', he confessed to Cottle.[13] He felt bereft of intellectual companionship, and longed for 'one companion to whom every serious thought might be freely communicated'.[14]

It is clear that Edith could not fulfil this need. She was his helpmate; but not his soulmate. That role was usually filled by men who were his intellectual peers, such as his uncle. Unfortunately Herbert was obliged to spend the summer in Lisbon, where his services as chaplain to the British forces were required. Southey had in the past shown an interest in women, like Mary Wollstonecraft, who could engage with him intellectually. There was an element of flirting in this engagement, for Southey was vain enough to think himself attractive to women, and was sufficiently handsome not to be deceiving himself altogether, either.

Although he pined for Miss Barker, he did not miss England. Sintra wanted 'only fresh butter and jacobinical company to make it an earthly Paradise'.[15] Southey's desire for radical companions was a sign that his own political position had not changed significantly during his absence from England. Ironically one of the authors of the *Anti-Jacobin*, John Hookham Frere, who had parodied Southey's poems, became envoy to Portugal in October 1800. Southey received a visit from him 'not without considerable embarrasment on his part even to a faltering of voice'.[16] He was alerted to the possibility of an imminent French invasion, in the event of which he and his uncle would probably be forced to leave. Yet he was reluctant to do so, and but for Edith would have been prepared to brave it out, for his second visit to Portugal found him much more at home there. The climate suited him, and his health improved. He was even prepared to tolerate Portuguese Catholicism, finding it though 'puppet-show popery' preferable to 'that execrable diabolism of Calvin'.[17] After his return to Lisbon at the end of October he regretted the approach of his departure for England, wishing he could stay another six or seven years in Portugal.

Once back in Lisbon Southey's preoccupation with *Thalaba* came to an end until January, when he received suggestions for changes to books eleven and twelve from Danvers and Davy. He was anxious to get the poem off his hands because he needed the money for his brother Henry's medical career. Henry was to be apprenticed to a surgeon, who required one hundred guineas as a premium. Now that he was free to concentrate on his 'History of Portugal' Southey found himself 'up to the ears in chronicles'. He had acquired access to the public archives, including the records of the Inquisition, though he was 'somewhat shy of laying heretical hands on those bloody annals'. He found the public library an excellent institution for an English researcher.[18] When his uncle left for England early in December, to take care of a living he had acquired, Southey and Edith moved into his house. There Southey had direct access to Herbert's well-stocked library. He supplemented its holdings by buying books, though some were very expensive. Southey hoped to recoup his expenditure from the sales of his 'History'. As usual he was optimistic about the prospects of remuneration. 'For six quartos Gibbon got 8000 pounds', he observed to Charles Danvers. 'I shall be satisfied if I get 1500 for three – tho I expect a more durable and deserved reputation than that even of Gibbon!'[19] Southey's frequent comparisons of his own genius with that of poets such as Milton and historians such as Gibbon, often claiming superiority, make one wonder whether he suffered from self-delusion, or was ironically mocking his own abilities.

By December Southey had found a substitute for the absent Mary Barker in a Miss Seton, 'an accomplished woman, whose society is pleasant and profitable'. He even made an implicit comparison between the two when he described the latter as 'a woman with brains, who draws well'.[20] In March 1801 she accompanied Southey and Edith on an expedition to Coimbra, along with other acquaintances they had made in Portugal, including Samuel Waterhouse. John Theodor Koster, a friend Southey had acquired in Lisbon, and whose son Henry was to help him in his *History of Brazil,* supplied them with an introduction to Timoteo Verdier, a cotton manufacturer at Tomar.

Verdier put the party up, and Southey was delighted to spend time with 'the sort of family that novels sometimes picture, and which I never elsewhere saw in real life'. He also enjoyed Verdier's company, and became intimate enough with him to challenge his making a living from machinery 'with a moral battery which neither he nor Adam Smith nor the whole race of commercialists could withstand'.[21] What his host made of this, one of Southey's earliest known onslaughts on the manufacturing system, is not recorded.

Despite France and Spain having declared war on Portugal on 27 February, following up the declaration with an invasion of Alentejo, in April Southey and Waterhouse set out on another excursion, this time to the Algarve. Part of the purpose of the trip was to familiarise himself with the country and to buy materials for the projected 'History of Portugal'. Southey's uncle, who had returned from England, was now actively encouraging his nephew's historical research. 'He was not perhaps quite aware of the literary rank which I hold in the world till he there learnt it', Southey conjectured. 'Now he forwards it in every way and hunts out books and information with as much zeal and assiduity as myself.'[22] Herbert knew the Bishop of Beja, and arranged for Southey to see him when he arrived there on 12 April. Southey met the Bishop, 'a little, chearful, large-eyed man', and bought two books.[23] The following day he took a letter from the Bishop recommending him to a priest at Castro Verde, and wrote in Portuguese to thank him for 'the courtesies received in Beja, as also the great advantage which we have derived from your recommendation'.[24] A Portuguese scholar observed that this is the only extant letter of Southey's in the language, and, despite some idiosyncrasies, justifies his 'own assertion that he was fluent in the language if not grammatically correct'.[25] When they reached Faro Southey found that the war was 'the most extraordinary one ever heard of. At Lisbon it has not been declared – here it has.' Despite the deteriorating situation they did not rush back to Lisbon but made their way to Monchique, 'the lovely Cintra of the Algarve'.[26] In Lagos at midnight on 23 April their 'chamber door was burst open and a party of soldiers entered with bayonets fixed'. The incident passed off when the Corregedor arrived the following morning and accepted their explanations for not having presented their passports to him the previous day. Southey dismissed it as being due to petty officialdom. Nevertheless the presence of Englishmen was becoming a problem to the Portuguese, as in negotiations to end the war Spain was insisting that Portugal close its ports to English shipping. By the time it was ratified in July Southey and Edith had returned to England. Though he hoped to go back one day, he never did.

One reason that brought Southey back to England was the prospect that Charles Wynn might be able to use his political influence to get him a job. Wynn had mentioned the possibility of a legal position in India that

Southey had toyed with, but was clearly not keen on. Finally accepting that Southey was not cut out for the law, Wynn now undertook to try to get him a post in the diplomatic service. Though an opportunity for one in Italy was investigated, nothing came of it.

On his arrival in Bristol Southey found letters from Coleridge awaiting him. During his absence his brother-in-law had moved into Greta Hall in Keswick, and invited him up to stay. Southey had disapproved of the move, since it made Coleridge and his wife Sara too remote from their families, and too close to Wordsworth. Nevertheless he responded enthusiastically to the invitation, telling Coleridge that he regarded him as his closest friend. Indeed, he even began to make flattering comments on the second edition of *Lyrical Ballads*. Southey and Coleridge discussed leaving England together were Robert to be posted overseas. Failing that Southey imagined them 'eating dates in a garden in Constantinople', adding 'and if our wives rebelled we would send for the chief of the black eunuchs and sell them to the Seraglio'.[27] 'A long absence from England [is] to me less an object of regret than it would be to most persons', Southey explained to William Taylor, 'not merely from my state of health but from my peculiar circumstances. I have never been settled in England – never had a home there. My friends are scattered – nowhere two in a place. From my family (excepting Henry's prospects) [I] receive no comfort and can communicate to none of them. Thus without anchor or cable it is but to hoist sail and away!'[28] At the beginning of September Robert and Edith visited the Coleridges in Keswick. Southey's initial reaction to the scenery was not favourable – not only was the weather cold and gloomy, but the Lakes at first disappointed him. 'They were diminutive to what I expected', he informed his brother Henry, 'and for beauty all English – perhaps all existing scenery must yield to Cintra. . . . Yet as I become more familiar with these mountains the more is their sublimity felt and understood; were they in a warmer climate they would be the best and most desirable neighbours.'[29] The weather, however, depressed him. 'In truth Grosvenor', he confessed to Bedford, 'I have lived abroad too long to be contented in England. I miss southern luxuries – the fruits – the wines – I miss the sun in heaven, and having been upon a short allowance of sunbeams these last ten days . . . these damned rainy clouds.'[30]

Southey took off from Keswick about the middle of September, leaving Edith with her sister and Coleridge. Wynn met him in Liverpool and they went on a journey through North Wales, which included a stay at Wynn's ancestral home, Wynnstay. 'The richness of the library in such books as were most useful to me', Southey wrote to Edith, 'and the goodness of the claret, made the delay very endurable.'[31] His trip was primarily with a view to acquiring background details for his poem *Madoc*, though he and Wynn no doubt discussed Southey's job prospects too. But it was John Rickman (who was then in Dublin as private secretary to the Chief Secretary of Ireland) who came up with a post for him. The Irish Chancellor of the Exchequer, Isaac Corry, offered Southey the position of his private secretary. Southey accepted, returned briefly to Keswick, and then on 7 October set out again, this time for Dublin. His many to-ings and fro-ings, between Portugal, the south and north of England, Wales and Ireland, in so short a space of time, led him to describe himself as 'the shuttlecock of fortune – so jolted from one spot to another'.[32]

It was also quite a jolt for Robert Southey, erstwhile leveller and republican, to occupy a place in the government. He had previously accepted that his radical politics disqualified him from any office in the administration. His readiness to accept one now stemmed partly from the fact that his *bête noire*, William Pitt the Younger, had resigned as prime minister in April 1801, and his successor, Henry Addington, was more acceptable to him. Southey approved of the new administration's negotiating peace with France at Amiens, the terms of which were agreed while he was in Ireland. Not the least of the merits of the political change, in Southey's eyes, was that Pitt had resigned because he could not persuade the king that the corollary to incorporating Ireland in a Union with Great Britain, in 1800, was the relief of Catholics from the penal laws. George III took the attitude that Catholic Emancipation would be a violation of his coronation oaths to uphold the Church of England. These were sentiments of which Southey thoroughly approved, as his exposure to Catholicism in Portugal had led him increasingly to disapprove of it, and what he saw in Ireland on this visit reinforced his prejudices against the Catholics: 'It will be difficult to civilise this people', he wrote to Edith.[33] Resistance to any deal with Catholics was becoming more of a priority to him than the radical causes he had previously espoused. He was also becoming more concerned about evangelicalism. When Rickman asked him to buy two copies of a book by Hannah More for him to give as Christmas presents, Southey protested against her 'wretched Calvinistical cant'.[34] Methodism too came in for his censure. 'There is a war brooding between our old Clergy, and these fanatics', he asserted, 'I take shelter in the Church that I may not be driven to the Meeting-House.'[35] Southey was aware that his political stance appeared to be shifting. 'It is not I who have turned around', he protested to Mary Barker, illustrating the claim with a metaphor he was increasingly to employ: 'I stand where I stood, looking at the rising sun, and now the sun has set behind me. England has mended – is mending – will mend. I have still faith enough in God and hope enough of man. But not of France! Freedom cannot grow up in that bed of immorality. That oak must root in a hardier soil – England or Germany.'

He then inveighed against Napoleon: 'a military despotism! – Popery re-established – the negroes again to be enslaved! Why had not the man perished before the walls of Acre in his greatness and his glory?'[36] Southey had not yet become a conservative, and there was to be much jolting from one position to another before he did. But his employment as private secretary to the Chancellor of the Exchequer in Ireland marked a step in that direction, even if it was not 'a baptism that purified me of all Jacobinical sins'.[37]

It turned out that he saw very little of Corry while he was in Dublin, and that there was no work there for him to do. So he worked on *Madoc* instead, and then learned that the Chancellor was returning to London, and wanted Southey to join him there 'to receive livery and seisin of the secretarian pen'.[38] He made his way back to Keswick, where he picked up Edith and took her with him to London. They stayed in town from the beginning of November 1801 until the end of May 1802, when Southey finally realised that Corry had no real need of a private secretary, and was really using him as a tutor to his son. The Irish Chancellor had to invent work for him, getting him to investigate such topics as the Corn Laws and tithes, and proposing that he write an official history of the war in Egypt rather than that of Portugal. Nevertheless Corry paid him a salary punctually in advance, though Southey later found out it came from the Irish revenues, and was very critical of this misuse of public money. He also found that people who had treated him like a pariah when he was regarded as a Jacobin accepted him now that he was working for the government: 'I did not myself know how like a scabby sheep I had been considered before the touch of the Irish Chancellor had purified me.'[39] While he was receiving a regular income he wrote no more than eighty lines of poetry, did very little reviewing, and concentrated on his historical research, finding it more rewarding than creative writing. He also brought to fruition the scheme to publish Chatterton's poems for the benefit of the poet's sister.

While he was in London, Southey's mother came on a visit with Mary Lovell, Edith's sister. They arrived on 30 November, later than they had indicated, much to his annoyance. But his irritation quickly vanished when he realised that his mother was terminally ill with consumption. 'This cursed disease is I now see a family one', he informed Danvers, 'an Uncle – an infant sister – my Cousin [Margaret] and my Mother are proofs enough. I shall be on my guard, and if ever I begin to cough ship myself in time for Lisbon.'[40] On 5 January his mother died, and she was buried on the 8th. Southey was devastated, pouring out his feelings the following day in a letter to Wynn. 'The moment of her release was welcome; like one whose limb has just been amputated, he feels the immediate ceasing of acute suffering; – the pain of the wound soon begins, and the sense of loss continues throughout life.' The sight of his mother's dead body momentarily deprived him of his belief in an afterlife, 'and it required thought and reasoning to recover my former certainty, that as surely we must live hereafter, as all here is not the creation of folly or of chance.'[41] 'I never had any feeling about a family grave till my mother was buried in London', he recalled, 'and that gave me more pain than was reasonable or right.'[42]

Southey sought escape from grief in work and company. 'Whenever anything distresses me', he maintained, 'I fly to hard employment, as many fly to battle.'[43] The 'History of Portugal' and the edition of Chatterton's poems kept him busy. He also threw himself into a round of meetings with what he called 'Living Remarkables'. Mary Barker introduced him to Charlotte Smith, the poet whom he regarded as 'the reviver of the sonnet in England'. He met Elizabeth Inchbald, who he described as 'very odd, very clever, very beautiful'; Isaac D'Israeli, to whom he took an immediate dislike, but later came to admire; and Sir Thomas Lawrence the artist, 'somewhat oily of tongue'.[44] Southey clearly enjoyed dropping the names of the eminent people he met socially while he was in London, and ran another list of them by Coleridge: 'Campbell . . . who spoke of old Scotch ballads with contempt! Fuseli . . . Flaxman, whose touch is better than his feeling . . . Bowles . . . Dr Busby. . . . Lastly Barry, the painter: poor fellow! He is too mad and too miserable to laugh at.'[45]

Southey had dinner with Coleridge while they were in London, even though he was scandalised that his brother-in-law was disseminating all over town the news that he had separated from his wife. Robert took Sara's side, but was not particularly offended by Coleridge's separating from her, since he admitted that 'he is of all human beings the most undomesticated'. It was his indiscretion in broadcasting the fact that Southey felt was 'very foolish & very criminal'.[46] Southey now found that he no longer wished to go abroad with Coleridge: 'Our habits are not enough alike', he admitted, 'I wish the similarity, or the dissimilarity were greater.'[47]

At the end of May Southey resigned his position under Corry and returned to Bristol with Edith, who was six months pregnant. The prospect of bringing up a child made him anxious to settle down, being 'weary of this unsettled vagabond life'.[48] Coleridge, temporarily reconciled with Sara, was putting pressure on his brother- and sister-in-law to move in with them at Greta Hall. Though the house was big enough for both families, despite Southey developing doubts on that score, he resisted the invitation, ostensibly because of the climate in Cumberland. Yet he was tempted by the mountains and lakes, and also by the low cost of living compared with other parts of England. Edith too wanted to go, though she was concerned about the effects the move might have on his health. The main objection to moving north in the summer of 1802 – his reservations about Coleridge himself – were scarcely hinted at.

On 31 August Edith gave birth to their first child, Margaret. 'There is an omission in the Book of Genesis', Southey announced to Mary Barker the following day, 'child bearing is mentioned as the woman's curse. The man's curse was forgotten – it is to be in the house at the time.'[49] He got out of it almost as soon as he could, leaving on 17 September to go walking in South Wales with his brother Tom. As they tramped along he looked around for a house to rent. A house near Neath, Maes Gwyn, attracted him and he entered into negotiations with the landlord to rent it. The idea of settling in Wales was appealing, as he toyed with the notion of learning Welsh, and bringing Margaret up there so she could act as translator. Already he was planning a future for the baby girl, an ominous hostage to fortune. Southey was a doting father: 'I talk nonsense very fluently to her', he boasted, 'and am a better nurse than you would perhaps imagine.'[50]

Following his return from Wales Southey himself became quite ill. 'For many days my eyes have suffered such "dim suffusion" that I am enjoined rigorous absence from book, pen, ink and paper', he observed, 'and to increase the comfort of this blind beetle state one side of my face so swoln . . . I cannot leave the house.'[51] Although the swelling soon went down, his eyesight continued to give him trouble. After many weeks when he had written little else but history, he now began to write poetry again, since he could compose verse with his eyes shut. As usual he divided his time between various projects, working on *The Curse of Kehama* and a translation of *Amadis of Gaul*. Apparently he was not discouraged in these undertakings by the critical reception of *Thalaba the Destroyer* that had been published in 1801. 'Poor Thalaba got abused in every review except the *Critical*', Southey recollected.[52] That in the *British Critic* was so dismissive that he guessed it was by Sir Herbert Croft, and attributed it to his own criticism of the baronet for appropriating the papers of Thomas Chatterton from the dead poet's sister. It was to rescue her from Croft's depredations, about which Southey had been outspoken, that he and Cottle were busy bringing out a posthumous edition of her brother's poems. Subsequent reviews had not been quite so damning, though they were at best lukewarm in their praise. Southey was 'not dissatisfied with the *Monthly Review* as to its quantum of praise, but very much so as to its quality. It is done with sufficient civility and fairness but it is not well done.'[53]

Southey was unaware that the anonymous reviewer was Francis Jeffrey, who was about to launch a second and far more devastating attack on *Thalaba* in the first number of the *Edinburgh Review*. After dismissing the plot as fantastic, Jeffrey criticised the way Southey had documented his romance. 'When he had filled his common-place book, he began to write; and his poem is little else than his common-place book versified.'[54] He concluded with some favourable observations that damned Southey with faint praise: 'We think it written, indeed, in a very vicious taste, and liable, upon the whole, to very formidable objections: But it would not be doing justice to the genius of the author, if we were not to add, that it contains passages of very singular beauty and force, and displays poetical conception, that would do honour to more faultless compositions.' Jeffrey then quoted several such passages, including the poem's opening lines.

How beautiful is night!
A dewy freshness fills the silent air;
No mist obscures, no little cloud
Breaks the whole serene of heaven:
In full-orbed glory the majestic moon
Rolls thro' the dark blue depths.
Beneath her steady ray
The desert circle spreads,
Like the round ocean, girdled with the sky.
How beautiful is night![55]

There was, however, a further sting in the tail: 'His faults are always aggressive, and often created, by his partiality for the peculiar manners of that new school of poetry of which he is a faithful disciple, and to the glory of which he has sacrificed greater talents and acquisitions, than can be boasted of by any of his associates.'[56]

Southey's connection with what Jeffrey called a 'new school of poetry' was his real sin in the eyes of the Scottish reviewer. Indeed Jeffrey used the review of *Thalaba* as a peg on which to hang his condemnation of the so-called school in general, and Wordsworth in particular. Had the *Edinburgh Review* existed in 1798, when *Lyrical Ballads* came out, he would surely have engaged with that, even though Southey did not contribute to it. By 1802 it was too late, but not too late to take a shot at the Preface Wordsworth had added to the edition of 1800.[57]

Southey was outraged at Jeffrey's treatment of his poem, and his including himself in a 'school' along with Coleridge and Wordsworth. 'Have you seen the Scotch review of Thalaba?' he asked Bedford. 'Of which what is good is not about Thalaba and what is about Thalaba is not good. The Critic says there is no invention in Thalaba. Now Grosvenor I will tell you what I think of the Critic – to speak mildly of him, as one always should in these cases, he is a damned lying Scotch son of a bitch.'[58] He objected to Jeffrey's idea of a 'new school', observing that there could be no 'stronger proof of want of discernment or want of candour than in grouping together three men so different in style as Wordsworth, Coleridge and myself under one head'.[59] 'It is ridiculous enough to be thus coupled with Wordsworth', he complained, 'a man who probably despises my talents as much as the Reviewers despise his.'[60] He did, however, concede that

> there certainly is a design in the most part of my poems to force into notice the situation of the poor, and to represent them as the victims of the present state of society. The object is to make my readers think and feel – as for the old Anti-Jacobin cry that it is to make the poor rebellious, that is too absurd to require answer. The poor do not read books of poetry upon fine paper nor are the poems addressed to their capacities or under-standing. The charge which the Scotch critic makes applies to me far more than to Coleridge and Wordsworth – for it is I who in the language of Mr Canning and Mr Cobbet am . . . the Jacobine poet.[61]

Southey denied however that he had 'exaggerated human misery, or ascribed it to wrong causes, or attempted to palliate the crimes of the poor by the plea of necessity – *a doctrine which I do not hold*'. What he did hold he explained to May a few weeks later: 'Some years and some observations have modified many of my opinions, but every thing that I have observed in the history of man and in the nature of the mind of man has tended to confirm and estab-lish the belief that the inequalities of property are now the cause of moral evil and human misery.' He considered this to be Christ's doctrine when he forbade his disciples to possess wealth: 'Poverty in the true sense of the word, actually physical want, is an evil of modern growth, unknown under the ancient regime of domestic slavery, unknown in the feudal times, the effect of the commercial system and increasing with it.'[62]

The exchanges over Jeffrey's review of *Thalaba* marked the opening salvo in a campaign between the editor of the *Edinburgh Review* and what he came in 1807 to call the 'Lake Poets'. As it developed, the vendetta became polit-ical as well as polemical. The *Edinburgh Review* had been launched by Jeffrey and his colleagues as a Whig organ opposed to what it regarded as a Tory ministry, and the 'Lake Poets' eventually were to be identified with the government. In 1802, however, this identification had still to be made, and their reputation was that of Jacobins. That label was in fact becoming less and less appropriate for all three. Southey was even prepared to 'forgive Pitt half the eternity of damnation to which he is doomed for the Union [of Britain and Ireland], and make over the remitted half to Bonaparte, who may enter upon his lease as soon as he pleases. Any Jacobine has my leave to put him in immediate possession.'[63] 'As for the politics of this wicked world', he wrote at the end of November 1802, 'his Majesty and his Majesty's ministers have certainly a very peaceable and well disposed subject in me. All my political irritation goes off in a curse or two at Bonaparte.'[64] He considered Addington to be 'an honest and well intentioned man' who handled the Despard conspiracy more liberally than Pitt would have done. Edward Despard was found guilty of treason and executed. Southey considered his fate harsh but deserved, and praised the ministry for not suspending Habeas Corpus and filling the prisons, as 'the old rascals' would have done.[65] Southey was well on the way to becoming a Tory. But Francis Jeffrey was not to know that when he committed what Southey dubbed 'Thalabacide'.

Another straw in the wind was Southey's agreeing to contribute to a new journal, the *Annual Review*, which was to be launched in 1803. Although its editor, Arthur Aikin, was a Unitarian, and a prominent chemist who had been associated with Joseph Priestley, his prospectus for the periodical was conservative. 'On all occasions', he announced, 'we shall be found the friends of good order, of domestic quiet, of that venerable constitution which has so long approved itself the bulwark of our liberties.'[66] Southey's first review for it, which he wrote before the end of 1802, was of *Periodical Accounts relative to the Baptist Missionary Society for propagating the gospel among the heathen*: 'A sect of dissenters neither numerous like the Methodists', he observed, 'nor powerful like the Quakers, have undertaken to preach the gospel in Hindostan, a duty shamefully neglected by the Church of England.' He could not resist, however, lambasting the Calvinism of the Baptists, calling it 'a miserable and mischievous superstition . . . for which bedlams as well as meeting houses should be erected'.[67] Despite his criticism of the Church of England for not being active in missionary work in the East he was now a committed Anglican. 'I who am a believer (and that upon the Socinian or low Arian ground)', he confided to William Taylor, 'were I now at three and twenty with the opinions that I hold at nine and twenty – would chuse the Church for my profession.'[68]

When the negotiations to rent the house in Neath fell through, Joseph Cottle recalled how 'before the final settlement Mr S[outhey] thought, on a second survey, that a small additional kitchen was essential to the comfort of the house, and required it of the proprietor, preparatory to his taking a lease. To so reasonable a request the honest Welshman stoutly objected; and on this slight occurrence, depended whether the Laureate should take up, perhaps, his permanent residence in the Principality, or wend his way northward, and spend the last thirty years of his life in sight of Skiddaw.'[69] Things did not work out quite like that. Although Coleridge visited Bristol at the end of January and urged Southey to join him in Greta Hall upon learning that he was not to rent the Welsh house, he still declined. His first thoughts were to settle in the Bristol area, and he even tried to persuade Coleridge to move back there, 'not wholly from selfish motives', but 'because the climate is far milder', which would be better for his health.[70] When William Taylor proposed that Southey moved to Norfolk, he replied that it was 'unhappily too far east . . . here in the west the intercourse with Portugal is far easier. There I must go in about two years and there if possible I will willingly fix my final abode, and spend my life speaking Portuguese and writing English.' Taylor responded that 'it would be an odd termination for you to select your home in the patria of the Inquisition and to make choice of the despotism of Portugal for the form of government.'[71] A more convincing reason for Southey's turning down Norwich was that Taylor was starting a newspaper there, the *Iris*, and wanted him to edit it. As he explained to Rickman, 'if I ever chose drudgery of that kind it should not be for a country paper'.[72]

In May 1803 the peace of Amiens broke down, and the renewal of hostilities with France scotched Southey's hopes to return to Portugal. That month he and Edith visited John May in Richmond, where he suggested they might move. This suggestion became more attractive after Southey spent two weeks in London early in July, negotiating the editorship of a survey of English literature to be called the *Bibliotheca Britannica*. 'I perceive that the great art of my generalship will be to do nothing beneath my commandership's dignity', he observed, 'my business must be to make others hew in the quarry and to erect the building myself.'[73] Among the stone hewers he had already lined up by mid-July were '[Sharon] Turner for the Welsh and Saxon; Carlisle for the surgery; Captain Burney for the voyages; Rickman for Roger Bacon and what else he may like; Duppa for books of art.'[74] He also hoped to engage Coleridge in some capacity. He was to receive £150 per volume as editor, and, calculating on contributing a quarter of the text, he estimated that he would clear £250 for each. The first volume was projected to appear by Christmas 1804. That was enough to live on, enabling him to drop reviewing and to concentrate on his 'History of Portugal'. With this in mind he got the first refusal of a house at Richmond that was to become vacant in November.

These plans all withered on the vine when Southey's daughter was taken ill and died in August. He poured out his heart to Mary Barker, who had become his main confidante. After Tom, who had lived with them as a half-pay officer for the duration of the peace of Amiens, left to join his ship Southey had offered his brother's bed to Mary, pointing out suggestively that it would have been improper to offer her half of it.[75] Nothing came of this, for Margaret began teething and with it her illness came on. She lost weight and then developed 'water on the brain', or hydrocephalus. In his distress,

Southey turned to Mary: 'I am struggling with the heaviest affliction that it has ever yet pleased God to try me with', he told her on 19 August when he realised that his daughter was dying. 'As soon as possible after her deliverance we shall set off for Keswick.'[76] The idea of going to Greta Hall to be comforted by the Coleridges had been suggested by Sara, Edith's sister: hearing of Margaret's illness she wrote to Southey that 'if the worst has happened you will come to Keswick, dear Southey both you and Edith know exactly our feelings on this subject and how ardently we here both wished to have you here. . . . Every thing that I can do for your comfort and for the consolation of you both – and for the happiness of us all, I will do – depend on it.'[77] The invitation determined Southey on a course of action which he outlined to John May.

> We are in heavy affliction; my poor child is dying of hydrocephalus and we have only to pray to God speedily to remove her. She is quite insensible, and that is our main consolation. Edith is suffering bitterly. I myself am recovering, perfectly resigned to the visitation, perfectly satisfied that it is for the best, perfectly assured that the loss will be but for a time.
>
> Never man enjoyed purer happiness than I have for the last twelve months. My plans are now all wrecked. Your letter was matter of some little relief to me. Longman's fears wish to delay the Bibliotheca and I am rejoiced to have no fetter upon me at present. As soon as it shall please God to remove this little object, I shall, with all speed, set off for Cumberland. Edith will be nowhere so well as with her sister Coleridge. She has a little girl some six months old, and I shall try and graft her into the wound, while it is yet fresh.[78]

'We hope to leave Bristol on Friday morning for Keswick', Southey informed William Taylor on 24 August, 'my poor child was buried yesterday and we are quitting a place where every thing reminds us of the loss. Poor Edith is almost heart broken . . . I have gone through more suffering than I ever before experienced – for I was fond of her even to foolishness.'[79] He was more forthcoming about Edith when he wrote to Mary the following day, telling her that his wife was ill. 'In all probability she has brought it on herself by refusing to take food for almost three days – now she takes medicine more patiently than she ever did (you know her mulishness of old) in the hope of getting well and departing.' As for himself, 'in truth I can be chearful and joyous even now, and shall soon be contented – but to be as happy as I was four weeks ago – so calmly and completely happy and so awake to that happiness as to break out into fits of boyish sportiveness as I then did – O Christ it must be a long time before that blessed state be restored to me.'[80] 'These things do one good', he told his brother Tom, 'they loosen, one by one, the roots that rivet us to earth; they fix and confirm our faith till the thought of death becomes so inseparably connected with the hope of meeting those whom we have lost, that death itself is no longer considered as an evil.'[81]

Southey seems to have been deliberately steeling himself to take the blow. After all, this was the third bereavement he had suffered since his return from Portugal, his mother and his aunt Margaret both having died the previous year. His behaviour in general, and his reaction to death in particular, strongly suggests that he was consciously guarding himself against misfortune. He had previously compared himself to a coconut and a hedgehog, impervious to the shafts of fate. A revealing insight into this frame of mind is provided by another letter he wrote to his brother at this time: 'I am like the boiling well – however agitated at bottom, the surface is calm.'[82] The loss of Margaret led him to vow never again 'to love anything of such uncertain existence'.[83] Instead he was determined to devote himself to more durable earthly objects. 'The old leaves are dropping from the family tree, and I see no bud upon its branches', he wrote to his brother Henry after the death of their mother. 'My books grow dearer to me. I cling to them with a comfortless feeling that it is the only safe attachment, that they are the friends whom there is no danger of losing, who must survive me.'[84] His love of books was to become a fetish. Notwithstanding this, as we shall see with his relationship to his son Herbert, his attempts to harden himself did not inure him to the loss of a child.

'As far as survivorship gives the feeling', Southey confessed to Mary Barker, 'I am old already.'[85] A year earlier he had admitted that 'ten years have materially altered me. The flavour of the liquor is the same – and I believe it is still sound – but it has ceased to froth and sparkle.'[86] This observation could also be made of his correspondence – the wit and warmth of his letters discernibly diminish, and a sober, almost pompous tone begins to intrude into them. 'I am growing old Bedford', he wrote in the autumn of 1803, 'not so much by the family bible as by all external and outward symptoms; the grey hairs have made their appearance; my eyes are wearing out . . . my limbs not so supple as they were at Brixton in '93; my tongue not so glib; my heart quieter; my hopes, thoughts, and feelings, all of the complexion of a sunny autumn evening.'[87] At the age of only twenty-nine, Southey's move to Keswick marked, not the beginning of the evening of his life, but the end of his 'morning of ardour and of hope'.

PART II

'A day of clouds and storms'

CHAPTER SIX

Laker (1803–1807)

Robert and Edith made their way north from Bristol, staying for five days with Mary Barker in Staffordshire, and on 7 September 1803 they arrived at Greta Hall. 'I have no fixture – feeling about me, no symptoms of root striking here', Southey confessed to Mary the following day. 'Alas! What am I but a feather driven by the wind, and God knows where the wind may drive me next.'[1] He could not have foreseen that in fact he was to spend the rest of his life there, for he did not determine to settle down in Keswick until 1807. Before that he was constantly making plans to live in the south of England, and to spend some time in Portugal working on his 'History' of the country. Until he abandoned these schemes he was little more than a visitor to the Lake District, like the summer tourists who came for a season and who were called 'Lakers'.

Yet, where he had not been particularly attracted to the house on his first visit two years earlier, this time he immediately enthused about Greta Hall. 'Nothing in England can be more beautiful than the site of this house', he claimed, boasting that it was 'situated on perhaps the very finest single spot in the whole of the lake country'.[2] It stands at the top of a slight rise to the west of Keswick, where it had originally been built as an observatory, since it commanded a magnificent view. Behind it is Latrigg, a hill attached to the majestic mass of Skiddaw, one of the highest mountains in England, from which flows the river Greta, murmuring incessantly at the back of the house to which it gives its name. Before it is the lake, Derwentwater, and other peaks, including Catbells, which Coleridge thought resembled the tents of giants. Southey soon fell under their spell. 'It is two years since we left this place', he noted a few days after his arrival, 'and in that time the Mountains and Lakes have not changed as I have done. There is something aweful in the unchangeableness and duration of these things of Nature to one who so lately felt the instability of human existence. I shall be the better for dwelling among them.'[3]

The builder, William Jackson, had added to Greta Hall, making it big enough for him to live in the back, and to rent out several rooms at the front to Coleridge. These comprised a kitchen, a parlour, a sitting room and two other rooms on the ground floor, three bedrooms and two drawing rooms on the first floor, and a large attic divided up into a servant's room and three nursery bedrooms.[4] When Coleridge initially invited Southey to move in with him, he had offered him only the ground floor, which Robert thought was not big enough, presumably because they were to be joined by Mary Lovell, sister to Edith and Sara Coleridge, and her son. In the event Mary got the sitting room on the ground floor and a small bedroom on the first, while Southey and Edith also obtained a bedroom there, and Southey acquired one of the drawing rooms as a magnificent study, which was to be his sanctuary for the next forty years. Coleridge probably agreed to this substantial concession because he had no intention of staying in the house much longer. He had intimated to Southey, when he first broached the idea of their sharing the house, that he was planning on going abroad, probably for two years, and he plainly saw the scheme to accommodate his brother- and sister-in-law as a solution to his own domestic difficulties. Before the end of the year he took off for Malta, leaving Southey to the company of the three Fricker sisters. Their presence in the house led Robert to call Greta Hall, in a typically grotesque pun, the aunt hill.

When Southey first arrived at Greta Hall, Coleridge was away in Scotland and did not join them until 15 September. Meanwhile Robert discovered that the wound inflicted by Margaret's death was not going to heal quickly by moving in with the Coleridges. On the contrary, the sight of Coleridge's infant daughter Sara made him feel more pain than he had apprehended. Her brothers, Hartley, then aged seven, and Derwent, three, must also have made him feel the loss of his daughter. When Coleridge arrived, his company cheered Southey up. 'Coleridge and I are the best companions possible in almost all moods of mind', he told Mary Barker, 'for all kinds of wisdom and all kinds of nonesense, to the very heights and depths thereof.'[5] They went walking together, climbing Skiddaw and going round Derwentwater. William Hazlitt, who had yet to make his reputation as the greatest critic of his generation and who was visiting the Lakes, joined them in a walk to Watendlath on 24 October. He was also to become notorious as a sexual predator, a charge that gained momentum from an allegation that he had been obliged to leave the Lake District abruptly, shortly after hiking with Coleridge and Southey, in order to escape the vengeance of the friends of a girl whose buttocks he had thrashed when she refused his advances. If the allegations had any foundation one might have expected Southey, with his rigid moral views, to have mentioned them with disapproval. But there is no hint of any impropriety on Hazlitt's part in the letter he wrote informing Richard Duppa that 'Haslitt . . . has been here, a man of real genius.'[6] A decade later, though, Southey did claim that Hazlitt 'owes me a good turn for enabling him to escape from Cumberland'.[7]

By then, however, Hazlitt had criticised Southey for apostatising from his youthful radicalism. When he encountered him in 1803 there were few overt signs of that change. Indeed, Hazlitt would surely have approved of Southey's reaction to the execution of Robert Emmet on 20 September. The twenty-five-year-old Emmet had led an abortive uprising of United Irishmen in Dublin in July, in the hope, though not expectation, that Napoleon would back it up with an invasion. Following its easy suppression he was brought to trial, found guilty, and hanged the next day. On the scaffold he delivered a short but impassioned speech that was to inspire Irish nationalists who followed him. It began: 'Let there be no inscription on my tomb. Let no man write my epitaph.' Southey responded with lines 'written immediately after reading the speech of Robert Emmet', which opened with a summary of it.

'Let no man write my epitaph; let my grave
Go uninscribed, my memory be at rest
Till other times come on, and other men,
They who will do me justice.'[8]

To this Southey replied 'Emmet, no!' and proceeded to write his own epitaph for him. It took a similar line to that which he had adopted towards Despard, that Emmet was only guilty of 'erring zeal', his 'feverish mind' having yielded 'to strong delusion'.[8] Had he been spared he would have learned the error of his ways. Southey sent the poem to the *Morning Post*, but when it failed to appear there he attributed it to the politics of the new editor, and published it in William Taylor's Norwich newspaper the *Iris* instead.

A further link with Southey's radical past appeared in the Lakes in the person of John Thelwall. The former orator, however, had learned his lesson from the treason trials of 1794 and no longer lectured on politics. Instead, he gave itinerant talks on elocution. 'We live in an odd world', Southey observed of this: 'They were going to hang and murder him for very intelligible Jacobinism and now when he rigmarolls them with a farrago of what he does not understand himself it is Oh Rare John Thelwall – and they give him three and sixpence apiece.'[9]

Southey was convinced that hanging was the likely fate of his scapegrace youngest brother Edward, who he nicknamed 'Hempstretch'. 'Few candidates for Tyburn have started with a better chance', he complained; 'if he only attains to transportation his destiny will be better than his deserts.'[10]

Edward had been a trial to him for some years, since he lived on his wits and had to be rescued from the scrapes this got him into. In the summer of 1803 Robert had contrived, with the help of Tom, to get him aboard ship as a seaman. Then on 1 December he learned that Edward had jumped ship, and was living with a Mr Barham in Exeter, running up debts that he expected his elder brother to pay. Robert was outraged by this impertinence, and detected behind it the influence of his aunt Elizabeth, who had befriended the fifteen-year-old Edward. He confided in Coleridge, who confirmed him in his determination not to pay the bills, thereby to teach his youngest brother a lesson. His younger brother Henry was also giving him trouble, for his tutor in Norwich had dismissed him for being too idle, and he had gone to Edinburgh to study medicine. 'Of the curses of life worthless relations are the worst', complained an exasperated Southey. 'It is a sad thing to have ties of duty where there is neither affection nor esteem. I love Tom for he has a warm heart and would go thro fire and water for me as I would for him. As for the other two Harry will be a spendthrift and a coxcomb – or rather is so – tho he will do well in a worldly way at last, the other bids fair to become either a swindler or a strolling player.'[11]

Coleridge left Keswick on 20 December to spend Christmas with Wordsworth in Grasmere, before heading to London on his way to Malta. Southey missed him, seeking solace in his study, to which only his wife was admitted. There he had already established a routine, having adopted 'the clockwork regularity of my father. After breakfast in my own room till dinner, unless fine weather tempts me to walk, from dinner to tea again and so again till supper, and this for the most part alone. In the morning I review, in the afternoon read and doze, in the evening either to *Madoc* or History.'[12] This was a very rare acknowledgement of his father's influence on him. Southey's habit of devoting different times of the day to different activities was to characterise his working practice for as long as he was able to work. It was a punishing schedule, into which he fitted his prolific letter writing and his prodigious reading. He reviewed no fewer than thirty-three books for the second volume of the *Annual Review* alone, which took up his mornings in the last weeks of 1803.[13]

Among these was a review of the *Essay on the Principle of Population* by Thomas Malthus, or 'Malthouse' as Southey called him in a letter to Rickman requesting ammunition against it.[14] Rickman duly obliged, though his observations reached Southey too late to be incorporated in the review. Coleridge also provided some notes, though they, too, came in characteristically late, causing Southey to rush his review because of their delay. The gloomy predictions of Malthus, that population would progress geometrically, while resources would merely increase arithmetically, resulting in a demographic catastrophe, appalled Southey. He held that they were based on the false premiss that man could not control the urge to reproduce, since 'the gratification of lust is a thing of physical necessity, equally with the gratification of hunger (a faith which we should laugh at for its silliness if its wickedness had not pre-excited abhorrence) nothing would be more easy than to demonstrate that abortion, or the exposure of children or artificial sterility on the part of the male would become virtues: – a thought which we turn from with loathing.' Southey clearly would have been outraged by the recourse to abortion and sterilisation for birth control today. 'But if the possibility of chastity be admitted', he maintained, 'the whole argument against the system of equality, against the perfectibility, or to use a more accurate and less obnoxious term, the improveability of man, falls to the ground.'[15] As somebody who was scarcely celibate himself, fathering no fewer than eight children, thereby consciously obeying the divine precept to be fruitful and multiply, Southey would no doubt have offended Malthus as much as he himself had been offended by the *Essay on Population*.

'One most complete scoundrel has been by God's judgement consigned over to my tribunal', Southey observed of another review he wrote that autumn, 'some fellow who writes under the assumed name of Peter Bayley Jun Esq. He has stolen from Wordsworth in the most wholesale way and most artfully, and then at the end of his book thinks proper to abuse Wordsworth by name. I mean to prove his thefts one by one, and then to call him rascal.'[16] 'Stop thief!' were the opening words of the review. Southey accused 'Bayley' of plagiarising from *Lyrical Ballads*. His own characterisation of some lines in 'Tintern Abbey' as 'one of the finest passages that ever was or can be written' suggest that Southey was using this review to try to redeem, in Wordsworth's eyes at least, the one he had written on *Lyrical Ballads* for the *Critical Review* six years before.[17] Southey claimed that the Preface to the second edition of *Lyrical Ballads* (1800), in which Wordsworth proclaimed his philosophy of poetry, articulated his own 'critical creed'.[18] As for Bayley, he vowed that 'every peacock's feather shall be plucked out and then his tail will be left – in the very fit and inviting condition for a cat-o-nine tails.'[19]

Southey wrote a much more sympathetic review of another poet, Henry Kirke White, who had published a collection of his verse with the title *Clifton Grove*. This had been critically noticed in the *Monthly Review*, which Southey thought was an unfair attack on a young man, the son of a Nottingham butcher, who deserved better. He observed that it was harder for a poet to be recognised in his day than it had been in those of Dryden and Pope, or even at the beginning of George III's reign: 'It is therefore with no common pleasure that we announce these extraordinary productions of early genius.'[20] He hoped that White would find a powerful patron.

'Will you not rejoice to hear that I am going to blow the Trumpet of alarm against the Evangelicals?' Southey asked Mary Barker, referring to another review he was to contribute to the *Annual Review* on *A Chronological History of the People called Methodists* by William Myles. 'Is it not a happy hit to call them the Ecclesiastical Corresponding Society?'[21] In the review he claimed that Methodism 'is a system which must necessarily darken the understanding, deaden the moral feeling, and defile the imagination; its immediate object is to destroy the church establishment . . . *The Church of England is in danger.*'[22] This was a theme he was to blow on his trumpet ever louder as the years passed.

'I look upon myself as a good reviewer', Southey boasted to Wynn about his reviews for the *Annual Review*, 'never losing sight of my text – pointing out always what is valuable, and sometimes enlivening what is dull. But it is dull work, and when I lay aside Madoc or the History of Portugal to write for a Review if I were a Catholic I should expect it to be set down to my mortification score on the creditor side of my account with Heaven.'[23] Yet to his brother, Southey admitted that he took 'too little pleasure and too little pride in such work to do it well – what there is good in my articles are the mere eructations from a full stomach. Their honesty is the best part.'[24] He always regarded reviewing as drudgery, essential for the money it brought in – his 'ways and means' – but distracting him from his preferred literary pursuits of poetry and history. He was even prepared to alter his routine if the chance came to concentrate on less financially but more intellectually rewarding writing. 'My reviewing, more than ordinarily procrastinated, stands still', he acknowledged in October. 'I began Clarke's book, and having vented my gall there, laid the others all by till the first of November, that I might be free till then for work more agreeable. My main work has been Madoc.'[25] The review he referred to was of J. S. Clarke, *The progress of maritime discovery from the earliest period to the close of the 18th century*, the first volume of a projected seven. Southey likened his treatment of it for the *Annual Review* to 'breaking [Clarke] upon the wheel for the crimes of pedantry, stupidity, jack-ass-ness and pickpocketing'.[26] The review was indeed scathing, concluding that the book was 'a national disgrace'.[27] This was the first of several dismissals of Clarke's historical works, which led to reciprocal hostile reviews from the man who was eventually to beat Southey to the post of historiographer royal.

Southey completed reviewing for the *Annual* in January 1804, when he found enough time to devote to finishing the first part of *Madoc*. The poem had endured a long gestation since he first thought of it at Westminster School. He had toyed with the idea of publishing it by subscription, but this was abandoned early in 1804 through want of sufficient subscribers. He also hoped that Mary Barker would illustrate it, and indeed she did send him a sketch in February that he rather tactlessly rejected. When the following month she sent him a drawing of a beaver he went out of his way to be complimentary, possibly mending fences with her. If so, he did not succeed in persuading her to visit Keswick that spring in order to work with him on the illustrations, and in the event the volume was illustrated by others. He also asked Tom to provide him with information on navigation for the second part of the poem, dealing with Madoc's return to America. The first part, some 3,600 lines concerning events in Wales, was completed and Southey planned to take it with him to give Longman when he went to London.

Southey's journey, however, was delayed until Edith, who was pregnant again, gave birth, as he was apprehensive about the imminent arrival of their second child. He was so fearful of it suffering the same fate as his first that he tried to stick to his vow not to become too attached to earthly objects. This perhaps explains his cool reaction to the arrival on 30 April of another daughter, Edith May. 'The young one is very very ugly', he opined to Mary Barker, 'so ugly that if I did not remember tales of my own deformity . . . notwithstanding my present pulchritude – I should verily think the Edithling would look better in a bottle than on a white sheet. She may mend and in about three months I may begin to like her and by and by I suppose shall love her – but it shall be with a reasonable love that will hang loosely upon me – like all second loves.' The double entendre of the final phrase was underscored by his adding *'make no comment upon this'*.[28]

A week later Southey was on the road to London, passing through Oxford at four o'clock in the morning, when 'the place never before appeared to me half so beautiful. I looked up at my own windows and . . . felt as most people do when they think of what changes time brings about.'[29] He not only took the manuscript of the Welsh section of *Madoc* with him to Longman, but also the idea of publishing *Specimens of the later English poets*. He had already sounded this idea out with them, and with Grosvenor Bedford, before he left Keswick. Unfortunately, as things turned out, he invited Bedford to be a joint editor of the work along with himself and Charles Lamb. When Longman accepted the proposal, Lamb declined to act as editor, leaving Southey to edit the volumes himself with Bedford. This was an unfortunate choice, as Bedford failed to apply himself to the task, which was to strain Southey's patience with his old friend before the book appeared in 1807. By October he was lamenting that he was 'a fool for trusting him'.[30] While he was in London he saw Aikin and arranged for more parcels of books to be posted to him in Keswick for him to review in the *Annual Review* for 1804. It pleased him to tell Edith that this hack work would bring in about £50.

Southey started back home from London on 29 May, 'being the most rascally day in the calendar', since it marked the restoration of the monarchy in 1660!'[31] He went north by way of Birmingham, staying at Mary Barker's home in Penkridge, though his hopes of persuading her to travel on with him to Keswick were disappointed, leading him to admonish her after his return home. 'How many years purgatory you are to undergo for the disappointment you occasioned must be left to some merciful Catholic Casuist to determine', he teased her. 'The Evangelicals would not let you off for any thing short of half eternity – and were the punishment at my discretion – or Edith's – or Mrs Lovell's – you would certainly be sentenced to vigorous cart's tailing, perhaps to travel in that fashion to Keswick instead of by the stage coach.'[32] He tried to inveigle her to visit Greta Hall that summer, imploring her to 'come to Keswick. Come – COME – COME – COME . . . here is a whole bed – make haste least there should be half one.'[33] Behind the teasing there is a note of desperation. After Coleridge left, Southey had found that he missed 'somebody to walk with in the morning and somebody to talk with in the evening'.[34] Clearly the womenfolk in the aunt hill did not, and in his eyes could not, fulfil this role.

This explains his willingness, even eagerness, to welcome summer visitors to Greta Hall. The summer of 1804 – the first that he spent there – saw the arrival of the Lakers, who were to visit every year in increasing numbers. It was a long hot summer, which lasted into early autumn. 'Fine weather has led me day after day mountaineering with a long succession of visitors', Southey recorded early in October. 'We have a round of company here which intrudes upon many an evening.'[35] Indeed, Southey even surprised himself by helping to organise a subscription ball at the theatre in Keswick. It is sometimes assumed that Southey became a virtual recluse in Greta Hall, and had little if anything to do with his neighbours in Keswick, yet shortly after his arrival in the town he was fully involved in its social life.

By mid-October the Lakers were all gone and Southey shut himself up in his study for the winter. He worked on completing the second part of *Madoc* and starting in earnest what was to become *Letters from England by Don Manuel Alvarez Espriella*. In it 'will be introduced all I know and much of what I think respecting this country and these times', he observed. 'The character personified that of an able man, bigotted to his religion, and willing to discover such faults and such symptoms of a declining power as may soothe the national inferiority, which he cannot but feel.'[36] 'What he most abominates here (apart from our heresy) is the spirit of trading which has poisoned every thing.'[37] Before the book appeared in 1807, Southey brought in many of his friends to help him to compose the letters, getting information on Joanna Southcott from Mary Barker, on art and architecture from Richard

Duppa, on contested elections and topography from John Rickman, and on naval matters from his brother Tom.

Besides these labours of love he also had to earn his bread and butter, and turned to the parcels of books that Aikin had sent him from the *Annual Review*. When the volume appeared in 1805 it contained no fewer than thirty-five contributions from his pen. The *Annual Review* was divided into several sections, such as 'Voyages and travels', 'History, politics and statistics', 'Geography', 'Poetry' and 'Biography'. Southey contributed to most of them, displaying an astonishingly eclectic range of subjects upon which he was prepared to pontificate. 'The great use of reviews', he thought, 'is that it obliges me to think upon subjects on which I had been before content to have very vague opinions, because there had never been any occasion for examining them.'[38]

One of the reviews he submitted to the *Annual Review* was of an *Address from the society for the suppression of vice*.

A society for the reward of virtue would be far more beneficial to the public than one for the suppression of vice. The orator of the society tells us that the times grow worse and worse, that decent manners, as well as good morals, have almost wholly disappeared. We look for proofs and are told of the French revolution and the corresponding society. The seven trumpets in the Revelation, according to him, will breathe nothing but sedition and the seven vials contain nothing but volatile essence of jacobinism. The more extravagant a fashion has been, the more ridiculous does the person appear who persists in wearing it, when all the rest of the world have left it off. An alarmist in England is as much out of fashion now, as a republican in France. Mr. Addington poured oil into the wounds of the nation, and the nation will not now be blistered by any state empiric who may want to open the old sores anew for the good of his trade.[39]

The work he imposed on himself by reviewing, finishing *Madoc*, collecting materials for his *Letters from England*, publishing a collection of his early ballads as *Metrical Tales*, not to mention writing letters, meant that Southey spent almost all his time in his study. He clearly found fulfilment in these tasks, for it was during this winter that he adopted as his motto 'In Labore Quies'.[40] His own translation of it was 'rest in labour'.[41]

In October 1804 Southey had discovered that Greta Hall had apparently been sold, and that he would have to move out by Whitsuntide. The putative purchaser was 'one White, a fellow all paunch, whom I therefore compare to Bonaparte as being the great belly-gerent' – one of his many excruciating puns.[42] In the event the sale of the house did not go through.

'After the deed was done Mr Jackson himself, the Southeys and the whole house were in trouble', Dorothy Wordsworth wrote to a friend, 'but luckily Mr White repented and all were glad, and I daresay Mr Jackson will never forget himself so far over any Glass or Bottle as to sell it again.'[43] Before the end of November Southey was reassured that he 'shall be lord of Greta hall as long as it suits me'.[44]

The end of the year found Southey still troubled by the antics of his brother Edward, who had again absconded and was running up bills he expected Robert to pay. On the other hand he had changed his mind about his brother Henry, whom he had previously dismissed as a 'coxcomb', when he became President of the Medical Society in Edinburgh. Southey then became very proud of him. 'He is a very fine young man', he boasted to Bedford, 'being the youngest President ever chosen.'[45] Conversely Tom, whom he had praised in the past, was now giving him concern, having been dismissed from his ship for insubordination to the captain, though fortunately he was made first lieutenant of another ship shortly afterwards.

Although the scare over the sale of the house had been short lived, the possibility that Greta Hall could be sold over his head seems to have strengthened Southey's resolve to move again. He felt isolated in Cumberland, unable to complete his 'History of Portugal' there, since it was far from the London libraries and even from his own books, which he had left with his friends Biddlecombe, Danvers and Rickman. He therefore resolved to live in the south of England and even to make another trip to Lisbon. News that British troops were being dispatched to Portugal early in 1805 led him to investigate the possibility of accompanying them in some administrative capacity. Unfortunately for his immediate plans, but surely fortunately for him and his family, the expedition was abandoned.

Another motive for wanting to move was the lack of intellectual companionship in Cumberland following Coleridge's departure – hence Southey's constant appeals to Mary Barker to come to stay in Greta Hall. The obvious neighbour to share his love of literature was Wordsworth, who lived only twelve miles away in Grasmere. However, though they had seen each other since Southey moved to Keswick, relations between them were cool, and Southey's review of Lyrical Ballads still rankled with Wordsworth. Then, in February 1805, news reached the Lake District of the death of John Wordsworth, William's brother, in the sinking of the Abergavenny on the coast of Dorset.[46] Drowning in a shipwreck struck Southey as being 'of all deaths . . . the most dreadful, from the circumstances of terror which accompany it'.[47] He immediately offered to visit Wordsworth 'whenever you feel or fancy yourself in a state to derive any advantage from my company'. On 12 February Wordsworth replied, 'if you could bear to come to this house of mourning tomorrow I should be forever thankful'. Southey went as requested and stayed for two days. When he left, Wordsworth wrote that he 'comforted us much, and we must for ever bear his goodness in memory', while his sister Dorothy found him 'so tender and kind that I loved him all at once – he wept with us in our sorrow and for that cause I must always love him.'[48] This marked the real beginning of friendship between Southey and Wordsworth, when cordiality replaced coolness. Yet though they saw each other more often, they never developed the close acquaintance that Southey had enjoyed with Coleridge in the heady days of Pantisocracy. Southey's cast of mind was more that of the historian than the poet, indeed he himself was aware that he was 'a good poet but a better historian'.[49] He was not so much a creative writer drawing on the imagination, like Coleridge and Wordsworth, as a scholar. Where Wordsworth's inspiration came from Nature and the outdoors, Southey's came from books and the study.

This was clearly the case with *Madoc*, which finally appeared in the spring of 1805. The two parts were liberally sprinkled with footnotes, as had been its predecessors *Joan* and *Thalaba*. Where those had been called epics, Southey disclaimed that 'degraded title' for his longest poem in the Preface to the first edition. There he outlined the plot, dating it towards the end of the twelfth century and claiming that Madoc, a Welsh prince, left Wales and sailed west. 'Strong evidence has been adduced that he reached America', asserted Southey, though in the *Annual Review* he had conceded that 'the first Europeans who saw the mainland of America were the English under Cabot, but the whole glory is due to Columbus!'[50] Nevertheless at the outset of the poem he invites his readers to 'listen to my lay, and ye shall hear how Madoc from the shores of Britain spread the adventurous sail, explored the Ocean ways, and quelled Barbarian power, and overthrew the bloody altars of idolatry and planted in its fanes triumphantly the Cross of Christ.'[51] *Madoc*, even though it had been on the stocks since 1789, can be seen as a significant indication of Southey's conversion from the anti-war sentiments of *Joan of Arc* and other poems of the 1790s, to his advocacy of what he considered to be a just war against the tyrant Napoleon.

'It would amuse you to hear how ambitious of the honour of England and of the spread of her power I am become', he wrote to Wynn, to whom the poem was dedicated. 'If we had a king as ambitious as Napoleon, he could not possibly find a privy-counsellor more after his own heart. Heaven send us another minister.'[52] In May 1804 Addington had been replaced as prime minister by Pitt, much to Southey's disgust, and when the following April he found out that Bedford had published a pamphlet in praise of Pitt he rebuked his old friend roundly. 'Whoever takes him for a great man', Southey protested, 'need never laugh at the Egyptians for worshipping a monkey as a

God.'[53] By contrast he sent a copy of *Madoc* to Pitt's great rival, Charles James Fox, who wrote to thank him for it.

The reviews were mixed. One compared *Madoc* to *Paradise Lost*, but others felt that its Welsh and Aztlan names made it unreadable. 'Goervyl and Ririd and Rodri and Llaian may have charms for Cambrian ears, but who can feel an interest in Tezozomoc, Tlalala or Ocelopan?' asked John Ferriar in a tetchy critique in the *Monthly Review*; 'how could we swallow Yuhidthiton, Coanocotzin and, above all, the yawning jaw-dislocating Ayayaca?'[54] Southey, who had altered the name of the king of the Aztecas from Huitziton to Yuhidthiton 'for the sake of euphony', was particularly incensed by this review. 'It is stupid and blunt ill nature', he protested. 'A bluebottle fly wriggling his tail and fancying he has a sting in it.'[55] He had misgivings about the poem himself, however, confiding to Cottle that 'I do not think I could have executed it better, but the subject is bad, it was chosen too soon, and has been too long in hand.'[56]

In July Southey learned that his uncle John had died, leaving everything to his brother Thomas and nothing to his nephews. When news reached him of the contents of John's will, Robert wrote bitterly that 'one skin of parchment has thus taken more from me than all the sheets of paper I shall ever live to fill can possibly produce.'[57] He hoped to make something from sales of the *Letters from England* when they eventually appeared, and was busy thinking of other projects more profitable than poems, including plays, which he never wrote, and an idea for a novel that was one day to produce *The Doctor*. Over the summer of 1805, however, he had to shelve his many literary projects due to the arrival of the Lakers. His Bristol friend Charles Danvers at last came to Keswick in July, and over the following month they walked through the whole of the Lake District, covering over four hundred miles. Mary Barker – whom he had tried to inveigle north in July, telling her that 'delays are dangerous in making a visit as well as in making love' – finally came on 24 September and stayed until 22 November. Having waited so long for her to visit him, Southey took off with Peter Elmsley, another Laker, on 4 October to visit Edinburgh, not returning until the 19th![58] On 7 October they arrived at Sir Walter Scott's house at Ashiestiel, and stayed there until the 10th. In Edinburgh he and Elmsley met Francis Jeffrey, who Southey found 'amusing from his wit; in taste he is a mere child; and he affects to despise learning, because he has none. . . . I really cannot feel angry with anything so diminutive; he is a mere homunculus.'[59] He also considered the other Scottish writers he met, with the exception of Scott, to be pygmies in comparison with Coleridge and Wordsworth, and, by implication, himself.

While he was in Edinburgh Southey wrote a very revealing letter to Edith. It opened by asking her not to read it aloud, until she had seen passages intended for her alone. By this he presumably meant that he did not wish Mary Barker, who was still staying at Greta Hall, to be made aware of its contents. He told his wife that he had been so lonely and homesick since leaving Keswick that he realised he could not face going to Lisbon without her. 'If on mature consideration, you think the inconvenience of a voyage more than you ought to submit to, I must be content to stay in England, as on my part it certainly is not worth while to sacrifice a year's happiness; for though not unhappy (my mind is too active and too well disciplined to yield to any such criminal weakness) still without you I am not happy.' He also felt it essential to bond with their daughter Edith May, which would be impossible if he were to be away from her for a year. 'But of these things we will talk at leisure; only, dear, dear Edith, we must not part.'[60] There was nothing unusual in his feeling depressed and vulnerable when he was away from her, as his previous letters to Edith when he was in London or elsewhere show. But there was more to this than his own psychological state when he was on his own. There is an element of trying to reassure her that he wanted her as his wife. Perhaps Coleridge's abandonment of her sister by going abroad had alarmed Edith, when her own husband indicated that he intended to go to Portugal alone if necessary. Then again, the curious use of the word 'criminal' suggests that she suspected that he would seek to assuage loneliness by seeking female companionship. Here her suspicions might well have fallen on Mary Barker, had she known that as recently as 4 September he had written to invite her to join him on a visit to Amsterdam, when peace made it possible: 'I am to make a book to pay my extra expenses', he had told her, 'and you to make drawings for it to pay yours.' He had added that 'you and I and Piggarel [by which he meant Edith] are all to smoke and talk Dutch together'.[61] There is certainly a sexual tension in Southey's letters to Mary Barker that cannot have been unintentional. 'I look upon novel reading as being exactly to the mind what rank debauchery is to the body', he once observed to her, 'over stimulation instead of true delight.'[62] At the same time, those letters that he wrote to both Mary and Edith tell them what he wanted them to know. He seems to have been trying to control a situation he himself was afraid might get out of hand.

Southey made his way back from Edinburgh on 18 October, taking the coach to Carlisle with Elmsley, then continuing alone on foot to Greta Hall. What he discussed with Edith about issues raised in his letter can only be guessed, though she apparently agreed to his going to Portugal without her after all, as he mentioned the possibility in letters to his brother Henry following his return. How he related to Mary Barker when he got back can, too, only be surmised. His time was presumably taken up entertaining Jeffrey, who visited Keswick before she left around 20 November. Attending to his Scottish visitor might have been the reason why he was unable to accompany her to Kendal to put her on the mail coach, for which he apologised when he wrote to her on the 27th. 'You are missed', he assured her, '*still more in my study than below stairs*. Your litter was become part of the furniture of the room, and I never like to lose what is become familiar.'[63]

'Our succession of visitors is over, the summer birds have taken flight', Southey announced on 22 November, adding that 'the season for reviewing is begun and I have put on my winter cloathes and commenced my hyber-nation.'[64] Once again he contributed over thirty reviews to the *Annual Review*, which he thought reflected 'more of the tone and temper of my mind than you can otherwise get at'.[65] After praising Hannah More's learning, good sense and good intentions he questioned her credentials for offering *Hints towards forming the character of a young Princess*. 'Her mind has never recovered from the French Revolution; in her dread of a heavy gale she longs for the pestilential and putrid calms of the Pacific', he claimed, insisting that 'the British sovereign must be of the Church of England, as it was in the days of our fathers, and as it is now, not as it would be if re-modelled by the Evangelicals.'[66]

Early in the new year Southey was still hankering after going to Portugal, as he told Sir Walter Scott in February, 'if Bonaparte will let me'.[67] Napoleon had in fact made the prospect remote by sweeping all before him in Europe, with his great victories at Ulm and Austerlitz in the autumn of 1805. Only Nelson's naval triumph at Trafalgar on 21 October had lightened the encir-cling gloom. Still, Southey held out hopes of revisiting Portugal. In March 1806 he announced that he was going to Lisbon in September with his brother Henry, 'but have some reason to think that Edith will remain here of necessity'.[68] The reason was that his wife was pregnant again, with a son, Herbert, who was to be born in October.

Southey's optimism about finding a position in Portugal arose from the political changes that had occurred following the death of Pitt in January. They had brought into office the so-called 'ministry of all the talents', led by Lord Grenville, with Charles James Fox as foreign secretary, and, much more relevant to Southey, his friend Wynn as an under secretary of state. 'The turn our politics have taken is very fortunate', wrote a buoyant Southey, 'it puts me in the road to fortune and makes my prospects very bright, far brighter indeed than they ever could have been had I stuck either to divinity or law.'[69] The rise of the Grenvilles to power, though they favoured Catholic Emancipation, of which Southey did not approve, and opposed parliamen-tary reform, which he still supported, reinforced his growing conservatism. 'What I ardently wished fourteen years ago from feeling, I now think inevitable, though at greater distance, and desirable, without wishing it', he wrote to Danvers. 'For myself, it is best that things should last out my time, so I suppose they may: being a tenant of an old house, I would rather suffer its inconveniences and its vermin, than be at the trouble and expense of repairs.'[70] The metaphor was perhaps suggested by the state of Greta Hall, of which Southey recorded that 'the rats nightly spring a mine in some part or other, and make me apprehensive of the fate of Bishop Hatto.'[71] As a reference to the British constitution, it captures essentially the conservatism of a former radical who has reached middle age. So did the reply he made to Nicholas Lightfoot's observation that time had moderated his opinions as it mellows wine. 'My views and hopes are certainly altered, tho the heart and soul of my wishes continues the same. It is the world that has changed – not I.'[72]

His attitude towards the established church had, however, undoubtedly changed. 'If I regret anything in my own life', he admitted to Lightfoot, who was an Anglican minister, 'it is that I could not take orders, for of all ways of life that would have best accorded with my nature, but I could not get in at the door. Still – without being in communion with any particular church or sect – I believe in Christ Jesus as the true teacher and derive my best hopes from that belief. It will be however necessary for me, for my daughter's sake, to join some church – and that will be the established one – I like everything belonging to it except the articles.'[73] Indeed, Southey needed to conform to the Church of England if he was to get a post or pension from the government. Wynn was soliciting on his behalf for the secretaryship to the embassy in Lisbon, and hoped that his friend's radical reputation would not blackball him, as it had done when he was at Oxford. When Wynn learned that Southey was to visit London in April 1806, he urged him not to see the radical Horne Tooke, which would jeopardise his chances of preferment.

On Southey's journey to London he was accompanied by Wordsworth until they reached Alconbury on the Great North Road, after which Robert diverted to take in Norwich, where he saw William Taylor. When he eventually arrived in the capital, he wrote to Taylor to tell him that '"Madoc" is doing well in all but the sale. If you do not know the current value of epic poetry at the present time, I can help you to a pretty just estimate. My profits upon this poem in the course of twelve months amount precisely to three pounds, seventeen shillings and one penny. In the same space of time Walter Scott has sold 4,500 copies of his 'Lay [of the last minstrel]' and netted of course above a thousand pounds. But', he added with characteristic conceit, 'my acorn will continue to grow when his Turkey bean shall have withered.'[74] As usual when he left her behind, Southey wrote long letters to Edith, and again his absence led him to feel insecure enough to assure her that 'upon my soul I do not think I can bear to go abroad without you', though this time he was careful to add 'at least I shall be thoroughly unhappy if I do'.[75] One reason for his visit to London was to inject some sense of urgency into Grosvenor Bedford about their joint edition of *Specimens of the later English poets*. Bedford's 'lazy loitering shilly-shallyness' over this had exasperated him for nearly two years, and he determined to get a grip on the project.[76] When he got back to Keswick, he wrote to his collaborator to let him know that he was working on the Preface. 'And now, Grosvenor, let me tell you what I have to do. I am writing, 1. The History of Portugal; 2. The Chronicle of the Cid; 3. The Curse of Kehama; 4. Espriella's Letters. . . . By way of interlude comes in this Preface.'[77] Though Southey was trying to shame Bedford, who had far less work on his hands, it was nevertheless a formidable agenda, and it did not even mention *Palmerin of England*, a sixteenth-century work that Southey had begun to translate from Portuguese into English that summer.

Progress on his writings was as usual delayed over the summer by the annual visitors. Henry, now 'the Doctor', having taken his degree at Edinburgh, spent the vacation at Greta Hall, and went hill climbing and boating on Derwentwater with his brother. Tom joined them, so that all three brothers were together for the first time in the Lakes. Southey was introduced to the bishop of Llandaff, who had a house in Ambleside, and with whom, he told Tom, 'I am more in favour than I should be likely to be with any other man who wears an apron, for he is a staunch Whig, and would wittingly see the Athanasian Creed and half a dozen other absurdities struck out of the liturgy as I should.'[78]

Southey's own Whig susceptibilities, such as they were, meant that he was shocked, perhaps more than he anticipated, by news of the death of Charles James Fox in September. 'I am grieved at his death', he wrote to Bedford, and 'sorry that he did not die before that wretched Pitt, that he might have been spared the disgrace of pronouncing a panegyric upon such a coxcombly insolent empty-headed long-winded braggadocio – sorry that he ever came into power except upon his own terms, and still more sorry that he has not lived long enough to prove that his intentions were as good and upright as in my soul I believe them to have been.'[79]

On 11 October, when the diversions of the summer were over, and the annual stint of reviewing had started, life at Greta Hall was disrupted by Edith giving birth to a son. 'He astonished the hour by his marvellous loud voice, roaring, they say, before he was born', Southey proudly informed Wynn, 'and am satisfied that he is lawfully mine.'[80] This was because of the great noise that the boy made, like his father, who enjoyed shouting at the top of his voice, and making loud animal noises. Southey was noted for his explosive sneeze, which he jokingly said prompted people miles away to exclaim 'bless you!' Herbert, as the boy was christened after Southey's uncle, became his pride and joy.

On 30 October Coleridge arrived at Greta Hall after an absence of nearly three years. He soon made it clear that he did not intend to stay long, much to his wife's distress. Southey on the other hand was relieved by his decision, as his behaviour was very trying. 'His habits are so murderous of all domestic comfort that I am only surprized Mrs C is not rejoiced to be rid of him', he told Rickman. 'He besots himself with opium, or with spirits, till his eyes look like a Turks who is half reduced to idiotcy by the practise – he calls up the servants at all hours of the night to prepare food for him.'[81]

Despite these distractions, Southey got down to his winter schedule. He reviewed only thirteen titles for the *Annual Review* this year, which was partly because he hoped to wind up his reviewing to leave him free to go abroad, and partly because he began to send in entries to a new journal launched by Longman, the *Athenaeum*. Many of his contributions to the *Athenaeum* were to reappear in *Omniana* (1812), a joint production with Coleridge. Southey was also quite prepared to reuse materials from the *Annual Review*. Thus, a passage he employed in a review of Thomas Moore's *Epistles Odes and other poems* was to reappear fourteen years later in the notorious Preface to *A Vision of Judgement*. 'The literature of the present reign has been distinguished by its moral purity, the effect and in its turn the cause of an improvement in national manners. A father might without fear have put into his daughter's hands any book which issued from the press if it did not bear either in its title page or frontispiece manifest tokens that it was designed as furniture for the brothel. This was particularly the case with our poets.'[82] Moore was here accused of breaching these conventions, as Byron was to be in 1821.

Even as reviewing came to an end, two new commitments delayed progress on the works Southey was engaged on. He had previously taken an interest in the poems of Henry Kirke White, and now, following White's death from consumption in October 1806 while at Cambridge, he determined on their posthumous publication. He began to edit them in two volumes that were to appear in 1807. White had been a student at St John's College, thanks to the help of Wilberforce and the arch-Evangelical Charles Simeon. As Southey put it in his account of White's life, which prefaced the edition of his poems, 'I must be permitted to say, that my own views of the religion of Christ Jesus differ essentially from the system of belief which he had adopted.'[83]

In addition to editing *The Remains of Henry Kirke White*, Southey set aside the text of the 'History of Portugal' he had written so far to devote himself to the materials he had collected for that project that concerned Brazil. This came about when he received two letters from his uncle in Lisbon in December urging him to concentrate on the Brazilian aspects of Portuguese history. Herbert had received enquiries from the British embassy about his nephew's work on South America, which led him to believe the government would be interested in it. He therefore instructed Southey to offer to the government such information as his papers contained. Accordingly Southey wrote to Wynn, who sounded out his own uncle, Lord Grenville. The prime minister's reply was 'that my materials relate to the wrong side of S[outh] America for their present views!' He nevertheless encouraged Southey 'to postpone the rest of my history and set immediately to work upon this, in consequence of the present bias of the public mind'. Southey agreed to concentrate on the *History of Brazil,* which decision made a visit to Portugal to do more research on the *History of Brazil's* mother country less urgent, as he was 'in possession of almost every printed book relating to the subject except such as may be in Dutch, and have made arrangements for procuring them'.[84]

These events made it easier for him to make another decision that arose early in 1807, when Coleridge, who had moved out of Greta Hall again (this time permanently), let Southey know that he should either leave it too or decide to stay; Southey decided to stay. 'My mind is made up to continue here indefinitely', he informed Tom in February. 'We are going to paper the parlour with cartridge paper, to have the abominable curtains there died a deep blue, and to fringe them. To buy a carpet and white curtains for my study – and to have my books round by sea. . . . Think of the joy it will be to arrange my books, and see them all together, and worship them every day.'[85] He was probably strengthened in his resolve by the fact that Edith had 'very much improved in health since she was in Hampshire', though he put that down to her nursing Herbert rather than to the move. At all events, he reported: 'she is grown fat and strong. I am as usual first cousin to a skeleton.'[86] Jackson, the landlord, was relieved that Southey had decided to stay, not least since Coleridge had suggested that the Wordsworths, whom he disliked, might move in should the Southeys leave. Mrs Wilson, Jackson's servant, also welcomed the decision as she enjoyed working for the Fricker sisters and their children too. Once Southey had resolved to stay in Greta Hall, he committed himself to it: 'Accordingly after living three years and a half in a house half finished and half furnished', he informed Wynn at the end of March 1807, 'we are now endeavouring to get as many comforts about us as are within our reach. . . . And unless I ever go to settle in Lisbon few things could excite a wish in me ever to remove from hence.'[87]

CHAPTER SEVEN

Lake Poet (1807–1809)

It was just as well that Southey had decided to stay in Keswick, for the hopes of Charles Wynn getting him a posting to Portugal came to naught. Instead, Wynn acquired a pension of £200 for him from the government. Southey supposed it had been 'asked for and granted to me as a man of letters, in which character I feel myself fully and fairly entitled to receive it.'[1] He was pleased with the award, even though it replaced the annuity of £160 that Wynn had paid him previously, and with taxes actually realised only £144 a year. 'By the Lord, Senhora!' he wrote to Mary Barker in April 1807, 'you *shall* smile at *my* having a pension from the Treasury. . . . Had Wynn his brother's fortune, or were he still a single man, I should have preferred receiving from him, rather than from the public; but as it is, it is best as it is.'[2] Now that he was settling down in Greta Hall, he was more anxious than ever for Mary's company, urging her to visit Keswick again, and she was to be one of the Lakers who visited him that summer. Meanwhile he took her more and more into his confidence. Thus he confided to her his views on Coleridge:

> There are few men with whom I have so many intellectual points of contact . . . and none with whom my habits, feelings, morals and affections are in more direct and hostile contrariety. We are so utterly opposite in all the outward and visible signs of men, and in the inward and spiritual grace as well, that in my conscience I do not believe any person whom we both know likes the one, without at the same time not liking, or positively disliking, the other. We are north and south and if the needle of any one's affections point to one, it must necessarily turn tail to the other. Strange, for two men who have been so closely connected by their opinions, and who at this time more nearly agree with each other than they do with any body else.[3]

What Southey had in mind with his last comment was their shared views on Catholic Emancipation, a subject that had just brought about the end of the Grenville ministry, when George III objected to its policy of promoting Roman Catholics to the army. Southey agreed with the king in this, though he had approved the ministry's introduction of limited rather than indefinite service into the regular army, and its abolition of the slave trade, 'two measures the best which I have seen, or will live to see'.[4] The ending of the slave trade even led him to break a five-year spell in which he claimed that he had not written a poem, composing one in praise of Lord Percy's motion that led to its being abolished.[5]

Southey was nonetheless unrepentant in his resistance to Catholic Emancipation, even though he conceded that he and Coleridge were the only ones among his acquaintance who opposed it. 'I am for abolishing the test with regard to every other sect – Jews and all – but not to the Catholics', he insisted in reply to Wynn's protest about his stance on the issue. 'They *will not tolerate*: the proof is in their present practice all over Catholic Europe: and it is the nature of their principles *now* to spread in this country; Methodism and the still wilder sects preparing the way for it.' As for Ireland, 'nothing can redeem that country but such measures as none of our statesmen, except perhaps Marquis Wellesley, would be hardy enough to adopt – nothing but a system of Roman conquest and colonisation, and shipping off the refractory to the colonies.' Concerning his own opinions, he claimed he was 'as to the essential points so very nearly a Quaker that if it were not for their non essential peculiarities I should quietly enter their fold, and no longer be a stray sheep in the land. But just as they, who hold all wars to be forbidden by Christ, think the British navy exceedingly useful, just so do I regard the Church Establishment; – it is our protection against the intolerance of Roman bigotry, or Calvinistic fanaticism.'[6]

Southey's religious susceptibilities made him acutely aware of the danger of antagonising the Quakers, and even 'the methodizing part of the reading world', in his publications. As he pointed out quite sharply to his old friend Grosvenor Bedford, who had selected 'coarse' passages to include in their joint edition of *Specimens of the later English poets*, 'the sale of the book would be affected by a whisper against it upon that score, and on the contrary what a wide field of sale is opened for it should it be noticed as free from all such taints.' It was not, he insisted, that he was concerned for his literary character, for even the errors that defaced every page of the book – another dig at Bedford – did not give him five minutes' unease. 'But this is not the case with respect to my character as a moralist – of that I am as jealous as a soldier of his honour.'[7]

When they appeared, the *Specimens* – despite Southey's private criticisms of Bedford – acknowledged his contribution fulsomely: 'Grosvenor Charles

Bedford, an old and dear friend, with whom I have lived in habits of unbroken intimacy since we were school-boys together, has been my co-adjutor in the work, has selected many of the specimens, supplied many of the prefatory notices and conducted the whole through the press, which in a situation so remote from London as that of my residence, it was impossible I could do myself.' Giving Bedford responsibility for the production of the collection was, perhaps, a sly way of escaping censure for its many short-comings. Southey added a Preface in which he developed his notions of the history of literature since the golden age of Spenser, Shakespeare and Milton. The era from Dryden to Pope he regarded as 'the dark age of English poetry', when it had been dominated by French influences. 'The Anglo-Gallican school which Pope had perfected died with him. . . . Even in his own days the Reformation began. Thomson recalled the nation to the study of Nature, which, since Milton, had been utterly neglected.'[8]

Besides the *Specimens* and *The Remains of Henry Kirke White*, 1807 was to see the publication of Southey's translation of *Palmerin of England* and *Letters from England by Don Manuel Alvarez Espriella*. He was more aware than ever of the need to make money from sales of his publications, 'what comes by the grey goose quill'.[9] For not only had his annuity been effectively reduced, but his pension was not paid promptly, while the charges of ship-ping his books and belongings from Bristol to Cumberland had to be. He was so short of cash that he had to ask Wynn to advance him £50 in antici-pation of his pension and proceeds from his publications. While he despaired of realising much from the other titles, *Letters from England* he hoped would be particularly profitable, as Longman had advanced him £100 against its sales.

The *Letters from England* were published in three volumes in July 1807.[10] They consisted of seventy-six letters purportedly written by Espriella, a Spanish visitor to England, between 21 April 1802 and September 1803. His 'visit' was thus spent mostly during the peace of Amiens, which he had heard 'called the great political thaw', an expression that Southey claimed to have coined and to have introduced 'because [it] had been remarked'.[11] During the peace many Englishmen took the rare opportunity to cross the Channel, and many foreigners availed themselves of the chance to go to England. There was a spate of published impressions of their experiences by both sets of tourists. Southey's employment of the device of a fictitious English journey by a Spaniard was presumably placed in that particular time to lend credence to the conceit that it was genuine. Certainly he was anxious to create the impression that the letters were translations, urging friends who knew the truth to keep quiet about his authorship of them, and adding spurious scholarly apparatus by 'the translator'.

'My object was to give a picture of the present state of England', Southey claimed, 'but for this I have not left myself room, having for the sake of preserving the assumed character taken up too large a portion in mere travelling.'[12] No fewer than twenty-two of the seventy-six letters describe journeys, the first five conveying Espriella from Falmouth to London and the last three conveying him back again, while fourteen take him on a tour of England as far north as the Lake District. Southey's main motive for impersonating a foreigner was his 'hope that it may pass unknown through the hands of those Reviewers who are sure to detract from whatever is mine'.[13] Espriella commented on the various reviews in England that 'of late years it has become impossible to place any reliance upon the opinions given by these journals because their party spirit now extends to every thing', and referred to reviewers as 'the baboons of literature'. Southey was remarkably condemnatory of publications that were essential for his own subsistence. As he put it in the mouth of Espriella:

> England is but a little country; and the communication between its parts is so rapid, the men of letters are so few, and the circulation of society brings them all so often to London, as the heart of the system, that they are all directly known to each other; – a writer is praised because he is a friend, or a friend's friend, or he must be condemned for a similar reason. For the most part the praise of these critics is milk and water, and their censure small-beer. Sometimes indeed they deal in stronger materials; but then the oil which Flattery lays on is train oil, and it stinks; and the dirt which Malevolence throws is ordure, and it sticks to her own fingers.[14]

Even though Southey glossed 'small-beer', saying that the original Spanish word was 'aquapie, which is to generous wine what small beer is to ale', there was no way that a visiting Spaniard could have acquired such views and inside information. It is one of the many passages in which the mask slips and Espriella is revealed to be his alleged translator.

Indeed the letters teem with Southey's own views and prejudices. Espriella shared his contempt for the younger Pitt and his respect for Addington;[15] he expressed concern about the social, economic and political impact of the manufacturing system;[16] he even employed a metaphor about its potential to cause a revolution that became almost a Southeyan cliché: 'Governments who found their prosperity upon manufactures sleep upon gun-powder.'[17] Above all, the Spanish visitor displayed a remarkable curiosity for, and knowledge of, the various manifestations of religious enthusiasm in England.[18] Southey informed Grosvenor Bedford that in the letters he would 'see more of the present history of enthusiasm in this country than any body could possibly suspect who has not, as I have done, cast a searching eye into the holes and corners of society, and watched its under currents, which carry more water than the upper stream.'[19] It does not seem to have occurred to him that it was absurd to expect people to believe that a Spaniard could have acquired such insights in a few months spent in England.

For all its flaws, *Letters from England*, Southey's first popular publication in prose, reveals him to have been more impressive as an acute and critical observer of English history and society than as an epic poet of past and remote cultures. Its relative success, by contrast with the poor sales of his poetry, led him thereafter to prefer publishing prose works rather than verse. As he put it, 'it was well we should be contented with posthumous fame, but impossible to be so with posthumous bread and cheese.'[20] It seems, too, that he himself was aware that his talents were more scholarly than creative, as about this time he began to covet the post of historiographer royal, which he would have preferred to the poet laureateship he eventually attained.

Before he could be considered for such a position he had to make his peace with the establishment by dropping his radical stance in politics. Though he had moved some distance from the radicalism he had espoused in his youth, there were still traces of it in his political views. He poured scorn on the unreformed electoral system in the *Letters from England*, even advocating the secret ballot as a cure for its abuses in Letter 48.

It must have been for his radical rather than his reactionary views that Southey, to his own surprise, came to be considered as a suitable contributor to the *Edinburgh Review*. In November 1807 Walter Scott wrote to tell him that he had raised the possibility with Jeffrey, who, despite his dismissive reviews of *Thalaba* and *Madoc*, raised no objection to it. Yet just before Scott approached Southey, Jeffrey had antagonised him afresh by dubbing him a 'Lake Poet'. The label was intended as a sneer, as Jeffrey made clear when he published a review of Wordsworth's *Poems in two volumes* in the *Edinburgh Review* for October 1807. 'This author is known to belong to a certain brotherhood of poets who have haunted for some years about the Lakes of Cumberland; and is generally looked upon, we believe, as the purest model of the excellences and peculiarities of the school which they have been labouring to establish.' Southey objected to Jeffrey's 'impertinence with which he alludes to my residence in the Lakes after having been my guest there'.[21] He did not, however, raise this objection in his reply to the letter in which Scott pointed out that the *Edinburgh Review* paid ten guineas a sheet to contributors, and 'doubted if the same unpleasant work is anywhere else so well compensated'.[22] It certainly appealed to Southey at this time, when he was desperately short of money, and the *Annual Review* paid only £7 a sheet. Yet he resisted the temptation. As he politely replied to Scott, Jeffrey's scornful reviews did not concern him, but his principles did. 'To Jeffrey as an individual I shall ever be ready to show every kind of individual courtesy; but of Judge Jeffrey of the Edinburgh Review I must ever think and speak as of a bad politician, a worse moralist, and a critic, in matters of taste, equally incompetent and unjust.'[23] In particular Jeffrey supported Catholic Emancipation and advocated peace with France. Southey by contrast was adamant in his stance on the issue of 'No Popery', and told William Taylor that he was angry with him for his tolerance of Catholicism. 'The measure of Lord Grenville was a foolish one which would not have satisfied the Catholics and would have introduced a Popish chaplain into every regiment and every ship in the service. I would rather have had the ministry turned out than they should have succeeded.'[24] He was pleased to discover that Rickman as well as Coleridge shared his views on Catholic Emancipation. He was also a passionate advocate of war against France as long as Napoleon was alive.

The war also meant that the British had to leave Portugal, including his uncle Herbert and his brother Henry, and Southey was anxious to get his reviewing out of the way before Christmas so that he could go to London to meet them. He had tried to stop contributing to the *Annual Review*, but the editor, Aikin, had ignored him and sent him a parcel of books to review. Since he needed the money anyway, he set to work on them rather than return them. He had no inhibitions about promoting his own works in his reviews. Thus Espriella found a reference in a very favourable review of his old friend Sharon Turner's *History of the Anglo-Saxons*, while he even contrived to mention the *Specimens of the later English poets* by himself and Bedford in one of Horace Walpole's *Catalogue of the royal and noble authors*.[25]

Although Southey did finish reviewing before the end of 1807, as he had only eleven books to review for that year, his journey to London was delayed, partly by severe weather, but mainly by Edith being pregnant and due to give birth early in 1808. The impending addition to his family gave rise to a temporary dispute between Southey and Mary Barker. She had asked her uncle Sir Edward Littleton if he would be godfather to the child, and while Southey was flattered to be so honoured by Sir Edward, he was dismayed when he learned that it was conditional on the child being named after him. In the event of its being a boy Southey had already bespoken the name of Danvers, after his best friend Charles. Fortunately a tense situation was defused when Edith gave birth to a girl in February, who they called Emma.

Shortly after Emma's arrival Southey took himself off to London for two months. His abrupt departure following his wife's confinement might seem callous, but he did confess to Anna Seward, whom he undertook to visit, that 'my habits have long been so domestic and so uniform that to set out upon any journey seems a more formidable undertaking and is a more unpleasant one than it ought to be. . . . My eldest girl clings to me and says don't go. . . . I had need think of Litchfield and what I shall see there . . . to counteract a melancholy I never yield to.' Fortunately he had company 'to lighten the wearisomeness of the way as far as Staffordshire'.[26] He was accompanied by his brother Tom, who was going to Bristol to see a surgeon about his piles. They stayed two days with Mary Barker and her uncle at his house at Teddesley in Staffordshire, and then Tom proceeded south towards Bristol, while Southey and Mary went to visit Anna Seward in Lichfield. Southey recalled their encounter with the celebrated poet many years later:

> Miss Seward was at her writing desk; she was not far short of seventy, and very lame. . . . The first scene was the most tragi-comic or comico-tragic that it was ever my fortune to be engaged in. After a greeting so complimentary that I would gladly have insinuated myself into a nutshell to have been hidden from it 'she told me that she had that minute finished transcribing some verses upon one of my poems – she would read them to me, and entreated me to point out anything that might be amended in them'. I took my seat, and, by favour of a blessed table, placed my elbow so that I could hide my face by leaning upon my hand, and have the help of that hand to keep down the risible muscles, while I listened to my own praise and glory set forth, in sonorous rhymes, and declared by one who read them with theatrical affect. Opposite to me sat my friend Miss Barker, towards whom I dare not raise an eye, and who was in as much fear of a glance from me as I was of one from her. The temptation to laugh at a time when you ought not is a terrible one.[27]

Fortunately Anna Seward does not seem to have noticed their discomfiture, for they remained good friends until her death the following year. After their visit to Lichfield, which lasted two days, Mary returned home to Penkridge while Southey carried on to London.

When he got there, as well as seeing old acquaintances, Southey made a new one, Henry Crabb Robinson, a literary critic whom Aikin invited to dinner. Robinson was delighted to make Southey's acquaintance: 'He has a most interesting figure, a very romantic countenance and an air of more elegance and tenderness than strength', he wrote to his brother. 'Our conversation was political and it did my heart good to find him the eloquent supporter of my favourite opinions. He . . . declared himself unqualifiedly for the war.'[28] Southey stayed in London until the end of April – one of the reasons for his visit was so that he could pack up books he had left with friends there to send home, now that he had decided to settle in Greta Hall. Indeed, no fewer than twenty-five boxes were sent north by waggon.

Southey himself went first to Salisbury, to visit his cousin, with whom he found himself confined to the house for two days because of rain. They talked together 'of old Bristol elections and old family affairs, subjects on which his knowledge was far greater than mine and in which the interest I felt was equal to his own'.[29] He then journeyed to Bristol, where he visited Joseph Cottle and Charles Danvers, picking up some more of his possessions that they had looked after. He also met there Walter Savage Landor, whose *Gebir* he had long admired. Its author impressed him hugely too. Above all Landor encouraged him to continue writing poetry, which Southey had virtually abandoned following the dismal sales of *Thalaba* and *Madoc*. Now he was motivated to finish poems such as *The Curse of Kehama*, which he had laid aside, not least since Landor offered to pay for their printing. Though Southey had no intention of accepting the offer, the fact that Landor had such confidence in his own poetic labours determined him to resume them. It also led him to criticise Wordsworth, who, as he complained to Mary Barker, 'thinks poetry exclusively the only worthy pursuit of any one who can succeed in it, and yet has never once expressed to me the slightest wish that I should not utterly abandon it, as I seemed to have done, and did in fact for three full years.'[30] Southey had visited Mary on his way north with his brother Tom, who had joined him in Bristol. They spent another night at Teddesley with Sir Edward Littleton and Mary Barker, before pressing on to Keswick. Southey's delight when he was reunited with his library of over four thousand books was mitigated only by the thought that he now had materials for more works than he was likely to complete in his lifetime.

Among those projects he was currently working on were the *History of Brazil*, which was nearly half done; *The Curse of Kehama*, which he had been encouraged by Landor to complete; and 'Pelayo, the Restorer of Spain', which eventually appeared as *Roderick the last of the Goths*.

Southey was inspired to write on a Spanish theme by the uprising in Spain against Napoleon in the spring of 1808. Spain had just been transformed from an uneasy ally of France into a French satellite. Napoleon had taken advantage of a dispute in the ruling Bourbon family, which had resulted in Carlos IV reluctantly abdicating the crown to his son Fernando VII, to depose Fernando and to place the country under Marshal Murat. On 2 May there was an uprising in Madrid against French military rule, which was easily suppressed by well-equipped troops who overwhelmed poorly armed rebels. The harsh suppression was vividly depicted by Goya in his haunting '3rd of May'. The aftermath, however, was the rising of almost the entire country against the French and in favour of the deposed Fernando. Napoleon responded by announcing that his brother Joseph had succeeded to the throne of Spain, and by sending more troops to suppress the uprisings. Forces sent under the command of General Dupont were defeated at Bailen, near Cordoba, on 19 July, a defeat that was followed by the withdrawal of Joseph from Madrid.

Southey was elated by these developments. 'Since the stirring day of the French Revolution I have never felt half so much excitement in political events as the present state of Spain has given me', he wrote. 'I never had any hope from the old confederacies of Austria, Russia &c. I never could have any from any of the old Governments of the continent. . . . Nothing but a spirit of liberty and of patriotism can check the power of France. That spirit is arisen, and in a country where it cannot easily be checked or overpowered.'[31] 'Great things have been done in Spain', he crowed in mid-August. 'I myself since the insurrection in Madrid and the carnage which took place there have never entertained a doubt of the eventual success of the Spaniards [and] the compleat deliverance of that peninsular.'[32]

Southey's translation of *The Chronicle of the Cid* came out that summer, and he also published a third edition of his *Letters written during a short residence in Spain and Portugal.* Work on other projects had to be set aside while he was incapacitated for nearly a month by a more than usually debilitating attack of hay fever, and even when he recovered from it he had to deal with the visits of Lakers. One of these was the American George Ticknor, to whom Southey gave two ballads he had translated from the Spanish.[33] Among the other visitors that summer were a family called Horton, friends of Mary Barker's. 'The daughter', Southey informed Mary, 'I named Miss Nobs from a strong likeness she bears to the hero of that noble story of Dr Daniel Dove of Doncaster.'[34] The story was eventually to form the basis of his novel *The Doctor*.

In the same letter Southey inveighed against the Convention of Sintra that had been negotiated between the British and the French earlier that month. The Spanish revolt against France encouraged similar demonstrations in Portugal against the rule of the French Marshal Junot. When the Portuguese cried out for help from Britain the government responded by despatching troops under Sir Hew Dalrymple and Sir Arthur Wellesley. On 21 August Wellesley inflicted his first defeat on French troops in the Peninsular War, overcoming Junot's army at Vimeira. The battle was followed by the Convention of Sintra in which the French agreed to quit Portugal, though with all their equipment, together with personal possessions, which could include plunder from pillaging, and on ships to be provided by the Royal Navy. There was a public outcry in England against the Convention by those who regarded it as a supine concession to the French. Southey swelled the chorus of complaint. 'There is a straight and easy way of proceeding in such a case', he told Mary Barker, 'which is to break the Convention and shoot those who made it; or else, after the manner of the Romans, deliver them up to the enemy with ropes about their necks. Sir Arthur ought to be shot for fighting when he did. He was afraid of being superseded before he won a battle, and for that reason fought with only half his own force – for fear if he had waited till the other half came up Sir Hew should land and take command.' In fact Wellesley had asked Sir Hew Dalrymple to join him in order to follow up the victory by pursuing the French, but the request had been refused by the cautious commander. Consequently, Dalrymple alone bore the brunt of the blame and was replaced by Sir John Moore. Southey was so indignant about Dalrymple's conduct that he even told Mary Barker that 'no man can possibly consent to let Junot carry off his plunder unless he had been promised a share of it for so doing. This will be laughed at . . . but the man who could subscribe such a Convention is capable of any degree of baseness.' He was so incensed by it that he agreed with Wordsworth and other friends in Cumberland to call a meeting to make a formal protest about it in an address from the county to the king asking him 'to appoint a day of national humiliation for this grievous national disgrace'.[35] In the event, they were dissuaded from doing so by Lord Lonsdale's opposition to a county meeting. 'Mum is the word of command from those who move his strings, and he moves the puppets in two counties', Southey told Landor, while to his brother he complained that 'he [Lonsdale] and the ministry (all ministers alike) never wish the people to come before the King with anything except professions that they are ready to kiss his Majesty's . . .'.[36] Southey and Coleridge vowed to keep the issue alive in the press, while Wordsworth wrote a pamphlet criticising the Convention of Sintra.

An opportunity to place his views on foreign policy before the public was offered to Southey in November with the launching of a new journal, which was to be called the *Quarterly Review*. It came about when Walter Scott, who had tried to persuade Southey to write for the *Edinburgh Review*, left it in protest at its pacifist leanings. He persuaded the foreign secretary George Canning to offset its pervasive and, to him, pernicious influence, with a rival journal that backed war against Napoleon. Canning asked William Gifford to edit and John Murray to publish the new journal, and Gifford approached Southey to see if he would contribute to it. This unexpected offer was ironic, since Gifford had edited the *Anti-Jacobin* in the 1790s, and Canning had mercilessly lambasted Southey in it. The title still existed, albeit under very different auspices, and as recently as 28 May Southey had told Anna Seward that 'the worthy wights who conduct that are at issue with me upon the simple question – whether they or I ought to be hanged.'[37]

Southey's views on the Spanish uprising, and the need to support it, however, now coincided with Canning's, which explains the approach from Gifford.

Southey accepted the offer, but with some misgivings. He was quite prepared to provide an antidote to what he regarded as the poison of the *Edinburgh Review*, but had no wish to become a paid hack of the government. He spelled out his position to Bedford: he would write for the new ministerial journal, but preferred to contribute reviews of books rather than to compose 'a political pamphlet upon the state of Spain; these things require a kind of wire-drawing which I have never learnt to perform, and a method of logical reasoning to which my mind has never been habituated, and for which it has no natural aptitude.' He wanted Bedford to make it clear to Gifford, however, that, while 'from my heart and soul [I] execrate and abominate the peace mongers ... I am an enemy to any further concessions to the Catholicks. I am a friend to the Church establishment – *not as a Churchman, for I am almost a Quaker* – but because an establishment is now and long will be necessary – and the one we have secures toleration to such hereticks as myself. I wish for reform because I cannot but see that all things are tending towards revolution, and nothing but reform can by any possibility prevent it.'[38]

He was well aware that the government took a different view of many subjects to those which he held.

> If Ireland be mentioned no hint must be given at the utter and almost irreclaimable barbarity of its population. When our finances are to be spoken of not a word of the burthen of taxation must be dropt, when the state of our army is alluded to not an innuendo will be permitted against the duke of York – his infamies, the disgrace which he has brought upon the army and the ruin which he may perhaps bring upon the nation must be kept out sight, for the duke of York is the king's favourite and the ministry are the king's ministry and the Review is the ministry's Review. Grosvenor I must put on my gloves when I write for it will be a dirty business.[39]

Despite the fact that the duke of York was acquitted by parliament of a charge by a former mistress that he had trafficked in army commissions, Southey was convinced of his guilt. 'Enough has been proved for the people of England', he felt. 'The thing has long been known and even notorious, but the Duke's character has now been blasted with all the virtuous part of the community.'[40] Southey was prepared to withdraw from the *Quarterly Review* if its politics went diametrically against his own. Nevertheless, despite his misgivings he urged Bedford, who was acting as a go-between with Gifford, to assure him that he would not be 'a troublesome man to deal with', for he was a quiet, patient, easy-going hack of the mule breed; regular as clockwork in my pace, sure-footed, bearing the burden which is laid on me, and only obstinate in choosing my own path. If Gifford could see me by this fireside where, like Nicodemus, one candle suffices me in a large room, he would see a man in a coat 'still more threadbare than his own' ... working hard and getting little – a bare maintenance, and hardly that; writing poems and history for posterity with his whole heart and soul; one daily progressing in learning, not so learned as he is poor, not so poor as proud; not so proud as happy. Grosvenor, there is not a lighter-hearted nor a happier man upon the face of this wide world.[41]

Southey often used such extravagantly optimistic expressions about his life, but usually they are underscored by a note of quiet desperation. Here for once, however, he seems to be entirely genuine. He was happy with his lot now that he had settled down in Greta Hall. The recognition by the government of his writing ability, and commitment to their cause in the Iberian peninsula, was psychologically as well as financially gratifying. He had a stable if somewhat tepid marriage, and delighted in his growing family. Edith May was now four years old; Herbert, on whom he himself admitted he doted to a fault, was two; Emma was nine months old, while Edith was pregnant again and due to give birth in spring 1809. His commitment to family life was expressed in a letter he wrote to Walter Savage Landor urging him to 'find out a woman whom you can esteem, and love will grow more surely out of esteem than esteem will out of love. Your soul would then find anchorage. There are fountains of delight in the heart of man, which will gush forth at the sight of his children, though it might seem before to be hard as the rock of Horeb, and dry as the desert sands.'[42] He also recommended it to his uncle Herbert on learning the unexpected news that he had married. 'I am truly glad at this change in your way of life', he assured him. 'The morning and the noon may well be past in solitariness, but for the latter part of the day it is an evil and a sore evil to be alone.'[43] Herbert was then fifty-eight years old. Southey himself, at the age of thirty-three, was enjoying the sunny noontime of his 'day of clouds and storms'.

Following his return from Portugal, Herbert lived in Staunton-on-Wye in Herefordshire. This enabled Southey to correspond with him much more readily than had been possible when his uncle resided in Lisbon. They corresponded mainly about the *History of Brazil*, upon which Southey was engaged whenever he could spare time from *The Curse of Kehama* and the even greater curse – to him – of reviewing. His last reviews for the *Annual* were sent off at the end of November 1808, and early December found him with his first books to review for the *Quarterly*. By the end of 1808 he had also written about 3,000 lines of *Kehama*, though for the next two months he was unable to add another, since illness afflicted first himself, then his children, and finally Edith, who took to her bed for a week. 'Anxiety unfits me for anything that requires feeling as well as thought', he admitted, 'I can labour, I can think, – thought and labour will not produce poetry.'[44] In March he sent to Walter Scott some lines from *Kehama*, in response to his request for something of Southey's to publish in a collection he was editing with the title *English Minstrelsy*.

> They sin who tell us Love can die.
> With life all other passions fly:
> All others are but vanity.
> In Heaven Ambition cannot dwell,
> Nor Avarice in the vaults of Hell.
> Earthly these passions of the Earth,
> They perish where they have their birth;
> But Love is indestructible.
> Its holy flame for ever burneth:
> From Heaven it came, to Heaven returneth.
> Too oft on Earth a troubled guest,
> At times deceiv'd, at times opprest,
> It here is tried and purified,
> Then hath in Heaven its perfect rest.
> It soweth here with toil and care,
> But the harvest time of Love is there.
> Oh! When a mother meets on high
> The babe she lost in infancy,
> Hath she not then, for pains and fears,
>   The day of woe, the watchful night,
>   For all her sorrow, all her tears,
>   An over-payment of delight.[45]

These were among the most lyrical lines Southey ever wrote. Yet he was in two minds whether to keep them in *Kehama* as he thought them out of character with it, though in the event he left them in.

Southey took the occasion to give Scott also his views on the *Quarterly Review*, which he thought was 'a little too much in the temper of the *Edinburgh*' to please him. 'No man dips his pen deeper in the very gall of bitterness than I can do', he admitted, 'but I do not like to see scorn and indignation wasted on trivial subjects – they should be reserved like the arrows of Hercules for occasions worthy of such weapons.'[46] He did not say what he thought of Scott's review of his own *The Cid*, though he complained of it to Rickman saying that Scott had criticised it 'as if it were not history but romance' and lacked love: 'he might as well look for love in the London Gazette!'[47] To his uncle, he was more critical of the new journal. 'I am fallen into company with whom I have no common opinions except Spain and the necessity of war ad internearnum with Bonaparte', he confided to him, though he was well rewarded for it. 'I get well administered praise from Gifford, flattery from the Bookseller and meet remuneration for the article in the shape of 21£-13 – better pay than I ever yet received for any former occupation.'[48] He received £16 8s for his second article, on Portuguese literature, which appeared in May.

An opportunity to defend the ministry's policy in Spain more effectively than his articles in the *Quarterly Review* soon arose. At the end of January 1809 he had been approached by James and John Ballantyne, Walter Scott's publishers, who had also printed *Madoc*. The Ballantynes were planning a new periodical, the *Edinburgh Annual Register*, and wanted him to contribute to it. At that stage the details of his contributions had not been decided, but in August Southey undertook to provide a survey of the political affairs of Europe during the year 1808.

He finished reviewing for the *Annual Review* in 1809, partly because he was not interested in the books that Longman sent him. 'There is much amusement in reviewing Travels, and much intellectual profit', he observed, 'but when our Fathers which are in the Row [Messrs Longman of Paternoster Row] send such books as can only serve as Texts to write from I begin to feel that their pay is not liberal enough to serve as a stimulus to exertion. . . . For whenever I yawn over the text I sleep over the sermon.'[49]

One text that he presumably did not doze over was Byron's *English Bards and Scotch Reviewers*, which appeared in March 1809. Byron lashed out at the *Edinburgh Review*, and also at his fellow English poets, especially the Lake or 'pond poets' as he contemptuously dubbed Coleridge, Southey and Wordsworth. He was particularly scathing about Southey's three epic poems.

> Oh! Southey, Southey! Cease thy varied song!
> A Bard may chaunt too often and too long:
> As thou art strong in verse, in mercy spare!
> A fourth, alas! were more than we could bear.

Southey affected indifference to such criticism. Of Byron's he observed, 'it is a safe game, and he may go on till he is tired. Every apprentice in satire and scandal for the last dozen years has tried his hand upon me.'[50] He was to take Byron more seriously when his attacks became more personal.

Edith gave birth to a daughter, whom they named Bertha, on 27 March. Shortly afterwards, Southey set off to Durham where he spent a week with Henry on a visit he had postponed until after Edith's confinement, on the grounds that 'there is no time when a man can be so conveniently from home as upon such occasions as this!'[51] His brother introduced him to his fiancée Mary Sealy. Among Henry's acquaintances whom he met was Thomas Zouch, author of *Memoirs of the life and writings of Sir Philip Sidney* (1808), a review of which was to form Southey's last contribution to the *Annual Review*. He also met Andrew Bell, the educationist, who he thought knew 'less about India than a man ought to know who has lived there!'[52] After staying a week at Henry's house in Old Elvet, Southey went up to Newcastle to visit James Losh, before returning to Keswick. Although he found all well on his return, soon afterwards he and several of the family were stricken by the mumps. This was followed by Herbert contracting croup, which alarmed Southey into thinking his son's life was in danger. He even looked forward to the time when he would himself be dead and undisturbed by such earthly afflictions. When the scare was over, however, he wrote to Mary Barker: 'I have but four of the fourteen yet', indicating how many children he wanted, 'and they bring with them a good deal of uneasiness, nevertheless I'se for the whole number. Piggarel [Edith] is not, but you know her of old, and I do not find that her grumbling about them before they come makes her like them a jot the less when they are here.'[53]

Then, on 21 May, Southey's daughter Emma suddenly died. The contentment with his lot was shattered. Southey had to communicate the sad news to his brother Henry, who had just married Mary Sealy. 'God bless you and your wife!' he began. 'That prayer will take away the ill omen of beginning a congratulatory letter with tidings of sorrow – for I have such to add. We buried Emma on Tuesday last. . . . This has been a heavy stroke – how heavy you will never know till you have children of your own, and then God grant that you may never know it otherwise than by the delight you take in them.' The letter continued on a much lighter note, so light indeed as to seem inappropriate. 'As soon as I can leave Edith I shall set off for Durham. . . . Your own feelings I doubt not will lead you to give Mary a hint (as delicately as may be) of my partiality for gooseberry pie, of the distinction between male and female pies, and of the heresy of eating them hot.'[54] Was Southey finding it difficult to combine congratulations to the newlywed couple with news of a death in the family? Or was he trying to come to terms with his own grief in a way which immunised him from it? Certainly his letters informing others of his bereavement seem surprisingly cool. Thus he wrote to Charles Danvers, 'do not suppose me more cast down than I really am. I am more sad than sorrowful and more thoughtful than sad.'[55]

To add to his problems at this time Southey was desperately short of money, so desperate indeed that he looked to the government to bail him out. Walter Scott interceded with Canning on his behalf for a professorship of history. Oxford and Cambridge were out of the question since they would require him to subscribe to the Thirty-Nine Articles. He had better hopes of Scottish universities, but found that even in Scotland professorial chairs were 'fenced about with tests'. In July Southey was tipped off by Richard 'Conversation' Sharp, a Whig MP who was among the Lakers who visited Keswick that summer, that the stewardship of the Derwentwater estates would soon become vacant by the death of its incumbent, a Mr Walton, who was seriously ill. These were the former estates of the Jacobite earl of Derwentwater that had been confiscated when he was convicted of treason after the rebellion of 1745. They were very extensive, with lands in Northumberland as well as Cumberland, and Southey was attracted by the prospect. 'Being on the spot it would suit me well', he enthused, 'and it would please me well, insomuch as it would give me the power of preserving the woods and improving both the property and this beautiful place by planting.'[56] He pulled all the strings he could to obtain it. As it was in the gift of Lord Lonsdale he had to approach him, even though he had fallen under his lordship's displeasure by seeking to convene a county meeting to protest against the Convention of Sintra. Southey asked his friend Sir George Beaumont to intercede with Lonsdale on his behalf. Sir George obliged, assuring the earl that 'he is certainly a man of talents, and although I doubt he has been periodically a "scurvy politician" yet I verily believe he has now been convinced of his error, thrown away his "glass eyes and no longer pretends to see the things he does not".' He then quoted from Southey's letter requesting his intercession and concluded, 'I shall only add that I believe him to be a worthy man, and I think we may take the word of a poet on the subject of preserving the woods. I must trouble you with one trait of the kindness of his heart. Although he writes for his bread himself last year he gave up some months to arranging the papers left by poor Kirk White for publication without the slightest compensation except the pleasure of serving that extraordinary young man's surviving friends.'[57]

Southey discovered from Bedford that the post was far from suitable, since Walton 'has always been employed for seventeen or eighteen hours out of the twenty-four, together with his first clerk. The salary is about 700l a year. The place of residence varies over a tract of country of about eighty miles. The Steward must be a perfect agriculturist, surveyor, mineralogist, and the best lawyer that, competently with these various duties, can be found.' Bedford concluded, 'for my own part I would rather live in a hollow tree all the summer, and die when the cold weather should set in, than undertake such an employment.'[58] Lord Lonsdale had nevertheless invited Southey to Lowther Castle to discuss the position, and he felt obliged to spend two fruit-less days there before declining it, writing to Beaumont that 'had I known anything more was required not a thought of asking for such a situation would ever have occurred to me.'[59] As he wryly put it in his reply to Bedford, 'so much for place hunting'.[60] He had himself intimated to Canning that he would like the position of historiographer royal, only to discover that a Frenchman, Louis Dutens, had held it 'with a salary of 400l for many years – upon what plea they who gave it him can best tell'.[61] Canning assured Southey that he would do all in his power to obtain the post for him when Dutens died, which emboldened him to seek Lord Lonsdale's help again through Sir George Beaumont. 'My object of pursuit must be changed. Mr Dutens holds the office of Historiographer; in the common course of nature he cannot hold it long, to that I shall have better claims than any other person.' Beaumont forwarded his request to Lonsdale, though observing that 'if I am not mistaken Mr Dutens, tho far declined into the vale of years, is a better life than Mr S seems to conceive.'[62] He was right. Dutens did not die until 1812, at the age of eighty-two. Southey was compensated for his failure to get the post by James Ballantyne, who visited Keswick that summer and offered him £400 for the task of chronicling the events of the year 1808 for the forthcoming *Edinburgh Annual Register*. As he told his uncle, 'to be historiographer to Mr Ballantyne is just as good a thing'.[63]

CHAPTER EIGHT

'Historiographer to Mr Ballantyne'
(1809–1813)

James Ballantyne's terms for Southey's contributions to the *Edinburgh Annual Register* put Robert's finances on a firm foundation for the first time in his life. It enabled him to sign a lease to be tenant of Greta Hall for twenty-one years, following the death of the landlord, William Jackson, in September 1809. He retained the services of Jackson's servant, Mrs Wilson, who was devoted to his own children. In order to provide for his family in the event of his death he took out an insurance policy on his life for £1,000. When doing so he had to declare his profession, and found that poet, historian and reviewer were not acceptable legal terms, so had to describe himself as Gentleman. He also had to make a statement about his health: 'I have had the small pox, I have not yet the gout nor is it in my family on either side', he assured John May, when asking him to pay the premium for him. 'The point of reference as to a medical man is easily answered – Mr Edmondson of this town will vouch for my being in as good health as I have been these six years – that is to say as long as he has known me.'[1]

Southey began work on the *Register* immediately after Ballantyne signed him up, and by mid-October he was correcting the proofs of his first chapter, which he boasted was 'a bolder chapter of contemporary history than anybody else would have produced. It is like Mr Southey's strong beer – wholesome, strong and stingo.' He had also completed the second chapter, which he half suspected 'will frighten the Scotchmen', i.e. the Edinburgh Reviewers, because he proposed that Britain should fight France until Napoleon was replaced by another government.[2]

Southey was so obsessed with Napoleon at this time that, when Coleridge wrote for advice about how to attract more subscribers to his recently launched journal the *Friend*, Robert advised him to publish a character of Bonaparte in it. He also urged him to be less long winded, since modern readers preferred short articles. In a very revealing comparison of his own style with Coleridge's, he observed that 'you yourself sometimes nose out your way, hound-like, in pursuit of truth, turning and winding and doubling and running when the same object might be reached in a tenth part of the time by darting straight-forward like a greyhound to the mark', that is, like himself.[3] His private views of the *Friend* were less favourable than those he communicated to Coleridge. 'My earnest advice to him has been not to begin till he was stocked with mater-ials for twenty weeks', he told May, 'twelve he thought sufficient and perhaps might I, had it not been for a suspicion that if twelve were the stock in hand resolved on he would begin with six, or probably half that diminished number.'[4] He also complained about Coleridge's 'affectation of humility even to downright canting . . . and the folly of talking as he does about his former principles is still worse. It is worse than folly, for if he was not a Jacobine, in the common acceptation of that name, I wonder who the Devil was. I am sure I was, am still and ever more shall be.'[5] It is hard to reconcile that statement with the place hunter who spent time with Lord Lonsdale at Lowther Castle. Yet Southey did feel a connection between his youthful enthusiasm for the French Revolution and his advocacy of total war against Napoleon, this link being the Spanish uprising against the emperor in 1808. 'At length a national resistance had been aroused against this iron tyranny! At length the cry of liberty had gone forth! Young men understood now by their own emotions, how their fathers had been affected in the morning of the French Revolution, and they who, having seen the hopes of that season blasted, were fallen in spirit as well as in age into "the sere – the yellow leaf", felt as though a second Spring had been vouchsafed them.'[6]

Southey made his own contribution to the war effort when he received James Stanier Clarke's life of Nelson to review for the *Quarterly*, for which he was to be paid the unprecedented sum of £60. It was admittedly a huge tome, which he vowed he would weigh to 'calculate its faults by the pound – or perhaps by the stone'.[7] He had previously crossed swords with the author, hostilely criticising his *History of Maritime Discovery* in the *Annual Review*. Clarke had got his revenge by savaging *Madoc* in the *Monthly Review*, and Southey was to get his own back by giving Clarke's *Nelson*, along with four other lives of the Admiral, a drubbing in the *Quarterly*. Having dismissed them all in five pages he then, acting upon a suggestion made by William Gifford, proceeded to write another forty on Nelson's career. This led John Murray to propose that he expanded it into what was to become his own *Life of Nelson*.[8]

Southey's chief contribution to the cause of fighting total war against Napoleon was to be the *Edinburgh Annual Register*, which absorbed much of his time during the early months of 1810. It turned out that the person Ballantyne had originally signed up to write the chronicle of the year's politics was 'a downright Courtling and a Pittite'. His contributions, however, were 'so very dull that it frightened the Ballantynes', Southey discovered: 'they applied to me in despair and to their own great astonishment are thus become the Editors of opinions manifestly unconnected with any party and hostile to all parties and delivered with a sincerity which the greatest knave cannot doubt, and a vehemence which the veriest dolt must feel.'[9] In his account of the parliamentary debates of the year 1808 Southey criticised the Whigs and radicals who opposed the policy. Thus against Samuel Whitbread, one of the leading lights in the opposition, he wrote 'a broadside of bitterness . . . for his base apologies for Buonaparte'.[10] Indeed, Whitbread's reasoning Southey actually dubbed to be 'insane'.[11] When Ballantyne sent him proofs in which he had used his position as editor to insert a eulogy of Pitt, Southey protested and had the passage removed. Yet he was so anxious 'to keep the peace-party out [that] Pitt himself (I was about to say the Devil, but that is from me a still stronger expression) should have my support were he living against any ministry that would abandon Spain and treat with Bonaparte'.[12] 'On this ground we should take our stand', he wrote in the *Register*, 'and openly proclaim to France, and to all Europe, that England never will, on any terms, make peace with Napoleon.' Southey remained true to his radical principles, however, in advocating that this policy of total war against Napoleonic France should not be pursued in alliance with corrupt courts 'whose hour must come and which have already cumbered the earth too long . . . the Corsican was not to be overthrown by corrupt courts and effete dynasties. Nothing but the force of good principles, loudly proclaimed and steadily pursued, will successfully oppose a power so gigantic, founded upon evil, supported by evil and steadily and strenuously pursuing evil.'[13]

By April 1810 Southey had finished his first stint as 'historiographer for Mr Ballantyne', and took a few weeks off from writing. The appearance of the first volume of his *History of Brazil* led him to hope to start work on the second before he resumed his contribution to the *Register*. Meanwhile he visited his brother Henry in Durham, and entertained Lakers who came to Keswick over the summer, including Grosvenor Bedford, Lord Holland and John Rickman. Another visitor was Coleridge. Fortunately his wife had moved into the part of Greta Hall previously inhabited by the late landlord Jackson, so that Coleridge's arrival did not cause disruption to Southey's household above that already visited on them by the birth of another daughter in August. She was christened Katherine along with her sister Bertha, born eighteen months earlier and whose baptism had been unaccountably delayed, in Crosthwaite parish church on 10 September.

By then Southey had started work on the second volume of the *Register*, in which he was offered a share by James and John Ballantyne, the publishers. At first he declined, telling his uncle that 'nature never meant me to have anything to do with financial accounts either of my own or the public's.' In October, however, he purchased a share 'which has taken up the only disposable sum I ever yet was master of. It gives me however a capital of 209£ producing an annuity of 80£ so long as this work maintains its sale.'[14]

He was determined that this would be the case, and worked enthusiastically on the history of 1809. James Ballantyne expressed some anxiety about his treatment of the affair of the duke of York, and so Southey undertook to treat the matter with 'careful decorum'. 'Concerning other individuals', he assured Ballantyne, 'I will endeavour to write more temperately provided every now and then I may be allowed to speak plainly concerning the admirers of Bonaparte, particularly Mr Whitbread. To think about them stirs the gall and pouring off two or three bitter sentences may prevent a bilious attack.' Ballantyne had clearly alluded to some passages in his chronicle of events for 1808 that had been criticised for having 'a democratical colouring', to which Southey responded 'that such a colouring must needs be the sunshine and the life of whatever proceeds from me'.[15]

Southey took his duties as 'historiographer to Mr Ballantyne' very seriously and searched far and wide for materials. Crabb Robinson put him on to Don Manuel Abello, the secretary to the Spanish embassy. 'I am engaged to write the historical part of the Edinburgh Annual Register', Southey informed Abello, 'a task which I was induced to undertake by my deep and ardent interest for the Spaniards and a desire of assisting, as far as it was in my power, to counteract the base calumnies and cowardly system of the Edinburgh Review and the opposition.'[16] Southey had been able to find sufficient materials for the history of 1808, but lacked Spanish documents for the following year, especially about the second siege of Zaragoza. He therefore asked if the secretary could obtain for him any relevant papers, a task which Abello undertook for him, while John Rickman provided him with copies of parliamentary and other papers, and Southey also obtained copies of official documents from the government through the secretary of the prime minister, Spencer Perceval, who had succeeded Portland in 1809. Southey's initial view of the new ministers was not flattering, dismissing them as 'not merely the servants of the Crown but the very menials, the sycophants, absolutely the Kissarcii of the King'.[17] However, he did come to respect Perceval. Thus in the *Edinburgh Annual Register for 1811* he was to observe of him that he was a 'man whose individual character was without a spot [and who] carried the pure principles of his privacy into public action, and possessed the steadiness and intrepidity of a statesman in as eminent a degree as the milder and most endearing virtues of domestic life'.[18] The prime minister's 'pure principles' were those of an Evangelical, yet he apparently appreciated Southey's views on Methodism that he had expressed in the *Quarterly Review*.[19]

Writing to Walter Savage Landor that he was 'at work upon the history of 1809 for the "Edinburgh Annual Register"', Southey remarked that it was 'a pleasant employment; there is some satisfaction in keeping up the heart of the country, in acquitting one-self of any participation in national guilt or national folly.'[20] His main reason for writing was to inform Landor that *The Curse of Kehama*, which was published towards the end of 1810, was dedicated to him, since without Landor's encouragement he might never have completed the poem. At the same time he was aware that he had left himself open to ridicule by choosing a subject involving Hinduism which, he claimed in the Preface, 'of all false religions is the most monstrous in its fables'. The reviews were mixed as usual. But even sympathetic reviewers tended to express bewilderment at the elaborate plot involving Hindu deities. Southey professed indifference to them, particularly Jeffrey's predictably scathing critique in the *Edinburgh Review*. One reviewer referred to a claim made in the *Edinburgh Annual Register* that Southey, Scott and Campbell were the leading British poets, but refused 'to subscribe to the belief in a Trinity of living poets of whom Mr S. is represented as entitled to the foremost honours'.[21] Southey himself thought that the *Register* was 'right enough in placing me upon an equality with two of my contemporaries, but he had not sense enough to find them out.' Thus the writer, 'God knows who he is', spoke 'ridiculously of Campbell . . . whose verses, one and all, are tinsel and trumpery.' As for Scott, he conceded that he was better than himself in 'conceiving fine stage situations', but denied they could be compared in any other way. The two with whom he revealingly felt himself to be the peer were Wordsworth and Landor, though he thought that 'Coleridge might have been added if he pleased'.[22]

Coleridge was at that time in London seeking to establish himself on the literary scene of the capital and to break his addiction to opium. Southey felt that his quest for a cure was hopeless unless he returned to Keswick, and allowed him to be his 'task-master for three months', at the end of which he would have kicked the habit.[23] Not surprisingly that prospect did not appeal to Coleridge, who refused to answer Southey's letters, and indeed left them unopened. This exasperated Southey, especially when one of them communicated news of their old friend George Burnett, who was languishing in a poor-house infirmary in Marylebone. Southey urged Coleridge to visit him and help get him back on his feet, but by the time he had read the letter it was too late, for Burnett had died. Southey blamed Coleridge for this neglect, and convinced himself that he had nothing to feel remiss about. There is certainly a smug insensitivity, perhaps covering

1 *Robert Southey (c.1798)*, portrait by John James Masquerier.

2 *Edith Southey* (1812), portrait by John Downman.

3 *Robert Southey* (1795), portrait by James Sharples.

4 Southey's bookplate.

5 *New Morality* (1798) by James Gillray.

6 *Robert Southey,* after a portrait by John Opie.

7 *Robert Southey* (1812), portrait by John Downman.

8 *Robert Southey* (1824), portrait by Samuel Lane.

9 *Robert Southey* (1828), portrait by Sir Thomas Lawrence.

10 *Samuel Taylor Coleridge* (1804), after a portrait by James Northcote.

11 *William Wordsworth* (1806), portrait by Henry Edridge.

12 *William Gifford* (*c.* 1800), portrait by John Hoppner.

13 *Walter Savage Landor* (1839), portrait by William Fisher.

14 *John Wilson Croker* (*c.* 1812), portrait by William Owen.

15 *Joseph Cottle* (1800), portrait by Robert Hancock.

16 *John Rickman* (1831), portrait by Samuel Lane.

17 *Charles Watkin Williams Wynn* (1835), portrait by Sir Martin Archer Shee.

18 *Self-Portrait* (undated), Caroline Bowles.

19 *South Window of Study, Greta Hall* (1841) by Caroline Bowles.

20 *The 'Cottonian Library'* (1926) by W. J. Wheeler.

21 *Greta Hall* (undated) by Caroline Bowles.

22 Effigy of Robert Southey, Crosthwaite Parish Church by John Graham Lough.

23 *Robert Southey, 'reartraiture'* (1848) by Edward Nash.

up some feelings of guilt, in his attitude towards his errant brother-in-law at this time.

Such feelings are all the more questionable since Southey was feeling something of the frustrations and temptations that had led Coleridge to go so spectacularly off the rails. Hearing that Mary Barker's uncle Sir Edward Littleton was ill, he wrote to her early in 1811 to warn her to make contingent plans should he die.

> What I have at heart is, that having this before your eyes, you should be prepared . . . whenever that event happens, to come and take up your abode here. I do not think any thing could conduce more to your own happiness – I am sure nothing could add so much to mine – and I am willing to believe that as you have no friend who possibly can love you better – so there should be none to whose society you should more naturally look for as much enjoyment as the untoward circumstances of your life have left to be your portion. Ten years intimacy, and more intercourse during those years than often falls to the lot of persons of different sexes who are not related have given us a thorough knowledge of each other, and mutual esteem. And without assenting to the system of your worthy uncle respecting the fitness of having two wives – there is certainly a very great fitness that my daughter and your god-child should have two mothers.
>
> This is not perhaps the sort of letter that you would expect on such an occasion – yet surely it is a fit occasion to say that there is one person in the world who feels for you as sincere an affection as if he were your brother, respecting your good qualities as thoroughly as he perceives and understands them God bless you.[24]

The language of this letter suggests that something more than brotherly love was on Southey's mind when he wrote it.

Sir Edward in fact recovered, so there was no immediate prospect of Mary's moving to Keswick. Instead Southey planned to visit her on a journey he was to undertake with Edith as soon as he had written the history of 1809 for the *Register*. The task was, however, to take him far longer than he had anticipated due to the sheer bulk of the materials he assembled for it. He also developed his role as commentator upon, as well as chronicler of, the events of the year. Thus he wrote a long account of the motion of Sir Francis Burdett for parliamentary reform, in which he observed that it might be admirable in principle, but in practice would be detrimental. His remarks reveal how far he had shifted from a radical to a conservative position in the year that had elapsed since he had commenced work on the Edinburgh journal. 'If you have seen the Register for 1809', he wrote to William Taylor, 'you will have seen that the Burdettites have cured me of all wish for Parliamentary Reform.'[25] Now he extolled the existing system as one which

> has made us the prosperous, the powerful, the free, the happy people that we are. Better systems, no doubt, are conceivable – for better men. The theory of a pure republic is far more delightful to the imagination; it is to our Constitution what a sun-dial is to a time-piece, simpler, surer, and liable to no derangement – if the sun did but always shine. When society shall be so far advanced in its progress that all men live in the light of reason, then we may have the dial; meantime, upon any pretext that it may require cleaning or repairing, let us beware how we trust the time-piece to a tinker.[26]

Southey indeed confessed that he had become more conservative: 'the gradual change in these opinions may be distinctly traced by those who think it worth while to trace it in my various operas – more especially in the ·Register.'[27] 'I was some years older than you are now before I gained firm ground for my political opinions', he informed Lord Ashley in 1832. 'They were rather feelings than opinions before that time – rather exacted by sympathy or provocation than taken up upon enquiry and reflection, and in that state they might have remained if I had not been required to write upon subjects which made it necessary that I should look into them and examine their foundation.' Such a requirement arose from his commitment to the *Edinburgh Annual Register*, and he began it 'with a persuasion that Reform in Parliament was a thing to be desired', but changed his mind by the time he came to write the second volume.[28]

His contribution to the *Register* grew accordingly. To the first volume he had contributed approximately 250,000 words. His text for the second amounted to over twice as many. Ballantyne was dismayed when he received it, and having failed to persuade Southey to cut it got him to pen an explanation for the subscribers to the annual. 'I finished the Register last night', Southey wrote to his uncle Herbert on 9 June 1811, 'and wrote an advertisement explaining the cause of its length and late appearance in a manner something different from a bookseller's apology.'[29] 'The year of which the annals are here presented was fertile in important affairs both at home and abroad almost beyond any other of modern times', he offered by way of explanation, adding that to collect sufficient documentation necessarily took more time than a mere chronicle of events would take.[30] 'Its enormous length has cost me at least three months' labour more than the former volume, the whole of which is dead loss of the only capital I possess in the world', he complained; 'half that time would have sufficed for the Life of Nelson, the other half have set me forward for the next three numbers of the Quarterly.'[31]

The delay cost Southey not only time but money: 'I have a twelfth share of the work which ought to produce 80£ for the year', he calculated, 'but the increased bulk will eat up almost the whole of the profit, if not quite, for the booksellers (foolishly as I think) are afraid to raise the price in proportion to the quantity . . . so that I expect to lose certainly three score and perhaps fourscore pounds by three months additional labour, the loss of the said three months being equivalent to 150£. At billiards it might well be very amusing to play the losing game so well; – in this case it is not quite so pleasant.'[32] He did not blame himself for the disproportionate bulk of the *Register*, asserting that 'the public must be very unreasonable if they do not perceive that its great increase of length is attributable to the greater number of events to be recorded, not to any prolixity in the writer!'[33]

After completing the text of his contribution to the *Register*, Southey set off for London with Edith, leaving the children at Greta Hall in the care of Mrs Wilson. He wrote the eldest, the seven-year-old Edith May, a very affectionate letter from London enclosing a book each for her brother Herbert and sister Bertha, and informing her that she was to have 'a large book, full of stories, and fit for a great girl; so I cannot put yours in a letter; but it will come to Keswick in a great box, with a great many other books which I have bought for myself.'[34] On 24 July Southey went to a dinner party given by Charles Lamb. Henry Crabb Robinson was there and noted that Southey had been with William Blake, who currently had an exhibition in Golden Square. Southey 'admired both his designs and his poetic talents, at the same time that he held him a decided madman'. He also spoke of Wordsworth in a way that convinced Robinson 'there is no great attachment between them. Wordsworth he says has the fault of overrating his works.' In a discussion of Southey's own works Robinson was clearly taken aback when he announced that he proposed to write a poem with a Quaker for a hero. Southey was indeed contemplating a work on King Philip's war in seventeenth-century New England in which the protagonist would be an English Quaker. 'I intimated the disadvantage he sustains from doing no homage to public opinion', observed Robinson. 'He said "I think nothing of it".'[35] While the subjects he chose for his major poems were not calculated to have a wide appeal, unlike Scott's, Southey was relieved that sales of *Kehama* were significantly better than those of *Thalaba*. Southey also dined at the Admiralty with John Wilson Croker, who congratulated him on Tom's promise of promotion that Perceval's secretary had procured. 'Perceval wrote me a very handsome note when it was done', Southey acknowledged, 'it is much to his credit that he should have thus interfered to oblige me after the manner in which I have spoken upon the D[uke] of York's business and the Walcheren expedition – for the sheets of the Register were at the Admiralty before the whole was printed.'[36]

Though Southey was pleased with this development, he was not happy about the way Croker had been commissioned by William Gifford to tone down a review he had contributed to the *Quarterly Review*. The review in question was of *An Essay on the Military Policy and Institutions of the British Empire* (1810) by Charles Pasley, a friend of Coleridge and Wordsworth, who appealed to Southey as being 'of the right political religion', while his book was 'our political bible'.[37] This message he thought had been blunted by the 'castrations' that the article had been subjected to. Southey was constantly complaining at Gifford's editorial cuts to his reviews, but on this occasion he vowed to get his revenge in the next *Edinburgh Annual Register*.

When they left London, Southey and Edith returned to Keswick by a circuitous route that enabled them to visit a number of their friends. They stayed with Landor and his wife, who were living at Llanthony in Wales. Then they went to Ludlow to stay with Wade Brown, a Laker whom they had entertained in Keswick. After that they visited Mary Barker in Teddesley, where they 'feasted upon the venison and pine apples'. From Staffordshire they made their way back to Wales, traversing the Potteries, which Southey thought were a 'sort of hell above ground'. Following a stay with Wynn at Llangedwyn they visited Henry Koster in Liverpool, and then went straight home to Keswick, arriving at Greta Hall on 4 September after an absence of twelve weeks.

Such a long interval from writing had led to a lot of work accumulating. Southey promised John Murray that he would produce the long-delayed *Life of Nelson*, which was to be 'the midshipman's manual, his moral and intellectual compass'.[38] He had received materials for the *Edinburgh Annual Register* from Spain, and had collected more in London, but before he began to write these up he finished an article for the *Quarterly Review* on the rival merits of the educational systems of Andrew Bell and Joseph Lancaster. In 1806 he had praised Lancaster's system in the *Annual Review*, but now came down heavily in favour of Bell's, in direct opposition to the advocacy of his rival in the *Edinburgh Review*. He now favoured it not least because Bell was an Anglican whereas Lancaster was a dissenter. 'The system of English policy consists of church and state', he asserted; 'they must stand together or fall together; and the fall of either would draw after it the ruin of the finest fabric ever yet created by human wisdom under divine favour. Now to propose a system of national education, of which it is the avowed and distinguishing principle that the children shall not be instructed in the national religion, is to propose what is palpably absurd.'[39] Southey was again outraged when Gifford cut his article, complaining that it 'would have been the heaviest blow the Edinburgh has ever received if all the shot of my heavy artillery had not been drawn before the guns were fired'.[40] He therefore proceeded to expand it to a pamphlet twice its length, adding passages suggested by Bell himself, who spent a few weeks in Keswick that autumn.

Another visitor towards the end of 1811 was Percy Bysshe Shelley, who was then nineteen years old. He had been expelled from University College, Oxford, for publishing a tract, the *Necessity of Atheism*. Subsequently he had further alienated his family by eloping to Scotland with the seventeen-year-old Harriet Westbrook, whom he had married in Edinburgh that August. The couple had then gone to York to stay with Thomas Jefferson Hogg, a college friend of Shelley who, like him, had been expelled, though when Hogg attempted to seduce Harriet they left abruptly and went to Keswick, where they took lodgings early in November. For some reason Shelley thought that Southey was not at home, and it was not until just before Christmas that they had their first meeting. Between then and Shelley's departure for Ireland at the end of January 1812 they had several conversations, during the course of which Shelley changed his mind about his fellow poet. Initially he looked forward to paying homage 'to a *really* great man'.[41] Before their first meeting Shelley had clearly found out more about Southey, and discovered that he was no longer a radical. 'I shall see him soon and reproach him for his tergiversation,' he wrote. 'He to whom Bigotry, Tyranny and Law was hateful has become the votary of those Idols in a form the most disgusting.' Southey upheld the constitution in Church and State and supported the war in Spain, which Shelley considered a 'prodigal waste of human blood to aggrandise the fame of Statesmen'.[42] Southey had shared that view of the French Revolutionary Wars, but the Napoleonic Wars had changed them. How far he had moved from his anti-war sentiments to advocacy of total war against Napoleon can be gauged from his observation in the spring of 1812: 'Thank God we are beginning at last upon the offensive. If this country once gets a liking for land war, as it has for maritime victories it will not be long before we shall have other Blenheims!'[43] What would old Kaspar have said to that? The first conversations between the two poets, however, reassured Shelley that, though Southey hated the Irish, and was opposed to Catholic Emancipation and parliamentary reform, he was still 'an advocate of liberty and equality'. In religion Southey claimed to be a Christian, though Shelley was convinced that he was a deist. Nevertheless he concluded that 'Southey, tho' far from being a man of great reasoning powers, is a great man.'[44] Shelley was full of intellectual assurance in his account of these conversations with Southey, who was reduced to saying that 'when you are as old as I am you will think with me'. The younger man dismissed Edith as 'very stupid' while 'Mrs Coleridge is worse'.[45] His dismissals smack more of youthful arrogance than acute observation, for

Edith, though uneducated, was certainly not stupid, while her sister Sara, for all her faults, was quite astute.

Southey's own reaction to his visitor was enthusiastic. 'Here is a young man at Keswick who acts upon me as my own ghost would do', he informed Bedford. 'He is just what I was in 1794.' No doubt he saw a parallel between Shelley's being expelled from Oxford for publishing an outspoken tract, and his own expulsion from Westminster for a similar offence. Southey confirmed Shelley's claim that he believed that the younger man would think as he did when he reached the same age by admitting that 'I tell him that all the difference between us is that he is nineteen and I am thirty-seven.'[46] 'Now that he is got to the Pantheistic stage of his progress', Southey told Mary Barker, Shelley 'is the very ghost of what I was at his age – poet, philosopher, and Jacobin and moralist and enthusiast. . . . His own heart will lead him right at last.'[47] 'To tell you all the odd things about him would fill a larger sheet than I have allowd myself for this whole letter', he wrote to Danvers. 'I hope he will continue here till you make us your visit in the summer.'[48]

Shelley, however, was already so disillusioned with Southey that he resolved to curtail his visit to Keswick and to leave for Ireland. What finally lost his good opinion of the older man was a passage in the *Edinburgh Annual Register* in which Southey had sarcastically dismissed Burdett and his supporters, and then gone on to extol the Spanish for showing themselves 'deserving of the best monarch that ever adorned a throne'. Shelley was so offended by 'this disgusting abominable flattery and horrible lie' that he wrote 'I cant contain myself'. To him 'Southey's conversation has lost its charm, except it be the charm of horror at so hateful a prostitution of talents.' He left Keswick shortly afterwards without seeing Southey again, and passed Greta Hall 'without *one* sting. He is a man who *may* be amiable in his *private* character stained and false as is his public one – he *may* be amiable, but if he is my feelings are liars.'[49]

Shelley was glad to shake the dust of Keswick from his heels for another reason. He did not like the town, finding that 'tho the face of the country is lovely the people are detestable'. Some of the observations that led to this conclusion presumably emanated from Southey. Shelley deplored the fact that a factory had been built there, whose debauched workers drowned their illegitimate children in the river. At the same time he appears to have taken against the town quite independently: 'Keswick seems more like a suburb of London than a village of Cumberland', he concluded.[50] His hostile view of it can only have been confirmed if, as Southey was assured, he 'was knocked down at his door – so close to it as to fall back senseless into the passage, and thus escape robbery'.[51] Southey had been alarmed at the threat of violence for some time. The previous spring he had written to John Spedding to complain of 'some mischief having been committed upon my outhouses'. This had led him to approach the local justices of the peace to take measures 'for putting some check to the outrages which almost every night are committed in Keswick'.[52] Now he thought that 'it may not be amiss to carry arms for some time to come'.[53] He loaded up 'an old Spanish fowling piece to keep up the courage of the family', and ordered a brace of pistols and a watchman's rattle from London.[54] These were to be used against the 'ugly fellows' who came to the town, mainly from Carlisle.[55] Such incidents, coinciding with the Luddite movement in the Midlands, reinforced his view that the factories were largely responsible for the disturbances, and the Luddites undoubtedly influenced Southey's growing conservatism. He was convinced that Jacobinism, which during the 1790s had been confined largely to middle-class intellectuals such as himself, had penetrated down in society to influence the lower orders, which made him apprehensive of class warfare. 'Whether the fiend who bestrides it and spurs it on have Jacobin or anti-Jacobin written on its forehead', he asserted in the *Edinburgh Annual Register*, 'the many-headed beast is the same.'[56] As Geoffrey Carnall observes, 'that sentence reveals the real continuity between Southey's earlier and later political sentiments. He was always haunted by a fear of the mob.'[57]

Southey's contributions to the *Edinburgh Annual Register* not only convinced Shelley that he had finally sold out to the establishment, but also persuaded his rivals on the *Edinburgh Review* to take up the cudgels with him. The first volume had passed virtually unnoticed by them. Indeed Southey was delighted to learn that Jeffrey himself had commended it to Ballantyne as 'the best piece of contemporary history which had appeared for twenty years. When the second volume appeared he knew who was the author!'[58] Henry Brougham, a prominent Whig lawyer who had launched the *Edinburgh Review*, recommended in it towards the end of 1811 that Southey's contribution to the *Register* should be raised in parliament. Southey imagined himself being arraigned at the bar of the House of Commons for breach of parliamentary privilege, and relished the notion of the consequent publicity. 'Such an event would do more for my books than all their intrinsic merit has done', he observed, 'for I should have something said in my behalf by Canning and perhaps Perceval, which would be worth all the praise of all the reviews that ever have been or will be written.'[59] In the event Brougham's proposition was prudently dropped.

Southey's new-found commitment to the constitution in Church and State led him to put to the publisher John Murray a proposal for a *Book of the Church*, which should be used as a text book in Bell's putative national schools. He outlined to Murray the work that he had discussed with Bell and the bishop of Meath.

The plan is this, to describe first the religions of our British, Roman and Saxon ancestors, and the consequences resulting from their respective systems, being the temporal ends from which our conversion to Christianity redeemed us. 2d. A view of Popery with its consequence – from which the Reformation delivered us. 3d. A picture of Puritanism rampant from which the re-establishment of the Church rescued us; 4th a picture of Methodism from which the Church protects us. Summing up the whole with an account of what the Church is, how it acts upon us, and how inseparably it is connected with the best interests of the country – the whole to form one little volume, the shorter the better, perfectly clear to a child's capacity, that is a child of 12 or 14 years of age. [Southey also proposed to follow it up with a second book on the constitution.] Two such books if they could be put into the hands of the rising generation would go far towards inspiring that ardent and devoted patriotism of which the ancients had so much and we have so little.[60]

On 10 January 1812 he signed a contract with Murray for both books.[61] His defence of the Church was almost entirely political, for he was still not a committed Anglican. 'I pay the price for not being in the Church', he admitted in March 1812, as 'I believe it to be the best possible establishment for men as they are, essential to the welfare of the country and to the very existence of the Constitution; – its Articles nevertheless exclude me. But I . . . am ready to stand at the door with a club in my hand to knock down those who would break it open and rush in for the purpose of destroying it.'[62] 'It would be impossible for me to subscribe to the Church Articles. Upon the mysterious points I rather withhold consent than refuse it – not presuming to define in my own imperfect conception what has been left indefinite. But the plenary inspiration of the Scriptures which is the established tenet of every Church except the modern Socinian I decidedly disbelieve and this is a gulph between me and the Establishment which can never be past', he confessed. 'But I am convinced that the overthrow of the Church Establishment would bring with it the greatest calamities for us and for our children. If any man could have saved it, it was Mr Perceval.'[63]

Unfortunately, Spencer Perceval had been shot dead in the lobby of the House of Commons on 12 May. He was killed by a lone assassin, a deranged Liverpool merchant, John James Bellingham, who blamed the government for his bankruptcy. But as more recently with the assassination of President Kennedy, people could not believe that an event so momentous could be the work of a solitary gunman. Southey considered the death of Perceval, the only British prime minister to be assassinated, to be 'the most fatal loss which has ever befallen the country'.[64] When he learned that the event had been greeted with rejoicing in various quarters, he was convinced that it threatened to precipitate the class war which he had already persuaded himself was imminent. His reaction was to recommend the muzzling of the popular press, which he held responsible for the spread of dangerous views among the populace.

Southey particularly dreaded that Lord Wellesley, Wellington's elder brother, would succeed Perceval as prime minister. In his view Wellesley was 'a vicious man and a tyrant at heart'.[65] Worse, he advocated Catholic Emancipation. In the event the Prince of Wales, who acted as Regent after George III finally went insane in 1811, chose Lord Liverpool as Perceval's successor, and Catholic Emancipation was shelved as a serious issue in British politics until the next decade.

These political changes affected Southey personally, for Dutens, the historiographer royal, died while they were in progress. Southey immediately made known his interest in the post, and did all he could to obtain it. The Regent, however, chose James Stanier Clarke, who was his chaplain, for it. Southey was convinced that had Perceval lived he would have achieved his ambition of succeeding Dutens. Instead, he had to content himself with being 'Mr Ballantyne's historiographer [which] is well paid, but the office is no sinecure'.[66] This work kept him busy again until the middle of June, when he wrote to tell Tom: 'Huzza! I have finished my third volume. Huzza! hay-go, jumpetum-down-derry-down, radderer-to, tadderer-tee, radderer-tadderer-tandoree! Huzza! Aballeboozobanganorribo!' His high spirits on completing the stint show how seriously he took his contributions to the *Edinburgh Annual Register*, which had led him to delay reviews for the *Quarterly* and his *Life of Nelson*. After that, he assured Tom, who was staying with Henry in Durham, he would pay them a visit.[67] He went there in July, accompanied by Charles Danvers. On his return he found a letter requesting that his copy for the next *Register* should be ready the following March, so that it could appear in April and not July. He therefore had to start work on the history of 1811 immediately. 'My yearly task is no sooner completed than I am called upon to begin again', he complained, 'to the lamentable delay of my own greater historical works.'[68] And there were other distractions from his making progress with the 'History of Portugal'. As usual the Lakers arrived with the summer. Among them was Andrew Bell, whose surname led to the choice of Isabel for the first name of the girl born to the Southeys that November, to whom he became god father.

A far more significant guest as far as Southey was concerned was Mary Barker. For some years he had pleaded with her to visit the Lakes again, but she had felt herself tied to Teddesley due to the illness of her uncle, Sir Edward Littleton, whom she had to nurse. Although Southey insisted 'that I am a very happy man I owe to my early marriage', he clearly felt that Mary supplied something that was missing in it.[69] Southey was frustrated at not being able to see her, and his frustrations found expression in indiscreet comments in his letters to her. These went too far for Mary when in January 1812 he insinuated that Colonel William Peachy, who was paying her a visit, intended to propose marriage to her. He also informed her that his son Herbert was 'so like you that scandal might find a pretty foundation for a pretty strong resemblance'. When she replied, she upbraided Southey for these remarks, which took him aback, and led him to apologise for whatever it was that had offended her: 'the Devil take it I say now'.[70] Yet in his very next letter the flirtatious innuendos began again. 'You are right honest Senhora', he wrote, 'an awkward sort of compliment to a lady, it must be confessed, considering what is meant by making an honest woman.'[71] When he heard that Sir Edward had died on 18 May, he wrote at once urging Mary to 'come here as soon as you can possibly quit the scene'.[72] Mary responded by indicating that she planned to move permanently from Staffordshire to the Lake District now that she was no longer tied to Teddesley: 'Write to me as soon as possible to tell me how I must send my furniture to Keswick'. She added, 'I wish Mrs Coleridge would give me up her end of your house and I think it very idle for her now to keep it.'[73] Southey was overjoyed. 'I have long had many day dreams of what was to be done when you came to reside among us', he told her.[74] He did not respond as enthusiastically to her idea that Sara Coleridge should make room for her at Greta Hall, however, for he began to look around for a house for her. In October Mary moved into Greta Lodge, right next door.

Despite these diversions Southey did make some progress with his writing. *Omniana*, a collection of miscellaneous notes by himself and Coleridge, most of which had previously been published in the *Athenaeum*, appeared that autumn. It would have been published earlier, but Coleridge characteristically kept the press waiting eighteen months, until Southey decided to go ahead, even though there were many more entries from his pen than from his collaborator's. He also found time to add lines to his Spanish poem, which he had now decided to call *Roderick the last of the Goths* and not *Pelayo*. His main priority, after the *Register*, was an article on the state of the poor for the *Quarterly*. 'It is an attack upon Malthus, upon the manufacturing system and upon the Cobbetts and the Hunts who have produced this Luddite feeling in the mob', he explained; 'the conclusion is to recommend modes of employment for those who want to work – further education upon a national establishment, military and naval schools to receive as many children as may be offered, extensive colonisation, and those means of improving our own stock at home and advancing the human race of which the operation would be without contingent evil or inconvenience and the effect certain.'[75] This was to advocate state intervention on a scale few contemporaries envisaged. On the contrary, the conventional economic wisdom of the age was the laissez-faire market system advocated by Adam Smith. The article was scathing about Smith's *Wealth of Nations*, which Southey dismissed as 'a tedious and hard-hearted book'. He objected to its reduction of a factory worker to the status of economic man.[76] He also repeated his concern that, where the middle classes had become disillusioned with the French Revolution, the poor in the manufacturing districts were uneducated, and vulnerable to demagogues preaching revolutionary doctrines.

John Reynolds informed a friend at the end of 1812 that Southey was 'writing a Life of Lord Nelson – hackney'd subject'.[77] However overdone it might have seemed, Southey's was to become the definitive biography for its generation, and one that is still in print today. He acknowledged in the Preface that his book was intended as 'a manual for the young sailor, which he may carry about with him till he has treasured up the example in his memory and in his heart'. Southey admitted that it was 'the eulogy of our great Naval Hero; for the best eulogy of Nelson is the faithful history of his actions.'[78] Southey spent considerable effort on the Admiral's great naval victories, for he was no seaman and needed the help of those who were, especially his brother Tom, who served in the navy. The biography concluded with a purple passage on Nelson's death at Trafalgar: 'The most triumphant death is that of the martyr; and the most awful that of the martyred patriot; the most splendid that of the hero in the hour of victory; and if the chariot and the horses of fire had been vouchsafed for Nelson's translation, he could scarcely have departed in a brighter blaze of glory.'[79]

'I shall always bear in mind the purpose and use of the book, that it is to be the midshipman's manual, his moral and intellectual compass', Southey promised John Murray, the publisher of his *Life of Nelson*. 'For this reason I shall avoid all detail of the dreadful scene at Naples – delivering my opinion, tho most intelligibly, in the gentlest terms and leaping as rapidly as possible over the whole disgraceful transaction.'[80] Towards the end of 1798, following his victory at the battle of the Nile, Nelson had sailed to Naples, where he fell in with the British ambassador Sir William Hamilton and his attractive wife Emma, who were close in the counsels of King Ferdinand and especially his queen, Maria Carolina. Nelson helped Neapolitan troops to attack the French in northern Italy, and when they were defeated, and the French advanced on Naples, he also assisted the Neapolitan court to retreat to Sicily. While Nelson enjoyed the hospitality of the exiled court, and the charms of Lady Hamilton, loyalists in Naples led a revolt against the French and regained it for the royal family. Shortly before they were reinstated, their supporters concluded an armistice with pro-French elements, granting them a safe passage to France. When Nelson arrived he cancelled the truce, insisting that there should be no truck with Jacobins, as he called the pro-French Neapolitans. On their release from jail they thought that they were going to be embarked on boats for France, and instead they were handed over to the restored regime to be tried, and in many cases executed. Nelson's role in their fate has ever since been controversial. Southey referred to it as 'the only blot on his public character' and 'a deplorable transaction'.

Southey tended, however, to ascribe this blot to Nelson's unfortunate liaison with Lady Hamilton, which 'ended in the destruction of Nelson's domestic happiness'.[81] As Richard Holmes has pointed out, treatment of Nelson's relationships with his estranged wife and his voluptuous mistress was one of the main challenges of the biography of his hero, one which Southey handled perhaps surprisingly well. Both ladies were still alive when he wrote it so he had to proceed with caution. While never condoning Nelson's behaviour, he nevertheless subtly conveyed his understanding 'that here was the grand passion of Nelson's life, an "infatuated attachment" of a supremely sexual nature'.[82] Southey's appreciation of the temptation presented to a man married to a dull wife by a beguiling woman surely owed something to his own relationships with Edith and Mary Barker.

Southey was disconcerted to discover that an error of Murray, the publisher, caused the *Life* to be printed in two volumes instead of one. This was, however, offset by the hundred guineas that Murray paid him for the copyright. It was a timely payment, as early in 1813 he had become aware of problems with the financial viability of the *Edinburgh Annual Register* that were to lead to his contribution to the volume published that year being his last. 'I am in bad hands with the bookseller Ballantyne, who is manifestly a shuffling fellow and a knave', he complained in February; 'luckily however he and his brother (who is a man of character) have more dependence upon me than I have upon them. But I shall cast about to get clear of the connection and emancipate myself as soon as possible from periodical labour.'[83] The fact was that the *Register* was losing money, a process not helped by the prodigious length of the volume published the previous year, which was largely due to Southey's prolixity. He himself, however, was totally unrepentant about it. 'I shall have done with Annual Registers when the "Edinburgh" fails', he told Wynn in April. 'The death will be owing to the London booksellers. . . . So that where ten copies sell in Scotland scarcely one is sold in England.'[84] Informing his uncle of his intention to make his contribution to the fourth volume of the *Edinburgh Annual Register* his last, he claimed to have 'long suspected Ballantyne the bookseller of intending to defraud me, and the intention is now pretty plainly avowed.'[85] Ballantyne declined to pay Southey for his contribution to the fourth volume on the grounds that it had lost money, while he had become a shareholder in the venture and must therefore accept the loss along with other shareholders. Southey objected that he thought the offer of the share had been a bonus, and that he should still be paid for his work, which he claimed came to £225. He pleaded with Sir Walter Scott to put pressure on Ballantyne to settle the dispute honourably and in the meanwhile resolved to withhold his work for the fourth volume until it was.

Southey hoped to salvage something from the collapse of the *Edinburgh Annual Register* by using materials he had contributed to it as the basis for a *History of the Peninsular War*. 'Had I been historiographer the booksellers would have jumped at such a proposal', he asserted, 'and I should have found it the most lucrative engagement of my life.'[86] When he approached Murray with the proposal the publisher enthused about it, offering him a thousand guineas should they publish it. Southey was hesitant at first, telling his uncle that he was going to give it some consideration: 'It is certain that tho what I have written in the Register must be recast, yet the materials there, and the knowledge which I have acquired, are of such import that my work is in reality half done. This however is not to be considered in the price.'[87] Southey undertook to get permission from Ballantyne to use copyright material, 'that I may not be thought to have acted otherwise than with perfect openness and propriety'.[88] His transparent honesty on this issue needs to be stressed, as he has been accused of recycling passages from the *Register* into the *History of the Peninsular War* without acknowledging it. Not that he merely re-used material from the journal in the text of the history, for he was eager to obtain fresh materials from any quarter that would be relevant. Murray undertook to procure copies of them for him.

When Southey went to London at the end of July he took with him all the papers relating to his dealings with the Ballantynes to put into a lawyer's hands, 'if they persist in this which is in direct contradiction to the letter and spirit of our agreement'.[89] Some settlement must have been agreed, for Southey's contribution to the *Edinburgh Annual Register for 1811* duly appeared, while he did get some compensation for his losses, albeit not for some years. However, the dispute did serve to bring to an unfortunate end his stint as historiographer to Mr Ballantyne.[90]

CHAPTER NINE

Poet Laureate (1813–1816)

'At thirty-five minutes after ten o'clock, on the 20th of July, in the year of our Lord 1813', Southey, having just extemporised for the fourth evening 'the story of the Doctor and his horse', looked at 'the Bhow Begum' (Mary Barker) and said, 'It ought to be written in a book!' Mary 'laid down her snuff box and replied . . . "It *ought* to be written in a book".' So the decision was taken to publish Southey's novel *The Doctor*, though this did not happen until many years later.[1] About four weeks afterwards Southey set off for London, where he stayed with his uncle in Streatham. Herbert had moved there in the summer of 1810 in order to take up a living to which he had been presented by the duke of Bedford. While in Streatham Southey entertained his uncle's three boys, whom he called 'Duke Bruin, Marquis Bruin and Earl Bruin', with 'the story of the Three Bears with universal applause'.[2] This, his most celebrated work, was to appear in print in *The Doctor*.

Southey had promised his uncle that he would visit him some months before, though his departure had been delayed by many considerations, not least the terminal illness of his brother-in-law George Fricker, who had been staying in Greta Hall since Christmas to be nursed by his sisters. George died of consumption on 27 June.

Before he left Keswick Southey had learned that the Poet Laureate, Henry James Pye, had died on 11 August, and as he journeyed south he reflected on whether the laureateship might be offered to him. Almost all his recent writings had been in prose, and he had come to prefer writing on history to composing poetry, even thinking that 'as a poet I am full grown. The quantity of my poems may be increased – doubled – quadrupled – decupled, if there were a demand for the article. But their value must be determined by assay – not by weight, and nothing that I can now produce will alter that.'[3] Nevertheless, he decided that he would accept, if it were offered to him and it did not incur the usual obligation to write on any and every royal episode, however trivial. Shortly after his arrival in town Grosvenor Bedford informed him that he had discussed the vacancy with John Wilson Croker, who thought Southey would accept the position if asked. Southey went straight to the Admiralty to consult Croker. He was pleased to learn that the Prince Regent had been in favour of his appointment 'because he had written some good things in favour of the Spaniards'.[4]

Southey must have been discomfited, however, to discover that the prime minister, Lord Liverpool, had written to Sir Walter Scott to offer it to him. The prince was disconcerted too, for he had not been consulted for a post that was in his gift, and he wished to bestow it on Southey. It was decided to leave things as they were, since Scott might refuse the offer. Southey wrote to Scott from Streatham to ask if he had accepted the laureateship, 'concerning which I dare say you feel as I do – that tho it may not be desirable to have it, it would not be decorous to refuse it.'[5] Pye, appointed by Pitt in 1790 more for his political than his poetical activities, had become a laughing stock for his excruciating verse, and had thereby brought the post into disrepute. In fact, Scott had declined the offer, and had recommended Southey instead. Scott had actually written to inform Southey about this recommendation, but the letter arrived in Keswick after his departure. Edith forwarded it to him in London, and when Southey received it he wrote to his wife quoting the contents. Scott had flattered him by saying that he hoped he would be offered the laureateship 'upon whom it would be so much more worthily conferred. For I am not such an ass as not to know that you are my better in poetry.' A relieved Southey was happy to accept it on condition that he 'would not write odes as boys write exercises at stated times and upon stated subjects'.[6] To his chagrin he was to discover that no such condition was in fact mentioned to the Regent, who expected him to produce poems to rote for such occasions as New Year's Day. In a typical pun, Southey was to term this the Laureate's 'odeous' duty.

Scott's letter became generally known. When Henry Crabb Robinson heard about it he thought that his candour in deferring to Southey was 'unusual in poets, but Southey evinced the same towards Wordsworth. His *Recluse* is to be published this winter, and it will, said Southey . . . establish Wordsworth as the first poet of his age and country.'[7] Southey is sometimes regarded as a self-centred poet, full of his own importance, and he left himself open to such criticism by his inflated claims for his own poems, though these were often deliberately overblown. So it is salutary to have this early recognition by him of the greatness of Wordsworth.

There were irritating delays before the ceremonies relating to the laureateship could be observed. Meanwhile Southey had a hectic social life in London, meeting Madame de Staël, then the lioness of the literary scene, and also Byron, for the first and only time, at Holland House on 26 September.

Southey reported to Edith that 'I saw a man whom in voice, manner and countenance I liked very much more than either his character or his writings had given me any reason to expect.'[8] For his part, Byron informed a friend that Southey was 'the best-looking bard I have seen for some time'. On 4 November Southey was sworn in as Poet Laureate in the Lord Chamberlain's office, and at last on 11 November he attended a levy presided over by the Prince Regent, who conferred the laureateship on him. Southey described his appearance 'in full buckle, bag, sword and ruffles' to Mary Barker, adding, 'would that you could see me in this masquerade dress!'[9] The following day he took a seat in the coach to Penrith, and forty-five hours later was back in Greta Hall after an absence of twelve weeks.

The return to reality after the masquerade was a sobering experience. Although he regarded the laureateship as an honour, it did not bring with it any great material reward, yielding only about £90 a year. Southey made this sum up to £102 to buy life insurance for £3,000. He put his friend John May in charge of handling the proceeds of the office, which did not make up for the loss of income from the *Edinburgh Annual Register*. At the same time his domestic expenditure was increasing with the needs of two growing families, his own and Coleridge's.

Adding to the demands on him from his own family was his feckless youngest brother. Edward surfaced again, this time as a strolling actor, claiming that he had recently married and needed money to support his wife. On investigation of his claim Southey discovered that he had not in fact undergone a marriage ceremony and was living in sin, and so Edward fortunately did not become yet another call on his overstretched resources.

Sara Coleridge and her three children, however, did. When he got back to Greta Hall he found Sara in distress, because she could not manage to support herself and them on an income of less than £70. Coleridge himself was then in Bristol, where he had gone in October after John Morgan, the friend he had been staying with in London, went bankrupt. There he had relapsed into his opium addiction, and sent nothing to his wife. Southey, who had little understanding and less sympathy for drug dependency, thought that Coleridge simply lacked will power and was guilty of 'moral imbecility'. When he learned through his Bristol friend Danvers that Coleridge proposed to set up a school he could hardly believe it. 'I advise him earnestly to come here and write for the theatre, and for the Reviews. From the Reviews alone he may get, if he chuses, as much as would suffice to keep Hartley at College.'[10] This of course did not happen. Instead Joseph Cottle approached Southey with a proposal to raise money for Coleridge from his friends. Southey was appalled. In his view Coleridge would only spend it on drugs and alcohol, and would be even less inclined to earn money from his writings, which he was perfectly capable of doing if he only got a grip on himself. Instead Southey proposed raising a fund to send Hartley Coleridge to Oxford, and during the course of 1814 he and Wordsworth raised enough from their friends to send him to Merton College.

Another domestic distraction occurred early in 1814 when Mary Barker had a quarrel with the Fricker sisters, the details of which are obscure. Dorothy Wordsworth visited Greta Lodge frequently between January and April to help Mary nurse a youth, Basil Montagu, who had become ill while visiting the Wordsworths and the Southeys. His symptoms, including vomiting blood, were so alarming that he had to stay in bed and be nursed round the clock by the two women. The very day that Dorothy arrived at Greta Lodge, 19 January, she observed a fierce argument between Mary Barker and the Fricker sisters, the upshot of which was that Mary was declared *persona non grata* in Greta Hall, while Southey was virtually banned from visiting Greta Lodge. Though what led to the quarrel is unknown, there is a cryptic letter that Southey wrote to Mary on 'Saturday evening' (14 May), while she was staying with the Wordsworths in Rydal Mount.

> The last four lines of your note, Senhora, are all that could have been wished, and all that should have been said; – but I am far too desirous of seeing things return to their former course to dwell upon any expression in the former part, however improper I may think them and however much I may wish they had not been there. – A chance meeting would at any moment have set all to rights, and this was so likely that it seemed the wisest and the easiest way to wait for it. The chapter of accidents turned out unluckily, but for this no person is blameable.[11]

It is a tantalising communication. To whom had Mary written the offending note? To Edith? And what had she said in it? There is no way of knowing, but it is clear that Southey was anxious to see things 'return to their former course'. They seem to have done so, for he wrote the Preface to *The Doctor* on 4 June, which it is hard to imagine he could do if relations were still strained with the 'Bhow Begum' to whom the novel was to be dedicated. He even contrived to work in a reference in it to snuff, which she habitually took. 'I have drawn up the window blinds (though sunshine at this time acts like snuff upon the mucous membrane of my nose).'[12]

As usual Southey found a refuge from these problems in his work. 'Here then I am once more at my desk with my books and papers about me, at my own fire side', he wrote to John Murray towards the end of November 1813, 'right glad to return to that rest in labour which I have taken for my motto, for in it I find my happiness.'[13] He had already started work on his prose *magnum opus*, the *History of the Peninsular War*, and requested several titles from Murray to forward his research into it. He had also commenced his stint as Poet Laureate with a poem intended to be published on New Year's Day, 'Carmen Annuum'. The opening stanzas were a versified history of the Peninsular War, an event Southey claimed had inspired resistance first from Russia and then from the German states, leading to the defeat of Napoleon. The original version included verses that vilified Napoleon as a tyrant and called for his execution. 'The burden of my poem is "Glory to God, Deliverance for Mankind"', Southey explained, quoting a recurrent motif, 'the concluding strain is "Down with the Tyrant"'.[14] Rickman, to whom he sent the ode for comment, advised against the inclusion of the 'concluding strain'. 'Put the case that, through the mediation of Austria, we make peace with Bonaparte, and he becomes of course *a friendly power*; – can you stay in office this Carmen remaining on record?'[15] Notwithstanding this objection Southey sent the poem as it stood to Croker, leaving to him the question of suppressing the verses calling for Napoleon's death. Croker did indeed request that they be cut, so Southey obliged and his poem appeared in the *Morning Chronicle* on 8 January as 'Carmen Triumphale'. Southey was so incensed by the cuts, however, that he thought it should be called 'Carmen Castratum'. After adding some verses to the censored lines he determined to get them published anonymously 'before it becomes a libellous offence to call murder and tyranny by their proper names'.[16] They appeared in the *Courier* on 3 February as an 'Ode written during the negotiations with Buonaparte in January 1814'. The peace negotiations left him 'very ill pleased at the aspect of public affairs', he complained. 'They must go to somebody else to write Odes upon peace for them.'[17]

Southey had anticipated that his acceptance of the laureateship would 'give occasion to the jests of newspaper jokesmiths'.[18] Sure enough, his critics attacked his first effusion. Among them was William Hazlitt, who entered the lists against the new Poet Laureate in the *Morning Chronicle*, describing 'Carmen Triumphale' as 'the irregular vigour of Jacobin enthusiasm suffering strange emasculation under the hands of a finical lord-chamberlain.'[19] Apparently Hazlitt was aware of the censorship it had suffered, and the truth that it had been the censored version that Hazlitt criticised led Southey to dismiss his review: 'the criticism is bad – the carmen is simply good for nothing'.[20]

Despite the feelers for peace, pressure was kept up on France. The Prussians invaded from the north-east while Wellington entered the south-west from Spain, with Blucher reaching Paris at the end of March, and Wellington defeating Marshal Soult at Toulouse in April. On 11 April Napoleon abdicated. 'Well Grosvenor the tragedy of five and twenty years is over', Southey wrote to his old friend. 'I shall never forget the sensation which the fall of the curtain gave me.'[21] On reading Byron's *Ode to Napoleon Bonaparte*, Southey recalled that, at their meeting in Holland House, Byron had asked him 'if I did not think Bonaparte a great man in his villainy. I told him, no – that he was a mean-minded villain. And Lord Byron has now been brought to the same opinion.'[22] He himself was in two minds about the restoration of the Bourbons: while he accepted that it was an inevitable consequence of removing Napoleon, he thought that they had been a threat to Europe since the reign of Louis XIV, and advocated the removal of the territory the king had acquired on the eastern frontier, including Alsace and Lorraine, from France.

Southey's objections to the occupation of foreign countries by alien invaders found expression in *Roderick the last of the Goths*, which he finished on 14 July 1814. This, the last of Southey's long poems, is also the greatest. James Losh thought it 'superior to any thing before written by Southey'.[23] It is a fine, swashbuckling tale, and told with zest. Too often Southey is linked with Coleridge and Wordsworth as one of 'the Lake Poets', a school he himself protested did not exist, and such a link is to his detriment, for he was not a 'Romantic' poet in the sense that they were. Instead he should be associated with other contemporary epic poets such as Walter Savage Landor and Sir Walter Scott. Curiously Landor in 'The Tragedy of Count Julian' and Scott in 'The Vision of Don Roderick' dealt with the same theme as *Roderick*. All three drew implicit if not explicit parallels between the invasion of Spain by the Moors and by Napoleon.

Alongside the main action of *Roderick* there is a sub-plot involving Roderick and Florinda, whom he had raped, a crime that led her father Julian to rebel against him. Florinda feels guilty about Roderick's fate, because she had led him on until he misread the signals and ravished her. She confesses her guilt to 'Father Maccabee', whom she does not recognise as Roderick. Others, including his mother, fail to penetrate his disguise, though his dog and his horse do. Southey was aware that some readers would find this implausible, but insisted that it was possible. He cited the example of his late friend Charles Danvers, whose death in May 1814 had devastated him. 'After a fortnight's absence, during which he had been very exposed to weather, sleeping out of doors, and in an open boat, and had endured the greatest anxiety (in assisting a man to escape to America, who would have been hanged for high treason if he had been taken) was so altered as literally not to be recognised at the end of that time by an old servant of the family.'[24] Nevertheless Florinda's failure to observe that Maccabee was really Roderick is still hard to believe. When describing her emotional involvement with him, Southey betrays an acute awareness of her predicament.

> I loved the King, . . .
> Tenderly, passionately, madly loved him.
> Sinful it was to love a child of earth
> With such entire devotion as I loved
> Roderick, the heroic Prince, the glorious Goth!
> And yet methought this was its only crime,
> The imaginative passion seem'd so pure:
> Quiet and calm like duty, hope nor fear
> Disturb'd the deep contentment of that love;
> He was the sunshine of my soul, and like
> A flower, I lived and flourish'd in his light.

Unfortunately Roderick was married, albeit unhappily. Florinda moved into the royal household. There she found that

> The passion, which I fondly thought
> Such as fond sisters for a brother feel,
> Grew day by day, and strengthen'd in its growth,
> Till the beloved presence had become
> Needful as food or necessary sleep,
> My hope, light, sunshine, life and every thing.
> Thus lapt in dreams of bliss, I might have lived
> Contented with this pure idolatry,
> Had he been happy: but I saw and knew
> The inward discontent and household griefs
> Which he subdued in silence; and alas!
> Pity with admiration mingling then,
> Alloy'd and lower'd and humanized my love,
> Till to the level of my lowliness
> It brought him down; and in this treacherous heart
> Too often the repining thought arose,
> That if Florinda had been Roderick's Queen,
> Then might domestic peace and happiness
> Have bless'd his home and crown'd our wedded loves.
> Too often did that sinful thought recur,
> Too feebly the temptation was repell'd.

One evening she was walking alone when she chanced to meet Roderick.

> He took my hand
> And said, Florinda, would that thou and I

Earlier had met! Oh what blissful lot
Had then been mine, who might have found in thee
The sweet companion and the friend endear'd.

He then kissed her, but, hearing somebody approaching, begged her to meet
him again the following evening. Although she agreed, she was struck with
guilt, and vowed to enter a nunnery and remain a virgin. When they met he
told her that he could divorce his wife and marry her. But then she told him
of her vow. They quarrelled about it

Till in the passionate argument he grew
Incensed, inflamed, and madden'd or possess'd, . . .
For Hell too surely at that hour prevail'd.[25]

Quite what happened next is obscure, but it seems that Roderick forced
himself on her, though she blamed herself more than him.

The passage is one of the most remarkable in the whole of Southey's
massive poetic output. Maurice Fitzgerald went so far as to claim that 'there
are few scenes in English poetry of a more intense dramatic feeling'.[26] The
question arises: what inspired Southey to sympathise so sensitively with a
woman who passionately loved a married man? A possible explanation is his
own intimate relationship with Mary Barker. He was working on this book
of the poem early in 1813, shortly after her arrival in Keswick, and was
having problems with it. When he sent a draft of it to Walter Savage Landor
he told him that 'here you have a part of the poem so difficult to get over
even tolerably that I verily believe if I had at first thought of making Roderick
any thing more than a sincere penitent this difficulty would have deterred me
from attempting the subject.'[27] He resolved the problem by making Florinda
partly responsible for Roderick's actions. This resolution, and the words he
put into Florinda's mouth, were feasibly based on a woman's experience
rather than a man's imagination. The only woman who could have communicated such emotions to him at that time was Mary. Whether they were
based on a previous relationship or her feelings for Southey himself can only
be surmised.

Although *Roderick* was in print by August 1814 it was not published until
November. Meanwhile Southey was appointed a member of the Royal
Spanish Academy, a credit he was able to add proudly to his name on the title
page of the poem. When he learned from James Hogg, the so-called 'Ettrick
shepherd', that Jeffrey intended to review *Roderick* savagely in the *Edinburgh
Review*, and Hogg apparently suggested that Southey should lay off his public
attacks on the journal, he replied on Christmas Eve that 'I despise his

commendation and I defy his malice'. He was scornful of Jeffrey's claim that he would crush Wordsworth's *Excursion*: 'Tell him that he might as easily crush Skiddaw.' Southey did not seek popularity, or he would not write such poems as *Roderick*. 'Jeffrey can no more stand in my way to *fame* than Tom Thumb could stand in my way in the street', he asserted, alluding to the Scot's diminutive stature, 'I consider him a public nuisance and shall deal with him accordingly.' He then went on to describe vividly the way he would respond to Jeffrey's criticism, revealing the violent inclinations he usually strove to suppress.

> *Nettling* is a gentle term for what he has to undergo. In due season he shall be *scorpioned* & *rattle snaked*. When I take him in hand it shall be to dissect him alive, & make a preparation for him to be preserved and exhibited *in terrorem*; an example to all future pretenders to criticism. He has a fore-head of native brass – I will write upon it with acqua fortis. I will serve him to the public like a turkey gizzard, sliced, scored, peppered, salted, kiann'd, grilled & bedevilled. I will bring him to justice; he shall be executed in prose & gibetted in verse & the Lord have mercy on his soul![28]

Having got that off his chest Southey informed Hogg that two days previously he had finished his official 'Ode for the New Year': 'Its object is to recommend as the two great objects of policy general education and extensive colonisation.' The other major poetic endeavour of the year 1814, an ode for the projected marriage of Princess Charlotte to the Prince of Orange, had to be aborted when the engagement was called off in December. Unfortunately he had already written fifty six-lined stanzas 'a good many of which are not convertible to any other Prince'.[29] He managed to laugh off his disappointment.

The new year found Southey 'close at work; sometimes upon Brazil; sometimes upon the Spanish history; sometimes reviewing in the service of Mammon'.[30] Among the reviews he contributed to the *Quarterly* was one of a French account of Napoleon's expedition to Egypt in which he inveighed against 'the impious hypocrisy, the systematic falsehood, the deliberate cruelty of this robber, this renegade, this Djezzar Buonaparte'.[31] When he learned that Napoleon had escaped from Elba and had been received with joy by his former troops in Paris on 20 March, Southey immediately urged that Britain should declare war on him, and scorned those who were opposed to renewed hostilities.

'After a burst of exhilaration' at the news that the allies had defeated Napoleon at Waterloo on 18 June, Southey found himself 'in a state of serious and thoughtful thankfulness for what, perhaps, ought to be considered as the greatest deliverance that civilised society has experienced since the defeat of the Moors by Charles Martel'. He thought that 'the cannon should be sent home and formed into a pillar to support a statue of Wellington in the centre of the largest square in London.'[32] Southey himself planned a celebratory bonfire on Skiddaw, which was originally to have taken place on 12 August, the Prince Regent's birthday, but unfortunately it rained, so it was postponed to the 21st. On that day a party took roast beef, plum puddings and rum to the summit for a celebration. Those who went included Southey and Edith, their daughter Edith May and son Herbert, together with their three maids. Also present were Mary Barker, Dorothy and William Wordsworth, William's wife Mary and their son John. The seventy-seven-year-old Lord and Lady Sunderlin, who brought James Boswell, the son of Dr Johnson's biographer, also accompanied them up the mountain along with sundry 'neighbours, Lakers, and Messrs Rag, Tag and Bobtail'. They sang the national anthem round the bonfire, 'fired cannon at every health . . . and rolled large blazing balls of tow and turpentine down the steep side of the mountain. The effect was grand beyond imagination. We formed a huge circle round the most intense light, and behind us was an immeasurable arch of the most intense darkness, for our bonfire fairly put out the moon.'[33] Mary Barker, clearly completely reconciled to Edith, was placed in charge of the festivities and named Colonel Barker by Boswell. She imposed her authority on the proceedings, which threatened to get out of hand when Wordsworth kicked over the kettle of boiling water intended for the punch. The boisterous party returned to Keswick at midnight after eight hours' carousing on the summit of Skiddaw.

Recounting the day's activities to Henry, who had recently remarried, Southey remarked that, contrary to his 'constitutional hilarity', he tended to be depressed by 'occasions of joy and festivity', which explained why he did not congratulate his brother on his marriage.[34] He did, however, arrange to join the couple on their honeymoon, which was to be spent in the Low Countries. Southey jumped at the chance to see the battlefield of Waterloo for himself, and travelled there with Edith, Edith May and Henry Koster. Henry and his new wife, fortunately perhaps for themselves, apparently gave them the slip, for Southey could find no trace of them eight days after landing at Ostend on 23 September. At Bruges he met Edward Nash, the artist, and Edward Hawke Locker. Locker, like Henry, was also on his honeymoon, having married Elizabeth Boucher, whom Southey dubbed 'the beauty of Cumberland'.[35] 'The most interesting object in Ghent to me', Southey recorded in a journal of his tour, 'and indeed the most remarkable, is the Beguinage'.[36] He sent a long description of it to Rickman, who shared his interest in the Beguins, an order of lay nuns. At various times they had devised projects for introducing a similar, albeit Protestant, order to find employment for women in England.[37] At Brussels Southey purchased 120 books from the bookseller Verbeyst and arranged to procure the fifty-two volumes of the *Acta Sanctorum* from him. When he reached the battlefield at Waterloo the still fresh reminders of the battle fought just three months before brought Southey face to face with the realities of war for the first time. Although some graves were already overgrown with poppies and pansies, others had been disturbed, probably by dogs or pigs, so that bones were visible. There was even one, he was told, 'in which the worms were at work, but I shrunk from the sight'.[38]

He shrank, too, from describing it in the poem he wrote to commemorate the Laureate's visit, 'The Poet's Pilgrimage to Waterloo', mentioning only that

> Sometimes did the breeze upon its breath
> Bear from ill-covered graves a taint of death.

In the second part, 'The Vision', he confronted the kind of pacifism he had himself upheld in his youth, notably in 'The Battle of Blenheim', which maintained that the victory was pointless and war unjustified. Now he expounded the view that the conflict with Napoleon was one between good and evil, and that right had triumphed at Waterloo. Indeed, had the wrong side won, Europe – the 'moral, intellectual heart of earth' – would have been plunged into darkness like the rest of the world. This outcome was not, however, inevitable, for although Providence guided the destiny of civilisation, in the end man's free will could choose barbarism over enlightenment. The poem reads like one written in fulfilment of his laureate duties. James Losh thought it a 'dull performance. It has all Southey's faults and but few of his beauties.'[39]

Southey returned to England on 28 October and spent November in London. On his way to the Continent he had dropped off the proofs of an article on the duke of Wellington for the *Quarterly Review*. When he returned he called in at Murray's offices in Albermarle Street expecting that the July issue, which had been delayed so that he could bring it up to date with an account of the battle of Waterloo, would have been published. To his surprise it was still in proof. He thought it could be because Murray wanted to include new material from his visit to the battlefield. However, when after three weeks he at last got the copy of half of the article, he was outraged to discover that changes had been made to his text. Some of them altered the sense of what he had written, for instance suppressing his assertion that Wellington had been surprised by the French, asserting instead that there had been no surprise, and dropping his acknowledgement that the Prussians deserved some of the credit for the allied victory. When he protested to the editor Gifford and to the publisher Murray, they replied that the changes had been made by Croker, which he had suspected, but at the instigation of Wellington himself, which came as a complete surprise. As Southey put it, 'I had been chosen as a fit mouthpiece for conveying falsehood to the public through an accredited channel.'[40] 'I will expunge all mention which I have made of the Duke's having been surprised', he conceded to Murray, 'but as to affirming there was *no* surprise and detracting from the Prussians, refusing them the praise which is their due, this I will never do, nor suffer myself in any way to be made instrumental in doing.'[41] This was a principled stand for Southey to take, especially when he was engaged on his *History of the Peninsular War*, which would certainly have benefited from a sympathetic attitude towards his research on Wellington's part. By demanding that the changes that the duke had made to his article be removed, Southey risked alienating any sympathy he might have had for his work on the war. That his views on how his article should appear in print were upheld is also a tribute to the esteem in which he was held by Gifford and Murray.

Early in December Southey left London with his wife and daughter for Keswick, where they arrived on the 6th. Their arrival is described in the 'Proem' to 'The Poet's Pilgrimage to Waterloo':

> O joyful hour, when to our longing home
>   The long-expected wheels at length drew nigh!
> When the first sound went forth 'They come, they come!'
> And hope's impatience quicken'd every eye!
> 'Never had man whom Heaven would heap with bliss
> More glad return, more happy hour than this.'
> Aloft on yonder bench, with arms dispread,
>   My boy stood, shouting there his father's name,
> Waving his hat around his happy head.[42]

These lines were echoed in another poem he wrote, in April 1816, 'Consolation'.

> Short time hath past since from my pilgrimage
> To this exulting home restored, I sang
> A true thanksgiving song of pure delight
> Never had man whom Heaven would heap with bliss
> More happy day, more glad return than mine.
> Yon mountains with their wintry robe were clothed

When from a soul that overflowed with joy
I poured that joyful strain. The snow not yet
From off those mountain sides hath disappeared
Before the breath of Spring, and in the grave
Is Herbert laid, the child who welcomed me
With deepest feeling on that happy day.
Herbert my only and my studious boy
The sweet companion of my daily walks
Whose sports, whose studies and whose thoughts I shared
Yea in whose life I lived . . . in whom I saw
My better part transmitted and improved
Son of my mind and heart, the flower and crown
of all my earthly hopes and happiness.[43]

Herbert had developed symptoms of an illness during the second week of March that had made Southey uneasy. They began with a cough and a fever that lasted five weeks. Mary Barker, now a welcome visitor to Greta Hall again, helped his parents to nurse him. They did their best to cheer him up, even though their spirits were sinking as he showed no sign of recovery. On 16 April they were so exhausted that Mary persuaded them to go to bed while she looked after Herbert. Years later she remembered him as 'that sweetest and most perfect of all children on this earth – who died in my arms at nine years of age – whose death I announced to his Father and Mother in their Bed. . . . When Southey could speak his first words were "The Lord hath given and the Lord hath taken away – Blessed be the name of the Lord!" Never shall I forget that moment! Present ever – ever! Until I rejoin that heavenly Child – and his heavenly Father.'[44] Southey 'had ever an ominous apprehension that he was not intended to grow up on earth',[45] and this is borne out in several letters in which he predicted that the son on whom he doted would make his mark in the world if he were spared. Thus the letter on which Mary Barker recalled the dreadful events of April 1816 Southey had written to welcome her to Keswick in 1812, telling her 'You will be much pleased with Herbert. He may best be characterised by calling him a sweet boy. You can hardly conceive anything more gentle and more loving. He has just learnt his Greek alphabet and is so desirous of learning, so attentive and so quick of apprehension, that if it please God he should live, there is little doubt but that something will come out of him'.[46] A notebook compiled to help Herbert learn Greek contains the poignant couplet

God grant O my son you may always enjoy
As happy a life as you do while a boy.[47]

Southey doted on his son to distraction, and his death was the cruellest blow he ever suffered. He bore his grief as a Christian stoic, clinging for comfort to the notion that he would see Herbert again in the next world. But his earthly happiness was shattered. 'The joyousness of my disposition has received its death wound', he confessed.[48]

Southey's immediate reaction was to contemplate quitting Greta Hall when the lease fell through a year later, for it had too many poignant reminders of Herbert. He would flee anywhere – to the south of England, or abroad. But he soon realised that flight was impractical. It would cost money, and he did not even have enough to bury his son, for he had to ask Bedford to pay the funeral expenses. Sara Coleridge wrote just after the burial service that 'never was child more lamented by a father than this, and will be to the latest hour of his life'. But then she observed how, more than ever, he found escape in work. 'Southey has, however, done great things even in the bitterest days of his most bitter sorrow – he never did so much in the same space of time.'[49] Thus he rewrote the poem on the marriage of Princess Charlotte, changing its title from 'Carmen Nuptiale' to the 'Lay of the Laureate'. The second volume of his *History of Brazil* was also completed in the weeks following Herbert's death. 'You see I have not been idle', he told his uncle, 'indeed at present there is more danger of my employing myself too much than too little.'[50] He even pressed the *Quarterly Review* to make room for an article on La Vendée in its April issue, which was not published until August. This was a review of no fewer than eight books on the counter-revolutionary uprising in the West of France during the French Revolution. In it Southey asserted that 'of all evils, of all miseries, of all curses which can befall a civilised country, revolution is the greatest.'[51]

Southey's retreat from his earlier enthusiasm for the French Revolution provoked Hazlitt to savage 'The Lay of the Laureate' in the *Examiner*. 'Mr Southey ought not to have received what would not have been offered to the author of *Joan of Arc*', he asserted, referring to the laureateship. 'Mr Southey himself maintains that his song has still been "to Truth and Freedom true;" that he has never changed his opinions; that it is the cause of French liberty that has left him, not he the cause.' Yet he applauded George III as well as the Prince Regent in the poem. 'The King has not changed', Hazlitt concluded, 'therefore Mr Southey has.'[52]

However, in his concern for the condition of the poor Southey had not changed. In the *Quarterly Review* that carried his article on La Vendée he published one of his more celebrated essays, on the subject of the poor. Although the hook on which he hung it was a review of four recent titles on the topic, the article was in many respects a sequel to one he had contributed to the journal four years earlier. He acknowledged that the eighteenth-century view that progress was inevitable had been severely set back by events since 1789, but still expressed confidence in a modified version of it. Evolutionary rather than revolutionary change for the better would almost certainly occur. The condition of the lower classes had not benefited from the general improvement, and unless it did the outlook for society was perilous. Education of the masses was the essential cure for this: 'The cost of national education is rendered so trifling by Dr Bell's intellectual steam-engine that the expense would present no obstacle.'[53] Southey's views were well received by Henry Crabb Robinson, who visited him in September. Robinson thought that the essay was 'a very benevolently conceived and well-written article abounding in excellent ideas and proving that though he may have changed his opinions concerning governments and demagogues he retains all his original love of mankind, and the same zeal to promote the best interests of humanity.' On 22 September Southey accompanied Robinson on his way from Keswick and convinced him 'of the perfect exemption of his mind from all dishonourable motives and views in the change of his practical politics and philosophy'.[54] The government, too, took an interest in his ideas, and no less a person than the prime minister, Lord Liverpool, made it known that he would welcome the launching of another journal to promote its policies, which Southey might edit. Tempted as he was, since he had become irritated with the constant cutting of his contributions to the *Quarterly*, Southey turned down the prospect. He did not want to be an editor himself, nor did he wish to move to London, which commitment to the proposed periodical would have necessitated.

The thought of moving from Keswick, therefore, that had occurred to Southey as vital in the immediate aftermath of Herbert's death, was now wholly abandoned. Indeed, he found consolation in the thought that he would one day be buried alongside his son in Crosthwaite churchyard. Nevertheless, Herbert's death – as Southey observed at the end of 1816 – had 'drawn a broad black line between the years which are gone and those which may be before me'.[55]

CHAPTER TEN

'Apostate' (1817–1822)

Notwithstanding his decision to stay in the Lake District, Southey continued to contribute to the debate on the post-war problems facing the country. Indeed, he diagnosed the basic cause of the depression that affected the economy after peace was declared. 'You will find much real distress in the country', he warned Colonel William Peachy, who was in Italy and about to return to England: 'No folly was ever greater than the cry for retrenchment. The main evil comes from an enormous diminution of public expenditure. A customer of 50 millions having suddenly left the market. Can stupidity go further than to recommend spending less as the remedy?' He instanced the demobilisation of the armed forces, for whom there were no jobs. 'So instead of paying them as soldiers you must support them as paupers; and you have them in the mob instead of in the ranks.'[1] He also advocated that the state promote public works in order to maintain high employment, whereby wages could increase the demand for manufactured goods. Such views were not widespread in 1817, and so Southey was ahead of his time in this respect, anticipating the Tory radicals of the Victorian era. The liberal Tory George Canning appreciated how advanced Southey's views on social problems were when he wrote to inform him that they were being considered by the government. A scheme to grant public money to parishes overburdened by paupers might run into objections, 'but the times are such that we must not, if we can help it, suffer Adam Smith to stand irremoveably in our way'; that is, laissez-faire policies were not to stop state intervention.[2]

In other respects, however, Southey was behind the times. His views on religion were akin to those of a seventeenth-century Anglican, seeing the Church in danger from Roman Catholicism on the one hand and enthusiasm on the other. The contemporary enthusiasts Southey feared most were the Methodists. As we have seen, he warned his fellow countrymen about the danger they posed to the establishment as early as 1804.[3] Yet in January 1817 he published an essay 'On the Life of John Wesley', which was remarkably sympathetic to 'the Founder of the English Methodists'.[4] His acquaintance with the Evangelical William Wilberforce seems to have led Southey to moderate his views on Methodism. Wilberforce initiated the relationship by writing to him in 1813 about missionary work in the far east. 'This is likely to lead to an acquaintance', Southey noted.[5] It led to Wilberforce approaching him in 1816 for advice about having Thomas Clarkson's *History of the Slave Trade* translated into Portuguese for sale in Brazil. Southey responded positively to the overture, arranging for his friend Henry Koster to make the translation. Shortly after, he observed that 'Wilberforce . . . has fallen in friendship with me'.[6] Southey's relationship with a former political ally of the younger Pitt, whom he never liked, indicates a distinct change in his political and religious attitudes, which made him more appreciative of Wilberforce's brand of moderate Evangelicalism.[7] This appreciation found expression in Southey's essay on Wesley, which concluded that he was 'a man of great views, great energy and great virtues. That he awakened a spirit of religion, not only in his own community, but in a church which needed something to raise it, is acknowledged by that church itself.' He was not uncritical of Wesley, however, maintaining that 'he encouraged extravagancies, lent too credulous an ear to false and impossible relations, and spread superstition as well as piety.' Yet he conceded that 'it would be absurd to deny that he was both a good man and a great man.' 'Whether more good or evil is to be expected from the progress of Methodism', Southey observed, 'is a question that I have no room for examining.'[8] He was to answer it in his *Life of Wesley and the rise and progress of Methodism*, which was not published until 1820. When it appeared it expanded his essay for the *Correspondent*, incorporating the text verbatim, without acknowledgement, in the longer biography of John Wesley.

Although Southey's contributions to the *Correspondent* were not widely known, those he made to the *Quarterly Review*, despite being anonymous, were public knowledge. These, too, became more overtly political and revealed his growing conservatism. The one he published on 'Parliamentary Reform' in the October 1816 issue, which appeared early in the following year, announced how far his views had moved to the right. Thus Burke, whom he had previously reviled, was now extolled as 'this great statesman'. He dismissed the advocates of electoral reform as 'some weak men, some mistaken or insane ones, and other very wicked ones'.[9] In his novel *Melincourt* Thomas Love Peacock satirised the tone of Southey's article as asserting that 'we, and those who think with us, are the only wise and good men'.[10]

Peacock depicted Southey in the novel as the poet Feathernest, grotesquely representing his shift from radical to conservative as being motivated purely by mercenary considerations. Though this was absurd, nevertheless the contrast between the politics of the Poet Laureate and those of the young Pantisocrat were by now so stark that some of Southey's former radical associates decided that the time had come to strike back. On 14 February 1817 Southey returned from spending an agreeable week at Netherall, the home of his friend Humphry Senhouse, to find a copy of the *Morning Chronicle* awaiting him. In it he read an advertisement for his own *Wat Tyler*, the radical play he had written in defence of the poll tax rebel in 1794.[11] He had left the manuscript with the publisher James Ridgeway, who had decided not to publish it. How it had got into print twenty-three years later was a mystery to Southey. 'The sins of my youth are risen against me', he informed Rickman; 'some rascal has just published a piece of sedition written in 1794 and peppered like a Turkey's gizzard. I have written to Wynn to know whether it be better to seek an injunction or let the brimstone burn out.'[12] In the event he decided to apply for an injunction to the Lord Chancellor, the reactionary Lord Eldon, who he doubtless thought would take the side of a fellow Tory. But his claim to the copyright of the play was disputed in a counter-affidavit by one William Winterbottom, a dissenting minister who claimed that Southey had given it to him in 1796. Southey was taken aback by this, insisting that he had done no such thing, and that Winterbottom was guilty of perjury. Eldon refused to grant an injunction, however, 'until after Mr Southey shall have established his right to the property by action'.[13] Southey 'did not chuse to incur further expence in establishing a claim which was opposed by direct perjury'.[14]

As a result, *Wat Tyler* was widely distributed and sold, some estimates of its sales being 60,000, making it far and away the best selling of Southey's works, ironically without him being able to claim a penny in royalties. Instead it earned him a savaging from radical critics. Among the most savage was William Hazlitt, who criticised it in the *Examiner* on 9 March, contrasting the radical sentiments of the play with the reactionary views expressed in the article on parliamentary reform. The cue was taken up by William Smith, a member of parliament, who made the same comparisons in the House of Commons on 14 March. Smith also emphasised a point many of Southey's radical critics made. While he was entitled to his change of opinions, he was not justified in attacking those who expressed views he himself had once held – this is what made him in Smith's eyes 'a renegado'. It was accepted as a fair criticism by some of Southey's own supporters, including Wynn, who rebuked Smith in the debate. Southey defended himself against Wynn's charge of intolerance, answering him by asserting that in the *Edinburgh Annual Register* he had only attacked those who supported Napoleon. As for the *Quarterly Review*, 'I have rarely had anything to do with politics, except in the two last numbers; and the man who censures the last paper must stand up for Hunt and Cobbett.'[15] His defence is not altogether convincing, however, for he undoubtedly condemned men whose opinions he once endorsed. In 1817 Southey would have sent the author of *Wat Tyler* to Botany Bay.

Smith's charging Southey with being a renegade stung him into publishing an open letter to the MP, which countered with the word 'slanderer'. *A Letter to William Smith M.P. from Robert Southey Esq* (1817), which the author called his 'billet doux', was his political testimony summing up the progress of his views since the heady days of Pantisocracy. He had expressed them in a single sentence in a letter to John Murray earlier in the year: 'I aim at lessening human misery and bettering the condition of all the lower classes.'[16] After rehearsing to Smith how his aspiration towards these ends had never altered, he concluded that 'the only charge which malice could bring against him was that as he grew older his opinions altered concerning the means by which that amelioration was to be effected.' A major reason for his changing his mind over the means was that the lower orders had become more revolutionary since his youth. Thus he claimed that *Wat Tyler* had been written 'when the mob were ferocious in their loyalty and the spirit of anti-Jacobinism was reigning in full vigour of intolerance'. Since then the sentiments it expressed had been 'long since discarded by men of my stamp and class in society', to be 'taken up by the rabble, and are threatening the utter overthrow of all our institutions'.[17] 'I should think revolution the greatest of all calamities', was Southey's considered view in 1817, 'and believe that the best way of ameliorating the condition of the people is through the established institutions of the country'.[18] As he expressed it in his *Letter to William Smith*, 'as he learnt to understand the institutions of his country, he learnt to appreciate them rightly, to love, and to revere, and to defend them.'[19]

Southey left Keswick on 22 April to visit London on the first leg of a journey to the Continent, hoping by travel to ease the pain left by the loss of Herbert. His son was still clearly on his mind when he wrote 'who could bear to look back, if he had not his deepest enjoyment in looking forward to that second birthday which will restore to us in another world, if we are found worthy, all that we have lost in this?'[20] On 9 May he set off for Dover accompanied by Humphry Senhouse and the artist Edward Nash. En route Senhouse and Southey diverted to the Artillery Barracks to visit Colonel Charles Pasley, where they witnessed a torpedo exploding in a pool of water, which 'threw up the water and the machine annexed to it sixty or 80 feet in the air'.[21] They joined Nash to cross to Calais, arriving there on 11 May, then continuing on to Paris, where they met Annette Vallon and the daughter she had by Wordsworth, Caroline. Southey kept a 'journal of a journey to and from the Alps in the summer of 1817', containing observations mainly about the sights he saw rather than the people and their manners. He did, however, observe that 'for everything what belongs to the public the French are much more civilized than we are. I acknowledge also in our mercurial neighbours, livelier countenances and among the lower classes a cleaner and cheerfuller costume and I like their animated features and their varied tone.'[22] This was quite a concession from a confirmed Francophobe. The journey took them next into Italy, where they visited Landor, and then back into France to Chamonix, where Southey read the entry that Shelley and his wife and her step sister had made in the visitors' book, against which somebody had added, in Greek, that they were atheists. Although he made no comment himself when he reported this to Edith, he clearly approved of the sentiments expressed by a later visitor, also in Greek, that 'if this be true these persons are fools and miserable ones, glorying in their lusts – but if it be not true, they are liars!'[23] Southey and his friends returned to England through Switzerland, Germany and Belgium, taking only sixteen days to get from Zurich to Brussels.

Southey returned to Keswick in August having benefited considerably from his continental excursion. 'Every person remarks that I look better than they ever remember to have seen me', he remarked.[24] He himself attributed it to 'early rising, continual change of air or copious libations of good wine'.[25] 'My long absence from home has drawn on me heavy arrears of work', he acknowledged in November:

I am proceeding in the press with my History of Brazil, the most laborious historical work which has ever been composed in our language. The history of the Peninsular war is now in progress; and I indulge myself at intervals by going on with a life of John Wesley upon such a scale and with such comprehensive views of the subject that it will include an important portion of ecclesiastical history. Then I have a poem in hand, a little volume it will form, its title 'A Tale of Paraguay'.[26]

He also wrote a 'Funeral Song' for Princess Charlotte whose death inspired him to project a dialogue between Sir Thomas More and himself when a radical youth. Initially he was to call More's companion 'Meipsum' (myself), though when their conversation eventually appeared many years later as *Sir Thomas More, or Colloquies on the progress and prospects of Society* the name had been changed to Montesinos.

Southey also contributed to the *Quarterly Review*. Despite the furore caused by his article on parliamentary reform he continued to write political reviews. The number for January 1817, which appeared much later in the year, was on 'The Rise and Progress of Popular Disaffection', in which he insisted that there was a conspiracy to overthrow the government. In 1818 the *Quarterly* published his essay 'On the Means of Improving the People', which was a sequel to one on 'The Poor' by John Rickman. They worked together on these articles, in which Southey attributed pauperism to 'misfortune in one instance, misconduct in fifty'. He referred to Napoleon and other philosophers 'of the Satanic school', an expression he was to use much more provocatively in *A Vision of Judgement*.[27] Southey's cooperation with Rickman revived their interest in the Beguines, inspiring Southey to gather materials for 'a paper upon the great advantages of establishing institutions of that kind by which the untold misery to which women who are left without friends or fortune are now inevitably exposed'.[28] Thus Mary Barker informed him of the 'Nuns of the desert'.[29]

Mary had moved from Greta Lodge the previous summer into a house she was having built in Borrowdale, so Southey lacked company in Greta Hall, where he virtually hibernated. 'I see no person during the winter except my own family and for weeks together do not stir beyond my own garden', he told Wynn in March 1818; 'the kitchen clock is not more regular in its movements than my life and scarcely more monotonous.'[30] As late as May he claimed to be 'living in as compleat seclusion as the monks of St Bernard during the winter'.[31] Even the offer of the post of librarian of the Advocates Library in Edinburgh failed to attract him from his Lakeland retreat.

The world outside, however, became busily engaged in preparations for the general election to be held in the summer of 1818. A contest loomed in Westmorland in which the Whig lawyer Henry Brougham announced his candidature at a meeting held in Kendal on 23 March. The county's representation was completely in the hands of Lord Lonsdale, whose sons William, Viscount Lowther and Henry Cecil Lowther held its two seats. Lonsdale's nomination of both knights of the shire had not been contested for forty years. Southey was incensed when Brougham attacked him by name at the hustings on 30 June, coupling him with Wordsworth as 'apostate poets'. Wordsworth had been involved in the campaign from the start, publishing diatribes against Brougham, who had retaliated by quoting the poet's lines 'they should take who have the power/ and they should keep, who can' as epitomising the Lowther creed.[32] Southey, however, had given Wordsworth 'no other assistance than that of sending him some quotations from B[rougham]'s writings'.[33] 'I have not written a line either in prose or verse about the Westmorland election', he protested, 'nor spoken of it out of my family (for this plain reason that I have not been out of my own family [i.e. in any other company] for more than six months).'[34] Yet 'as Wordsworth and myself, Heaven knows why, seem destined to be coupled together like

... Robin Hood and Little John, this fellow with his characteristic impudence has chosen to make war upon me in return – Be it so then! War he shall have. I am giving him a WilliamSmithiad.'[35] He did indeed write a riposte to Brougham, though in the event he was dissuaded from publishing it. In it he maintained that his dearest ambition would be fulfilled 'if I should go down to future ages not only as the biographer of Nelson and the historian of Wellington but as the compeer of Wordsworth also'.[36] At the polls Brougham lost the election, but vowed to fight the seat again as long as he lived, which led Wordsworth to organise the splitting of freeholds to procure more votes for the Lowthers. Even Southey looked into the possibility of buying a freehold to qualify himself as an elector, if he were not disqualified by his pension or his post of Poet Laureate.

The electioneering did not disrupt Southey's sedentary habits. 'I know not whether we shall have any guests this year or not', he wrote to his uncle in July; 'they will be welcome however if they come for without some such cause of locomotion I shall grow to my chair.'[37] Perhaps fortunately for his health the Lakers did arrive, including Wilberforce along with his wife and servants, who created quite a diversion with their demands. On 26 October Southey went up Saddleback with General Peachy and Chauncy Townsend. He had hoped to visit London before the end of the year, but his plans had to be set aside when he learned that Edith was pregnant. It had been six years since the birth of their youngest child, so Southey had not expected to become a father again, and the prospect filled him more with foreboding than with joy. If it were to be a boy, he did not know how he could apply himself to bringing him up as he had done the incomparable child Herbert. The birth was expected in February or March, and so Southey could not set off from Keswick before that.

He therefore settled down to his many writing tasks. They were almost all prose works, for, apart from the expected New Year's Ode, and sporadic work on *Oliver Newman*, which he never finished, he wrote hardly any poetry. He did, however, maintain a keen interest in the work of other poets. Caroline Bowles, encouraged by his efforts on behalf of Henry Kirke White, approached him for criticism of her own efforts in the spring of 1818. He responded positively, assuring her that she had 'the eye, the ear and the heart of a poetess'.[38] They had struck up a correspondence that was to cement a firm friendship. He also offered constructive criticism to Ebenezer Elliott, and among other new poets he was particularly impressed by Keats. When Croker savaged *Endymion* in the *Quarterly Review* Southey protested to Murray that he 'was very sorry to see the way in which Keats was handled'.[39] One poet whom Southey was not inclined to encourage, however, was Byron, especially when he learned that his lordship had prefaced his latest poem, *Don Juan*, with a dedication to himself. In the event John Murray, who published both their works, persuaded Byron to drop the offending preface. Southey heard about it, however, from Wynn, and told his brother that 'His Lordship would find me an ugly customer if I were to enter the lists with him'.[40] He nevertheless wrote to thank Murray. 'For tho I fear or care for Lord Byron as little as I do for the Devil to whose service he has devoted himself I do not like to have my tranquillity disturbed by engaging in polemics of any kind, least of all when they are of a personal nature.' His tranquillity would certainly have been disturbed had he read the suppressed passage. It began 'Bob Southey! You're a poet – poet laureate'.[41] The abbreviation of Southey's name allowed Byron to make a double entendre that would have made him shudder even more:

And then you overstrain yourself, or so,
    And tumble downward like the flying fish
Gasping on deck, because you soar too high, Bob,
And fall, for lack of moisture, quite adry, Bob!

A 'dry bob' was a colloquial expression for coition without emission. What would probably have offended Southey most of all were Byron's references to him as a 'renegade' and 'apostate' who 'turned out a Tory at last'. Fortunately, the suppressed dedication did not appear in print until 1833, by which time Byron was long dead and Southey past caring.

That one at least of Byron's charges was unwarranted was proved by Edith's eighth pregnancy. She gave birth to a boy on 24 February 1819. 'Edith is in bed with a son after a tremendous labour', Southey informed his brother Henry. 'The child is one of the largest that Edmondson ever saw born into the world and came stern foremost. At one [time] he believed it would be lost and was under no little apprehension for the mother. Thank God all seems to be going on well at last.'[42] The boy was named Charles Cuthbert: Charles after his godfathers Bedford and Wynn; Cuthbert, by which he was to be known, and 'if any one asks why', Southey told Bedford, 'it is reason enough that I like genuine English names.' However, he then went on to tell him the real reason for his choice. Bedford would 'find the secret feeling that leads me to choose it in a legend which Wordsworth has versified, as an inscription for St Herbert's Island'.[43] The island is in Derwentwater, and on it, according to Wordsworth's inscription, stands the ruins of a cell inhabited by St Herbert, who had prayed that his companion St Cuthbert might die at the same time as himself, and his prayer had been answered. Thus Southey, in a rather macabre, almost morbid way, linked his new son's name with that of his saintly dead brother.

Cuthbert was born in his father's study, for Edith had to move out of their bedroom when the chimney threatened to collapse into it. Southey therefore moved temporarily into what had been Coleridge's study, which he dubbed All Saints' Room, for in it he had shelved the multi-volume *Acta Sanctorum* that he had bought in Brussels the previous year. He proposed to write a 'History of the Monastic Orders' based largely on the information they provided. This addition to his many projects led him to contemplate reducing his contributions to the *Quarterly Review*. One of his major enterprises, however, indeed the one he felt would make his reputation as a historian, was completed in June. The birth of his son was still clearly on his mind, not surprisingly since Edith suffered for three months after the breech delivery of Cuthbert, and so he informed his uncle that 'on Wednesday last I was delivered of the H[istory] of Brazil and am as well as can be expected.'[44]

The completion of his *History* took Southey longer than he had expected, and left him with no time to visit London that summer. Instead he went on a tour of Scotland with John Rickman and Thomas Telford, examining some of the latter's engineering feats there. Southey arrived in Edinburgh on 17 August, where he met up with his travelling companions. Although he was troubled by a carbuncle on his head, which he dubbed 'the volcano', he enjoyed a journey that took them up to Inverness and across to Fort William. Southey showed a Romantic appreciation of the scenery. Thus of that in Eskdale, north of Langholm, he observed 'it has a quiet sober character, a somewhat melancholy kind of beauty, in accord with autumn, evening and declining life', while a glorious sunset over Morvern affected him such 'that I could almost have wished I were a believer in Ossian'. He was, however, much more struck by the piers and harbours that Telford had constructed in various Scottish ports, details of which, obviously imparted by the engineer, he recorded. Above all he was impressed by the construction of the Caledonian Canal. Of a series of locks through the Great Glen he noted 'such an extent of masonry, upon such a scale, I have never before beheld. . . . It was a most impressive and remarkable scene.' Viewing the work in progress between Fort Augustus and Loch Lochy, he observed 'what indeed could be more interesting than to see the greatest work of its kind that has ever been undertaken in ancient or modern times?'[45] 'Never was any country in the world in a more rapid state of improvement', Southey wrote from Dingwall, 'and never was so much done to improve a country in so short a space of time by Government conjointly with the people. Besides the canal within the last 15 years 1,000 miles of the finest roads in the world have been made and 1,500 bridges great and small.'[46] He expressed his admiration of Telford's achievements in three inscriptions for the canal. One enshrined his advocacy of public works undertaken by the state, which marked him out from the currently fashionable disciples of Adam Smith. 'Humanity', he asserted,

> May boast this proud expenditure, begun
> By Britain in a time of arduous war;
> Through all the efforts and emergencies
> Of that long strife continued, and achieved
> After her triumph, even at the time
> When national burdens bearing on the state
> Were felt with heaviest pressure. Such expense
> Is best economy. In growing wealth,
> Comfort, and spreading industry, behold
> The fruits immediate![47]

On his way home Southey visited New Lanark, where he was shown round by Robert Owen himself. Robert Owen had visited him in Keswick in 1816, and had struck him as a modern Pantisocrat. Although some of his notions seemed to Southey to be verging on the insane, he had felt they could be useful to the government as an alternative to laissez-faire principles. Southey, though, was not convinced when he actually witnessed the factory, concluding that Owen had deceived himself. Although Owen tried to make them happy, nevertheless he treated his employees as mere machines. 'But I never regarded man as a machine . . . I never for a moment would . . . suppose, as Owen does, that man may be cast in a mould (like the other parts of his mill) and take the impression with perfect certainty.' Yet he admired Owen, and thought that his operatives were better off than the 'Yahoos who are bred in our manufacturing towns'.[48] 'He is wrong in all his principles except one – but that is of main importance', Southey opined after his visit to New Lanark. 'It is this, that the national character will always be what the institutions of the country make it, and that men are as clay in the hands of their legislators. At present indeed we have a great stock of coarse crockery in hand made in the very worst pattern and applied to the vilest purposes. With this nothing can be done – but we must learn to model better for the future.'[49]

While he was in Scotland Southey learned of the Peterloo massacre, which to him was a sign that the 'Yahoos' were threatening society. A crowd estimated at 60,000 assembled in St Peter's Fields in Manchester on 16 August to hear Henry 'Orator' Hunt advocate parliamentary reform. Since the meeting had been banned beforehand by the magistrates, they ordered a militia company of Manchester yeomanry to arrest Hunt. To effect this the militia had to make their way through the crowd, which obstructed them until the magistrates had to send in regular troops to rescue them. In the ensuing mêlée fifteen people were killed, while hundreds were seriously injured. The 'massacre' divided English society. Those sympathetic to the crowd protested that the authorities had acted with draconian severity, while those hostile to the demonstration applauded their handling of the situation. Southey was among the latter. When James Brougham, the Whig lawyer's brother, tried to organise a petition in Cumberland to protest against Peterloo, one of those he approached, William Calvert, refused to sign. As a friend of Southey, Calvert requested that he draw up a counter petition.

Southey agreed and penned an address to the Prince Regent in terms that condemned Hunt and his supporters as revolutionaries, and praised the government and the magistrates for their stance: 'However much we regret the lives that were lost at Manchester', he wrote, 'we cannot but see that greater and far more extensive evil must arise if multitudes are allowed to assemble under such circumstances in contempt of the established authorities.' He then sent it to prominent people whom he thought would share his sentiments for their signatures.[50] Some fifty obliged, but others who might have been expected to do so balked at his extreme reaction to Peterloo, and preferred to sign a more moderate petition drawn up by Thomas Wallace, a privy counsellor. Although this incorporated some of Southey's terminology, it was much more restrained in its tone.[51] Reporting on the dropping of the first address, the radical *Carlisle Journal*, though it was unaware of its author, crowed: 'we can pronounce it an abortion; it has been stifled in its very birth and buried in haste with shame.'[52] Southey was chagrined that his address had been rejected, but took some comfort from the information that it had been well received by both the prince and the Cabinet. Even he came to accept that the incident was more complex than he had previously understood. 'The fault at Manchester', he admitted in mid-November, 'according to what I have heard, was in employing the yeomanry instead of the regular troops. This was obviously done as appearing the least obnoxious, but after bearing a great deal of outrage and injury, they lost their temper, which disciplined soldiers would not have done, and did more mischief than was necessary in dispersing the rascally rabble.'[53] When he was asked what he thought of Peterloo, Southey replied that he 'looked upon it as an unfortunate business, because it has enabled factious and foolish men to raise an outcry and divert public opinion from the great course of events to a mere accidental occurrence'.[54]

Winter found Southey hibernating in his study as usual. Early in 1820 he put the finishing touches to his *Life of Wesley* and wrote two articles for the *Quarterly Review*, one on William Coxe's *Life of Marlborough* and the other on a proposal to build new churches. His review of Coxe showed how far his opinion on the 'Battle of Blenheim' had changed since he wrote his pacifist poem on the subject. He now described it as 'the greatest victory which had ever done honour to British arms', claiming that, so far from being futile, 'had it been lost by the allies, Germany would immediately have been at the mercy of the French, and their triumph would have been fatal to the Protestant Succession in England.'[55] He welcomed the projected new churches, remarking that 'our forefathers built convents and cathedrals – the edifices which we have erected are manufactories and prisons, the former producing tenants for the latter.'[56] Hopes of escaping from the drudgery of reviewing by inheriting his uncle John Cannon Southey's estate were raised once again when his heir Lord Somerville died. Sadly for Southey, his lawyer friend Sharon Turner advised him not to pursue his claims in the courts. As Poet Laureate he could not escape the yearly task of composing a New Year's Ode. The death of George III in January, however, provided a more auspicious occasion for his official duties. He was not totally unprepared for this event, and by early February had made a serious start on what was to become *A Vision of Judgement*. Southey was to take his time over it, not publishing his response to the king's demise for over a year. It was to earn him notoriety, not least from the riposte he provoked from Byron by alluding to him as a member of 'the Satanic school' of poets.

Mary Barker has been credited with coining this expression, though Southey had used it in his article for the *Quarterly Review* in 1818. Moreover, he was not in close touch with Mary when he composed *A Vision of Judgement*, for she had run into serious financial difficulties with the building of Rosthwaite, her house in Borrowdale, and in April 1819 had left the Lake District to go to live in Boulogne. It could also have been that the hopes raised by moving to Keswick to be near Southey had withered on the vine. Whatever the reason, Mary settled permanently in France and eventually married a Mr Slade Smith. Thereafter she and Southey drifted apart. Replying in February 1820 to a note she had sent him, he admitted that he had not been in touch with her 'for a very long while', pleading pressure of work.[57]

Southey informed Mary that the severe winter had seriously affected the health of his housekeeper, Mrs Wilson, and that she might not survive much longer – in fact she died shortly afterwards and was buried on 11 March. The death of 'Wilsey', as she was affectionately known in Greta Hall, was a great blow to all its residents. She left £5 to each of Southey's children and to Edith's sisters, Sara Coleridge and Mary Lovell.

One of the works that Southey claimed had taken up too much of his time to write to Mary Barker was his *Life of Wesley*, which he finished in March 1820. 'It is written with too fair a spirit to satisfy any particular set of men', Southey claimed. 'For the "religious public" it will be too tolerant and too philosophical; for the Liberals it will be too devotional; the Methodists will not endure any censure of their founder and their institutions; the high Churchman will as little be able to allow any praise of them.'[58] 'My Life of Wesley, I hear, has been noticed in the Literary Gazette before it is published', he informed John Murray on 5 April. 'I suppose it will be ready next week. It will not please any particular set of men, and will violently offend the bitter part of the dissenters, who are the larger part. Attacks no doubt will be made upon me from all quarters and of course I shall reply to none.'[59] Southey was quite right to anticipate that his *Life of Wesley* would meet with hostile criticism. An anonymous reviewer in the *Monthly Magazine* accused him of propagating 'secret, and insidious and poisonous doctrines'.[60] 'There is an entertaining account of my "Wesley" in the last "Evangelical Magazine"', Southey informed his publishers Messrs Longman. 'They set me down for a book-maker, treat me with great contempt for my ignorance of theology and ecclesiastical history, and hint, at the close, that what I must expect for such a book is – *damnation*.'[61] Despite the strictures of some Methodist reviewers, the *Life of Wesley* was remarkably free from the kind of diatribe Southey had been wont to make against Methodism in print and in private on previous occasions. It developed the essay he had contributed to the *Correspondent* in 1817, which had been much more balanced in its assessment of the Methodist leader.

Southey waited in Greta Hall until the printer finished the Wesley volumes before setting off in the middle of April on a journey that was to keep him away from Keswick for eleven weeks. He first visited Wynn at Wynnstay and celebrated his return to parliament at the general election required by the accession of George IV. Although Cumberland had not been contested, Southey had noted mob activity in Keswick associated with the elections, and was alarmed that a radical had been returned for Carlisle. While staying with Wynn he met their mutual friend Reginald Heber, who was about to go to India as bishop of Calcutta. He was to recall the occasion in 1830 when he wrote an 'Ode on the portrait of Bishop Heber'. The poem records that

> Ten long years have held their course
>   Since last I look't upon
>   That living countenance
> When on Llangedwin's terraces we paced.[62]

Yet it was not in fact the very last time they met, for Heber was to be present at a ceremony held that June in Oxford to confer on Southey an honorary degree. Indeed, it was probably while they were in Wales that Heber let

Southey know that the vice-chancellor of Oxford University had intimated to him that the university wished to offer him a Doctor of Laws (LLD). Southey, delighted that his old Alma Mater had recognised his contributions to poetry and history, accepted. From Wales he made his way over to Shrewsbury and thence to London, where he arrived on 1 May. While in town he stayed with his brother Henry in Queen Anne's Street and his uncle Herbert at Streatham. Southey made the rounds of his acquaintances, including Grosvenor Bedford, Isaac d'Israeli, John Kenyon, Edward Nash, John Rickman and Henry Crabb Robinson. He recited many lines from his *Vision of Judgement* to Robinson, who noted that 'they sounded well-better than his extreme political opinions'.[63] On 10 May Southey attended a levee at court and kissed the new king's hand. The following morning he had breakfast with the bishop of London at Lambeth, when they discussed his *Life of Wesley*. The work was also praised by the bishop of Durham, and by Lord Liverpool, the prime minister, whom Southey met when he visited George Canning. At the end of May he went on a brief visit to Cambridge, where he saw Neville White. Back in London at the beginning of June he met for the first time Caroline Bowles, with whom he had begun to correspond two years previously. Overcome with shyness she scarcely spoke a word.

On 13 June Southey went up to Oxford for the honorary degree ceremony, which was held on the following day. John Keble recorded meeting him on the 14th. 'Luckily for me (though I am afraid rather irksomely for him) he has hardly any acquaintance resident in Oxford, having completely out-lived all his old contemporaries, so that I had a good deal of him to myself; and that indeed was delightful.' Keble noted that of all the honorary graduands Southey and Lord Hill received the most applause. Southey himself was very gratified with his reception, telling Edith that 'the place rang and thundered with applause and acclamations when my name was pronounced.' The vice-chancellor entertained the new graduates to a cold collation in Brasenose College, after which Southey spent the afternoon wandering round Oxford, which he had only passed through twice since he was an undergraduate there. Walking through Christ Church meadow, he reflected wistfully on how many of his contemporaries were no longer alive. He later reflected that 'my heart was never heavier than during the only whole day which I passed in that city.'[64] That night he dined in his own college, Balliol. It says a lot for Southey's reputation that the wife of a porter, who knew him when he was a student, stayed up until midnight, when the dinner ended, in order to see him. Keble hoped Southey could stay for dinner the following day, and was sorry when he returned to London, noting that he 'left a most excellent name behind him, for his kind and unassuming manners, with every one who had been in his company for five minutes'.

Back in London Southey had breakfast with Charles Lamb, where Mary Betham chanced to call, 'perfectly sane in her conversation and manner', Southey reported to Edith, 'tho she has written me the maddest letters I ever saw.'[65] For once he did not upbraid his wife for not writing to him, though he did comment on the tone of her letter, for it seems that she was burdened with domestic problems while he was enjoying himself. The children were ill, and his brother Tom was making financial demands on him. In his response, Southey observed that his own family would be provided for when he died, and informed Edith where to find his will, of which his brother Henry, John May and Neville White were the executors and trustees. Although Edith had indicated that she would like them to spend some time alone together when he returned, he let her know that he would be accompanied by Edward Nash and his aunt Mary Southey. Hartley Coleridge, who had been stripped of his fellowship at Oriel College for drunkenness, had also hinted when they met in Oxford that he would be going home, though Southey was surprised that he had the nerve to think of visiting Keswick in the circumstances.

On his return home Southey resumed his voluminous literary labours. He continued the *History of the Peninsular War*, the first proofs of which arrived at Greta Hall on Christmas Day, and contributed an account of Derwentwater to William Westall's *View of the Lakes*. Where these demanded immediate attention, less pressing projects kept him occupied too. He added lines to *Oliver Newman* and made a start on *The Book of the Church* and *Colloquies on Society*. Relatively new projects were also initiated, and thus he began serious discussions with Longman to write a biography of George Fox, along the lines of his *Life of Wesley*, and with Murray to write another on Warren Hastings, whose widow had asked the publisher to raise the subject with Southey. Although he began seriously collecting materials for both, neither came to fruition. Nor did a projected 'History of English Literature and Manners', though Murray had agreed to pay him 1,000 guineas a volume. The *Quarterly Review* kept him occupied with a review of the *Works* in twenty volumes of the Reverend William Huntington, who added the letters 'S. S.', standing for 'Sinner Saved', to his name.

Occasionally Southey complained that articles in the *Quarterly* were attributed to him that he had not written, and which expressed views he did not hold. One who was misled was Shelley, who attributed to Southey a savage review of Leigh Hunt's *Foliage* that appeared in the journal in 1818. The following year Shelley was informed by friends that a review of his own poem *The Revolt of Islam* was also by the Poet Laureate. He was not inclined to believe them, though the possibility rankled enough for him to write to Southey in June 1820 to clear up the matter. While giving Southey the benefit of the doubt, Shelley nevertheless pointed out 'the arts practised by that party for which you have abandoned the cause to which your early writings were devoted'. This stung Southey into replying that he had not written the hostile review, while denying that he disavowed it because of the menacing tone that Shelley had adopted. This in turn provoked Shelley into disclaiming any menace, and into asserting that his 'only real offence is the holding opinions something similar to those which you once held respecting the existing state of society'. The repeated charge of apostasy infuriated Southey, who delivered a magisterial rebuke to the younger poet, accusing him of having changed since their meeting in Keswick in 1812. Then Shelley had feelings that 'were humane and generous, and your intentions good'. The circumstances that led to his wife's suicide, however, revealed that he had put his own interests before all others. 'Ask your own heart, whether you have not been the whole, sole and direct cause of her destruction.' Southey then denied that his own adolescent views had been the same as Shelley's 'in any other point than that, desiring, as I still desire, a greater equality in the condition of men, I entertained erroneous notions concerning the nature of that improvement in society, and the means whereby it was to be promoted. Except in this light and darkness are not more opposite than my youthful opinions and yours. You would have found me as strongly opposed in my youth to Atheism and immorality of any kind as I am now, and to that abominable philosophy which teaches self-indulgence instead of self-restraint.' This blistering denial was prompted not just by self-righteousness, but from the consciousness Southey had that it was only by the most rigorous self-control that he himself had avoided the fate of hedonists like Byron, Coleridge and Shelley. Having delivered it there was really only one way to end the letter: 'here, Sir, our correspondence must end.' It did.[66]

Southey would have had his view of Shelley's politics and morals reinforced by the publication of the latter's *Swellfoot the Tyrant* towards the end of 1820, though it was swiftly withdrawn when the Society for the Suppression of Vice threatened to prosecute the publisher. Shelley burlesqued the prosecution of Queen Caroline, the estranged wife of George IV, by her husband, who initiated divorce proceedings in the House of Lords on the grounds of her alleged 'licentious, disgraceful and adulterous intercourse in various places and countries', particularly in Italy. The Whigs and the populace took her side in the dispute, especially when she was denied access to the coronation in Westminster Abbey. Southey emphatically supported the king and denounced the queen as 'Carolina purissima'.[67] 'This infernal woman will raise a rebellion if she can', he complained to his uncle Herbert, informing him of a threat by 'King Mob' to break windows that were not illuminated with candles on her behalf. 'I stand in a conspicuous situation, and thought it not unlikely that my windows might have been attacked, in which case I should certainly have faced the assailants and have tried what fair words and a resolute avowal of opinion would have done. Much to my satisfaction they let me alone.'[68] It was just as well, for Southey's 'fair words' would doubtless have provoked the crowd to assail more than his windows.

The Queen Caroline affair persuaded Southey to dedicate his long-delayed poem on the death of George III to his successor. 'My blood is up', he wrote to Bedford at the end of 1820, 'and it would gratify me at this time to wear the King's colours.'[69] The Dedication alone guaranteed Southey a drubbing from those who regarded him as a political apostate. He praised George IV for presiding over an era that brought Britain 'to the highest point of glory', with a government of 'perfect integrity', which had done more 'than was ever before attempted for mitigating the evils incident to our stage of society', while the constitution was 'the happiest form of government which has ever been raised by human wisdom under the favour of Divine Providence'.

The poem itself might have passed muster for a performance of his duties as Poet Laureate if Southey himself had not taken it so seriously. 'When I accepted the Laureateship', he insisted, 'it was with a hope of being exempted from the ordinary worthless trashwork which degrades the office and a determination of exerting myself in a manner which . . . might redeem the office from contempt. Time enough has now elapsed since the death of the king to allow of treating the subject in an imaginative manner.'[70] Unfortunately, he risked ridicule by imagining the resurrection and ascension into heaven of the late king. As he rises from the vault, no longer blind and mad, George III is greeted by Spencer Perceval who updates him on events since he lost his mind. The war had been won, but radicalism was still a threat. When he arrives at the gates of heaven his entry is briefly delayed while witnesses are heard against him, but these, John Wilkes and 'Junius', are quickly discredited. Southey had considered calling George Washington as another, but instead included him among the 'Absolvers' who vouch for the king's worthiness to pass the portals. His glowing testimonial, coming from a former foe, is enough to clinch the case for King George's entry into heaven. He is welcomed by a host made up of former sovereigns, elder worthies, worthies of the Georgian age and 'the young spirits'. Conspicuous by their absence were Whig worthies such as John Hampden, Lord Russell, Algernon Sidney and Charles James Fox. Although Southey left out Pitt too, whom he still could not accept as a statesman, and even toyed with the idea of including Oliver Cromwell, the whole poem reads as a paean to the Tory tradition.

Southey anticipated criticism of the poem, but more for its experimental hexameter metre than for its politics. He defended his choice of metre in a long Preface to the poem. It proved a weak defence against Byron's satire of his hexameters as 'spavin'd dactyls', 'not one of all whose gouty feet would stir'.[71]

Byron was responding not just to the passages in the Preface explaining the experiment with metre, but to the digression that Southey inserted in it on the 'Satanic school' of poets. He added this in January 1821, after the composition of the poem and at the proof-reading stage. Although he did not name them, Southey told friends that he meant to attack Byron and Thomas Moore as leaders of the school. Shelley was not included in it since 'guilty as he is, he is not wicked enough to be so flagitious a writer as his friend Lord Byron.'[72] Moore, another friend of Byron, was associated with him because Southey wanted to settle a score with them both. Byron's was on account of *Don Juan*, but it is unclear why Moore was coupled with him. Whatever the reason, a passage Southey had written in a review of Moore's *Epistles Odes and other poems* in the *Annual Review* for 1807 was recycled for present purposes: 'For more than half a century English literature had been distinguished by its moral purity, the effect and in its turn the cause of an improvement in national manners. A father might, without apprehension of evil, have put into the hands of his children any book which issued from the press if it did not bear either in its title page or frontispiece manifest signs that it was intended as furniture for the brothel. This was particularly the case with our poetry.' However, this was no longer so. There were poets with 'diseased hearts and depraved imaginations', who 'labour to make others as miserable as themselves by infecting them with a moral virus that eats into the soul!' These formed 'the Satanic school'.[73]

Reaction to the political implications of the poem were predictable. Southey was delighted to learn that the king, to whom his brother Henry presented a copy, was pleased with the poem. William Cobbett, on the other hand, marked Southey down as the first man to be hanged when the Radicals came to power. On the whole though Southey was satisfied with the poem's reception. 'Some very gratifying opinions have reached me concerning it', he wrote to his uncle, 'and likewise concerning the manner in which I have alluded to Lord Byron's abominable writings – for which many persons have thanked me.'[74]

Apart from visits to Netherall and Lowther, Southey spent the summer of 1821 at home, entertaining Lakers. Edward Nash, a constant visitor in recent years, was, however, no longer among them. After returning with Southey from London the previous year, he had stayed at Greta Hall until November, when he returned to the capital, where he had suddenly died in January 1821 to Southey's great grief. Among those who did visit Keswick was 'a cart full of females', who went on an excursion to Buttermere, with Southey as 'the footman of the party'.[75] It was not until 11 November that he could report that 'Lakers and visitors have now disappeared for the season'.[76] He never-theless found time to work as usual on several projects at once. Thus he completed a revision of the first volume of his *History of Brazil*, adding a hundred pages to the original for a second edition, and worked on the proofs of his *History of the Peninsular War*. News that he had been elected to the Massachusetts Historical Society spurred him to blow the dust off *Oliver Newman*, his poem on an episode in colonial New England that he thought would sell more in America than in England. His need for money kept him busy until July on an article for the *Quarterly Review* that dealt with four works on Oliver Cromwell. His mind was the more concentrated on this as Murray held out the prospect of it being expanded into a full biography in six volumes, for each of which Southey would receive £500. The review was sympathetic to Cromwell, whom Southey described as 'the most fortunate and least flagitious of usurpers'. A passage in his account of Cromwell's career after the execution of Charles I reads like a defence against the charges of apostasy levelled at himself: 'The present danger was from the levellers whom Cromwell had at first encouraged and with whom it is very possible that at one stage of his progress he may sincerely have sympathised. But being now better acquainted with men and with things, his wish was to build up and repair the work of ruin.'[77]

Byron repeated the familiar charge in the third Canto of *Don Juan*, which appeared in August, accusing the Lake Poets of 'renegado rigour' though Southey claimed that it did not disturb his peace since he did not read it. He could not, however, ignore Byron's next assault in *Two Foscari* when it was published in December, for Wordsworth drew it to his attention on Boxing Day. It included an Appendix in which Byron castigated Southey as a 'pitiful renegado' and referred to his 'shifting and turncoat existence'. He had been provoked to attack the Poet Laureate not just for his *Vision of Judgement* but also for his 'calumnies on a different occasion, knowing them to be such, which he scattered abroad on his return from Switzerland, against me and others'.[78] The nature of the alleged calumnies, Byron had communicated to John Cam Hobhouse in 1818, explaining why he wrote the suppressed dedi-cation of *Don Juan* to Southey: 'the son of a bitch on his return from Switzerland two years ago – said that Shelley and I "had formed a League of Incest and practised our precepts with &c" – he lied like a rascal – for they were not sisters – one being Godwin's daughter by Mary Wollstonecraft [Mary Shelley] – and the other the daughter of the present Mrs G[odwin] by a former husband [Mary Jane Clairmont]. . . . He lied in another sense – for there was no promiscuous intercourse – my commerce being limited to the carnal knowledge of Miss C.' He repeated his denial to John Murray, insisting that 'Southey was a damned scoundrel to spread such a lie'.[79]

Southey himself had ignored these accusations until they were alluded to in this fresh onslaught. Now he wrote an angry riposte, 'with a direct and positive denial' to them that he sent to the *Courier*, where it appeared on 5 January 1822. He attributed Byron's libel on him, not to hearsay reports of his conversations four years earlier, but to the attack on the Satanic school of poets that he had made in his *Vision of Judgement*. He now explicitly named the author of *Don Juan* as the head of the school, where before his leadership of it had only been implied. 'One word of advice to Lord Byron before I conclude. When he attacks me again let it be in rhyme. For one who has so little command of himself, it will be a great advantage that his temper should be obliged to keep tune.'[80]

These concluding remarks raise the possibility that Southey was aware that his adversary had already composed a reply, *The Vision of Judgement*. For although it was not published until October 1822 when it appeared in the *Liberal*, Byron had written it the previous year and had tried to get Murray to publish it, but had been refused. When he read the *Courier* he was beside himself with fury. Thomas Medwin recorded his reaction 'as he glanced rapidly over the contents. He looked perfectly awful: his colour changed almost prismatically; his lips were pale as death. . . . He paused a moment, and said "You have not seen *my* Vision of Judgement".'[81] It was a devastating composition. The conceit of having Southey wafted up to heaven from the foot of Skiddaw, 'where as usual it still rain'd', answered the Poet Laureate's heavy solemnity with light hilarity, and at the same time with a supreme control of verse, which exposed the leaden quality of Southey's hexameters. Above all, it was deadly in its condemnation of the political apostasy of that 'poor, insane creature, the Laureate'.

> He had written praises of a regicide;
>   He had written praises of all kings whatever;
> He had written for republics far and wide,
>   And then against them bitterer than ever;
> For pantisocracy he once had cried
>   Aloud; a scheme less moral than t'was clever;
> Then grew a hearty anti-jacobin –
> Had turn'd his coat – and would have turn'd his skin.[82]

CHAPTER ELEVEN

'The most powerful literary supporter of the Tories' (1822–1829)

'My career as a poet is almost at an end', Robert Southey announced early in 1822.[1] He continued to publish some poems, including one of his more well-known verses, 'The Cataract of Lodore', an impressive exercise in onomatopoeia he completed that June. Nevertheless, his major poetic works had all appeared before 1822, and his main publications thereafter were to be in prose. 'The love of writing poetry is departed from me', he confessed in June 1823.[2]

Instead Southey became more a historian than a poet. He worked on two major historical projects throughout 1822, his *History of the Peninsular War*, and *The Book of the Church*, both of which were contributions to the Tory cause he had now completely espoused.

In the Preface to the first volume of the *History of the Peninsular War* Southey asserted that 'it was as direct a contest between the principles of good and evil as the elder Persians, or the Manicheans, imagined in their fables: it was for the life or death of national independence, national spirit, and of all the holy feelings which are comprehended in the love of our native land.'[3] He had thought hard about a dedication for the work, sending his uncle Herbert three possibilities: 'to the Memory of Spencer Perceval'; 'to Lord Sidmouth'; and 'to the King'. In the draft inscription to Sidmouth he admitted that 'I am one of the many persons who, at the beginning of the French Revolution, were deceived by its specious promises. . . . Youth, igno-rance and an ardent mind rendered me easy to be deluded.' He had believed that war against revolutionary France was immoral. The Peace of Amiens, however, transformed his attitude. 'It restored in me the English feeling which had been deadened, it placed me in sympathy with my country, bringing me thus into that natural and healthy state of mind upon which time, and knowledge and reflection was sure to produce their proper and salutary effect.'[4] His uncle persuaded Southey to dedicate the *History* to George IV.

The Book of the Church was written 'with the hope of imbuing young minds with those principles which ought to be their best inheritance and their surest support'.[5] It was intended to instruct youth in the ecclesiastical history of England, which in Southey's view had seen the Anglican Church emerge as the bulwark of the state against Roman Catholicism and Protestant fanaticism. 'If the friends of the Constitution understand this as clearly as its enemies', he concluded, 'then will the Church and State be safe, and with them the liberty and the prosperity of our country.'[6] 'Here was a dangerously providentialist theme', observes Sheridan Gilley, 'with the British constitution as the embodiment of the hòly ghost, and God an English tory.'[7]

Apart from a brief visit to Harrogate in May, to bring home his daughter Edith May, who had been to the spa for her health, Southey did not leave the Lake District in 1822. The summer was unusually hot, and he suffered more than ever with hay fever. Sometimes he could do little more than lie on a sofa for much of the day. While this incapacitated him from making progress with his military and ecclesiastical histories, he was able to work on his *Colloquies on Society*. Visitors also distracted him from his study. One was the Reverend Nicholas Lightfoot, a college friend he had not seen for twenty-eight years. Among the rest were Alexander Bell, John May and his own brother Henry. With these companions he went for long walks on the Lakeland fells, a routine that his doctor brother encouraged him to keep up. Nevertheless, once he had got over his hay fever, he was able to bring his historical works to fruition, even making progress on the 'History of Portugal'. 'It is in more forwardness than any work that I ever yet committed to the press', he informed his uncle at the end of August, 'and, as soon as the "Peninsular War" is finished, to the printer it will go.'[8] He also worked on a review of Grégoire's *Histoire des sectes religieuses*. By the time he came to write it Byron's *The Vision of Judgement* had appeared in the *Liberal*. In it Byron had mocked Southey for being prepared to write anybody's biography, even the Devil's. This inspired him not just to contribute a review of Grégoire to the *Quarterly* but also to write a whole article on 'The Progress of Infidelity'. 'If Gifford will let me', he told Wynn, 'I may possibly touch on the "Liberal" here, and show Lord Byron that there can be no better preparatory exercise for writing the memoirs of the Devil than by attempting a sketch of his Lordship's own character and conduct.'[9] Sure enough, when the article appeared the following year it did touch on Byron. 'One Liberal (we are thankful for the word – it is well that we should have one which will at once express whatever is detestable in principle and flagitious in conduct) one Liberal who produced a "Catechism for the human race" affirmed that property in land and property in women, that is to say marriage, were the two greatest violations of natural liberty and the bane of human happiness.'[10]

Towards the close of 1822 Gifford's health was giving serious cause for alarm, and the need to find a successor to edit the *Quarterly Review* appeared urgent. Southey persuaded John Murray, the proprietor of the journal, to accept John Taylor Coleridge, Samuel's nephew, as editor. In the event Gifford's health improved, and so Coleridge's appointment was delayed until 1824.

In November Southey arranged for his brother Henry to present a copy of the first volume of his *History of the Peninsular War* to the king. He informed the keeper of the privy purse to George IV, Sir William Knighton, who would make the presentation, that 'the whole pack of Liberals will presently be upon me in full cry. Let them! You know my brother will have it that I like to be abused. The truth is that not being of the *genus irritabile*, I am not annoyed by it: moreover use goes for something; and I am so used to these things that if I did not now and then think it proper to take the whip in hand, anger alone would never rouse me to the exertion.' He concluded his letter by conceding that 'for many years I have been so much devoted to historical pursuits that, were it not that I wear the bays, and am proud of wearing them, I should almost forget that I am a poet. A villainous commutation (made I suppose when my predecessor was a water drinker) prevents me from trying what inspiration there may be in sack.'[11] 'I am commanded by the King to convey to you the estimation in which His Majesty holds your distinguished talents, and the usefulness and importance of your literary labours', Knighton replied. 'I am further commanded to add that His Majesty receives with great satisfaction the first volume of your valuable work on the late Peninsular War.' Southey was immensely gratified with this letter, especially since the king had written at its head 'entirely approved, G. R.'[12]

The first review of Southey's *Peninsular War*, which appeared in the *Literary Gazette* for 14 December 1822, must have pleased him too. 'For it is a noble History', it observed, 'and if the name of its author had not already stood so eminently high, this production alone would have engraved it on that splendid roll where the names of Gibbon, of Hume, and of Robertson, are inscribed in immortal characters.' The anonymous author examined the work for signs of political bias, and concluded that 'the evident leaning of his mind to what for want of a better understood appellation we must call Tory principles, does not in any material degree affect the impartiality and integrity of his work.'[13] His opponents did not see it like that. 'The Whigs I hear are up in arms against the book', Southey informed Rickman on 4 January; 'they will like the second volume worse, for there I shall write their misdeeds and put them upon record where they will be read.'[14] He was right to think that he had annoyed the Whigs. Sir William Napier reacted angrily to the book. 'His malignity exceeds that of any other writer who has yet attacked Sir John Moore', he protested, and 'his History is despicable being

a compilation of all the absurd stuff he wrote himself in the Edinburgh
Annual Magazine [*sic*] and extracts from the inflated Spanish papers and the
catchpenny publication of . . . others whose froth was received in England at
the time instead of good ale.'[15] Unfortunately for Southey, Napier had served
in the Peninsula, and the comments on Moore provoked him to write a rival
*History of the War in the Peninsula and in the South of France from the year
1807 to the year 1814*. When the first of six volumes appeared in 1828 it
immediately replaced Southey's as the standard history of the campaigns in
Portugal and Spain. Southey was of course unaware of Napier's initial reaction to his work, while the private views that reached him were mostly
complimentary to a fault. He took umbrage, however, at an implication in a
letter from Crabb Robinson that he was not sufficiently independent in his
political views to give an objective account. 'You express a wish that my
judgement were left unshackled to its own free operation', he replied. 'In
God's name what is there to shackle it? I neither court preferment nor popularity, and care as little for the favour of the great as for the obloquy of the
vulgar.'[16] Yet he was conscious of his own major deficiency as a historian, that
being his tendency to get bogged down in detailed narrative, admitting 'that
a love of detail is my besetting sin'.[17]

This weakness affected progress on his *Book of the Church*: 'As usual my
book grows under my hands and what was intended for a small duodecimo
will be a full-size octavo volume.'[18] On 23 April Southey wrote to the
publisher John Murray asking if he could bring it out in two volumes: 'For I
have yet to handle the parts which are of deepest interest', he explained,
'Q[ueen] Mary's reign and the overthrow of the Church by the Puritans.
. . . Unawares I have been led to produce a work of more importance than
either you or I intended.'[19]

'I am staked down to the book upon which not my ways and means, but
Tom's also for his expedition, are dependent', Southey wrote to Henry on
5 May.[20] Their brother Tom, who had fallen on hard times after being
discharged from the navy, with an ever growing family, relied upon them to
make ends meet. Southey had done what he could on his meagre resources.
Henry, a successful London doctor who was appointed physician in ordinary
to the king that summer, could afford more. Tom had tried farming, but that
had not worked out, and now decided to emigrate to Canada to seek his
fortune there. Meanwhile, his wife and eight children would stay behind in
England until he got settled. Southey was a keen advocate of emigration,
even feeling that the state could ship people to the colonies compulsorily. But
when he learned of the primitive conditions that Tom and his fellow passen-
gers endured on their voyage out he protested at their inhumanity to Wynn.
His old friend had become president of the Board of Control over India, with

a seat in the Cabinet, in 1822. Southey's complaints led to enquiries from the Colonial Office.

Tom's demands, and some masonry work he was having done on Greta Hall, left Southey critically short of money at this time. He relied not only on projected sales of the *Book of the Church* but also on the £100 he antici-pated from the *Quarterly Review* for the article on 'The Progress of Infidelity', which he had submitted for the January issue. Unfortunately, because of Gifford's continuing health problems it did not appear until July. It was even more of a misfortune that when it appeared it offended his old friend Charles Lamb, who had published his *Essays of Elia* that January. Shortly after their publication Southey urged Wynn to read them: 'There are some things in it which will offend, and some which will pain you', he warned him, 'but you will find in it a rich vein of pure gold.'[21] Southey also referred to them in his essay for the *Quarterly*, observing that Lamb's book 'only wanted a saner reli-gious feeling to be as delightful as it was original'. Re-reading the passage he felt that the adjective 'saner' was insensitive given Lamb's mental state, and changed it to 'sounder'. He later claimed that this was the first word that came into his head when he decided to make the change, and that he intended 'to re-model the sentence when it should come to me in the proof; and that proof never came.'[22] Yet he wrote on 22 March: 'I have to-day received the proofs of my paper upon the Theophilanthropists in France and the Rise and Progress of Infidelity.'[23] Moreover, he mentioned the article to Gifford in April, asking him not to cut the 'praise which is bestowed upon Elia. . . . It is written in kindness, and carries with it a monition, which may be felt as it is intended.'[24] There is no mention of the offending adjective. It certainly offended Lamb who wrote a long and blistering attack upon Southey in the *London Magazine* that October. For some reason copious extracts from the 'Letter from Elia to Robert Southey' were quoted in the first issue of the *Lancet* on 5 October 1823 'to show the real character of that "pretended moralist" Mr Robert Southey'.[25] Southey, who felt guilty about the unfortunate reference to Lamb's views, responded magnanimously, offering to forgive the 'Letter from Elia' if he would forgive a passage that was never intended to offend. The gesture was reciprocated. Years later Lamb was to write to Southey 'look upon me as a dog who went once temporarily insane and bit you'.[26] When Southey went to London in November 1823 he visited Lamb in his house in Islington, where the two were emotionally reconciled.

Southey's journey to London had been delayed over the summer while he worked on the *Book of the Church*. There was again the usual influx of visi-tors. Among them was Caroline Bowles, visiting Keswick for the first time, staying in lodgings and not at Greta Hall, probably because of the building work that was taking place there. When she left in October, Southey wrote a letter informing her of the good impression she had made on the ladies of the house, and then followed it up with another suggesting that they write a poem on Robin Hood together. There are echoes in it of the intimate language he had previously employed when writing to Mary Barker. 'Will you form an intellectual union with me that it may be executed?' he asked her. 'The secret itself would be delightful while we thought proper to keep it; still more so the spiritual union which death would not part . . ... As there can be no just cause or impediment why these two persons should not be thus joined together, tell me that you consent to the union.'[27] Citing the words of the marriage service implied that it was more than just a business proposal. He arranged to visit her in Lymington on the great tour he undertook that winter, when he travelled 1,500 miles in fifteen weeks.

Southey set out from Keswick on 6 November, going first to Sheffield – where he at last met Ebenezer Elliott, the 'Corn Law Rhymester' – and then to Coleorton in Derbyshire, where he stayed with Sir George Beaumont, before proceeding to London. He was accompanied to the capital by his nineteen-year-old daughter Edith May, who was to stay there for two years. They clearly enjoyed a close, easy relationship. Indeed Southey's affection for all his children, and his respect for them as individuals, bespeaks a loving father who earned their trust and companionship. While he was away he wrote to them engaging, often humorous letters. On this trip he confided to Cuthbert, his youngest child, not quite five years of age, 'you know we are both very fond of you, tho your Mamma does not tell you so quite as often as I do.' One wonders what Edith thought when she read this, especially when Southey went on to tell his son that 'on Saturday I hope to see Miss Bowles and Rover her dog and Donna her cat'.[28] After the usual whirl of visits in London Southey spent Christmas with his uncle at Streatham. Early in 1824 he went first to the West Country, and then to East Anglia, visiting friends, acquaintances and, as he put it to Edith May, 'all the grandees of the neighbourhood, the Whatsisnames, the Whatdyecallums and the Thingambobs'.[29]

As ever when returning from a long journey, Southey found himself with a backlog of work to catch up with. His *History of the Peninsular War* demanded attention, while reviewing for his 'ways and means' kept him writing for the *Quarterly Review*. As usual, too, he was busy with other projects, such as his *Colloquies on Society* and his novel *The Doctor*. He even found time for poetry. Despite his feeling the previous year that the Muse had deserted him, something inspired him to write verse again. 'I have written some forty stanzas in the "Tale of Paraguay"', he informed Wynn in May, 'and have brought myself more into the run of verse than I have been for many years.'[30] He had been working on the poem for some time, but had struggled to produce it in a demanding Spenserean stanza. He might have been tempted to blow the dust off it by the publication of a translation of a book by Louis Dobrizhoffer, *Account of the Abipones,* in which the original tale was recorded, for the translator was his niece Sara Coleridge, and Southey was so anxious to promote her edition that he reviewed it, anonymously as always, in the *Quarterly Review.* But it seems that it was his increasing involvement with a fellow poet, Caroline Bowles, that rekindled his poetic ambitions. Referring to their relationship he told her that 'if as a poet I am to have a second Spring (there is still sap enough in the trunk – enough life in the root) to this it must be owing.'[31] When he got home after seeing her he wrote to tell her that he had 'returned to my old habit of writing verse before breakfast (at which time nine tenths of Thalaba, Madoc, Kehama and Roderick were written)'.[32]

Southey also worked again on his poem set in colonial New England, *Oliver Newman,* which he was determined to finish, since he now had many friends in the United States. Indeed he claimed that he had more friends in Boston than in any town in England apart from London, many of whom beat a path to his door during the summer season. In July 1823 Southey informed George Ticknor, a professor at Harvard who had visited him as long ago as 1808, that five of his fellow countrymen had arrived in Keswick so far that summer, assuring him that 'no country can send out better specimens of its sons'.[33] Ticknor, who had supplied Southey with American books over the years, was instrumental in getting him elected to the Massachusetts Historical Society in 1821 and to the American Antiquarian Society in 1823. This had made Southey anxious about what he perceived to be the hostile posture of the *Quarterly Review* towards the United States. To offset it he wrote a review of Timothy Dwight's *Travels in New England* for the *Quarterly,* 'written in a better temper than those which have excited so much irritation in the Americans'.[34]

Besides paying attention to his own writings Southey helped his brother Tom with a *Chronological History of the West Indies.* Tom had failed to settle in Canada, and had returned to England even more dependent upon Robert's goodwill to maintain his family. Southey tried desperately to find him a post, and did eventually help him obtain one in the customs service in Cromer, Norfolk, where he went to live in 1825. Meanwhile Southey suggested that he write the history of the West Indies, assisted him in the research, and when it was published reviewed it favourably for the *Quarterly Review.*

There were mixed reactions, however, to his own *Book of the Church.* The *Universal Review* damned it, while the *British Critic* praised it. But friend and foe alike criticised it for its lack of references: 'I could have wished for refer-ences to the original writers', the bishop of London told Southey, adding that a 'wish had been expressed by many judicious persons, that the work might be published in a reduced form, for the benefit of the lower classes'.[35] Ironically, the reason for the lack of references was precisely that the original intention had been to produce a succinct work for use in Dr Bell's schools. It was Southey's incurable prolixity that had swollen it to two volumes.

In December 1824 Gifford finally agreed to give up the editorship of the *Quarterly Review* and Murray accepted Southey's recommendation of John Coleridge as his successor. Murray had wanted Southey to obtain references from John Wilson Croker and George Canning to add to his own glowing testimonials for Coleridge. While Southey was quite willing to approach Croker for one, he declined to ask Canning, since he claimed that he was not on such familiar terms with the foreign secretary as he was with the secretary to the Admiralty. 'There is another motive which would withhold me from addressing him upon this topic', he admitted to Murray. 'The time cannot be far distant when the QR must take its part upon a most momentous subject, and chuse between Mr Canning and the Church. I have always considered it as one of the greatest errors in the management of the Review that it should have been silent upon the subject [Catholic Emancipation] so long. . . . Let us take our stand upon the rock of high constitutional princi-ples and we shall have with us the integrity and the talents and the heart of the country.'[36]

At the turn of the year Southey found himself still under attack for the views he had put forward in his *Book of the Church*. One anonymous salvo in the *Morning Chronicle* in December was so virulent that he actually contem-plated suing the paper for libel, but was dissuaded from doing so. 'The only answer that could be given to such an assailant', he felt, 'would be to spit in his face, call him liar and knock him down.'[37] He described the author as 'a raving Irish Roman Catholic'.[38] John Milner, the elderly Catholic bishop and vicar-apostolic of the western district of England, also entered the lists with *Strictures on the Poet Laureate's Book of the Church*, which Southey dismissed as 'short and abusive'.[39]

A more formidable opponent was Charles Butler, an eminent English Catholic lawyer. Southey was acquainted with him, and had a great respect for his *Philological and Biographical Works*, the five volumes of which Butler had donated to him in 1818. Thanking him for the gift Southey wrote, 'you have indeed Sir written in a spirit of true Catholic charity, in the true accep-tation of the word. And did the question of a reunion depend upon such minds as yours, that most desirable of all objects would easily be effected. As yet, according to human judgement it is far distant, yet sooner or later we shall be one fold under one shepherd.'[40] He was less charitably disposed, however, to Butler's *Book of the Roman Catholic Church in a series of letters addressed to Robert Southey Esquire*, which appeared early in 1825. 'I shall treat Mr. Butler with all the courtesy & true respect to which he is eminently & every way entitled, but at the same time I shall again open my batteries upon the walls of Babylon.'[41]

Despite his bullish tone Southey felt beleaguered by all the opponents ranged against him. 'What a pleasant catalogue of enemies have I, living here in retirement', he observed in January 1825. 'The Whigs, the Reformers, the Radicals, the old Buonapartists, the Methodists, the Dissenters, the Roman Catholics and the Gentlemen of the Press, whom I call the Press Gang.'[42] It was some consolation for the opprobrium he had brought on himself by it that *The Book of the Church* sold better than most of his publications. The first edition realised 3,000 sales, and Murray published a second in 1824 of 1,500, which quickly sold out, prompting him to print a third in 1825. Southey was also gratified by requests from leading churchmen that he should reply to Butler's criticisms, which had been endorsed by the Catholic Association. 'Do you not think the King should appoint me sub-Defender of the Faith?' he asked his uncle.[43] He began immediately to respond with his *Vindiciae Ecclesiae Anglicanae*, the first sheets of which he sent off to the press as early as March. 'I am at war with the Roman Catholics', he exulted, 'and having been attacked by Mr Butler, who writes with all the civility of a Jesuit and by Milner, who breathes fire and brimstone like a Dominican high in the Holy Office, I am about to prove, in the teeth of these persons and the rabble who are raising their hallo against me, that the Romish religion is a system of imposture and wickedness.'[44] Southey's *Vindiciae* did not appear, however, until January 1826, as he wanted to take the opportunity to supply references he had been criticised for omitting from the *The Book of the Church*, which would require research in London, and a visit to Brussels to buy books that summer.

Southey therefore arranged to visit the Netherlands if he could find a companion to go with him since, while he was content to work alone, the prospect of travelling on his own did not appeal to him. Eventually he persuaded three friends, all much younger than himself – Arthur Malet, Henry Taylor and Neville White – to accompany him. Southey left Keswick towards the end of May and met up with them in London. They set out on 8 June and went by 'steam packet' from Dover to Boulogne, where Southey sought out Mary Barker, who lived there, but she had 'gone on a pic-nic party'. As soon as she heard he was in Boulogne, however, she hurried to his hotel and invited him and his friends to join her the next day on an expedition to see a chateau. While his companions travelled separately,

Southey went in a carriage with Mary. One wonders what they discussed. 'Miss B looks not an hour older than when we saw her last', Southey wrote to Edith, 'nor does she appear changed in any respect.'[45] The following day the party set out for Brussels.

Although his hay fever was less severe this summer, he nevertheless suffered on his journey. Before he left Keswick he had walked up Latrigg, and had rubbed up a blister on the second toe of his right foot – as he told his daughter Bertha, the piggy who stayed at home. When he stayed overnight in Bouchain the blister was bitten by a bed bug, and became seriously infected. Although he joked that it was a Popish bug punishing him for his *Book of the Church*, he was genuinely concerned when he reached Antwerp, with his foot so swollen that he thought it might need surgery. Having rested it with a poultice he felt well enough to proceed to Leiden. By then, however, it was so painful that he asked his host, the Dutch poet Willem Bilderdijk, to send for a surgeon. He was advised to rest until the inflammation subsided, and stayed three weeks as a guest of Bilderdijk and his wife, who had translated his *Roderick* into Dutch. Henry Taylor stayed at a nearby hotel to keep an eye on him, while Arthur Malet and Neville White continued on their journey. Southey found his enforced confinement with his Dutch friends a surprisingly satisfying experience. 'I can truly say', he claimed, 'that unpleasant as the circumstance was which brought me under their roof, no part of my life ever seemed to pass away more rapidly or more pleasantly.'[46]

Southey's injury healed sufficiently for him to set off home on 15 July, and by the 23rd he was staying with his brother Henry, who now lived in Harley Street, as became a king's physician. Southey was still sufficiently troubled by his foot to avoid travelling to Keswick by night, since he needed to rest it. This led him to abandon a visit to Caroline Bowles that he had arranged on his return. 'This is a great disappointment', he told her, 'for, with all my eagerness to be once more at home, the prospect of seeing you was one of those things to which I looked on during my confinement with most pleasure.'[47] His foot was to trouble him for months after his return to Greta Hall early in August, for he could not walk for more than half an hour without it becoming swollen. However, he found it a good excuse for the sedentary life that he preferred and that was necessary while he caught up with his writing, especially when the books he had bought on his travels began to arrive at Greta Hall in October.

Upon the books' arrival Southey enjoyed one of the great delights of his life, that of unpacking them and arranging them on his shelves. He wrote to Caroline Bowles to share his pleasure, again expressing it in terms that suggest he wanted her to share far more.

The honeymoon is not over yet. O dear Caroline what a blessing it is to have an insatiable appetite of this kind, which grows by what it feeds on, and for which food can never be wanting! With such pursuits nothing is wanting to my enjoyment and the only thing I wish for is – now and then – the presence of some one who could fairly enter into my views and feelings and partake the interest which I take in such literature. But of all my friends the only one who does this is my uncle and he is in the last stages of bodily infirmity from old age – but with his faculties perfect and his love of these things unabated.[48]

Had the sight of his elderly uncle Herbert, bent double with arthritis, put these thoughts into Southey's head when he visited him on his way home from the continent that summer? Or had his brief encounter with Mary Barker reminded him that she had once been his soulmate? Now Caroline supplied the intellectual companionship he craved and could not get from Edith. In November Southey sent Caroline a lithograph of a party on Honister Crag in which they were among the group depicted. 'It is a very pleasant memorial and likely to be valued one of these days for your sake, and for mine, when we shall be far off in our celestial journey, travelling, I hope, together.' Caroline replied, 'Yes I hope we shall travel together that journey after Time.'[49]

The books that Southey had acquired abroad enabled him to resume work on his *Vindiciae*. One, *La Vie et Révélations de la Soeur Nativité*, instead of incorporating in the book he decided to review for the *Quarterly*, since 'it will appear sooner, get into wider circulation, and have more effect'.[50] Sister Nativity, the name she chose when she entered a convent in her native France, had died in 1798 after giving an account of her visions to an abbé. 'She was as ignorant as Joanna Southcott', Southey asserted in his review, 'and very probably as diseased both in body and mind.' He drew from her 'Apocalypse' the conclusion that it was one of 'a series of impostures' by which 'the corruptions of the papal church have constantly been supported'.[51]

By the time it appeared in 1826 the editorship of the *Quarterly Review* had changed again. Murray had dismissed John Coleridge and replaced him with John Gibson Lockhart. Southey was appalled at the treatment of his protégé. On 25 November 1825 he wrote to Sir Walter Scott, Lockhart's father-in-law, protesting about it. He felt angry on John Coleridge's behalf, since he had recommended him for the editorship. 'Murray probably thinks that I am bound by necessity to his *Review* and may be transferred with it, like a serf who is attached to the soil', Southey told Scott. 'He is mistaken.'[52] Southey also let John Coleridge know that his replacement was due not to any intrigue on the part of Scott or Lockhart, but to Murray's 'double dealing'.[53] 'I lose by the change an editor whom I knew, and on whom I could rely', he told Rickman, 'but I am released from any motive for continuing to work at that occupation longer than my own convenience may render necessary.'[54] By January 1826 Southey was cooperating fully with the new editor, recommending contributors and articles for the *Quarterly*. His own on 'Sister Nativity' was now definitely to appear in it and not in his *Vindiciae*.

When the book came out in the spring, it was dedicated to his old friend Charles Wynn, even though he was in favour of Catholic Emancipation. Southey wrote to him to explain how he had used a flail – a metaphor he frequently employed for his treatment of his Catholic critics in the book – to scatter all of Butler's assertions 'like chaff'. He also pointed out that the subtitle was 'Essays on the Romish Religion' and not 'Essays on Popery'. 'It is not from fear of giving offence that I have used two words where one would express the meaning', he insisted, 'but if I had said Popery it would have looked like addressing myself to a popular feeling – a feeling I must assuredly wish to strengthen but never will court. My appeal is not to the ignorant but to those who may be willing to read, learn, mark and inwardly digest.'[55] 'Every Roman-Catholic proclaims in his creed that none can be saved out of the Romish Church', he declared in the Preface to the *Vindiciae*, 'and vows in that creed, that he will, by all means in his power, bring those, over whom he has any influence, to believe in it . . . this principle it was which rendered the Revolution of 1688 necessary for the preservation of our civil and religious liberty. By that event our twofold Constitution, consisting of Church and State, as it now exists, was established and secured. It would therefore be a solecism in policy were we to entrust those persons with power in the State, who are bound in conscience to use it for subverting the Church.' He predicted that Catholic Emancipation would ultimately result in 'bringing upon Ireland the horrors of a civil and religious war'.[56]

Southey was no longer quite so confident about the imminence of a revolution in England. Though he was still 'fully persuaded, that the manufacturing system cannot be carried on as it is at present without producing . . . a more tremendous convulsion than these kingdoms have ever yet sustained', he now predicted that it would occur 'in the course of half a century at farthest'.[57] Putting forward his prophecies by fifty years was to extend them way beyond his own lifetime. The relative prosperity of the 1820s, following the privations of the previous decade, had led to a diminution in radical activity that even Southey recognised. He compared the current 'commercial manufacturing prosperity' to 'the vegetation on the side of a volcano', but did not predict an imminent eruption.[58]

In the spring of 1826 Southey set off on another journey to the Netherlands. On his way south he visited Caroline Bowles in Buckland. While staying there he wrote to Edith giving details of his meetings with relatives and friends in London. His uncle Herbert was now so crippled with arthritis that he was confined to the upstairs rooms of his house in Streatham. He himself was suffering severely from piles, a condition that had afflicted him for some time, and which caused him to lose a great deal of blood, though he did not seem concerned about it. However, he did express concern about the state of Edith's health. She had shown signs of depression when he left her, and he urged her to 'take due means for keeping yourself in a healthy state by regular exercise, generous food, and occasional medicines, cheerful thoughts and wiser ones will put an end to all unhappiness of mind'.[59]

In June Southey visited the Bilderdijks in Leiden, accompanied by John Rickman and Henry Taylor. The previous year he had promised Mary Barker that 'the next time I visit Leyden I shall go by way of Rotterdam and take Boulogne on my way home.'[60] Before setting out he wrote to let her know that 'I shall see you please God in June, very early in the month if on my way out, or by the 20th if on the way back.'[61] He also told John May that he planned to visit Boulogne in June, 'having the intention of spending six or thirty hours there for the sake of my old friend and neighbour Miss Barker'.[62] Unfortunately it was not to be. 'The weather rendered it impossible to move abroad on the day we were at Boulogne', he informed her long after his return home, 'tho I went there wholly for the sake of seeing you.' He claimed that the intense heat inflamed his foot, so that he could not walk. Despite his assurances that 'I will visit you one of these days', he never did, and there is no evidence that he ever communicated directly with her, let alone saw her, again.[63]

When Southey was in Brussels on his way home he learned to his astonishment that he had been returned as member of parliament for Downtown in Wiltshire during his absence from England. On his arrival in London at the end of June there was a letter waiting for him from the earl of Radnor, whom he had never met, informing him that his lordship had returned him for his pocket borough, having been so impressed by *The Book of the Church* that he rewarded its author with a seat in the House of Commons. Southey instinctively decided to decline it, since it was 'neither consistent with my circumstances, inclinations, habits, or pursuits in life'.[64] He then thought of several reasons he could give his benefactor for turning down the seat. As Poet Laureate he was a crown pensioner and therefore ineligible by Act of Parliament. He also lacked the statutory property qualification. It would not have been difficult to circumvent these obstacles, but he was determined not to take his seat at Westminster since 'for me to change my scheme of life and go into Parliament, would be moral and intellectual suicide.'[65] His return was subsequently declared void, but until that happened he could add 'M.P.' to the numerous titles after his name. When he arrived in Keswick there was a civic honour for the new member. A band played and a crowd assembled to welcome him home.

The shine soon rubbed off this reception when Southey discovered that his daughter Isabel was dangerously ill with a sore throat. Robert and Edith watched in anguish for over a week, as Isabel's condition made them alternate between hope and despair. On 16 July he was on his knees praying for her recovery or release when she died. The letters he wrote to his family, and particularly to his surviving daughters, witness the desolation he felt at the loss of a fourth child, 'the flower of a fair flock'.[66] His loss concentrated his mind on his own mortality, leading him to appoint Henry Taylor as his literary executor. Though he was badly shaken he did slowly recover, unlike Edith. Her mental state, already fragile, was shattered by the blow. As their son Cuthbert observed, 'from this shock my mother's spirits, weakened by former trials, and always harassed by the necessary anxieties of an uncertain income, never wholly recovered.'[67] By the end of November Southey was aware that Edith 'has not recovered from the affliction of last summer nor will she soon recover it'.[68] His own usually buoyant spirits were also still low at the end of 1826. 'In truth if they were better disposed to rise, my wife's spirits would weigh them down', he confessed to John May. 'The best I can say of myself is that I am as well as a man can be with a thorn in his side and an unclosed wound in his heart.'[69] Early in the new year Southey was still lamenting the death of Isabel – 'a lovelier flower this earth never produced'. His spirits were still low, while Edith's, 'I have but too much cause to apprehend, have received a shock from which they will not recover'.[70]

On top of all these troubles Southey received a letter from the wife of his brother Edward, informing him that 'he had left her, had spread a false report of her death, and was living with another woman'.[71] He was glad that he had washed his hands of Edward. When he heard that his friend John Kenyon was standing for election at the Athenaeum, and needed to mobilise all the votes he could influence, Southey pulled out all the stops on his behalf, writing to many of his friends and acquaintances urging them to support Kenyon. 'I cannot say that I have moved Heaven and earth for you on the present occasion', he informed Kenyon, 'for tho there are Saints in the Romish Kalendar who may be applied to for the cure of any particular disease . . . or for assistance in any ordinary business, I cannot find that there is one who takes any concern in the management of a ballot.'[72] Whether or not it was due to Southey's efforts, Kenyon's application for membership of the Athenaeum was successful in the election held on 5 February 1827.

In the spring of 1827 the Royal Society of Literature awarded Southey a gold medal, and invited him to London to receive it. Though he thanked them for the award he declined to travel to the capital to accept it. Instead in June he took his wife and daughters to Harrogate, hoping that the spa waters and change of air would act as a tonic. Sara Hutchinson, Wordsworth's sister-in-law, accompanied them, having been assured that her company would be 'of great service to poor Mrs Southey'.[73] It was the first time Edith had been away from Greta Hall since 1815, but though the visit did Southey and the girls good, it did nothing for her. Edith continued in 'the melancholy and almost hopeless course of her habitual thoughts and feelings', which were to Southey, he confided to Caroline Bowles, 'a sore grief, of which I never before said as much as is now expressed here to any human being, but which presses upon me more than my bodily infirmities'.[74] That was a rare and revealing insight into the true state of his marriage. When they returned to Keswick they were plunged into a constant stream of visitors, 'shoal after shoal' from the beginning of July to the end of September. What effect this had on Edith can only be imagined. Even Southey acknowledged that he had 'not been able to settle fairly to work for a single day'.[75]

Southey did get round to writing an article to the *Quarterly Review* in reply to Butler's attack on his essay on Sister Nativity. He had once claimed that he had killed off Butler, and that his ripostes resembled those 'who even after they are buried and a stake driven through them, choose to get up and play the vampire'. Yet, although he had asserted that 'I will have nothing to do with vampires', he could not let Butler alone.[76] In his reply he claimed that the vitals of his antagonist's argument 'have been pierced through and through, its bones broken, its limbs lopped, its head severed, its brains beaten out; and yet . . . here he is still in the field.'[77] In that case one wonders why he bothered to reply. Lockhart apparently took this view, for he delayed publishing the essay for two issues of the *Quarterly*. Southey felt slighted, and that his connection with the journal could be at an end. He was also desperately short of money again, with his finances being in their worst state for ten or fifteen years. When he received an invitation to contribute to a new periodical, the *Foreign Quarterly Review*, he responded positively. 'After trying to cajole me into writing for 10 guineas a sheet and then screwing themselves up to an offer of 50£ for an article', he wrote to Henry, 'they were glad to come to my terms and pay 100£. And I am glad to have this string to my bow, not knowing how long my other string might last.'[78] This prompted John Murray to intervene in the dispute between Southey and Lockhart, bringing about a reconciliation.

Southey thought that the political changes, or 'cabinet quake' as he put it, of 1827 would have an adverse effect on the *Quarterly*. Lord Liverpool, the

Tory prime minister, had a stroke on 17 February that forced him to resign. When he was succeeded by George Canning, who showed his willingness to ally with the Whigs, four Tories, including Robert Peel and the duke of Wellington, resigned from the Cabinet. Southey thought that Canning was now more in sympathy with the *Edinburgh Review* than with the *Quarterly*, and that the Scottish journal would become the ministerial organ. He had been finally reconciled to Lockhart's editorship of the *Quarterly* when he learned that John Coleridge had converted to the cause of Catholic Emancipation. Had Coleridge remained as editor Southey would have resigned. Now he feared that Murray would fall into line with Canning and pursue a liberal line. He wrote to him from Harrogate to warn him that 'if the *Quarterly* abandons those constitutional principles of Church and State which it has maintained another journal will be started upon them, with ample funds for establishing it.'[79] When the intention to launch such a journal was announced in July Southey wrote to inform Murray that he had been approached to edit it.

> I will fairly tell you that if it had come six weeks ago it would have found me very much disposed, not indeed to have acted as Editor, but to have taken an efficient part in it, under a feeling that I could not depend upon the Q for a certain income, and that I had been treated with a disrespect which was in no degree deserved. That feeling is past – more willingly dismissed than it was entertained. And the change of party or rather of principle which might have separated me from the QR is no longer to be apprehended.[80]

Lockhart had assured him that the journal would not change its political stance despite the accession to power of Canning and a coalition ministry.

Notwithstanding Southey's distrust of Canning, the new prime minister indicated to him through Sir Walter Scott that he would like to do something for him. A Chair in history at one of the Scottish universities was apparently on his mind. Southey indicated that he would prefer the post of historiographer he had long craved were it to become vacant. The approach proved abortive when on 8 August Canning fell ill and died. He was succeeded as prime minister by Viscount Goderich, who headed a weak ministry that collapsed early in 1828 without ever meeting parliament. 'The main business is that our ministers should support the constitution of the country', Southey commented. 'If that be certain it would be of little consequence who might figure in and who figure out. The whigs assuredly will not do this: some of them are ill affected to the church. Others (the majority I believe) have no religious belief.'[81]

Southey demonstrated his credentials for being historiographer, and bolstered the *Quarterly Review*'s Toryism, with a critique of Henry Hallam's *Constitutional History of England*, 'a sort of whig's Bible', as he described it.[82] 'At present I am finishing a review of Hallam's book and hitting him as hard as he deserves', he wrote in October. 'No Jesuit has ever more villainously advanced the doctrine that the end justifies the means as this modern whig has done in defending the execution of Strafford. It is very well that he has attacked me in some of his notes, for otherwise personal acquaintance must have prevented me from treating the book with just severity.'[83] When John Murray took exception to some of the severer passages in the review, and asked him to soften them, Southey undertook 'to strike out any passage . . . which bears the slightest appearance of angry feeling or of personal incivility'. But he thought Hallam's book displayed 'the worst and sourest spirit of whiggery throughout' and therefore deserved to be censured. 'My dear Murray, do not think me *prejudiced* because I hold clear opinions and have a strong sense of their importance', he insisted. 'This neither renders me unjust or uncharitable.'[84] When it appeared in the *Quarterly Review* for January 1828, Southey's sustained critique of Hallam concluded that his book displayed 'the spirit and the feeling of the party to which he has attached himself, its acrimony and its arrogance, its injustice and its ill temper'.[85]

During the year 1828 Southey appears to have been back in harness like a horse, as he imagined himself, 'patiently at work, in the mill, round and round, and never the nearer the end of his labours'.[86] He had reviews in hand not only for the *Quarterly* but also for the *Foreign Quarterly Review* and a new journal the *Foreign Review and Continental Miscellany*. He himself did not think that two rival periodicals dealing with foreign publications would survive, but was quite happy to make hay while the sun shone. His *Colloquies on Society* and the third volume of the *History of the Peninsular War* were also demanding his attention. He was so occupied with his writing that when he was approached to contribute to yet another magazine, the *Keepsake*, he could only promise to do so when the pressure of his other work eased. Nevertheless, he undertook to publish a poem in it, *All for Love or the sinner well saved*, which he had started a year before, and he had written about twenty stanzas. The prospect of being paid fifty guineas for the ballad concentrated his mind on finishing it. Two weeks after agreeing to finish it he had already added fifty more stanzas to the poem. 'Will you wonder that Pegasus prickt up his ears at this?' he asked Caroline Bowles, ' for . . . money makes the mare to go, and what – after all is Pegasus but a piece of horse-flesh?'[87] When towards the end of February Allan Cunningham asked him for something for the *Anniversary*, yet another new magazine he was launching, Southey could only offer him a Pindaric Ode 'upon a gridiron'. If that was not appropriate then he told him, in words reminiscent of the Southey of Byron's *Vision of Judgement*, 'I can write for you a life of John Fox, the Martyrologist, which may, I think, be comprised in five or six and twenty of your pages. This, however, you cannot have in less than three months from this time.'[88]

Southey was anxious to clear the decks so that he could go to London for a few weeks. He wanted to see his uncle Herbert, knowing it would probably be for the last time. While in town he declined an invitation to Longman's 'beautiful abode in Hampstead' because he had to be 'with my poor uncle, who has been more than two years confined to his chair bent like a bow by rheumatism and in that hopeless condition is waiting for death'.[89] Southey also had an appointment with a surgeon, Thomas Copeland, for an operation to cure the haemorrhoids that had troubled him for thirteen years, and were now so bad that they made walking painful. He reached town in the last week of May. On the 28th he attended a dinner party thrown by Edward Quillinan, friend and future son-in-law of William Wordsworth. Henry Crabb Robinson, who was also there, observed that Southey 'would have burst out on the Catholic Question if he had not been at a Catholic's table. He abstained from talking offensively.'[90] He also visited Robert Peel, the home secretary in the new ministry headed by the duke of Wellington. 'I liked Mr Peel better than I had expected', he remarked. 'His manners were very agreeable and his house more beautiful than I supposed any house could be in London.'[91]

Following his operation Southey went down to Buckland to stay with Caroline Bowles while he recuperated. Anticipating his visit, in February he had written to her 'I must talk'.[92] What they talked about can only be conjectured. Health was probably one item they discussed, with Southey a convalescent, while Caroline was a chronic invalid whose 'bodily frame [was] so frail', as he himself put it, 'that you would suppose her to be on the brink of the grave'.[93] Edith's condition was doubtless also mentioned, for she had never recovered her mental stability since the death of their daughter Isabel. Presumably they conversed about poetry, and their plans to compose a poem on Robin Hood together. Perhaps they also discussed their 'celestial journey' together.

On Southey's return home he was delighted that he had recovered sufficiently from his operation to enjoy fell walking with his son, and even ascending mountains again. Three years earlier he had come to the conclusion that 'I am sadly afraid my climbing days are over.'[94] Now the renewed experience seems to have determined him to spend the rest of his life in the Lake District. 'I have nothing to look for or to desire in life further than to remain where I am and as I am so far as the course of nature will permit', he told Tom. 'The way is all down hill and I must not expect to reach the resting place at the bottom without some shaking and some shocks.'[95] His thoughts of death had no doubt been intensified by news that his uncle Herbert had died on 19 September. Curiously he had had a vivid dream the night before in which he saw his uncle, who had reproved him for being so affected by his suffering.

Southey had been very struck with the resemblance between his uncle and a portrait of Sir Thomas More by Holbein, as engraved by Houbraken, and urged John Murray to publish it as the frontispiece to his *Colloquies on Society*. This long-heralded work, complete in two volumes, finally appeared, with the portrait, in spring 1829. Its full title was *Sir Thomas More, or Colloquies on the progress and prospects of Society*. They took the form of fifteen dialogues between the shade of More and Montesinos, who represents the young Southey who had given the course of lectures in Bristol in 1795 on 'The Origin and Progress of Society'. The naive optimism of Montesinos is crushed by More's chastened pessimism. Thus his belief that society constantly progresses is offset by More's observation that the French philosophers believed that the Enlightenment would bring about a new era of peace and prosperity. But their belief was confounded by the Revolution 'which, for its complicated monstrosities, absurdities and horrors is more dreadful to human nature than any other series of events in history'.[96] This leads on to an examination of many aspects of contemporary life that Southey felt were not an improvement on conditions in the sixteenth century. All the prejudices that he had nurtured for twenty years are here distilled. Above all, his conviction that the manufacturing system had brought into existence a new exploited class of industrial workers who threatened the very fabric of society found its most forceful expression. Unless the condition of the poor was addressed, so that their material, intellectual and spiritual needs were satisfied, they would be susceptible to the oratory of demagogues who could goad them into class warfare. That was the basic message of 'the most powerful literary supporter of the Tories'.[97]

CHAPTER TWELVE

'The Doctor' (1829–1834)

In the Preface to his *Colloquies on Society* Southey denied an assertion that he had once espoused Catholic Emancipation: 'I have ever maintained that the Romanists ought to be admitted to every office of trust, honour, or emolument, which is not connected with legislative power; but that it is against the plainest rules of policy to entrust men with power in the state whose bounden duty it is to subvert, if they can, the Church.'[1] He dated the Preface 9 March 1829. Already the defences of the Protestant constitution, as he saw it, had been breached. In February 1828 a Tory ministry presided over by the duke of Wellington had repealed the Test and Corporation Acts, passed in the reign of Charles II, which had effectively kept Roman Catholics out of power. They were still not allowed to sit in either House of Parliament by a second Test Act passed in 1678. Their disqualification became a major issue when the Catholic Daniel O'Connell was elected as MP for County Clare in a by-election held in May 1828. Wellington was faced with serious disturbances in Ireland verging on civil war if he did not allow O'Connell to take his seat. Consequently in the spring of 1829 he repealed the Act. The triumph of Catholic Emancipation shattered the Tory party. The 'Ultras', as opponents of the movement were called, castigated Wellington and Sir Robert Peel as traitors to the Tory cause.

Among the 'Ultras' Southey was prominent. As recently as December 1828 Coleridge had criticised him for allowing himself 'to be flattered into servility by that one testicled fellow Peel. He writes most servilely though very honestly.'[2] Now, however, Southey was outraged at what he saw as the betrayal of the Constitution in Church and State perpetrated by the prime minister and Peel. While he could sympathise with Wellington's dilemma, he could 'have no commiseration for Peel who by his imbecility and half measures has suffered the danger to grow up to which he now yields. He has neither bottom nor brains.'[3] 'We have been betrayed by imbecility, pusillanimity, and irreligion', Southey complained. 'Our citadel would have been impregnable if it had been bravely defended.'[4] He sent up a petition from 'the inhabitants of Keswick' to the House of Commons to protest about Catholic Emancipation.[5] He also circulated two more, one to the House of Lords and another to the king, 'praying him to dissolve parliament because the House of Commons does not represent the wishes of the people'.[6] It was ironic that Southey, along with many who opposed parliamentary reform, now used the argument that the Commons was unrepresentative, because the majority of the people were opposed to Catholic Emancipation. Hundreds of petitions signed by thousands of protesters were presented to both Houses and George IV. Among those whom Southey approached for his support was the bishop of Bath and Wells, one of whose predecessors in the see was Bishop Ken, who had stood up to James II in 1688. 'At this time', Southey informed him, 'I feel it is an honour to be addressing a Prelate who has proved himself so worthy to be his successor in times but too similar.'[7] It is remarkable how in his defence of what he termed the Protestant constitution Southey was fighting seventeenth-century battles in the third decade of the nineteenth.

Yet it is also remarkable that Southey's social ideas were still progressive rather than reactionary. Where his resistance to Catholic Emancipation aligned him with the Ultra-Tories, his concern to ameliorate the lot of the working class allied him with radical Tories such as Michael Thomas Sadler and Lord Ashley, who later became the seventh earl of Shaftesbury. Southey supported Sadler's bid to enter parliament in March 1829 and was pleased when he was returned for Newark. Sadler was expected to visit Lord Lonsdale at Lowther Castle in the autumn and Southey looked forward to meeting him there. In the event he was disappointed as Sadler did not make it. Lord Ashley got in touch with Southey in June 1829 to communicate a 'fact drawn from an official document to justify a remark made in the Colloquies, thinking such appropriate information could not fail to gratify a learned and enquiring student of mankind'.[8] When he learned that summer about the nascent cooperative movement Southey was enthusiastic about its aims. 'You have heard of the Cooperative Societies', he wrote to Mrs Opie, 'with whom in my judgement the most important movement has begun that has ever yet affected the political world.'[9] Although he became apprehensive that they would be pushed to the conclusion of 'a community in land and goods', he nevertheless felt that 'if we can keep this principle within its proper bounds so as to secure the well-being of the whole lower order, without pulling down the higher orders, leave full scope for that desire of bettering our own condition, which is the main-spring of improvement in every thing, and at the same time prevent that desire from making its own gratification by injuring or defrauding others; – if this could be done, I should then gladly sing my *Nunc dimittis*!'[10]

When Sara Coleridge married her cousin Henry Nelson Coleridge that September, Southey thought that the wedding was as gloomy as a funeral. This feeling doubtless arose from the knowledge that Sara and her mother would move out of Greta Hall, which they had shared with him since his arrival there twenty-six years earlier. Nor was it retrospection alone that made him uneasy, for he would be left with Edith, now clinically depressed, with only her sister Mary Lovell and his children to share the burden. Perhaps to cling on to the past as long as possible he accompanied Sara and her husband on their honeymoon journey as far as Ripon. His trip to Yorkshire and back took ten days. In November he spent another three days away from Keswick visiting an old Westminster friend who had married an heiress and lived at Levens Hall in Westmorland. Christmas 1829 must have been one of the gloomiest Southey spent at Greta Hall since he moved into it. To add to his woes his sister-in-law, Henry's wife Louisa, died early in the new year, as did his friend Robert Gooch, 'one of the men in the world of whom I thought most highly, and in whose company I took most pleasure'.[11] Caroline Bowles was so ill that he thought she was close to death too.

'Thank God I generally continue to be in good humour with my employment', Southey observed early in 1830.[12] He was busier than ever, taking on two volumes of *Lives of the British Admirals* for Longman, which he undertook 'not for love but for lucre', as he was to be paid £760, or a shilling a word. A life of John Bunyan, which he wrote to accompany a lavish edition of *Pilgrim's Progress* to be published by John Murray, by contrast was 'a task not of lucre but of love'.[13] Meanwhile he still depended for his 'ways and means' on reviewing. Thus he wrote an essay on Ignatius Loyola for the *Foreign Review* that he hoped would be useful for a projected study of the Monastic Orders, and contributed three reviews to the *Quarterly* in 1830. He also revised former reviews selected for inclusion in *Essays Moral and Political*, as far as possible with the cuts made by the 'prose-gelder' Gifford restored. Although Murray did not publish these until 1832, they were substantially completed by November 1830. Throughout the year he continued to work on the final volume of his *History of the Peninsular War*.

Southey also completed a long introduction to *Attempts in Verse by John Jones*. Jones had sent a volume of his poems to Southey when he was in Harrogate in the summer of 1827, asking his opinion of them. Southey had resolved not to offer his view on the poetry of those who solicited it, and in his introductory essay 'On the Lives and Works of our Uneducated Poets', he warned other poets that any further application to him for poetical preferment 'might as well be addressed to the man in the moon'.[14] He had made an exception in the case of Jones, however, whose poems pleased not only his wife and daughters but also Sara Hutchinson, 'a lady of our party whose approbation in the case of my own writings has long been to me an earnest of the only approbation which I am desirous to obtain . . . that of the wise, the gentle and the good'.[15] He therefore undertook to get Jones' verse published by subscription, a task that took time. Southey obtained 108 subscribers, over half of them from Mrs Anne Watts Hughes, the wife of a canon of St Paul's. Jones himself persuaded over eighty friends to subscribe. The list when it was published included such names as Grosvenor Bedford, Mrs Rickman, Humphry Senhouse, Henry Southey and William Wordsworth. Among other subscribers whom Southey had also clearly enlisted was John Wood Warter of Christ Church, Oxford. Warter had visited Greta Hall, when he had doubtless been solicited to subscribe to the volume. His visit was to result in far more than a subscription, for he was attracted to Edith May, and by the time he went as chaplain to the British embassy in the summer of 1830 he was betrothed to her.

Following the death of George IV on 25 June 1830, the Poet Laureate declined to write a poem commemorating him, or greeting the accession of William IV. 'For what could I say', he asked, 'when in the one case there is so little that can be praised and in the other nothing to anticipate but what is fearful?'[16] What he feared most was the appointment of a Whig ministry determined on parliamentary reform. 'I do not think there ever has prevailed in any country a more general opinion that some great political changes were at hand than may now be observed in England', he asserted. 'I do not mean such changes as our fathers were used to, merely between *ins* and *outs*, but changes which affect the very fabric of society.'[17] Although William IV, unlike his predecessor, was Whiggishly inclined, he retained the duke of Wellington as prime minister, even after a general election that increased Whig strength in the House of Commons. Their success in popular constituencies led Southey to conclude that 'the old ground of defence . . . that the system works well, is no longer tenable'.[18]

Southey hoped that the Tories would close ranks around the duke's standard and preserve his administration as a barrier against reform. He felt so strongly that he could rally them that he went to London at the end of October to try to persuade them to hold firm. En route he stayed overnight in Doncaster where he gathered materials for use in *The Doctor*. On 2 November, the day after Southey's arrival in London, Wellington announced in the House of Lords that there would be no reform bill while he headed the ministry. It is possible that Southey was present, for he attended as many debates as he could while he was in town. Wellington's announcement provoked a reaction, even from the Tories, which led to the duke's resignation and the formation of a Whig administration under Lord Grey. Southey hoped that it would soon collapse, and that Peel would return to power 'upon a strong tide of public opinion'.[19] He deliberately sought out influential individuals, such as the duchess of Kent, and leading politicians from all parties, to impress upon them his case against reform. His young friend Henry Taylor, a senior clerk in the Colonial Office, was a great help in gaining access to influential figures, inviting him to a breakfast party where Charles Greville and John Stuart Mill were among the guests. Greville, a social gossip with a waspish tongue, found Southey 'remarkably pleasing in his manner and appearance, unaffected, unassuming and agreeable'.[20] Mill was later to observe shrewdly that 'he seems to me to be a man of gentle feelings and bitter opinions'.[21] Southey even corresponded with the radical William Hone, formerly his virulent critic, on the 'Captain Swing' riots then raging in the countryside. Where Hone advocated a reduction of rents to alleviate the rural distress, Southey thought they had been reduced enough, and proposed more equitable taxation, state education and public works. The outgoing Tories proposed to launch an opposition paper, and apparently invited Southey to contribute to it. However, though he encouraged their efforts, he declined to join them, being 'no Oppositionist by choice'.[22] Instead he decided to communicate his views on the current state of affairs in an essay for the *Quarterly Review*. He began to write it in London, but found the hectic life he led there not conducive to composition, and so arranged to finish it in the retreat of Caroline Bowles' house at Buckland, in Lymington, Hampshire. He was there from 29 December to 10 January 1831, during which he completed the article. When urging his daughter Bertha to write to Caroline, Southey asked her to 'thank her for making me feel myself so much at ease there that I could go on with my work morning noon and night. I never before got through so much in eleven days.'[23] They never went out 'except when she mounted her Shetland pony, and I walked by her side for an hour or two before dinner'.[24]

Initially Southey gave his essay for the *Quarterly Review* the title 'Letter to the People', preferring this to 'To the Lower Orders' because, as he explained to Murray, 'though mainly intended for them it will allow of my addressing high and low'.[25] When it appeared in the issue for January 1831 it carried the heading 'The Moral and Political State of the British Empire'. It merits Southey's own judgement of it as 'one of the best political papers which I have ever written'.[26] In it he surveyed the course of events during the previous decade, providing astute assessments of its leading politicians. For the first time in the *Quarterly Review* the issue of Catholic Emancipation was openly addressed, since previously Canning and Gifford had suppressed it. Southey deplored the capitulation of Wellington and Peel to those who advocated it. Those who resisted it felt 'disappointed by those in whom they trusted . . . disappointed we say, preferring to use an inadequate rather than an offensive word, because we write in sorrow, not in resentment'.[27] Clearly Southey felt betrayed, not so much by Wellington as by Peel. He nevertheless praised the latter for his introduction of a police force in London, calling it 'the greatest benefit which has been conferred upon the country by any minister within the memory of man'.[28] His main attack was on his now familiar targets of the ignorance of the masses and its exploitation by revolutionary demagogues. He concluded by appealing to the Whigs to defend the constitution. 'It was time that the appellations of Whig and Tory should be dropped, because they no longer designated the same difference of opinion which they had formerly denoted. There were but two parties in the country – that which sought to overthrow the constitution, and that which was resolved to support it: in these broad distinctions, all minor ones must, sooner or later, be merged; and this truth could not be recognised too soon for the constitutional cause and the general good.'[29]

When he left Buckland Southey journeyed to Crediton, where he spent three days with Nicholas Lightfoot. He turned down an invitation from Derwent Coleridge to visit him in Helston, since the trip to Cornwall would extend an already protracted journey. It was not just that it would prolong his absence from home, but that he needed rest. 'The continual excitement which is kept up by change of place, persons, occupation etc in this over-active life, cannot long be borne with impunity', he wrote to Derwent. 'No man stands constitutionally more in need of a good allowance of sleep than I do, and I shall have no sound sleep till I am at rest in mind and body under my own roof. I would not go into the West at all were it not for the sake of seeing my Aunt Mary at Taunton. Her age is such that it becomes a duty to do this and I should reproach myself were I to leave it undone.'[30] On leaving Taunton he visited Bristol for the first time in twenty years. Nostalgia took Southey to his father's shop, 'buying a coloured neck handkerchief as an excuse for entering it, and then asked leave to go upstairs, telling the owner who I was'. Informing his wife of this, he went on: 'God bless you my dear Edith make yourself easy about all things for all things work together for the good of those who take the best thankfully, the ordinary ones cheerfully and the saddest religiously.'[31] Edith apparently was still anxious and depressed, or she would not need such reassurance. Southey also visited his grandmother's house at Bedminster, where 'nothing recognisable is left, tho many of the apple and other fruit trees are standing which my grandfather or my uncles planted.'[32] On 21 January after dining with Joseph Cottle he set off for Shropshire, where he stayed with John Warter's family. He eventually arrived home at the end of January after an absence of three months. While he had been away Mary Barker, who had recently married, becoming Mrs Mary Slade Smith, had visited her old friends in Keswick, including those at Greta

Hall. Shortly after his return Southey wrote to her friend Miss Fletcher: 'I need not say anything of my own family as you have probably seen the ci-devant Miss Barker since she saw them.'[33] He does not appear to have been distressed at missing her visit.

One of the politicians whose hand Southey found himself shaking when he was in London was Lord Brougham, the Whig lawyer whom he had previously castigated. Brougham had been appointed Lord Chancellor by the incoming prime minister Grey. When Southey was in Crediton he was surprised to receive a letter from him seeking his advice on how the government could best encourage scientific and literary pursuits. 'With this view I have applied to two men at the head of the physical and mathematical sciences', Brougham wrote, 'and I cannot look into the department of literature without being met by your name.'[34] 'Strange things happen in strange time', Southey observed to Wynn, 'and that he should write to me upon this subject is one of them.'[35] To Rickman, who had forwarded Brougham's letter to him from London, Southey wrote that 'it has a good deal the air of offering me a sop, at which I shall neither bite, nor snarl and show my teeth, but answer him at leisure with sufficient care.'[36] On returning to Keswick Southey replied to acknowledge that state aid could assist some cooperative ventures such as the compilation of an English dictionary. He also proposed an academy with salaries for its members. Brougham had alluded to a suggestion for the creation of an Order of Merit, but preferred an existing order of knighthood such as the Guelphic. Southey's response to this suggestion was 'for myself if we had a Guelphic order, I should choose to remain a Ghibelline.'[37]

In his reply to Brougham Southey referred to the Lord Chancellor as being 'now on the Conservative side'. That was a curious sentiment for him to use of a Whig minister, but he was convinced that 'the Whigs will become Conservatives *ex officio* now that they are in power'.[38] He believed that the political struggle came down to a conflict between the propertied elite and the masses. In a way he saw the alignment of forces in British politics very much as Marx did, as a class war. Almost every change in the electoral system was seen by Southey as a betrayal of their class interests by propertied Whigs who ought to have known better. As he put it to Lord Ashley, 'if anything could reconcile me to an experiment in English government which should divest rank and property of their proper influence it would be the part which is now taken by men whom nothing but the influence which they derive from rank and property could ever have made considerable enough to be mischievous. But for the sake of the country and of all that is worth preserving we must labour to preserve their rank and their property in spite of themselves.'[39] Southey was not opposed to all reform, however. On the contrary, he felt that if minor reforms had been conceded earlier, it would have avoided major concessions having to be made. 'If you continue to represent the property of the nation and not mere numbers I should not care what alterations were made', he admitted to Wynn, who supported the reform bill. 'But base it upon numbers, make all elections popular, and nothing can avert a revolution in the fullest extent of the word.'[40] He even conceded that, were he seventeen rather than fifty-seven years old, he might welcome 'a general revolution in society, looking only at the evils which it was to sweep away and the good with which I thought it would replace them'. However, he had lived long enough to know that this was merely a short-term view, and that in the long run a revolution would lead to military dictatorship, and ultimately to 'a despotism of institutions which, when once established, stamps a whole people in its iron mould and stereotypes them'.[41]

The bill that the government presented to parliament on 1 March provided for the abolition of over a quarter of the existing seats in the Commons, representing small boroughs, and their redistribution to counties and large towns. It also abolished a plethora of voting qualifications in boroughs, replacing them with a uniform £10 household franchise. Although many historians are inclined to consider it a moderate measure, it was regarded by contemporaries as sweeping. Southey was not alone in talking about 'the revolution which this bill (should it pass without essential alterations) must produce'.[42] It ran into immediate difficulties, passing its second reading by only one vote. Southey took heart that the Conservative cause was reviving. He was particularly pleased by the maiden speech of Philip Henry Stanhope against the measure on 22 March, of which Stanhope, more generally known by his courtesy title Lord Mahon, sent him a copy. When thanking him for it, Southey assured Mahon that he would 'be looked to with hope by all who wish to preserve the institutions of our country'. This began a correspondence between the two, who shared not only ultra-Tory politics but an interest in the history of the Iberian peninsula.[43]

The hopes raised by the opposition to the reform bill in the House of Commons were dashed when Grey asked the king to dissolve parliament on 22 April in order to seek a mandate for the measure from the electorate. In the ensuing general election those who supported it generally defeated its opponents where there was a contest. Anticipating this result, Southey predicted, in a strikingly topical metaphor, that 'we shall presently be on the railroad to ruin and with the Devil for driver'.[44] He himself stayed 'out of the way of all electioneering bustle and being without a vote either in this county [Cumberland] or anywhere else shall not be carried into it'.[45] It is worth noting that this arch-opponent of parliamentary reform was not defending his own narrow self-interest by his stance, but what he took to be the general interest. It is odd that he could not see that its supporters might be similarly altruistic. When he learned that the outcome of the election was as he had anticipated he took a Mr Micawber attitude towards events, hoping that something, anything, the death of a minister, or the outbreak of a war, or the arrival of cholera – then raging on the continent – would turn up to derail the bill. For such an intervention he put his faith in Providence 'with almost as implicit reliance as a child places upon its mother', though the thought of emigrating to Denmark, Portugal, Spain or Sweden crossed his mind too.[46] He still saw the struggle as one 'between property and the levelling system'.[47] Landed proprietors such as Lord Lonsdale were full of gloom, while common people were predicting that they would become grand. 'The white inhabitants of Jamaica are not in more danger from the negroes', Southey exclaimed, 'than we are from our servile population.'[48]

Despite these anxieties Southey was able to continue working. John Rickman had agreed to collaborate with him on a new volume of *Colloquies on Society*. Through his parliamentary connections Rickman arranged to have them printed by Hansard, and by September nearly two hundred proof pages had been set up, when Murray, who was to publish them, objected to this arrangement, and his misgivings about the project eventually led to its abandonment. Meanwhile he kept Southey busy writing no fewer than six reviews for the *Quarterly Review* that year. Southey also spent as much of the summer as he could spare from the attentions of Lakers on the final volume of his *History of the Peninsular War*, and by autumn he was adding material to his novel *The Doctor*. 'I am going to write a chapter which will include the story of the "Three Bears"', he informed his eldest daughter. 'The effect can be given by printing in type of different sizes, and it will be a noble chapter for which the author will be blest by all who love to tell stories to their children.'[49]

Southey was temporarily distracted from these labours in June by a journey he undertook to Cheltenham to see Andrew Bell, who had been incapacitated by a stroke. He found Bell 'in full possession of all his faculties except the power of speech', adding that 'the same paralysis which renders him speechless makes him drivel like a teething infant.'[50] Bell was anxious to make him an executor of his will in which, apart from some legacies – including £1,000 each for Wordsworth and Southey – he intended to leave all his wealth to the University of St Andrews and his schools. Southey tried unsuccessfully to persuade him to leave something to the Church of England. Bell's sister was outraged by the will's provisions and threatened to contest it on the grounds that her brother was insane. For this and other considerations Southey declined to be an executor. He even suspected that Bell would in the end also leave the legacies earmarked for himself and Wordsworth to educational purposes: 'if he weighs me in the balance against a Madras school in any part of Scotland, my scale will kick the beam.'[51]

Southey went on a much more agreeable journey in October, taking his daughter Edith May to the home of her prospective parents-in-law in Shropshire. On his return he learned that his brother Henry had married again and congratulated him: 'That you have once more a home to which you return in chearfulness and comfort is among the pleasantest of my thoughts at this time.'[52] That he himself felt the same sentiments on returning to Greta Hall might be doubted, for although Edith's spirits had risen in the spring, she fell into a depression again in the autumn, one from which she was never to recover.

Southey took heart about the political prospects facing the country from conversations he had on his journey. 'Only one of all the persons with whom I conversed in stage coaches or inns professing himself a Reformer', he claimed, 'and that one was a Londoner. But the others did not declare their opinions till they heard me broadly deliver mine.'[53] One suspects that any supporter of the reform bill kept quiet when Southey spoke his mind. The bill had sailed through the newly elected Commons with majorities of over a hundred. However, it was rejected by the House of Lords on 8 October, at which Conservatives rejoiced while the bill's supporters protested. In Bristol the protests took a violent turn, when the episcopal palace was gutted by fire. 'The insurrection in my native city', Southey concluded, pointed to 'the danger in which this country continually exists and must continue to exist while the servile classes are left in such a state of thorough brutality'.[54] His spirits were strangely lifted when the cholera finally arrived in England towards the end of 1831. 'I have for some years been looking forward to such a visitation', he admitted.[55] He believed it was a judgement of Providence on the nation, and even accepted an invitation to sit on the Board of Health, set up in Keswick to monitor and try to control the spread of the disease: 'my reason for doing this is to make the people conclude that a matter must be serious which induces me to come forward in it.' The spread of the disease was in his view inevitable, as there was no controlling the movements of vagrants carrying it from cities such as Carlisle into the surrounding coun-tryside. He was glad that Greta Hall was on a hill some way out of Keswick, which the contagion might not reach, though it was a target for beggars. Hearing that 'the ministers are heartily frightened', he commented on 'whether any of them will have grace to turn away from the wickedness which they have committed remains to be seen'.[56] It did not prevent them reintro-ducing an amended reform bill, which was easily carried through the Commons in December. 'I am a good hoper', Southey nevertheless insisted, 'and trust that tho we are under the most profligate ministry that ever misconducted the affairs of a great nation and the most besotted sovereign that ever governed a free people, Providence will preserve us.'[57]

The new year brought further confirmation that the country was heading towards disaster, in Southey's view, when the reform bill went up to the House of Lords. Lord Grey put pressure on the king to create as many peers as would be necessary to get it through the upper chamber should the peers reject it. 'The King I am told will make as many peers as his Ministers choose', Southey observed on 10 January 1832, 'and nothing then remains for us but to await the course of revolution.'[58] He nevertheless felt with Lord Ashley that 'it is much better the Peers should be overpowered by an invasion than that they should betray themselves.'[59] In March, just after writing 'Laus Deo at the conclusion of the Pen[insular] War', Southey took his daughter Bertha to Rydal to stay with the Wordsworths.[60] He found William even more despondent about public affairs than himself, which he ascribed to his having no work to keep his mind otherwise occupied. On 13 April the Lords succumbed to the threat of increasing their numbers if they did not pass the reform bill by approving its second reading. Southey blamed it on 'a litter of rats' who had gone over to the Whigs.[61] There was a sufficient rallying of Conservatives to inflict a defeat on a crucial clause in the bill on 7 May. Grey told the king he required the creation of fifty peers to get it through the Upper House, failing which he would resign. William IV for once stood his ground and accepted the prime minister's resignation. Southey expressed his delight that 'the king is no longer the tool of the Revolutionists'.[62] But when the king called upon Wellington to form a ministry, and bring in a more moderate measure of reform, the duke failed to do so since other Tories, including Peel, refused to accept office under him. There were mass demonstrations against this political reversal, and Southey was not alone in thinking they presaged civil war. In the event Grey came back into power and the reform bill became law on 7 June, in Southey's view 'by means which are flagrantly unconstitutional'.[63]

The cholera, which Southey was convinced came as a judgement upon the political follies of the nation, reached Carlisle at the end of June, 'where it manifested itself', he observed, 'immediately after some drunken rejoicing for the Reform Bill'.[64] He insisted, against the objections of brewers and publicans, that similar scenes would not disturb Keswick by persuading the Board of Control to suppress the horse races there in July. When Charles Swain, a Manchester poet whose verse had so impressed Southey that he invited him to Keswick that summer, failed to appear when expected he became alarmed, 'considering how widely the cholera has extended itself'.[65] The danger did not deter other Lakers from making the trip, 'and they have about as much mercy (most of them) upon my all-too-precious time',

Southey complained, 'as the flies and gnats have upon my flesh and blood.'[66] He himself spent a few days in August at Lowther Castle, where Lord Lonsdale had invited him to meet Lord Mahon. They got on well enough for Southey to invite him to Greta Hall to look at his Spanish books and papers.

A rumour reached Southey that he had also received a visit from Lord Nugent, which he thought might have been a mistake for Mahon, for he was at the time at loggerheads with Nugent over a review he had written of his lordship's two-volume work *Some Memorials of John Hampden, his party and his times.* Southey had opened his review by stating that no historian could be impartial about the English Civil War, since such impartiality 'would be to show himself indifferent to right and wrong'. He himself as a Tory was on the whole partial to the royalists, while Nugent, a Whig, supported the parliamentary side. This in itself set them on a collision course. Southey might also have been getting his own back for Nugent's critique of his review of Hallam's *Constitutional History*, which accused him of writing it 'in a mere spirit of political controversy'. Southey riposted by asserting that 'Lord Nugent is lamentably bewhigged.'[67] Nugent took umbrage at this review and published *A Letter to John Murray touching an article in the last Quarterly Review.* Murray did not send Southey a copy until his brother Henry ordered one for him. Southey was offended by the attack upon him, describing 'the tone and language of his pamphlett' as 'those of a bully, a blackguard and a liar'.[68] He was particularly annoyed because it exposed his authorship of a review that had appeared anonymously. He therefore decided to write a reply to it 'not in my own person but as the Reviewer'. His review had addressed the circumstances of Hampden's death indicated by the exhumation of what Nugent believed was his corpse. It even dwelt on such gruesome details as the discovery of maggots eating the brains. 'This was ghastly enough for persons who were neither accustomed to act as resurrectionists, nor had gone through a course of experiments like Frankenstein in his laboratory when he manufactured his monster.'[69] However, Southey did not then dispute the identification of the body as that of Hampden. The more he thought about it, though, the less convinced he became that Nugent had exhumed Hampden's and not somebody else's remains. He now determined upon 'proving what he denies, and pressing upon him now as intellectual dishonesty what I had before provided him with possible excuses for'.[70] 'Not being of an irritable temper and being in this case completely in the right', he maintained, 'I deal with him coolly and quietly. Nevertheless, the exposure will be such that I am almost sorry for him. Many a man has hanged himself for less.'[71]

Southey's disgruntlement with John Murray at this time extended beyond the publisher's rather underhand dealing with Nugent. The collapse of the scheme to publish a new series of *Colloquies on Society* in conjunction with

Rickman still rankled. The delays in payments for reviews also irked. Southey attributed Murray's eccentric behaviour to 'incoherent transactions', a euphemism for a drinking problem.[72] He was informed that the publisher 'is generally drunk half the night and muzzy the whole of the morning'.[73] His relations with Longman's, however, were much better. In December they offered him £1,750 towards a projected multi-volume work on *Lives of the British Admirals*. This relieved Southey of financial pressures that had been building up over the year. His brother Tom had again needed to be bailed out of his difficulties, costing Southey £5 a month. Other demands had increased his debts to £750. This situation had made the possibility of a professorship of history at the new University of Durham seem attractive, even though he was loath to leave Greta Hall – as he told a peripatetic American poetess, 'to be as happy as this world will allow us to be we must be at *rest*.'[74] Fortunately the Chair was never offered him. The Longman advance, which was quickly followed by the legacy from Dr Bell, gave his finances 'a better prospect than has ever been before me till now'.[75]

At the end of 1832 Southey summed up his bodily and mental state in a letter to Derwent Coleridge thus: 'I have not lost much either of my activity or strength, and nothing of my spirits', he told him, 'but I have no longer the digestive powers of an ostrich. I require the aid of a glass for distant objects and even for distinguishing faces across a room; and sleep and I are not hand in glove as we used to be when I derived my descent from one of the Seven Sleepers. Age, however, is leading me *gently* down the hill.'[76]

'Last year you might well call the Wicked Year', Southey wrote to Mrs Hodson in February 1833. 'What epithet will the present one deserve? The Bloody – will probably be it[s] proper designation in Ireland. I do not see what is to avert a Rebellion there.'[77] The fact that his increasingly pessimistic prophecies failed to materialise does not appear to have given him pause. Like the millennium to apocalyptic sects, the revolution was to him always just round the corner. If it was averted, it was due to Providence and not to human agency. Yet he did not withdraw from the world. On the contrary, his new-found friendship with Lords Ashley and Mahon drew him further into politics than he had been before. He offered them his advice on the two great issues which arose during 1833, the abolition of slavery in the British Empire, and the Act that limited the daily labour of children in factories to ten hours. On the first he was more cautious than he had been in the campaign to abolish the slave trade. He thought that it should be done gradually and not precipitately. On the second he would have gone further, for he considered the plight of factory children to be even more offensive than that of the slaves. He organised a petition in support of the Ten Hour Bill, even getting his fourteen-year-old son Cuthbert to sign it, but refused to support one for the immediate emancipation of the slaves. When Sadler's Report on the factories brought to light what Southey considered to be systematic cruelty on the part of manufacturers, he concluded that 'a plantation in Jamaica [is] Paradise to an English factory'.[78] A copy of one of the Colloquies he had composed in collaboration with Rickman, which dealt with the factory system, Southey sent to Lord Ashley, who introduced the Ten Hour Bill into parliament. He also sent a copy of Caroline Bowles' poem on the same subject, adding, 'No one in any age or country ever wrote with truer feeling than she does.'[79] Southey was actively contributing to the parliamentary debates, even urging the Conservatives to cooperate with the ministers to offset their dependence on the radicals in 'Parldaemonium', as he called the reformed parliament, but not to coalesce with them.

All Southey's advice was issued from his armchair in Greta Hall, for he did not stir from Cumberland the whole year. He was kept too busy to travel far with his *Lives of the British Admirals*, the first two volumes of which were published in 1833. By March, two volumes of his novel *The Doctor* were also ready for the press. Southey took elaborate steps to preserve his anonymity as author, thinking that, like the *Letters of 'Espriella'*, this would arouse curiosity and increase sales. The manuscript sent to Messrs Longman was not in his handwriting but in that of others, principally Sara Hutchinson, who had persuaded him to publish it. Clearly the Wordsworths were in on the secret, as was Coleridge, who annoyed Southey by divulging it to his family. 'S.T.C has acted not in indiscretion but in malice', he complained to Bedford. 'What must be said is that *if* I had a secret *he* was not the person to whom it would have been entrusted.'[80] Apart from Bedford only a very small number of his acquaintance was aware of the conceit, including Southey's brother Henry, Henry Taylor and the Wordsworths. Though the Longmans were to publish them, the volumes were to be printed by William Nicol, who was to deal with Bedford and Henry rather than directly with Southey himself. Duplicate proofs were to be sent to him, so that one set could be returned with the corrections written by one of his daughters. 'Like the Yankee servant who, when the bell had been rung three or four times, opened the parlour door, looked in and said "the more you ring the more I won't come",' Southey joked to Taylor, 'so the more I may be convicted of having written this book the more I won't own it.'[81] 'It cannot fail of exciting notice', Southey felt assured, 'for I have put into it as much queerness and as much knowledge as ever entered into the composition of a book, jingling my bells to draw people round and then telling them wholesome truths in sportive earnest or in severe jest.'[82]

Another task that Southey undertook at this time was to edit Dr Bell's literary remains for the compilation of his biography. He was overwhelmed by the sheer volume of letters and other papers that arrived at Greta Hall, fortunately accompanied by a Mr Davies, an amanuensis who 'was established in lodgings at the bottom of the garden'.[83] Southey spent two hours with him before breakfast every day to try to get a grip on the undertaking. In the event it proved too much for him, and the three-volume *Life of the Reverend Andrew Bell* did not appear until a year after his death.

As usual the summer brought a break in Southey's schedule with the arrival of the Lakers. 'In no former year have they ever come in greater strength', he observed in 1833.[84] Among them was Henry Crabb Robinson, who visited Greta Hall several times in late June and early July. He 'had a cordial reception from the Laureate and found the whole family amiable. With Southey I had a long and amicable chat on all kinds of subjects. On politics he was by no means as anxious and earnest as, but if anything more violent than Wordsworth.'[85]

Towards the end of the summer Southey was able to resume his literary labours. He completed the second volume of his *Lives of the Admirals* and after a respite began work on the third. Although the biography of Bell still took up much of his time he felt that he could take on new assignments. Thus he accepted an approach from the publishers Baldwin and Cradock to edit the works of William Cowper, a commitment that was to cause him considerable trouble. He even proposed to Edward Moxon an ambitious scheme to write 'Lives of the English Divines' to be published in monthly parts, though nothing came of this.

At the beginning of January 1834 the first two volumes of *The Doctor* arrived at Greta Hall with the inscription 'from the author'. Southey was able to test how firmly his anonymity would survive the scrutiny of readers. Among those in the house at the time was the Reverend James White, who had come to officiate at the marriage of Edith May to John Warter on the 15th. While his daughter and future son-in-law were aware of Southey's authorship, White was not, although he suspected that he might have written it. His suspicions were allayed, however, when Southey's son Cuthbert, who had not been let in on the secret, revealed his ignorance. It amused his father when he exclaimed: 'the author, whoever he is, must be a clever man, and he should not wonder if it proved to be Charles Lamb.' Retailing this story to Bedford, Southey added, 'You may imagine how heartily we have enjoyed all this.'[86] The joke was carried to tedious lengths when Southey pretended to guess who had written it, even when the third volume appeared in 1835. Indeed, though he never explicitly denied it, so he never openly acknowledged his authorship. He got a curiously perverse thrill out of teasing people about it. Thus in 1837 he wrote anonymously to a lady, signing the letter with 'the mark of the author of the Doctor'. In it he told her, 'Whatever you may think of Dr Dove, the book represents his disciple and biographer to the very life, neither less playful, nor less pensive, nor more wise, nor more foolish than he is, an old man with a boy's heart.'[87]

Among those Southey suggested as possible authors were Henry Coleridge, hoping it would explain away why the Coleridges were identifying himself as the author, Isaac D'Israeli and John Hookham Frere. His feigned conjectures for his bogus suspicions betray an exaggerated estimation of his own writing skills, which were characteristic of 'the heavy magniloquence of his own self-esteem' as an author.[88] For instance he dismissed D'Israeli from his calculations because 'upon a perusal, I was satisfied that he could not write a style which is at once so easy and so good.'[89] Again to John Gibson Lockhart he pressed the case for Frere's authorship, on the grounds that he did not know 'in what other person we should find the wit, the humour, the knowledge and the consummate mastery of style'.[90] Lockhart was to hoist Southey on his own petard when he reviewed the novel in the *Quarterly Review*. Discussing the conjectures about the authorship he noted that most people suspected Southey, but he dismissed him, no doubt with tongue in cheek, since 'of the real author of the work we happen to know he is ignorant'. This enabled Lockhart to savage *The Doctor* without seeming to attack Southey. 'It is broadly distinguished from the mass of books recently published', he wrote, 'both by excellencies of a very high order, and by defects, indicating such occasional contempt of sound judgement, and sense, and taste as we can hardly suppose in a strong and richly cultivated mind unless that mind should be in a certain measure under the influence of disease. . . . two thirds of his performance look as if they might have been penned in the vestibule of Bedlam. . . . 'The Doctor' is the work of a man who stands more in need of physic than of criticism.'[91]

The novel, like Sterne's *Tristram Shandy*, on which it was loosely modelled, is one that readers either love or loathe. Cuthbert Southey pointed out that 'there is not much in the book about the Doctor' and that 'it was very proper to put &. in the title-page'.[92] The 'etcetera' indeed overwhelm the tale of Dr Dove of Doncaster and his horse Nobbs. They were accumulated over many years, the first hint of the book being as early as 1805. 'Interchapter II', with the heading 'Aballiboozobanganorribo' – which Southey confessed was meaningless – he had read to his son Herbert, 'who entered fully into the humour of it'.[93] Although it was published in seven volumes, the last two posthumously, each contains materials collected painstakingly for decades as well as during composition. Thus there is a reference to Queen Victoria's coronation in 1837 in the one-volume edition that John Warter published in 1848, while its penultimate chapter is a delightful 'Memoir of the Cats of Greta Hall', dated 18 June 1824. In it Southey paid tribute to

Hurlyburlybuss, Rumplestiltzchen and the other cats to whom he acted as 'historiographer'. The most famous chapter, 'The Story of the Three Bears', as we have seen was written in 1831. Southey scribbled quotations and extracts from books as he read them, on scraps of paper as well as in commonplace books, hoping that one day they would become useful. Although his son-in-law published much material from them in four volumes, many still survive in collections in several repositories. Scholars seem to be at a loss to know how to make use of them, as they are bewilderingly eclectic in their subject matter. But Southey found a use for them in this bewilderingly eclectic book, more a disquisition than a novel. 'I am much mistaken if you do not find a great deal of it after your own heart', Southey wrote to Grosvenor Bedford, 'and I am sure you will recognize that the whole of it is after mine.'[94] It is, to such an extent that it is hard to think how anybody could be convinced he was not its author. Above all, perhaps, it gives the lie to those who claim that Southey had no sense of humour, being characterised throughout by those 'boyish spirits' that he still displayed at the age of sixty.

These spirits were to be severely tested by Edith's continued depression. Following her marriage to John Wood Warter, Edith May went with her husband to West Tarring in Sussex, a living to which he had been presented following his return from Denmark. Such a distance from Keswick, almost as many miles as there are days in the year by Southey's calculation, depressed her mother even more than usual, so that her spirits sank alarmingly. Southey sent his brother Henry regular reports of her symptoms. Thus in May he reported that she felt 'a weight in the abdomen (where however there is no enlargement) a sense of lightness in the head which makes pressure seem a relief to it, frequent and tremulous agitation, depression of spirits sometimes to a hysterical degree – and failing appetite tho a sense of weakness makes her frequently take food, and little sleep. This has now continued so long as to make me uneasy.'[95] Southey's uneasiness about Edith possibly explains his remarkable indifference on hearing the news of Coleridge's death in July. 'He had long been dead to me', he coolly told Mrs Hughes, 'but his decease has naturally wakened up old recollections.'[96] Henry visited Keswick that summer to see the patient at first hand. After he returned to London, however, Southey told him that 'Edith is worse than when you left us.' He became aware that the entertainment of visitors – in August there was 'a house full of guests' – so far from lifting her spirits, subjected her to stress, and began to feel guilty about his lack of consideration for her.[97] The poet Charles Swain, who had been obliged to cancel his visit two years earlier, finally got to Keswick that June. Southey later told him that he was 'the last guest whom my dear Edith received with pleasure'.[98] 'Next week when our guests depart the House will be quieter', he confided to his brother Henry in mid-September, 'but our then near departures will counteract for a while any good that this might produce – It is however from quiet that I can hope anything.'[99] He had arranged for Cuthbert to stay with his sister- and brother-in-law in West Tarring in order to study for Oxford, and planned to accompany him there on a circuitous route taking in the West Country in October. Unfortunately the plan had to be abandoned on 25 September when he informed Henry that Edith's 'sleeplessness has now produced mental derangement'.[100]

Dionysius Lardner, the editor of the Cabinet Cyclopaedia to which Southey contributed his *Lives of the British Admirals*, was among the usual throng of visitors who went to the Lakes that season. He turned up at Greta Hall and 'on passing the drawing-room he noticed several ladies apparently in a very cheerful mood; on giving his name, after waiting about five minutes, Southey came to him, the very image of distraction, took his hand and led him into his study. For a long time he remained silent – at length he told him he believed he must dismiss him; in fine, he disclosed to him that within the last five minutes, since he rang the bell at the lawn gate, Mrs Southey had, without previous indication or symptom, gone raving mad, and to that hopeless degree that within an hour he must take her to an asylum.'[101] The claim that there had been no 'previous indication or symptom' was erroneous. As we have seen, Edith had been clinically depressed for some time. Reporting her condition to Wynn in December, Southey observed 'now that the malady has manifested itself I can refer to its lurking seeds numberless circumstances which for several y[ears] indicated a gradual change of character and disposition.'[102] Nevertheless that some sudden and dramatic change for the worse took place on 25 September is clear. After telling his brother that lack of sleep had deranged her, Southey added 'this morning she was perfectly insane'.[103] It seems that Edith became violent, for Southey took her to the Retreat, a mental hospital at York, on 1 October, where she had to be restrained.

PART III

'An evening of gloom closed in by premature darkness'

CHAPTER THIRTEEN

Widower (1834–1837)

'I have been parted from my wife by something worse than death', Southey wrote to Bedford from York on 2 October 1834. 'Forty years has she been the light of my life; and I have left her this day in a lunatic asylum.'[1] Although a recovery was not ruled out he did not bank on it, warning his daughters that 'two circumstances . . . are very unfavourable: – her time of life; and her natural want of chearfulness.'[2] On his return to Greta Hall he found it hard to cope, not least because Edith had previously managed routine domestic tasks that he had now to do. Fortunately the four guineas a week it cost to keep her in the Retreat, which required a quarter's payment in advance, he found affordable since his finances, helped by a legacy from Thomas Telford, were in better shape than they had been for years.

Southey's financial situation had benefited from an unexpected quarter early in 1835. Sir Robert Peel had formed a minority government in December, and had called a general election in January, hoping to obtain a majority in the House of Commons. Although the Tories gained 290 seats, becoming the largest single party, they were outnumbered by the other parties. Nevertheless, Southey was heartened by the revival of Tory fortunes, and even cast his first vote ever, having been enfranchised by the Reform Act. The poll book for Cumberland records the votes of Robert Southey of Greta Hall 'near Keswick' for Messrs Irton and Stanley, the Conservative candidates standing against Major Aglionby.[3]

Peel used his authority as prime minister to see what assistance he could give to artists and writers. This led him to offer Southey a baronetcy. The Poet Laureate was at first taken aback by this largesse, but decided on reflection to refuse it, on the grounds that he could not sustain the dignity of the title from his own limited resources, which he spelled out. Peel took the hint and offered instead a pension of £300 a year, which Southey gratefully accepted. Together with the pension he had been granted by Grenville, and his income as Laureate, it made him financially independent for the first time in his life.

He had always said that if he could afford it he would drop the hack work that had been essential for his 'ways and means', in order to concentrate on works he hoped would last. Thus he gradually phased out his reviewing for the *Quarterly Review*, which he had been inclined to do anyway following his disagreements with Murray. The latest had arisen following an article that Southey had contributed on the Corn Laws, which placed tariffs on imported cereals to protect British farmers from foreign competition. It had included a passage on Ebenezer Elliott, the 'Corn Law Poet', which Lockhart had excised. Southey was not particularly annoyed at this, since he accepted that poetry and the price of grain could be considered separate entities. However, he was offended when Murray offered him only £70 rather than the £100 he had been promised, on the grounds that his contribution was not as long as it should have been. Southey put it down to Murray's 'incoherent transactions'.[4]

Southey's financial independence left him free to concentrate on his work on Bell's biography, with the assistance of William Davies, who had become a close friend, accompanying him and Edith on their forlorn journey to York. He also made slow progress with the *Life and Works of William Cowper*, though anxiety over his wife interrupted his labours. Thus he found it impossible to give the publishers Baldwin and Cradock a date for the delivery of Cowper's biography, which was to comprise the opening volumes of his edition. They were anxious for dispatch, since a rival publication edited by the Reverend T. S. Grimshawe in eight volumes was published by Saunders and Otley in the opening months of 1835. Grimshawe claimed to have acquired the copyright of 221 of Cowper's letters published in 1824. This left Southey at the disadvantage of quoting them in his life of Cowper rather than providing an edition of them in the works.[5]

The rivalry between the two editions was exacerbated by the Evangelicals backing Grimshawe, one of their number, in his view of Cowper, who was another. Southey's animus against them was no doubt reinforced by the effects on Edith of Evangelical sermons preached by the Reverend John William Whiteside, curate at Crosthwaite parish church, which, he told Henry, 'I suspect had much to do with the "horrible thoughts" that possessed her when she was sleepless in the night or when she awoke in the morning – That race of Evangelicals should be called Dysvangelical preachers of ill tidings!'[6] When Whiteside moved to Ripon in 1835, Southey felt 'his removal from this place to be a great deliverance'.[7] Had Edith returned home before he left Southey vowed that he would 'never allow her to hear another of Mr Whiteside's sermons. On that point I am fully resolved.'[8] His own treatment of the causes of Cowper's mental breakdowns was not surprisingly rather different from that of Grimshawe's. Indeed he attributed the second and most serious to the impact of Evangelicalism on Cowper's delicate sensibility. Southey felt that his understanding of the poet's insanity was helped by his having to cope with Edith's. 'There are passages which . . . would not have been written', he claimed, 'unless I had had something more than a theoretical knowledge of this most awful of all maladies.'[9]

In February Betty, a servant who had accompanied Edith when Robert took her to the Retreat, and who stayed with her there, informed him that Edith had recovered sufficiently to go back home. On receiving this welcome news Southey resumed his plan to take Cuthbert to West Tarring, and set off with his son on a hectic journey. They stayed for a few nights in London, when Southey had his first meeting with Thomas Carlyle, who remembered him being 'a serious, human, honest, but sharp almost fierce-looking thin man'.[10] Southey accompanied Cuthbert to Sussex, then went on alone to visit Caroline Bowles in Hampshire, before heading up to York. There he found Edith in no condition to be taken straight to Greta Hall. To his brother Henry he admitted that, in his opinion, 'the case is irremediable'.[11] 'Since I came this morning', he informed his daughter Bertha, 'she has gone on in a rambling strain with scarcely a gleam of sanity'. The patience that Southey had shown in his relationship with his wife seems to have worn thin under the strain. He complained that 'the leaven which is now at work is no other than the evil old habit of not allowing that she is pleased with any thing.'[12]

Instead of taking Edith straight home, Robert took her to Scarborough, more for the sake of his own health than hers. He was suffering from a very irritating rash on his arms and thighs, which he thought bathing in hot salt water would ease, if not cure. No doubt he was also hoping that a short stay there would help improve her state of mind, and prepare her to return home. Again he expressed irritation with her when she 'objected greatly to the journey, the place and the lodgings, all in that old unhappy habit of objecting to every thing, which perhaps was an indication of the malady which she now suffers'.[13] A week in lodgings with Mrs Ling on the Cliff did not procure any improvement, and he had to warn his daughters that 'your poor mother's state is that of complete imbecillity'.[14] He was indeed very concerned about the impact her return would have on them. 'I do not think that your dear mother will manifest any pleasure at seeing you', he warned them, 'and I am sure it will give you great pain if she does not, and even if she does to see how her intellects are shattered. On the other hand the likelihood that home may do her good . . . will be much lessened if you are not there at first.' He was clearly agonising over the dilemma, for he assured them that 'if . . . after a very short trial I find that there is no good to her in your presence I shall accept Miss Fenwick's most friendly invitation to both of you' to stay with her.[15]

When they eventually reached Keswick, however, Edith responded so positively to familiar surroundings that Southey entertained hopes of a recovery. He resorted to his old stoical conviction that duty was inseparable from happiness, informing Cuthbert that 'your sisters will find themselves supported in the performance of their duties', and Henry Taylor that he 'had never any thought of leaving the girls with their mother, and transferring to them a duty which I am better able to bear'.[16] Not that the girls were left to bear the burden alone. Betty, the maidservant, who had attended to Edith in York and Scarborough, was there to help. So too was Martha Fricker, Edith's unmarried sister who normally lived on the Isle of Man with another spinster sister, Eliza. She was at the house when Southey brought Edith home. When arranging to do so he stipulated that 'if Miss Lovell would go to the Isle of Man . . . and leave your aunt Martha at Keswick the only objection to your mother's return would be removed.'[17] Mrs Lovell went to live with Eliza the day Edith returned to Greta Hall. Early in April, shortly after her return, Southey learned from Sir Robert Peel about the award of his pension. It was ironic that he no longer faced financial problems, since both Southey and his son Cuthbert attributed the decline of Edith's mental faculties to anxiety about money over the previous twenty years.

In his reply to the prime minister, thanking him for the pension, Southey assured Peel that 'while we have you to look to I cannot doubt that the nation will be saved from revolution and that, under Providence, you will be the means of saving it.'[18] This was a significant softening of his previous apocalyptic vision. There are signs of mellowing, too, in his religious beliefs. Thus he felt that now he 'could most conscientiously subscribe to the Articles in which the doctrine of the Trinity is stated'.[19] However, he still could not bring himself to believe in Hell. 'As for eternal torments', he maintained, 'God forgive those who suppose that it can be for His glory to believe in such a tenet!'[20]

'What Sir Robert Peel has done for me will enable me to employ the remainder of my life upon those works for which inclination, peculiar circumstances and long preparation have best qualified me', he informed Murray. 'They are the History of Portugal, the History of the Monastic Orders and the History of English Literature.'[21] He even contemplated a second edition of his *Life of Wesley* and the 'Lives of the English Divines'. But none of these projects was ever to result in publication.

By the summer the hopes raised by Edith's responsiveness to familiar surroundings were 'gradually sinking'. 'A settled melancholy possesses her when she is most herself', Southey admitted; 'if I could but see any dawn thro this cloud I should think all might yet be well.'[22] So far from light breaking through he observed in July that 'our domestic prospects are darkening upon us daily. I know not whether the past or the present seems most like a dream to me, so great and strange is the difference.'[23] The death of Sara Hutchinson, Wordsworth's sister-in-law, who had been such a comfort to Southey and his daughters during his wife's sojourn at the Retreat, deepened the gloom. They had no guests that summer, other than Cuthbert, who stayed ten weeks for a vacation and returned to West Tarring in October. Southey thought it 'an evil to [his daughters] that our house should be closed to those who used to be our summer visitors', though it could not be helped given Edith's sad state.[24] When Henry Taylor visited Keswick in November, he stayed at an inn.

That month the first volume of Southey's edition of *The Life and Works of William Cowper* appeared, comprising the biography of the poet from his birth to about 1780. It cannot compare with Southey's lives of Nelson and Wesley, not least since the need to quote from Cowper's letters forced upon him by Grimshawe led much of it to read like an edition of his correspondence. There is also much scene setting, and digressions about Cowper's contemporaries, which interrupt a narrative that in any case lacks the action of that of the life of an admiral or of the founder of a sect. Yet, as the acute observations of one poet for another whom he admired, it has considerable interest. Its appearance was well received by all but the Evangelicals. 'I have seen nothing for some years equal to the account of the first [volume] in the Evangelical Magazine', Southey asserted. 'They say I shall be known to posterity in the words of a noble poet as an incarnate lie. On the other hand I see by Baldwin and Cradock's advertisement that I have been puffed as high as the power of bellows blowing can carry praise.'[25] Southey's account of Cowper's education at Westminster was particularly pleasing to the school, whose reputation had fallen since the days when he himself was a pupil there. The dean of Westminster wrote to ask him if he could write a poem about the school for a public meeting. Southey declined, however, on the grounds that he was too busy, while he had 'outlived the inclination of writing poetry. To be asked for an epitaph, or to contribute something to a lady's album, gives me much more annoyance than I ever felt at hearing Dr. Vincent say to me "Twenty lines of Homer, and not go to breakfast".'[26]

The second volume of *Cowper* was published in February 1836. Southey was greatly helped in his task of checking the accuracy of the transcriptions of the poet's letters by his daughters, to whom he read them aloud. Bertha and Kate also passed the time by binding some two hundred of his books in cuttings from their cast-off frocks, which led to their being called the Cottonian Library. Colourful though the end result was, the process speaks of a certain desperation to render the depressing task of tending to their mother agreeable. Southey, too, felt penned in that winter, going out only for his daily constitutional walks. He dared not leave his wife even for a day. 'We are thankful when one day passes quietly, and most days, thank God, do so', he told Wynn. 'The angry fits do not last long; they are immediately forgotten, and appear to have the effect of exercise (of which she takes none) in producing better sleep.'[27] Southey's female relatives seem to have done most of the work of ministering to his wife, for he found plenty of time to write. 'Leisure I may look for when "Cowper", and the "Admirals", and the revision of "Wesley", are off my hands', he wrote in April. 'That I never am idle for five minutes which it is possible to employ, I may truly say; and it is not less true that more time is employed in increasing my materials intended or in progress, than in using the abundant collections already made.'[28] In the summer friends came to see them, though even Grosvenor Bedford, paying a long-awaited visit, had to stay in lodgings, and not in Greta Hall itself.

Southey's brother Henry came too, though he presumably stayed in the house. They no doubt discussed their feckless brothers. Edward had returned from Spain the previous year, and at Christmas had written to tell Robert that Henry had admitted him as an outpatient, and given him two sovereigns. Southey refused to deal with him directly, but asked Henry to give him the same amount on his behalf. In the summer of 1836 Edward claimed he had been offered a position in Guernsey. He had misled them on so many previous occasions that Henry and Robert were wary about paying his way there, though Southey thought that a gift of £5 would 'not be thrown away in removing him to a distance'.[29] Tom's family, too, was giving them concern. He had gone to be harbour master at Demerara in British Guiana, leaving them in Canterbury laden with debt. In March Tom's wife had informed Southey that he hoped to pay it off. 'The way to do this is not by having an establishment in England and another in Demerara', Southey complained, though he did undertake to give her £20 if she asked for help.[30] When Henry returned to London after visiting Keswick he reported to John May that 'I left my brother quite well and he appears to bear his calamity better than I could have imagined. His youngest daughter [Kate] seems most depressed and nervous, but not more so than is quite natural under the circumstances. As for Edith herself she is in a state approaching to fatuity from which there is no chance of her ever recovering.'[31]

Henry urged Robert to take a break from attending upon his wife for the sake of his own health. Southey was longing to take Cuthbert, who again spent the summer at home, with him on an extended tour of the West Country to see the scenes of his own youth. Still he could not bring himself to leave Edith. Then an opportunity presented itself to test her reaction to his going away. In September he was summoned, along with Wordsworth, to be a witness at the trial of a disputed will in Lancaster. In the event their testimony was dismissed, but it meant that Southey had to leave home for several days. Although Edith was upset at first, she soon settled down, indicating that he could take his brother's advice and quit the house without his absence affecting her adversely. He was nevertheless afraid that 'the thought of our departure – or rather feeling (for she often says "I have lost my thought") will soon begin to disturb her. The journey is likely to do me good – but I shall be wishing it were over all the while.'[32]

Before leaving Southey had to plan their route carefully. It was to be a research trip as well as a holiday. He arranged to visit Egerton Bagot in Warwickshire in order to see Cowper's letters to his father, and to consult the poet's correspondence with Joseph Hill, left by Hill's widow to a Mr Jekyll of Spring Gardens, London. But his 'main object was to show Cuthbert the scenes of my childhood and early youth, and introduce him to the few old friends whom I have left.' Outstanding among these was Joseph Cottle, with whom they were to stay for a week, 'being the longest tarriance we shall make upon our whole circuit'.[33] When arranging this Southey had to exercise considerable tact, for he found himself involved in a bitter row between Cottle and the family and friends of S. T. Coleridge. Since Coleridge's death Cottle had written a *Memoir* of him for publication, which they learned would divulge episodes, not least Coleridge's addiction to opium, which they were anxious to suppress. Southey wrote to Cottle on 10 October 'urging him to leave out what is objectionable and offering to read over the Memoir when we meet'. He also wrote to Sir John Coleridge, Coleridge's nephew, to assure him that 'you shall hear what my success may be and see me (I trust) in London. Our departure is postponed for a week, for I have been distanced in writing against Time.'[34]

They left Keswick on 24 October and stayed the night at Kendal, after booking places on the coach to Liverpool that left at half past five the following morning. From Liverpool they made their way to Chester, where they 'walked round the walls before breakfast' on the 26th.[35] They stayed with Lord Kenyon at Gredington in Flintshire; with Mr Parker, a friend of Dr Bell, and his amanuensis Davies, at Sweeny Hall in Shropshire; with the parents of his son-in-law John Warter near Shrewsbury; and Egerton Bagot near Birmingham, where Southey spent two mornings transcribing letters of William Cowper. By 3 November they had arrived at Cottle's home in Bedminster. Southey was delighted to show Cuthbert his grandmother's house, 'which was the very paradise of my childhood'.[36] Cuthbert 'was much struck with his strong attachment to his native city, and his appreciation of all the beauties of the neighbourhood.'[37] They spent some time in the company of Walter Savage Landor, who lived at Clifton. While at Bedminster Southey discussed the *Memoir* of Coleridge with Cottle, and wrote to reassure

Derwent Coleridge that 'he will be induced to omit whatever is most objectionable – whatever I can convince him would be painful to your father's nearest connections.'[38]

From Bristol Southey and his son made their way through Bath to Chippenham to spend three days with the poet William Bowles, whom they found delightfully eccentric. After that they went to Taunton to see Robert's aunt Mary, who at the age of eighty-six was his only living relative older than himself. Then they proceeded along the Somerset coast to stay with Thomas Poole in Nether Stowey and Sir Thomas Acland at Holincot. From Somerset they made their way to South Devon, where they visited Mrs Hodson at Dawlish, Lord Devon at Powderham Castle and Nicholas Lightfoot at Crediton. They then returned to North Devon before striking west to Cornwall to stay with Derwent Coleridge in Helston, where 'a host of people in the street being asked what they were looking at replied "that they were waiting to see Lord Southey get into a carriage".'[39] After visiting Land's End they returned to Devon to spend Christmas with Mrs Bray in Tavistock. Advising her of their impending arrival Southey admitted that he was 'a good traveller as far as regards patience, capability of exertion and endurance. But travelling (and still more absence from home) makes larger demands upon my spirits than they can at all times answer.'[40] He was apparently warning her that he would not particularly enjoy Christmas, for after his departure, writing to thank her for her hospitality, he admitted that he had not been cheerful, 'and you must judge of what my spirits have been rather from my writings (which have always faithfully represented them) than by what you have seen of me, for you have only seen what is left.'[41] Cuthbert and Southey were then on their way to Lymington to stay with Caroline Bowles at Buckland, where they were to spend a week. Cuthbert made no comment on it in the *Life and Correspondence*. One wonders what he made of it in view of his later hostility towards Caroline. Southey claimed that Caroline 'says she never saw so lovable a creature; and he says of her that he never took so much to any one in so short a time.'[42] But he was inclined to see the world through rose-coloured glasses.

Cuthbert left Lymington on 13 January, proceeding directly to his sister at West Tarring, while Southey stayed until the following night, when he went to London. Edith May had given birth while they were at Buckland, and Robert wanted her to be given time to recover before he imposed himself upon her. After spending three weeks in the capital he, too, made his way to his son-in-law's home. He spent about ten days with his daughter's family and Cuthbert, then returned to London for a few days before getting on the mail coach for Penrith on the 17th. He arrived home three days later, after an absence of seventeen weeks. It was a sad homecoming, as 'Edith manifested no emotion of any kind at my return'.[43]

True to his motto 'In Labore Quies', Southey plunged into a demanding schedule of work. In addition to his work on Bell with Davies, his editing of Cowper and his *Lives of the British Admirals*, not to mention the fourth volume of *The Doctor*, he took on the task of revising all his poetry for publication in a new edition by Longman. The publisher had long been annoyed at a pirated French collection of his poems, and now retaliated by launching a definitive version of them to appear in monthly volumes, starting that autumn. Southey began with his first epic, *Joan of Arc*, which in view of the two editions of 1796 and 1798 gave him most difficulty. It was while he was commencing labour on it that he replied to a letter he had received out of the blue from the young Charlotte Brontë when he was at Buckland, asking his opinion of some of her verses. On the one hand he told her that she evidently possessed 'and in no inconsiderable degree, what Wordsworth calls "the faculty of verse"'. On the other, he discouraged her from seeking to make a career as a poetess, asserting that 'Literature cannot be the business of a woman's life, and it should not be.' It seems incredible that he should write such a reply to a letter he had received in the home of Caroline Bowles. However, he was not discouraging Charlotte from writing poems. Indeed he urged her to 'write poetry for its own sake'. What he was advising was that she should not make it her profession. She seems to have taken the advice well, for she replied to thank him, a reply that he told her gave him great pleasure.[44]

To add to his domestic worries at this time Southey learned that the arrangement for Cuthbert to receive tuition from John Warter, preparatory to applying to Oxford, was not working out well. Warter thought that his brother-in-law had not been well taught by his father, and even Cuthbert admitted that his education at home had not been systematic. Southey got wind of this and communicated his unease at it to Henry Taylor: 'the good and evil of public education and of private, as compared with each other, are so nearly balanced, that it would be difficult to say on which side the advantages preponderate. But life is uncertain, and it was a great object with me, feeling that uncertainty, to make his boyhood happy. Moreover the expense of a public school would have cost me no little anxiety, and must have put me to my shifts.'[45] He began to wish he had not sent Cuthbert to Tarring, not least because Warter had two other students, neither of whom were to his son's liking. 'One of these pupils is a thing to be loathed like toad or asp, – and the other not much more to be loved than frog or slow worm', Southey told Mrs Bray, passing on Cuthbert's opinion of them, and claiming 'that I never knew him to take liking or disliking without just cause'.[46] Cuthbert returned to spend July and August in Greta Hall. Southey was very anxious about the effect his departure would have on Edith. 'She will never have us out of her sight, if it were possible. There is a total wreck of every thing but her affections – those will remain while any glimpse of consciousness is left.'[47]

Tom's family, too, was creating problems again. In July his daughter Mary Hannah came to stay in Greta Hall on her way from Glasgow to Canterbury. 'My poor Edith took to her', Southey told Henry, 'and we were very desirous of keeping her as long as we could, looking upon her as a sort of God-send.' The girl's presence relieved Bertha and Kate of some of the burden of caring for their mother. She wished to stay too. 'But her mother, with characteristic temper, expressing herself as very severely hurt that she did not come home directly', ordered her to return. To add insult to injury she showed her total lack of understanding of Southey's predicament by insisting that he accompanied her daughter to Canterbury. He understandably refused.[48]

Cuthbert returned to West Tarring early in September to resume his preparations to enter Christ Church. When he presented himself there in October, however, he failed to gain admittance. His father put it down to the competition he had to face, for Cuthbert was one of thirteen out of twenty-five who were rejected. Southey's 'sole motive for fixing on Ch. Ch. first', he admitted, 'was because of Edward's [Edward Hill, Cuthbert's cousin] being there; otherwise so far am I from having any predilection for it, that I should prefer any respectable college; any except those halls which are either a refuge for the destitute, or a nursery for Evangelicals.'[49] In the event Cuthbert was accepted at Queen's College. 'I am sorry he is to be at Queen's owing to the society, which he must now seek out of college', John Warter observed. 'In his own they are mostly North-countrymen and sadly unpolished.'[50] Southey had banked on the thousand guineas he had been offered by Baldwin and Cradock to edit Cowper's works to pay for his son's college education. Unfortunately the publishers went bankrupt, and though the terms of the bankruptcy enabled them to pay him £800, there was an inevitable delay before he received it.

By mid-October Edith was 'sinking fast – thank God without any suffering either of body or mind'.[51] Early in November Southey noted that 'for several days when I have supported her downstairs, I have thought that it was for the last time; and every night when she has been borne up, it has seemed to me that she would never be borne down alive.'[52] In the morning of 16 November Edith died. 'All is over', Southey wrote immediately to Henry. 'Life lasted much longer than I could have thought possible. But thank God she is now at rest.'[53] 'It is a blessed deliverance!' he confessed to Cottle.[54] 'In the midst of that anguish of mind which must be experienced by a heart like yours, in the severance of the nearest of earthly ties', Cottle replied, 'what abiding sources of consolation you possess in the recollection of the most exemplary and affectionate conduct displayed by you, towards the dear deceased, and that under the most trying circumstances.' He had not abandoned her in the Retreat, but taken care of her himself. 'This is precisely the conduct which those who knew you best, might and did expect. To the end of your days, your mind will be sustained by those consolatory recollections, and the Inspector of human actions has noticed, and will reward it!'[55]

CHAPTER FOURTEEN

Old Man (1837–1839)

Although Southey had long anticipated Edith's death, and resigned himself to his loss, when it came it affected him more than he had expected. 'The truth is that I am much shaken', he confided to Henry, 'I am full ten years older than when you saw me in the summer.'[1]

The loneliness of Greta Hall became increasingly unbearable. In January 1838, when Cuthbert left for Oxford, Kate went with him as far as London to stay with her uncle Henry. Southey was left with his sister-in-law Mrs Lovell and his daughter Bertha. Mrs Lovell usually spent the day in her own room, always had breakfast alone, and rarely appeared for other meals. Since in Southey's view her 'state of health and spirits would weigh down even more buoyant spirits' than his he did not miss her presence, though it meant that he was virtually alone in the house, as Bertha saw him 'scarcely ever but at meal-times'.[2] This marked 'a great change from what was formerly a large and cheerful family circle'.[3] The house had become desolate, and his 'habits, which were always domestic, might now be called recluse'.[4] He withdrew into his own world. Before Edith's illness came on he had admitted that 'I never talk much in company and never carry abroad with me the cheerful spirits which never forsake me at home.'[5] Now he was 'as much disposed to be silent in my own family as I ever was in company for which I felt little or no liking; and if it were not plainly a matter of duty to resist this propensity, I should never hear the sound of my own voice.'[6] His taciturnity was to be remarked on more and more in subsequent months.

Southey felt that he had to get away from Keswick for a while. 'This will be the most expensive year I have yet had or am likely to have on account of travelling', he anticipated, 'but the Admirals will cover all extras, and I shall not leave home till the means are secured.'[7] At that time he was planning to travel south with Bertha, who was to join her sisters in West Tarring in May, 'and spend the summer in the West'. He was also toying with the idea of going with Cuthbert for a holiday in France during the long vacation, if, as he hinted to John Kenyon, 'we could meet with a companion to our liking who had a French tongue in his head'.[8] However, a sudden crisis over his own health led him to go unexpectedly to London in March. He suspected that he had developed a hernia in his groin, a suspicion that a local physician confirmed. Southey was alarmed to learn from Wordsworth that failure to wear a truss properly could be fatal. Lying awake with anxiety he convinced himself that the diagnosis had been wrong, and sought a second opinion from a young doctor, who assured him that there was no rupture. Nevertheless the doctor advised him to seek expert advice from surgeons in London. Southey left Keswick on 20 March, and for the first time in his life went part of the way by train. In London he stayed with Isabella Fenwick, with whom Kate was also staying. While in town he consulted Sir Benjamin Brodie and Mr Copeland, both of whom 'confirmed the young surgeon's opinion and thus relieved me from very serious apprehensions'.[9]

Just before he left Keswick he learned that his brother Tom had died while sailing home from Demerara, where he was the harbour master. 'This event will bring on anxieties and vexations that come at an ill time', he commented. 'In London I found a letter telling me of my aunt's death at Taunton, a most remarkable and admirable woman . . . I am now the eldest of my race.'[10] While he was in town he encountered Thomas Carlyle again. 'It was our second and last piece of intercourse', Carlyle recalled, 'and much the more interesting, to me at least.' He was delighted to learn that Southey strongly approved of his *French Revolution*. They began to talk of Shelley, of whom Carlyle remarked 'a haggard existence that of his'. Southey replied 'it is a haggard existence', which Carlyle took to be a reference to his own as well as to Shelley's life.[11]

Southey returned to Keswick the way he had gone, again taking the train between Birmingham and Warrington. Cuthbert met him in London and accompanied him to Greta Hall for a month's holiday. After his son's return to Oxford, Southey welcomed the arrival of a late spring. 'The sun shines; the birds are busy, the buds beginning to open', he reported to his fellow poet Charles Swain, 'there is a vernal spirit abroad which carries joy to young hearts and brings the best substitute for it to those whose season for joy is past, never to return again.'[12] He took advantage of the good weather to go on longer walks than usual, 'because I am less sensible of the want of spirits when engaged in walking than at any other time and therefore spend more time out of doors than I might otherwise do.'[13] The consequence was the neglect of his literary labours, for which he felt less and less inclination. 'If locomotion be conducive to health', he remarked to Henry, 'I take never less than four miles for my daily dose, and twice a week make a morning's walk of from ten to twelve or fourteen without any fatigue. But my spirits give way under a perpetual sense of loneliness.'[14] His lowness of spirits led to despond. 'Whether Hope and I shall ever become intimate again in this world is very doubtful', he reflected, a remark made more poignant given his belief that without hope 'life is but a living death'.[15] Despondency had led him literally to despair. In his desperation he turned to Caroline Bowles.

'Early in the year 1838', Caroline recorded, 'Mr S[outhey] made proposals to me which (circumstanced as I then was) greatly distressed me, for I felt myself under the necessity of declining them, from a conviction that my infirm health, still more than my advanced age [she was then fifty], wholly unfitted me for entering into the married state. . . . My refusal sorely disappointed him, and after a faint show of acquiescence in it, he set himself to work with all his powers of heart and head to bring me to revoke it.'[16] He wrote her a series of letters begging her to become his wife, which she found hard to resist. Her replies clearly encouraged him, for he wrote to Henry Taylor at the end of May, 'I am in good health and good spirits – and in earnest correspondence with one whose health is of more consequence to me than my own. I intimate this to none but yourself as yet. If the result be as there seems reason to expect, the last chapter of my life will be the most interesting in the book.'[17]

Caroline, however, sustained her resolution, until 'at last he so far yielded to circumstances as to follow my advice and give up his purpose of coming immediately to Buckland, projecting in its stead a foreign tour.' About the end of May Southey committed himself to the projected trip to France with Cuthbert, when John Kenyon and Henry Crabb Robinson volunteered to accompany them. This put paid to the proposed excursion with Bertha and Kate, especially since work on the *British Admirals* required him to stay at home until July. He still continued to bombard Caroline with letters, hoping to break down her defences. 'My main business for the last two months', he confided to Henry Taylor on 22 July, 'has been correspondence the most remarkable that I was ever engaged in. All's well that ends well, and if this ends as seems probable I shall have good reason to be thankful.'[18] The pressure he put on Caroline was immense. 'The last miserable years have I know told upon me', he admitted, referring apparently to the period between Edith's going mad in 1834 and her death; 'but it is not too late. If you do not take me I shall assuredly break down . . . all will be over for me in this life and I care not how soon I join the departed.' Caroline, who had been so incapacitated that she spent 'half my time lying half dead on a sofa', began to feel 'a revival of health'. When Southey learned this he 'wrote day after day'. 'This has made me another creature', he assured her. 'It is not too much to say you have given me new life.' He looked to her to lift the depression he had sunk into. When she raised doubts about late marriages, he insisted that they had known each other intimately so long that 'we are already one. All that I desire in woman I should find in you. . . . You would participate in all my thoughts and feelings. There would be but one heart and one will. The one person in the world to whom I could look with perfect confidence for advice in all things, for encouragement in all my pursuits and material help and cooperation in many of them, would be the wife of my bosom.' These were Southey's criteria for the ideal partner, ideals that Edith, for all his praise of her as a spouse, had patently not matched. When he wrote to say that were he to marry Caroline he would 'be repaid . . . for long years of misery' he was surely not just referring to those which had elapsed since 1834.

Southey was responding to Caroline's undertaking, at the end of June, to marry him twelve months later 'provided the amendment in my health continued and his wishes remained unchanged'. He assured her that 'were life long enough and we young enough to afford it' he would 'wait as long as Jacob waited for Rachel with such a reward in view'. The Biblical allusion is instructive. Jacob had wished to marry Rachel, but was told by her father to wait for seven years, at the end of which he was tricked into a marriage with her sister Leah. It was not until another seven years had elapsed that he was at last united with Rachel. Again Southey was surely contrasting the years he had passed with his first wife, and those he anticipated spending with his second. He was prepared to abandon the planned visit to the Continent that summer, and to spend the time with Caroline, 'now that he had no wish and as he said no need to travel farther than to Buckland'. But she insisted that he should keep his commitment to his companions, who now included Humphry Senhouse and Captain William Jones, a friend of John Kenyon's. Before joining them in London in mid-August, however, Southey 'passed a few days to my heart's content with my old friend Miss Bowles, on the skirts of the New Forest'.[19] 'His hopefulness, his happiness were infectious', Caroline recalled. 'Never had I seen him so happy – never in better health of mind or body.'

It is curious that Caroline noticed no deterioration in Southey's physical or mental condition on this visit, since he had been encouraged to travel abroad by his son, and others in the party, because they were worried about the state of his health and spirits, and hoped that the holiday would improve them. There are signs that he himself was aware that his memory was not all that it had been. Just before he left London to go to France he wrote to Henry to ask him to 'discharge a commission which I forgot to discharge myself, my wits having taken of late to the unprofitable practice of wool-gathering'.[20] Yet that in itself indicated little more than the normal forgetfulness that comes with advancing years. His friends were to notice more ominous signs of senility. 'None of us in setting out were aware to how great

a degree the mind of the Laureate was departed', Crabb Robinson wrote in his
diary. 'He had lost all power of conversation and seldom spoke.'[21] Cuthbert,
too, 'could not fail to perceive a considerable change in him from the time we
last travelled together – all his movements were slower, he was subject to
frequent fits of absence, and there was an indecision in his manner, and an
unsteadiness in his step, which was wholly unusual with him. The point in
which he seemed to me to fail most was, that he continually lost his way, even
in the hotels we stopped at; and . . . although he himself affected to make light
of it, and laughed at his own mistakes, he was evidently sometimes painfully
conscious of his failing memory in this respect.'[22]

Yet the journal that Southey kept betrays no signs of failing mental faculties.
The confusion which his companions observed did not at that time extend to
his ability to express coherent thoughts on paper, either in the journal or in the
letters that he wrote while on his travels.[23] On the contrary, his descriptions of
the places they visited in their journey through Normandy and Brittany, and
down to the Loire, are lucid, informed and perceptive. When they were at
Vannes Southey realised that it would be possible to take in Chinon, though
they had not originally intended to visit that town. 'Upon mentioning this to
Kenyon, and expressing a wish . . . to see the place where Joan of Arc was introduced to the King, all the party agreed that such a diversion from our route was
worth making', he recorded. 'Indeed no travellers ever accommodated themselves more readily to each other's wishes.'[24] He seems to have been unaware
that his companions had 'resolved that Southey should be our single object of
attention. We would comply with his wishes on all occasions. And we never
departed from this.' Thus, as well as agreeing to go to Chinon, they had also
accepted his request to see the battlefield at Crecy.[25] It is a remarkable tribute
to his capacity for friendship that old acquaintances such as John Kenyon,
Crabb Robinson and Humphry Senhouse, as well as Captain Jones, whom he
met for the first time that summer, should be so solicitous for his welfare as to
accompany him on this excursion, and to acquiesce in his every desire.

After visiting Chinon they made their way to Paris, where they parted
company. Crabb Robinson and Senhouse stayed in Paris, while Kenyon and
Jones journeyed to the Netherlands, and Southey and Cuthbert went down
the Seine to Le Havre. 'Do not suppose that I am in bad spirits, or any way
given to depression', Southey wrote to Bedford from Paris. 'On the contrary
I am in good heart and hope, and look with more confidence to compleating
unfinished works, and executing others which have been long projected, than
I have for many years.'[26] On 11 October he and Cuthbert sailed from Le
Havre to Southampton, from where his son went on to Oxford, while he
hastened to Lymington. Caroline, to whom he had written at every resting
place on his continental tour, and who had written to him frequently, could

hardly believe that Cuthbert was totally ignorant of his father's feelings for her, especially since he had stayed with her to the very last minute before joining the party in London, and now returned immediately to her for an indefinite stay. She also hoped he might have worked it out, since she was particularly anxious about how Southey's children would react to their engagement. When she asked him 'if he thought Karl [the family nickname for Cuthbert] guessed how it was with us, his answer was "he must be a fool if he does not".' For the next eight weeks they settled down to 'that life of calm companionship in all things, of inseparable association to which he looked forward with humble hope as the portion of his latter days'.

Caroline decided that she could no longer keep their engagement secret from her friends and neighbours. They expressed their delight at it, their only concern being that she would leave them and go with him to Keswick. Southey was prepared to stay in Buckland, but she thought it best for his family that they lived in Greta Hall. When she persuaded him to inform his children about their projected marriage, Southey duly wrote to them. On 15 October he informed Bertha, concluding his letter with 'some natural tears it will call forth. But that I have done well and wisely for myself I am sure you will perceive, and that the change in my condition when it takes place, which will not be till June, will be to Kate's comfort and yours. I am perfectly satisfied Caroline will be to you as an elder sister. . . . You will love her the more for having made me myself again which under any other circumstances I never should have been.'[27] For some reason he waited five days before writing to Edith May, by which time he was aware she might have heard from her sisters. 'My home, I trust, may thus once again be made a cheerful one', he pointed out to her; 'as far as human foresight extends, I have provided against that loneliness which I must else have felt when any farther diminution of my reduced household might take place.'[28] The latter reference was to the proposed marriage of Bertha to her cousin Herbert Hill, a fellow of New College, Oxford, which was to take place when he got a living that would support them. Southey might also have been wishfully thinking of the death of his sister-in-law Mrs Lovell, whom Caroline was aghast to discover still resided in Greta Hall, having assumed that she had moved permanently to the Isle of Man. His letter to Cuthbert has not survived. Caroline noted of the replies that Edith May sent, 'the kindest – most frank-hearted – most feeling', while those from her sisters were 'the most proper – all I could expect'. However, 'from the son – the most undutiful and improper I have reason to believe, for [Southey] would never let me see it.' She was taken aback by this, since he had led her to anticipate that his children would welcome their marriage. When she eventually told this to Kate, who was to become her most bitter opponent in the family, she replied,

'I wonder you could be so credulous'. 'Cuthbert has written intemperately', Southey complained to Bertha. 'I shall take no notice of his letter, and in due time he will be sorry for having written in such terms, and the silence which I shall observe for some time shall be sufficient reproof.'[29]

Caroline's first impulse was to call off their engagement, but Robert responded so frantically to this that she became alarmed, and did not raise the subject again. It was the first sign she saw that he could easily be unbalanced. Another was his increasing gloom as the time for his departure to Keswick came near. She knew that one word from her would be enough to keep him at Buckland, but felt that he ought to spend the winter in Greta Hall, to finish his work on the admirals, and make provision for their arrival there after their wedding. Given what she later learned about the effects that the separation from her had upon him, she came to regret that she had refused his pleas to get married at once, and return to Keswick for Christmas as man and wife.

Instead Southey departed for Keswick on 3 December alone. 'I am in good condition', he wrote to inform Henry after his return to Greta Hall, 'and enter this day in good spirits and with good will upon my winter course of work and exercise.'[30] In January he renewed his subscriptions to the Church Missionary Society and the Society for the Propagation of the Gospel, though not to the Society for Promoting Christian Knowledge, since that 'was paid to Dr Jackson during my absence'.[31] Cuthbert recalled that 'on returning home for some of the winter months he partly occupied himself in hearing Mr Davies read over the notes and memoranda he had made during a visit to Swanage' to incorporate in the biography of Andrew Bell.[32] 'I pursue my habitual course of life with as much contentment, tho not with as much ardour, as in the days of my youth', Southey maintained. 'It will not be long before I shall have the History of Portugal in the press, and I continue to collect materials for a History of the Monastic Orders, for which I have long been preparing, and which I believe to be the most useful work on which I can employ the remainder of my life.'[33]

However, he was deceiving his friends if not himself. His motto 'In Labore Quies' was no longer efficacious. He added nothing to the life of Bell beyond what he had written before he went on the continental tour, and it was published as the first of three posthumous volumes. Even then Caroline had to edit it, while Cuthbert wrote the other two. The works he himself referred to were never finished. Above all he did not find peace. On the contrary, he wrote to Caroline every day saying that he would return to Buckland as soon as possible. She was worried that his obsession with communicating with her was bound to disrupt his other writings. When he announced that he intended to leave in February, before Bertha's wedding, she dissuaded him, feeling that his daughter would resent his missing her marriage to Herbert Hill. Southey acquiesced impatiently, and duly attended the ceremony on 12 March. Then 'immediately after the ceremony he took post for Penrith and there stepping into the London mail never set foot on ground but to get into the Southampton coach', Caroline recorded, 'and from thence into the carriage which brought him to my door by half past 10 on the second night after leaving Keswick.' He might have got there even more quickly if he had not come to a decision never to travel by train again, since 'the rapidity of railway travelling, if long continued, has a tendency to bring on a determination of blood to the head!'[34]

'When he arrived at Buckland his happiness, his full contentment at finding himself there again, is indescribable', observed Caroline. At first she and her friends noticed nothing unusual in his demeanour. 'But early in April some of those persons as well as myself perceived that there was a look of illness and debility about him.' Caroline also noted a 'languor' about him, a disinclination to write letters, let alone to work on his histories, 'though he transcribed for the press and made extracts as diligently as ever.' She put his languor down to influenza, which had affected them all, but was prolonged in Southey, who developed a persistent cough, with considerable phlegm. Caroline thought a change to the mountain air of Cumberland would do him good, and was prepared to bring forward the date of their wedding so that they could get away. Southey, too, looked forward to his daily walks around Keswick. Although he took them in Sussex, he found that he had to keep to the roads, since the fields were all hedged round and gated against trespassers. 'It will not be long before we shall have some walks together again', he wrote to William Davies on 24 April.[35]

The previous day Robert and Caroline had each written an epithalamium, on the same sheet of paper. His read

Moments there are in life, alas, how few!
When casting cold prudential doubts aside,
We take a generous impulse for our guide,
And following promptly what the Heart thinks best,
Commit to Providence the rest;
Sure that no after reckoning will arise
Of shame or sorrow, for the Heart is wise;
And happy they who thus in faith obey
Their better nature; err sometimes they may
And some sad thought lie heavy in the breast,
Such as by hope deceived are left behind;
But like a shadow these will pass away
From the pure sunshine of the peaceful mind.

Hers, after denying that she loved him for his land, money or lineage, continued:

> For all these things I loved thee not;
> But that thy noble mind,
> (Divinely framed, divinely taught)
> Left all so far behind,
>
> That when thy faith was pledged to me,
> I knew the bond was given,
> For time and for eternity
> For this life and for heaven.[36]

It is a bitter irony that both should lay stress on his mind, for the shadows that were darkening it were not to be dispersed by sunshine.

Caroline persuaded her close relatives Sir Harry Neale, who was to give her away, and the Reverend George Burrard, who was to preside over the service, to marry them about the middle of May. Unfortunately her aunt, Lady Rooke, died suddenly, 'and instead of our wedding Mr Southey had to attend with a long train of family mourners at her funeral almost on the very day he had hoped to be so differently occupied. It was an ill omen verily, and when he came home from the sad ceremony in a mourning coach with his crape scarf and hatband the sight chilled my blood, and it seemed to me as if Death came too near us at that time – almost a wedding guest.'

Robert and Caroline were married at last in Boldre Church on 4 June. 'A lovely day that was when it arrived', Caroline recalled. 'He was thoughtfully, deeply happy, and expressed his happiness as only he could have expressed it.' They went for a brief honeymoon on the Isle of Wight. On their return to Buckland they arranged to let the house before setting out for Keswick. Unfortunately no tenants were forthcoming, which delayed their departure. Meanwhile Southey's debility increased to the point at which Caroline became alarmed and sent for his brother Henry to examine him. She had almost resorted to that step a few days before her wedding when Southey had woken from a deep sleep under the impression that it was the day of the ceremony, and asked why she was not dressed for it. This had alarmed her so much that she had burst into tears, at the sight of which he came to his senses, and assured her that it was just a waking dream. Now she felt that his behaviour merited a medical diagnosis. Henry came at her bidding, but so as not to alarm his brother pretended that he was on business in the neighbourhood. His observations of Robert's conduct led him to conclude that there was mental disturbance, but that it was not due to anything organic, and would probably be cured by his return to Cumberland. Caroline was not altogether reassured by Henry's optimistic diagnosis, and asked Sir Harry Neale if he had noticed any signs of mental disturbance in her husband, only to be assured that he had observed nothing that could not be ascribed to the effects of influenza. Henry had not only given Caroline similar reassurance, but wrote to John May to tell him that Southey 'is not in a state to excite any present alarm and he would be much annoyed if he thought I had gone to Buckland on his account. So pray do not allude to his illness when you write to him.'[37]

Henry was right to feel that his brother would be annoyed if his friends raised the question of his health. 'Every one who writes to me supposes I am out of health', Southey complained to Henry Taylor, 'and instead of any more agreeable topic enquires what complaint has seized me.' As was his wont in responding to such enquiries, he denied that he had any other symptom than mild influenza. But the very letter that contains these denials documents his mental confusion. It goes on to inform Taylor that Kate was glad that Cuthbert's holidays were over, and quoted a letter from her in which she admitted that 'an idle man about a house is enough to drive me wild'. This then led Southey to assume that he was replying to her. 'I hoped to have heard by this time that I had received my quarter pension', the letter continues, 'in which case you would have had money and tea to your heart's content.' Having opened by addressing Taylor it concludes, 'God bless you Kate'.[38]

By August Caroline accepted that they would not be able to let her house at Buckland, and arranged for it to be taken care of in their absence. Two days before they set out she noticed that Southey had fallen into a gloomy silence. They then left Lymington, to her great distress and that of her neighbours, friends, and not least servants whom she had to discharge. Southey offered no word of solace when she shut the door of her cottage for the last time, and indeed uttered no word at all on their journey to his son-in-law's at West Tarring, their first stop. They then stayed in Harley Street with Henry, who again reassured Caroline about his brother's health. But a friend who saw Southey there was shocked by how much he had changed. 'The animation and peculiar clearness of his mind quite gone, except a gleam or two now and then. . . . The appearance was that of a placid languor, sometimes approaching to torpor.' According to Henry, Southey was 'aware of his altered condition and speaks of it openly'.[39] Still Henry was sanguine that 'the quiet of his own house and the constant care of a very sensible wife will much improve his bodily health, and as he gets stronger in body the powers of his mind will also revive. At present he is a very old man of his age – a year or two ago he was quite the contrary.'[40]

Henry's optimism proved to be ill founded. Southey's daughter Kate was appalled at how much his mind had changed for the worse since he had left home in March. 'My father did not know me', she claimed; 'twice shortly after his return, he looked me full in the face and asked me, who I was.'[41] Southey had anticipated 'much pleasurable penwork as soon as we reach home, where the books of which I stand most in need will be within arms length'.[42] A few days after his arrival at Greta Hall he wrote to tell Charles Wynn: 'I am now fairly settled with my books about me, resuming my wonted occupations, and about to proceed with certain works which have too long been left unfinished.'[43] On the other side of this letter Caroline added what she called 'a supplement' to it. She confided to Wynn what she was 'inexpressibly anxious to keep from general knowledge, that with a visible sinking of the physical frame there has been for some time past a weakening of the mental powers, not in the slightest degree pertaining to *irrationality* but causing a degree of confusion and bewilderment which makes it difficult – at times impossible – for him to arrange his ideas on paper, and for the present absolutely precludes all literary labour.' Although she hoped he would recover, 'in the mean time my only comfort is – and it will comfort you to hear it – that he is *perfectly happy* except when making fruitless efforts to employ himself with his pen.'[44]

The letter Southey wrote to his old friend Charles Wynn is recognisably in Southey's hand, but written so carefully and neatly that it is as if he were trying desperately to keep it under control. Previously letters to Wynn had been signed off with his initials, 'R. S.'; this one concludes with his signature, 'Robert Southey'. It is the last piece of writing known to have come from his pen. The rest is silence.

Epilogue

Anybody who has ever witnessed a friend or relative descend into the darkness of Alzheimer's knows that a point is reached when the patient is effectively lost to the world, long before he or she actually dies. For that cruel disease robs people not only of their memories but of their personalities, and all that made them unique individuals. The story of their last years is not really theirs but that of those who minister to them.

So it was with Southey, although whether he succumbed to Alzheimer's or some other form of dementia cannot now be diagnosed. After 6 September 1839 we can no longer document his life with his own words, but only draw on those of his family and friends. These follow a curiously similar pattern to those of Southey and his daughters on the progress of Edith's illness. At first they were optimistic of a cure. Henry was pleased to hear from Caroline in October that his brother 'reads and converses as usual, but is inclined to sleep always when left alone and never attempts to write. She thinks (not unreasonably) that he is resolved to give his mind perfect rest.'[1] Caroline even thought she detected an improvement in Southey's condition in November, though she accepted that 'we can look only to a very gradual amendment and I have prepared myself for a long season of anxious suspense.'[2] By the following summer, however, she had come to realise that her hope was ill-founded, when 'the sad conviction pressed itself upon me that all rational ground for it was giving way – that "the night when no man can work" was closing in on my husband's moral usefulness.'[3] Despite Henry's assurances to the contrary, there was 'an apprehension that organic affliction of the brain *may* be working its slow insidious course'.[4] At the end of 1840 there was no doubt in her mind that 'it has pleased God for many months past to afflict Mr Southey with serious and I fear hopeless illness, the nature of which (an organic disease of the brain) precludes him from all use of his pen to application of any sort.'[5] When Henry Crabb Robinson visited Wordsworth in January 1841 he offered to go to see Southey in Greta Hall, but Caroline did not wish him to visit. Robinson was relieved, writing to a friend, 'I should have no pleasure either in the sight or in the recollection of a man, once the object of my admiration for great and varied powers of intellect, in a state of all but idiotcy [*sic*].'[6] By July Caroline was complaining that 'it would seem (so profound is our solitude and isolation) as if it were forgotten that he is still of the number of the living', though she had to admit that 'my dear husband is not now capable of reading or taking cognisance of any book whatever.'[7] On Southey's sixty-seventh birthday, 21 August 1841, she wrote a poem to him which contained the lines

> I dare not pray
> That the mysterious veil be drawn away
> Which parts thee from this world and all its woes[8]

By then even Henry appreciated that 'the mind is gone; there remains mere animal life and that may exist for a long time. He does not suffer, thank God, but his best friends must now rejoice to hear that he is released from the trammels of the flesh by which his immortal mind is now bound down.'[9]

Henry visited Keswick in the autumn of 1842, but Robert did not recognise him. He then diagnosed 'organic disease of the brain'.[10] Ironically, the morning after he had gone, Caroline heard Southey cry out 'Brother! Brother!' – 'surprised and affected as I was by this unexpected indication of a sort of consciousness', she wrote to John May, 'I drew no flattering reference from it – from time to time the mind seems thus to flash into momentary light – an expiring sparkle – and then all is dark again.'[11] Henry arranged to send a wheelchair to Keswick so that Caroline could take her husband outdoors, as the 'apology' for one she had borrowed in Keswick that summer, when the weather was glorious, had been inadequate, while one she had made by a local craftsman had proved to be unusable.

Henry's gesture was welcome to Caroline, for her husband's relatives were not all supportive of her in her ordeal. On the contrary, Cuthbert and Kate took against their step-mother, accusing her of taking advantage of their father's mental illness to trap him into a second marriage. Bertha was still in mourning for her mother when her father wrote to inform her that he was engaged to Caroline. Kate left behind a bitter memoir in which she laid the blame for the divisions in the family firmly at Caroline's feet. Thus she recorded their first quarrel towards the end of September 1839. When she saw her father about to leave the house she asked him where he was going. His response, that he was going to see Mr Davies, led her to offer to accompany him, as she felt he could not find the house on his own. Upon seeing her about to leave with him Caroline commanded her not to do so, as she did not wish him to become dependent. Kate told Mrs Lovell that Southey's new wife was in denial, as a newborn baby was not more helpless. As this was said in the presence of the servant Betty, Caroline took particular exception to it. They exchanged angry words. Kate told her step-mother that 'the truth is Mrs Southey you have married an old man, and do not choose to allow it', a remark she later regretted. Caroline replied, 'God forgive you of that speech Miss Southey.'[12]

Clearly there were strong wills, and tempers, on both sides. At one time it almost came to blows, when Cuthbert stood up for Kate and Caroline accused him of threatening to strike her, an accusation he indignantly denied. Cuthbert and Kate objected to Caroline's presence in Greta Hall, which they regarded as an intrusion on their space. Their sisters were divided on the matter. Bertha, who lived nearby at Rydal, though she seems to have tried to stay out of it, came down on Kate's side. Edith May, however, sided with Caroline. Southey's friends found themselves drawn into the quarrel. Wordsworth admired Caroline, but felt she had treated Kate badly. Caroline for her part was critical of Wordsworth's reaction to her husband's illness. 'It will be two years next month since Mr Wordsworth has given any other token of remembrance of his old friend, except doing his utmost to misrepresent and injure his unhappy wife', she complained in July 1842. 'He has passed thro' Keswick, but never so much as sent an enquiry for Mr Southey to this house.'[13] Landor, on the other hand, was very sympathetic to Caroline's plight.

The unfortunate dispute was even prolonged after Southey's death. In February 1843 he had a seizure that so alarmed Caroline that she sent for Doctor Irvine, who drew a pint and a half of blood from Southey, then declared him '*safe for the present*'. Caroline reported that 'his nights have been sadly distressing for two months and more with convulsive agitation and other ill symptoms – very lately he has been hours of every night in a strong convulsive state, and I fear with suffering in his head.'[14] On 21 March Southey died, apparently of typhoid. Caroline 'closed his eyes for their long sleep'.[15] 'It has pleased God to remove my father to a better world', observed Cuthbert piously, 'an event which in the state of unconsciousness in which he had for so long been plunged we can but look upon as a happy release.'[16]

Southey's funeral took place in Crosthwaite Church on 24 March. The mourners were divided between the feuding factions. Caroline did not even invite Wordsworth, but he went anyway, driven over the hills by Edward Quillinan, his son-in-law. They joined Cuthbert, Bertha and Kate in the churchyard, while Caroline, Edith May and her husband John Warter stood apart. Quillinan recalled that the gloom was lifted by a pair of robins:

As the bearers bear the dead
Pacing slow with solemn tread
Two feather'd choristers of Spring
To the dark procession sing:
Heedless of the driving rain,
Fearless of the mourning train,
Perch'd upon a trembling stem
They sing the poet's requiem
Some sacred frenzy has possesst
These warblers of the russet breast,
To honour thus with friendship brave
A Poet's passage to his grave.[17]

Southey's requiem was also sung by Wordsworth, who composed lines that
were engraved on a memorial stone in Crosthwaite Church. They begin

Ye vales and hills, whose beauty hither drew
The poet's steps and fixed him here, on you
His eyes have closed! And ye, loved books, no more,
Shall Southey feed upon your precious lore,
To works that ne'er shall forfeit their renown
Adding immortal labours of his own.[18]

Caroline thought the lines 'utterly heartless and spiritless'.[19]

Caroline left Keswick shortly after the funeral, feeling that she had been
driven out of Greta Hall. Southey's family no longer had any need for it.
Cuthbert had married and taken up a living in Cockermouth, where Mrs
Lovell joined him and his wife. Kate had moved into a house on Vicarage Hill
in Keswick. They decided not to renew the lease on their former home, and to
sell its contents. Southey's beloved library of 14,000 volumes was put under
the hammer. He was so fond of his books that when Wordsworth last saw him
he was patting one, like a cat on his knee. When Southey informed Cuthbert
of the provision he had made for his family in his will, he told him that he had
made 'no estimate of my library, because if it please God that you should make
use of the books . . . they would be of more value to you than any sum that
could be raised by dispersing them'.[20] Cuthbert, who had more interest in field
sports than in study, had so little regard for his father's wishes that he sold the
books that Southey had devoted a lifetime to collecting. He had even bought
between seventy and eighty while they were together in Paris in October 1838.

Cuthbert had no compunction either in publishing the letter in which his
father had expressed his wishes, perhaps not appreciating that it reflected

badly on himself, though he suppressed any correspondence that he thought might cast a poor light on Southey. His *Life and Correspondence of the late Robert Southey*, published in 1849 and 1850, also perpetuated the family quarrel, for it airbrushed Caroline Bowles out of the story almost completely. Her role in Southey's life had to be asserted by her ally, John Wood Warter, in his *Selections from the Letters of Robert Southey*, which appeared in 1856.

It was on the basis of these editions that William Makepeace Thackeray formed his judgement that 'Southey's private letters are ... sure to last among us, as long as kind hearts like to sympathize with goodness and purity, with love and upright life.'[21] Jack Simmons reached a similar conclusion. 'Beyond dispute and without qualification', he maintained, Southey 'belongs to the great English letter-writers ... his letters show all his powers in turn at their highest. ... There he stands to the life: independent, irritable, generous, tender, kind-hearted, loyal – above all, intensely human.'[22] Recently, however, Southey's correspondence has been disparaged. 'He searingly records significant (even low) details about many of his contemporaries', writes Robert Woof. 'One enjoys the anecdotage but marvels at the acid candour with which he pronounces his judgements.'[23] It is true that Southey had very firm views about people, and expressed them strongly in his letters. Those he disliked could indeed be dealt with savagely. After his first encounter with Lord Somerville he described him as 'very amusing and certainly does not want talents, but his mind and his manners are coarse and vulgar; he is a nondescript mulish compound of butcher and courtier, both bad breeds, and the mixture worse than either.'[24] Similar pen portraits of people he took a dislike to could be multiplied. Yet, as Kenneth Curry observed, 'Southey's descriptions of most persons whom he met are good humoured.'[25] And alongside the negative dismissals of those he could not stand could be placed at least as many positive portrayals of those he admired. 'Charles Lamb is a person for whom all who know him entertain great regard', he acknowledged. Despite the fact that Lamb made one of the most vicious attacks on him in print, even more cutting than those of Hazlitt, Southey did not resent it. 'Except during that moment of irritation there never existed in him a feeling of unkindness towards me, nor even for a moment did any such feeling ever exist on my part.'[26]

Above all, what emerges from a reading of his letters is his ability to sustain a correspondence, and to maintain a friendship, over many years with so many correspondents. He wrote regularly to Grosvenor Charles Bedford and Charles Watkin Williams Wynn from their days at Westminster School together until Bedford's death in 1839, the year when his own malady incapacitated him from further correspondence with Wynn. It also brought an end to his exchange of letters with Joseph Cottle, whom he met in Bristol in

1794; John May, with whom he became acquainted in Portugal in 1796; and John Rickman, whom he first encountered in 1798. A close friendship he made later in life, that with Walter Savage Landor, which began in 1808, was one based on mutual admiration between the two poets. Landor's high opinion of Southey found expression in a memorial poem, which can serve as a fitting epitaph.

> In maintaining the institutions of his Country
> He was constant, zealous and disinterested
> In domestic life he was loving and beloved
> His friendships were for life and longer
> In criticism, in dialogue, in biography, in History
> He was the purest & most candid writer of his age
> In Thalaba, Kehama and Roderick the most inventive Poet
> In lighter compositions the most diversified.[27]

Abbreviations

BL	British Library
Cabral	Robert Southey, *Journals of a Residence in Portugal 1800–1801, and a Visit to France in 1838*, ed. Adolfo Cabral (Oxford, 1960)
CD	Charles Danvers
CW	Charles Watkin Williams Wynn
Dowden	*The Correspondence of Robert Southey with Caroline Bowles*, ed. Edward Dowden (Dublin, 1881)
GB	Grosvenor Charles Bedford
JM	John May
JR	John Rickman
Kirkpatrick	Robert Galloway Kirkpatrick junior, 'The Letters of Robert Southey to Mary Barker' (Ph.D. Thesis, Harvard, 1967)
LC	*The Life and Correspondence of Robert Southey*, ed. Charles Cuthbert Southey (6 vols, London, 1849–50)
NL	*New Letters of Robert Southey*, ed. Kenneth Curry (2 vols, Columbia, 1965)
NLS	National Library of Scotland
NLW	National Library of Wales
NYPL	New York Public Library
PW	Robert Southey, *Poetical Works, 1793–1810*, ed. Lynda Pratt (5 vols, London, 2004)
QR	*Quarterly Review*
Ramos	*The Letters of Robert Southey to John May 1797 to 1838*, ed. Charles Ramos (Austin, Texas, 1976)
RS	Robert Southey
Simmons	Jack Simmons, *Southey* (London, 1945)
SL	*Selections from the Letters of Robert Southey*, ed. John Ward Warter (4 vols, London, 1856)

Stanton	Michael Neil Stanton, 'An Edition of the Autobiographical Letters of Robert Southey' (Ph.D. Thesis, University of Rochester, New York, 1971)
STC	Samuel Taylor Coleridge
Storey	Mark Storey, *Robert Southey: A Life* (Oxford, 1997)
TPL	Thomas Philips Lamb
TS	Tom Southey
WT	William Taylor
WW	William Wordsworth

Notes

PREFACE

1. W. A. Speck, 'Robert Southey's Letters to Edward Hawke Locker', *Huntington Library Quarterly* 62 (2000), 170.
2. Robert Southey, *A Vision of Judgement* (London, 1821).
3. *QR* 12 (1815), 509.
4. *LC*, i, 2: RS to JM, 26 July 1820.
5. Bodleian Library, MS English Letters d. 110. f. 22: RS to Nicholas Lightfoot, n.d. [1816].
6. *LC*, iv, 327–8: RS to GB, 5 Dec. 1818.
7. Lionel Madden (ed.), *Robert Southey: The Critical Heritage* (London, 1972), pp. 461–3, 466.
8. Thomas De Quincey, *Recollections of the Lakes and the Lake Poets*, ed. David Wright (London, 1970), pp. 221–2.
9. Robert Southey and Caroline Bowles Southey, *Robin Hood: A Fragment* (Edinburgh, 1847), p. x.
10. BL, Additional MSS 30927 f. 106v: RS to TS, 17 Feb. 1804.
11. Madden, *Robert Southey*, p. 454.
12. Ibid., p. 157.

CHAPTER 1

1. Unless another citation is given, all quotations in this chapter are from the series of letters RS wrote to JM between July 1820 and January 1826, which were published in *LC*, i, 1–157.
2. The prints are described in Southey's *Letters from England* (3 vols, 1807), i, 19. In his own interleaved copy, now in the Brotherton Library, Leeds University, Southey observed 'how well do I remember these in my father's bed-chamber! He was a passionate hunter. I have heard him say that when he was apprenticed in London a boy past the shop-door with a hare in his & [*sic*] he burst out a-crying at the sight of it. London made him so miserable that he was soon taken from it.' Southey was to adopt his father's view of the city.
3. Stanton, p. 14. Southey made two versions of these letters, a fair copy, which he kept and which his son Cuthbert used in *LC*, and drafts that he sent to JM. The latter, now in Rochester University Library, were edited by Dr Michael Stanton for his doctoral dissertation.
4. See Simmons, p. 230.
5. Stanton, p. 40.
6. Ibid., p. 44.

7. *NL*, i, 151: RS to GB, 30 Sept. 1797.
8. See the interleaved copy of Southey's *Letters from England*, Brotherton Library, Leeds University (3 vols, 1807), i, letter 35, note by RS.
9. *NL*, i, 150: RS to GB, 30 Sept. 1797.
10. Stanton, pp. 49–50.
11. Bodleian Library, MSS Eng. Lett. c. 22. f. 76: RS to GB, 8 Nov. 1793.
12. Southey rarely mentioned his 'father's house' by contrast with those of his aunt at Bath and his grandmother at Bedminster. He did, however, confide to Grosvenor Bedford 'how much more accurate and perhaps a thousand years hence more valuable a book it would be [than the 'History of Portugal'] were I to write the History of Wine Street below-the-Pump, the street wherein I was born.' Bodleian Library, MSS Eng. Lett. c. 24. f. 3: RS to GB, 6 March 1806.
13. *NL*, i, 150: RS to GB, 30 Sept. 1797.
14. *SL*, iv, 473: RS to Mrs Bray, 6 Nov. 1836.
15. Robert Lovell and Robert Southey, *Poems* (Bath, 1795), 'Retrospect', p. 6.
16. 'Hymn to the Penates', *PW*, v, 130.
17. *Attempts in Verse by John Jones . . . with . . . an introductory essay on the lives and works of our uneducated poets, by Robert Southey* (1831), p. 158.
18. Southey, *Letters from England* (interleaved copy), i, 307. RS mistakenly calls his aunt's friend 'Mrs Delamere', presumably because he had just mentioned Isaac Delamere, who rented a house at nearby Buntingford 'when I was a school boy & I have been there with him'.
19. Cabral, p. 127.
20. Elizabeth Rowe, *Letters Moral and Entertaining* (3 vols, London, 1729–33).
21. Robert Southey, *The Life and Works of William Cowper* (15 vols, 1836–7), iii, 32 note.
22. Houghton Library, MS bMS 265.1: RS to GB, 2 Jan. 1803.
23. *LC*, i, 134: RS to JM, 29 Aug. 1824.
24. Simmons, p. 230 note 13.
25. NYPL, Berg Collection: RS to James Montgomery, 29 May 1815. Southey had encountered Sparrow's widow, who he 'understood . . . was not happy with him. Indeed it was impossible that she should be. It was mating the falcon and the dove.'
26. Southey, *William Cowper*, i, 16 note.
27. *NL*, i, 381: RS to CW, 11 April 1805.
28. *PW*, v, 264.
29. In May 1830 Southey dreamed that he was at a dinner 'and directly opposite me was my old schoolfellow and friend poor Bean', of whom he had heard that he had been killed by Malay boatmen while taking money from one island to another in his capacity as paymaster to a regiment. 'Presently Bean came round and stood by me. I asked him if he were dead or alive. "Dead" he said.' Dowden, p. 383.
30. Ernest Betham, *A House of Letters* (London, 1905), p. 112: RS to Mary Betham, 2 July 1809 (misdated 1808).
31. John Wood Warter (ed.), *Southey's Common-place Book* (4th series, 1851), p. 515.
32. Robert Southey, *Vindiciae Ecclesiae Anglicanae* (London, 1826), p. vi.
33. Ibid., p. 6.
34. The original edition of Picart's text was published as *Cérémonies et coutumes religieuses de tous les peuples du monde* (8 vols, Amsterdam, 1723–43).
35. *LC*, iii, 351: RS to J. M. Longmire, 4 Nov. 1812.
36. Southey, *Vindiciae* p. vii.
37. Dowden, p. 379.
38. *PW*, v, 102.
39. The manuscript of the three-volume novel is in the Bodleian Library, MS Eng. misc. e. 114. It was written between 13 July and 6 August. See Simmons, p. 24.

40. *The Byrth, Lyf, and Actes of Kyng Arthur*, with an Introduction and Notes by Robert Southey (2 vols, London, 1817), i, xxviii.
41. Bodleian Library, MS Eng. misc. e. 114. ff. 81–82v.
42. Ibid., ff. 44v–45.
43. Roland Baughman, 'Southey the Schoolboy', *Huntington Library Quarterly* 7 (1944), 254: RS to Charles Collins, 10 Dec. 1791. Southey refers to their school friend William Rough.
44. The first five were printed by T. and J. Egerton of London, and the last four by E. Jeffery. The only extant copies of *The Flagellant* are apparently a full set in the British Library and the first five numbers in the Beinecke Library at Yale University. All quotations are from the British Library copy. This is possibly the edition that Southey's uncle Herbert requested be sent to him, and which his son Cuthbert used for his account of the episode in *LC*, i, 167–8.
45. *LC*, iv, 320: RS to JM, 16 Nov. 1818.
46. Bodleian Library, MSS Eng. Lett. c. 22. f. 39: RS to GB [Dec. 1792].
47. John Field, *The King's Nurseries: The Story of Westminster School* (London, 1987), p. 54.
48. *NL*, i, 293: RS to JR, 18 Oct. 1802.
49. Bodleian Library, MS Eng. Lett. c. 22. ff. 5–6: W. Vincent to E. Dolignon, 9 April 1792; E. Dolignon to RS, 11 April 1792; E. Dolignon to W. Vincent, n.d. (copy).
50. *NL*, i, 4–5: RS to GB, 13 April 1792.
51. Houghton Library, MS Eng. 265.1.33. However, he still hoped to bring out another volume in a few months!
52. Bodleian Library, MSS Eng. Lett. c. 22. ff. 1–2.
53. Ibid.
54. Duke University Southey Papers: RS to TPL, *c.* 30 Sept. 1792.
55. Bodleian Library, MSS Eng. Lett. c. 22. f. 1.
56. *NL*, i, 14: RS to GB, 26 Dec. 1792.
57. W. A. Speck, 'Robert Southey and *The Flagellant*', *Harvard Library Bulletin* 14 (2003), 25–8.

CHAPTER 2

1. Bodleian Library, MSS Eng. Lett. c. 22. f. 9: RS to GB, 'Sunday at Theobalds' [16 April 1792].
2. Duke University Library: RS to TPL, *c.* 30 Sept. 1792.
3. See above, Preface p.xi.
4. *LC*, vi, 344: RS to S. Mackenzie, 3 Nov. 1837.
5. Roland Baughman, 'Southey the Schoolboy', *Huntington Library Quarterly* 7 (1944), 252–3, 267.
6. Dowden, p. 368.
7. Keswick Museum: RS to Edith May Southey, n.d.
8. *NL*, i, 8: RS to GB, 30 May 1792.
9. Baughman, 'Southey the Schoolboy', p. 262. RS to Charles Collins, 4 June 1792. The creed of St Athanasius, as it appears in the Anglican *Book of Common Prayer*, expounds the doctrine of the Trinity, commencing with the assertion 'that we worship one God in Trinity, and Trinity in Unity; neither confounding the persons; nor dividing the substance'.
10. Huntington Library, MS HM 4834: RS to WT, 26 Feb. 1802. Southey recalled that he undertook this voyage when he was the same age as his brother Henry had reached when he wrote the letter, i.e. eighteen.
11. Bodleian Library, MSS Eng. Lett. c. 22. f. 17: RS to GB, endorsed 'recd. June 21st 1792'.
12. *LC*, iv, 320: RS to JM, 16 Nov. 1818.

13. Duke University Library: RS to TPL, College Green, n.d. This letter was published by John Warter (*SL*, i, 5) with a PS – 'if you will have the goodness to write before the fourteenth of October' – which belongs to another letter. Many Southey scholars have been misled by this error into giving it a later date than it could have been written on, as it refers to events in France that took place around 20 June.

14. Bodleian Library, MS Eng. Lett. c. 22. f. 23: RS to GB, 29 Sept. 1792. Southey claimed that Vincent called him an atheist and that Jackson 'proscribes me as a pest of society'. *NL*, i, 17: RS to GB, 8 Feb. 1793.

15. NLW: RS to CW, [Aug.] 1802.

16. *LC*, i, 167: RS to GB, 20 Nov. 1792. Southey long remembered 1 March 1792, when the first issue of *The Flagellant* appeared. Even though it was written by Bedford, 'that circumstance did not prevent me from feeling that I was that day borne into the world as an author.' *LC*, iv, 319.

17. Duke University Library: RS to TPL, n.d. [?July 1792].

18. *LC*, i, 169: RS to GB, 20 Nov. 1792.

19. Duke University Library: RS to T. D. Lamb, n.d. [?July 1792].

20. *NL*, i, 10: RS to GB, 21 Oct. 1792.

21. *NL*, i, 12: RS to GB, 26 Dec. 1792.

22. Robert Lovell and Robert Southey, *Poems* (Bath, 1795), p. 14.

23. *LC*, i, 169: RS to GB, 20 Nov. 1792.

24. Dowden, p. 27: RS to Caroline Bowles, 7 July 1822.

25. *LC*, iv, 320: RS to JM, 16 Nov. 1818. Talus was a character in Spenser's *The Faerie Queene*, whom Astraea left behind on earth when she returned to heaven after sin began to abound. He was 'an yron man . . . made of yron mould, immoveable, resistless, without end'. He held an iron flail in his hand, 'with which he threshed out falsehood and did truth unfould.' Book V, canto I, verse 12.

26. NYPL, Pforzheimer Collection: RS to Anna Seward, 25 July 1807.

27. *LC*, i, 181: RS to GB, 4 April 1793.

28. *LC*, i, 174: RS to GB, 14 Feb. [1793].

29. NYPL, Pforzheimer Collection: RS to Anna Seward, 25 July 1807.

30. Bodleian Library, MSS Eng. Lett. c. 22. f. 64: RS to GB, 25 July 1793. On 4 August Southey wrote to GB that he had 'just met with a passage in Rousseau which expresses some of my religious opinions better than I could do it myself'. *NL*, i, 33.

31. *NL*, i, 13: RS to GB, 26 Dec. 1792. 'Ought not . . . that wretch who styles himself a philosopher to be shunned like pestilence, who, because Christianity has to him no allurement, seeks to deprive the miserable of their only remaining consolation?' *LC*, i, 174: RS to GB, 14 Feb. [1793].

32. *NL*, i, 64: RS to GB, 20 July 1794. RS had previously noted of Howe, 'God bless my tutor – but Duce take his lectures.' Bodleian Library, MSS Eng. Lett. 453 f. 191: RS to Nicholas Lightfoot, 22 Dec. 1794.

33. *NL*, i, 20: RS to GB, 5 May 1793.

34. Interleaved copy of Southey's *Letters from England*, Brotherton Library, Leeds University (3 vols, 1807), ii, 90.

35. Duke University Library, RS to TPL, 3 April 1793.

36. See ibid.; RS to Charles Collins, 31 March 1793: Baughman, 'Southey the Schoolboy', p. 270.

37. Baughman, 'Southey the Schoolboy', p. 270.

38. Duke University Library: RS to TPL, 3 April 1793. How far Southey missed female company might be deduced from his being distracted from a church service by 'terrestrial angels'. Baughman, 'Southey the Schoolboy', p. 273. In his poem 'The Chapel Bell', written in 1793, he compared Balliol College to a monastery.

39. Bodleian Library, MSS Eng. Lett. d. 9. ff. 127–8: RS to Henry Taylor, 7 April 1838.

40. Houghton Library, MSS Eng. 265.1.33: RS to T. D. Lamb, 17 May 1793.

41. W. Frend, *Peace and Union* (1793), p. 29.

42. Storey, p. 31.

43. *An account of the proceedings of the University of Cambridge, against W. Frend* (Cambridge, 1793), p. 92.

44. Richard Holmes, *Coleridge: Early Visions* (London, 1998), p. 48. Coleridge was then a student of Frend's at Jesus College.

45. Pierpont Morgan Library, attached to extra illustrated copy of Boswell's *Life of Johnson*: Edmund Seward to RS, 3 June 1793 (Seward wrote 'Wedn 5th May', but as 5 May was a Sunday and 5 June a Wednesday, and events discussed in the letter clearly occurred in May, this was obviously an error).

46. Duke University Library: RS to TPL, 3 April 1793.

47. *NL*, i, 22: RS to GB, 5 May 1793.

48. *NL*, i, 26: RS to GB, [1 June 1793].

49. *The Annual Anthology* (1799), p. 116. Yet immediately before this poem appear 'verses intended to have been spoken in the theatre to the duke of Portland at his installation as Chancellor of the University of Oxford in the year 1793'. In 1805 Southey published a review of poems by William Grove, public orator to the University of Oxford, in which he quoted the verses again, claiming that they 'were rehearsed in the theatre but not permitted to be spoken because the University of Oxford did not approve the [anti-war] sentiments which they express'. *Annual Review* 3 (1805), 593–4. The verses were written by Southey himself, despite his disclaimer here. *PW*, v, 432–5.

50. *NL*, i, 314: RS to CW, [7 June 1803].

51. Bodleian Library, MSS Eng. Lett. c. 22. f. 59: RS to GB, 8 June 1793.

52. Christopher Smith, *A Quest for Home: Reading Robert Southey* (Liverpool, 1997).

53. *NL*, i, 30: RS to GB, 31 [July] 1793. Southey must have discussed this with Bedford when they met in Oxford.

54. Keswick Museum: RS to Herbert Hill (junior), 12 May 1831.

55. Cabral, p. 262. The comment was made to Henry Crabb Robinson by a Mrs Hawker in 1838. She had been introduced to the Southeys when they visited Portugal, and she never saw Edith again after they returned to England. When she made the remark Robinson had just informed her that Edith had died. It could therefore be taken as flattery, though Southey himself was not present when the exchange took place.

56. *NL*, i, 31: RS to GB, 31 [July] 1793.

57. Ibid. Southey here echoes the charge of the sixth article against Frend that he had 'profanely reviled and ridiculed the most sacred offices of religion, as enjoined by the Church of England, and performed by its ministers'. *Proceedings of the University of Cambridge, against W. Frend*, p. 10. Frend unconvincingly defended himself by arguing that in this passage he was referring to the Roman Catholic Church. Ibid., pp. 145–51.

58. *NL*, i, 36–7: RS to Horace Bedford, 11 Dec. 1793. He made no mention of a girlfriend when he told Horace on 12 December of the attachments that made it impossible for him to emigrate to America singly. Ibid., p. 39.

59. *NL*, i, 42: RS to Horace Bedford, 12 Dec. 1793.

60. Robert Southey, *Joan of Arc* (1796), p. v.

61. As Lynda Pratt has shown, '*Joan* actually emerged over a period of two and a half years.' Lynda Pratt, 'Patriotic Poetics and the Romantic National Epic: Placing and Displacing Southey's *Joan of Arc*', in Peter J. Kitson (ed.), *Placing and Displacing Romanticism* (Aldershot, 2001), p. 89. Not the least of the changes were the lines contributed by Coleridge. See below pp. 54–5.

62. *NL*, i, 27–8: RS to GB, 14 July 1793.

63. Bodleian Library, MSS Eng. Lett. c. 22. f. 71.

64. Bodleian Library, MSS Eng. Lett. c. 22. f. 77: RS to GB, 8 Nov. 1793.

65. Bodleian Library, MSS Eng. Lett. c. 22. f. 79v: RS to GB, 13 Nov. 1793.

66. *NL*, i, 39: RS to Horace Bedford, 12 Dec. 1793. 'The visions of futurity are dark and

gloomy', he wrote to Horace on 22 December, 'and the only ray enlivening the scene beams in America.' Bodleian Library, MSS Eng. Lett. c. 22. f. 91.

67. *LC*, i, 187: RS to GB, 26 Oct. 1793.
68. Bodleian Library, MSS Eng. Lett. 22. f. 88v: RS to GB n.d. [endorsed 'rec'd 20 Dec. 1793']. The youthful Southey's knowledge of the United States seems a little sketchy to say the least. Americans might encounter hostile natives but scarcely tigers.
69. Huntington Library, MSS HM 4820: RS to WT, 12 March 1799. 'They did me some good', he added, 'but time has done more.'
70. Baugham, 'Southey the Schoolboy', p. 178: RS to Charles Collins, 7 Nov. 1793.
71. *NL*, i, 49–50: RS to GB, 2 Feb. 1794.
72. Bodleian Library, MSS Eng. Lett. c. 453. f. 191: RS to Nicholas Lightfoot, 22 Dec. 1793.
73. *NL*, i, 49: RS to GB, 2 Feb. 1794.
74. *NL*, i, 50: RS to GB, 2 Feb. 1794.
75. *NL*, i, 44: RS to Horace Bedford, 24 Jan. 1794.
76. *NL*, i, 51: RS to GB, 2 Feb. 1794.
77. Houghton Library, bMS Eng 265.1.2: RS to GB, 23 March 1794.
78. *PW*, v, 7–8.
79. NLS, MS 845. f. 101: RS to J. Horseman, 16 April 1794.
80. *NL*, i, 57: RS to GB, 12 June 1794.
81. *LC*, i, 205–7.
82. *NL*, i, 194: RS to Edith Fricker, 19 May 1799.
83. *NL*, i, 59: RS to GB, 25 June 1794.

CHAPTER 3

1. Yale University, Beinecke General MSS 298. 21: RS to James Montgomery, 6 May 1811.
2. *NL*, i, 58: RS to GB, 12 June 1794.
3. Yale University, Beinecke General MSS 298. 21: RS to James Montgomery, 6 May 1811. The letter claims that the utopia was 'to be founded in the wilds of America', but this destination was not decided upon, as Southey made clear to his brother Tom in 1810, 'till after I left Oxford'. *SL*, ii, 194: RS to TS, 11 Feb. 1810.
4. *NL*, i, 56: RS to GB 12 June 1794.
5. On 8 July 1794 he borrowed Hartley's *Observations on Man* from Bristol Library.
6. Bodleian Library, MSS Eng. Lett. c. 453. f. 197: George Burnett to Nicholas Lightfoot, 22 Oct. 1796.
7. *NL*, i, 60: RS to GB, 25 June 1794.
8. The complete poem was never published in Southey's lifetime. There is a manuscript in Southey's hand signed with his initials in the Pierpont Morgan Library MA 1472. A version was sent in a letter to William Smith MP in 1817 in an attempt to discredit the author. Duke University William Smith Papers: John Horseman to Smith, 15 July 1817. This was dated according to the French Republican calendar 'the sixth day of the first decade of the fourth month the third year of the French Republic, one and indivisible', i.e. 26 Dec. 1794. Nine verses of the poem were quoted by Coleridge in his introduction to a series of lectures he gave in Bristol in February 1795, and published in his *Conciones ad Populum* (1795), pp. 23–4.
9. Bodleian Library, MSS Eng. Lett. c. 453. f. 197: George Burnett to Nicholas Lightfoot, 22 Oct. 1796.
10. Joseph Cottle, *Reminiscences of Samuel Taylor Coleridge and Robert Southey* (London, 1847), p. 404; William Haller, *The Early Life of Robert Southey, 1774–1803* (New York, 1917), p. 128.
11. Bodleian Library, MSS Eng. Lett. c. 453. f. 197: George Burnett to Nicholas Lightfoot, 22 Oct. 1796.

12. *NL*, i, 61: RS to GB, 20 July 1794.
13. *PW*, i, 160.
14. *NL*, i, 69: RS to GB, 1 Aug. 1794.
15. Margaret Ellen Sandford, *Thomas Poole and his Friends* (2 vols, London, 1888), i, 101. Mrs Sandford, née Poole, recorded the anecdote as being 'according to tradition', p. 100.
16. *NL*, i, 73: RS to Horace Bedford, 22 Aug. 1794.
17. Richard Holmes, *Coleridge: Early Visions* (London, 1998), pp. 69–70.
18. *NL*, i, 72: RS to Horace Bedford, 22 Aug. 1794.
19. *NL*, i, 68: RS to GB, 21 Aug. 1794.
20. Sandford, *Thomas Poole*, i, 96–9.
21. James C. McKusick, '"Wisely Forgetful": Coleridge and the Politics of Pantisocracy', in Tim Fulford and Peter J. Kitson (eds), *Romanticism and Colonisation: Writing and Empire 1780–1830* (Cambridge, 1998), p. 116.
22. *Collected Letters of Samuel Taylor Coleridge*, ed. Earl Leslie Griggs (6 vols, Oxford, 1956–71), i, 85: STC to RS, 13 July 1794.
23. Sandford, *Thomas Poole*, i, 103. John Poole does not seem to have paid close attention to what the two said as he recalled that both 'had left Cambridge and had walked nearly all through Wales'.
24. Yale University, Beinecke General MSS 298. 21: RS to James Montgomery, 6 May 1811. A Socinian was a follower of the sixteenth-century Italian Unitarian Sozzini, Latinised to Socinus, who denied the divinity of Christ, but accepted the divine purpose of his ministry.
25. *NL*, i, 70, 71: RS to Horace Bedford, 22 Aug. 1794.
26. Nigel Leask, 'Pantisocracy and the Politics of the "Preface" to *Lyrical Ballads*', in Alison Yarrington and Kelvin Everest (eds), *Reflections of Revolution: Images of Romanticism* (London, 1993), p. 41.
27. Sandford, *Thomas Poole*, i, 99.
28. *NL*, i, 71: RS to Horace Bedford, 22 Aug. 1794.
29. Bodleian Library, MSS Eng. Lett. c. 453. f. 195: George Burnett to Nicholas Lightfoot, 22 Oct. 1796.
30. *Collected Letters of Samuel Taylor Coleridge*, i, 106. Coleridge did offer to add Southey's name if he insisted, but since he prefaced it by saying that 'it would appear ridiculous to put two names to such a work', it is not surprising that the offer was not taken up.
31. Simmons, p. 47. 'Elinor' and 'To a Nettle', the poems that appeared in the *Morning Chronicle*, were the first Southey published.
32. *NL*, i, 80: RS to GB, 27 Sept. 1794. Unfortunately Johnson chose not to publish them, and they did not appear until Southey published *Poems* in 1797.
33. *NL*, i, 72: RS to Horace Bedford, 22 Aug. 1794.
34. Robert Lovell and Robert Southey, *Poems* (Bath, 1795). Despite the date in the imprint, the volume appeared before the end of 1794. Poems by Southey were signed 'Bion' and those by Lovell 'Moschus'.
35. *NL*, i, 52: RS to GB, 13 Aug. 1794. The stream also inspired a sonnet, 'Corston', written in the Bowlesian manner.
36. *NL*, i, 81–2: RS to TS, 12 Oct. 1794.
37. Bodleian Library, MSS Eng. Lett. b. 4. f. 133: Edmund Seward to Nicholas Lightfoot, 3 Oct. 1794.
38. Bodleian Library, MSS Eng. Lett. c. 453 f. 195: Edmund Seward to Nicholas Lightfoot, 2 Jan. 1795.
39. Harry Ransom Humanities Research Center, University of Texas: RS to [Sara Fricker], 1794.
40. *LC*, i, 224–5: RS to TS, 19 Oct. 1794.
41. *Collected Letters of Samuel Taylor Coleridge*, i, 114.
42. Ibid., p. 123.

43. *NL*, i, 85–6: RS to TS, 6 Nov. 1794.
44. *The Poetical Works of Robert Southey* (10 vols, 1837–8), ii, 25. Southey seems to have become confused about the time of its composition, for in 1817, when a pirated edition came out to his great embarrassment, he claimed that it was written 'in the summer of 1794'. *NL*, ii, 153. See below pp. 171–2.
45. This reinforces the dating of the composition of the play to November, for the trials were held between 28 October and 22 November. The three were charged with treason for their support of the so-called British Convention, which met in Edinburgh in 1793 to advocate parliamentary reform. See John Barrell, *Imagining the King's Death: Figurative Treason, Fantasies of Regicide 1793–1796* (Oxford, 2000).
46. Bodleian Library, MSS Eng. Lett. c. 22. ff. 138–9: RS to GB, endorsed 'rec'd 23 Nov' [1794].
47. Cottle, *Reminiscences*, p. 12. Cottle slanted his version of events when he wrote this volume, and can only be relied upon when, as here, his facts can be corroborated from contemporary sources.
48. Ibid., p. 5.
49. *Collected Letters of Samuel Taylor Coleridge*, i, 132.
50. Harry Ransom Humanities Research Center, University of Texas: RS to [Sara Fricker], n.d.
51. *NL*, i, 91: RS to Edith Fricker, 12 Jan. 1795.
52. *LC*, i, 232: RS to GB, 8 Feb. 1795.
53. *PW*, v, 105.
54. Ibid., i, p.4.
55. *NL*, i, 93: RS to TS, 21 March 1795.
56. *NL*, i, 92: RS to TS, 21 March 1795.
57. *NL*, i, 94: RS to TS, 9 May 1794.
58. Quoted in *NL*, i, 42.
59. Dowden, p. 379.
60. *NL*, i, 93: RS to TS, 21 March 1795.
61. Cottle, *Reminiscences*, pp. 28–9.
62. *Collected Letters of Samuel Taylor Coleridge*, i, 164. Unless otherwise indicated quotations are from the long letter that Coleridge wrote to Southey on 13 November 1795. Ibid., pp. 163–73.
63. Bodleian Library, MSS Eng. Lett. c. 22. f. 191: RS to Horace Bedford, 12 June 1796.
64. Pierpont Morgan Library, MS MA 63/2: RS to Richard Duppa, n.d.
65. *LC*, i, 247: RS to GB, 1 Oct. 1795.
66. Bodleian Library, MSS Eng. Lett. c. 22. f. 142: Herbert Hill to RS, Lisbon, 24 Jan. 1795. RS was clearly so stunned by his uncle's letter that he sent it to Bedford.
67. *Collected Letters of Samuel Taylor Coleridge*, i, 158.
68. *LC*, i, 245: RS to GB, June 1795.
69. *NL*, i, 101: RS to GB, Oct. 1795.
70. *The Letters of William and Dorothy Wordsworth*, ed. Ernest de Sélincourt, vol. 1: *The Early Years*, second edition, revised by Chester L. Shaver (Oxford, 1967), pp. 153–4.
71. *NL*, i, 102: RS to GB, 17 Nov. 1795.
72. *NL*, i, 102–3: RS to GB, 17 Nov. 1795.
73. *LC*, i, 258: RS to Joseph Cottle, Falmouth, 1795. Coleridge would have appreciated the rectitude of this remark!
74. *LC*, i, 255–6: RS to GB, 21 Nov. 1795.
75. *LC*, i, 261: RS to GB, 'Falmouth Monday evening' [30 Nov. 1795].

CHAPTER 4

1. Joseph Cottle, *Reminiscences of Samuel Taylor Coleridge and Robert Southey* (London, 1847), p. 191: RS to Cottle, 15 Dec. 1795.
2. NLW, MSS 4811D: RS to CW, Lisbon, 29 Jan. 1796.
3. This was to appear in three editions, in 1797, 1799 and 1808. Robert Southey, *Letters written during a short residence in Spain and Portugal* (Joseph Cottle, Bristol; G. G. and J. Robinson and Cadell and Davies, London, 1797).
4. 'Lines upon Christmas Day 1795'. *PW*, v, 144–5.
5. *LC*, i, 260: RS to GB, 'Falmouth Monday evening' [30 Nov. 1795].
6. Southey, *Letters*, p. 267. The very title RS chose for his book echoes Wollstonecraft's *Letters written during a short residence in Sweden, Norway and Denmark* (1796), a work he much admired. *LC*, i, 311.
7. See below p. 85.
8. Southey, *Letters*, p. 59. RS is quoting from Wollstonecraft's *Historical and Moral View of the Origin and Progress of the French Revolution* (1794), p. 9.
9. Southey, *Letters*, p. 72.
10. Ibid., p. 81.
11. Ibid., p. 61. *PW*, i, 155.
12. *LC*, vi, 207: RS to A. Alison, 17 April 1833; *PW*, i, 5, 44.
13. Lionel Madden (ed.), *Robert Southey: The Critical Heritage* (London, 1972), pp. 41–2. Wordsworth thought the Preface was 'a very conceited performance'. Ibid., p. 40.
14. NLW, MSS 4811D: RS to CW, Lisbon, 29 Jan. 1796.
15. *LC*, i, 267: RS to GB, 24 Feb. 1796.
16. See Malcolm Jack, *Sintra: A Glorious Eden* (Manchester, 2002).
17. Southey, *Letters*, p. 547.
18. *NL*, i, 108 note.
19. Houghton Library, MSS Eng. 265. 1: RS to Horace Bedford, 13 Oct. 1796.
20. Ramos, p. 47.
21. *NL*, i, 118: RS to GB, [17 Nov.] 1796.
22. Carlisle Public Library, Diaries of James Losh, entries for 13 and 14 Nov., 4 and 13 Dec. 1796, 2 February 1797. For Losh see Jeffrey Smith, 'James Losh: His Ideas in Relation to his Circle and his Time', Ph.D. Thesis, University of Northumbria, 1996.
23. John Wood Warter (ed.), *Southey's Common-Place Book* (4th series, 1851), p. 45. As Warter comments in a note, he had begun the poem in 1794, and started to revise it on 22 Feb. 1797.
24. *On the French Revolution by Mr Necker translated from the French* (2 vols, 1797). John Aikin translated the first volume. Neither translator is acknowledged in this English edition.
25. *NL*, i, 134: RS to GB, 16 July 1797. 'Three or four such jobs would furnish me a house' Southey observed to his brother Tom. *LC*, i, 307: RS to TS, 31 March 1797.
26. Dr Williams' Library, Crabb Robinson MSS: Henry Crabb Robinson to Thomas Robinson, 11 April 1797.
27. Bodleian Library, MSS Eng. Lett. c. 22. f. 192v: RS to Horace Bedford, 12 June 1796.
28. Cottle, *Reminiscences*, p. 203: RS to Joseph Cottle, 6 March 1797.
29. Peter Cochran, 'Why did Byron hate Southey?', paper read to the Newstead Abbey Byron Society, pp. 6–7. Byron was reacting furiously to Southey's accusation that he had an affair with Mary Godwin, Wollstonecraft's daughter by William Godwin.
30. Cottle, *Reminiscences*, p. 204.
31. Ibid., p. 200: RS to Joseph Cottle, Nov. 1796.
32. Princeton University Library, MSS, Robert Taylor Collection RTO1/RHT: RS to STC, 16 Jan. 1800. When Southey heard of Babeuf's execution he wrote to Horace Bedford on 11 June 1797: 'She [France] has now no man left whom we may compare with the Gracchi'. Bodleian Library, MSS Eng. Lett. c. 22. f. 194 (out of chronological sequence).

33. Cottle, *Reminiscences*, p. 213: RS to Joseph Cottle, 14 June 1797.
34. Ibid., pp. 214–15: RS to Joseph Cottle, 18 June 1797. Cottle added that when he met Rickman he found him 'seditious enough, that is, simply anti-ministerial'.
35. Princeton University Library, MSS, Robert Taylor Collection RTCO1/RHT: RS to Edith Fricker/Southey, 21 June 1797.
36. NLW, MSS 4811D (*SL*, i, 32): RS to CW, 2 June 1797.
37. Princeton University Library, MSS, Robert Taylor Collection RTCO1/RHT: RS to Edith, 21 June 1797.
38. Princeton University Library, MSS, Robert Taylor Collection RTCO1/RHT: RS to JM, 24 Aug. 1797.
39. *NL*, i, 148–9: RS to CW, 22 Sept. 1797.
40. *SL*, i, 46: RS to TS, 11 Nov. 1797.
41. A. S. Cottle, *Icelandic Poetry or the Edda of Saemund translated into English* (Bristol, 1797), pp. xxxiii, xxxvii.
42. Bodleian Library, MSS Eng. Lett. c. 23. f. 25: RS to GB, 7 Nov. 1797.
43. W. A. Speck, 'Robert Southey and the *Anti-Jacobin*', in H.T. Dickinson and Ulrich Broich (eds), *Reaction to Revolution: The 1790s and their Aftermath* (forthcoming).
44. Robert Southey, *Poems* (Bristol and London, 1797), p. 31.
45. *PW*, v, 64–5.
46. George Canning and John Hookman Frere, *Poetry of the Anti-Jacobin* (Woodstock, 1991), p. 6.
47. Madden, *Robert Southey*, pp. 59–60.
48. Samuel Taylor Coleridge, *Biographia Literaria*, ed. George Watson (London, 1975), p. 14.
49. *NL*, i, 160: RS to TS, 24 Jan. 1798.
50. Cornell University Library, Wordsworth Collection: RS to Joseph Cottle, 9 Dec. 1797.
51. RS to H. G. Standert, 14 Dec. 1809, quoted in Simmons, p. 71.
52. Bodleian Library, MSS Eng. Lett. d. 9. ff. 75–6: RS to Henry Taylor, 9 Oct. 1838. I am grateful to Dr Lynda Pratt for a transcription of this letter.
53. *LC*, i, 326: RS to TS, 24 Dec. 1797.
54. *NL*, i, 156: RS to Charles Biddlecombe, 24 Dec. 1797.
55. Keswick Museum: RS to TS, 12 March 1798.
56. Diaries of James Losh, quoted in E. P. Thompson, *The Romantics* (Woodbridge, 1997), p. 58.
57. *PW*, i, 52–3.
58. Ibid., p. 276.
59. Ibid., pp. 13–20.
60. Simon Bainbridge, *British Poetry and the Revolutionary and Napoleonic Wars* (Oxford, 2003), pp. 86–7. Bainbridge places the poem between June 1798 and 19 January 1799, when it appeared in the *Morning Post*, claiming that only later did Southey date it 'Westbury 1798'. However, the holograph manuscript in the Huntington Library is so dated. Dating is significant since the poem repeats the question 'was it for this?', which Wordsworth posed in the first line of 'The Prelude', also composed in 1798. It could be that he picked it up from Southey, although both probably came across it independently elsewhere. Among several sources claimed, that of Ariosto's *Orlando Furioso* cited by Howard Erskine-Hill is the most convincing. Ibid., 97–8. *The Contributions of Robert Southey to 'The Morning Post'*, ed. Kenneth Curry (Alabama, 1984), p. 20.
61. Ramos, p. 33: RS to JM, Norwich, 6 June 1798.
62. *LC*, i, 336: RS to Edith, 4 June 1798.
63. *LC*, i, 340: RS to TS, 27 June 1798.
64. *PW*, v, 226–8.
65. BL, Add MSS 47890 f. 20v: RS to TS, 29 Aug. 1798 (*LC*, i, 347), *Catalogue of Personal and Political Satires in the British Museum*, ed. Dorothy George, number 9240. 'New Morality – or – the promis'd installment of the High Priest of the Theophilanthropes,

with the homage of Leviathan and his suite', i.e. the English 'Jacobins'. The asses' ears were a reference to Coleridge's poem 'To a Young Ass'.

66. *LC*, i, 345: RS to CW, 15 Aug. 1798.
67. Huntington Library, MSS: RS to WT, 5 Sept. 1798; Houghton Library, bMS Eng. 265.1 (24): RS to JM, 26 Sept. 1798.
68. *The Critical Review* (1798), 197–204.
69. Christopher J. P. Smith, *A Quest for Home: Reading Robert Southey* (Liverpool, 1997), p. 271; Bainbridge, *British Poetry*, p. 96.
70. Bodleian Library, MSS Eng. Lett. d. 110. f. 5: RS to Nicholas Lightfoot, 4 Dec. 1798.
71. *LC*, i, 350, 352: RS to WT, 14 Dec. 1798.
72. NLW, MSS 4811D: RS to CW, 27 Jan. 1799.
73. *PW*, v, 270.
74. *LC*, ii, 12–13: RS to WT, 12 March 1799.
75. *Minnow among Tritons: Mrs S. T. Coleridge's Letters to Thomas Poole 1799–1834*, ed. Stephen Potter (London, 1934), p. 1: Sara Coleridge to Thomas Poole, 11 Feb. 1799.
76. Robert Southey (ed.), *The Annual Anthology 1799, 1800* (Woodstock, 1997), p. [i].
77. Huntington Library, MSS 4817: RS to WT, 12 March 1799.
78. *NL*, i, 183–95: RS to Edith, 13, 15, 16 and 19 May; Boston Public Library, MS Acc 461: RS to Edith, 20 May 1799.
79. *NL*, i, 191: RS to Edith Southey, 16 May 1799.
80. *NL*, i, 193: RS to Edith Southey, 19 May 1799.
81. Boston Public Library, MS Acc 461: RS to Edith Southey, 20 May 1799.
82. *SL*, i, 78: RS to CD, 20 Aug. 1799.
83. Warren U. Ober, 'Southey, Coleridge and "Kubla Khan"', *Journal of English and Germanic Philology* 58 (1959), 414–22. I am grateful to Professor Ober for an offprint of his article. He assumes that Coleridge was aware of the notes Southey had made in his commonplace books of sources for *Thalaba*. His assumption is supported by a reference to 'Sommona-Codom', which Southey made in a letter to Coleridge of 11 Oct. 1799, an allusion that could only be made to him if he were familiar with quotations from that Siamese deity from two books he had annotated. *NL*, i, 201.
84. *PW*, v, 395.
85. Cabral, p. 63: RS to GB, 12 Nov. 1838.
86. John Davy (ed.), *Fragmentary Remains, Literary and Scientific, of Sir Humphry Davy* (London, 1858), p. 43: RS to Humphry Davy, 12 Nov. 1799.
87. Huntington Library, MS HM 4826: RS to WT, 3 Feb. 1800.
88. Boston Public Library, MS c. 1.22.4: RS to JM, 27 Dec. 1799.
89. *NL*, i, 191: RS to Edith Southey, 16 May 1799.
90. Yale University, Beinecke General MSS 298. 14: RS to JM, 20 Oct. 1799.
91. Huntington Library, MS: RS to JR, 9 Jan. 1800.
92. *NL*, i, 215: RS to STC, 16 Jan. 1800.
93. *NL*, i, 221–2: RS to TS, 2 Feb. 1800.

CHAPTER 5

1. Cabral, p. 68: RS to TS, 23 March 1800.
2. Ibid., p. 71: RS to STC, 1 April 1800.
3. *NL*, i, 224: RS to JR, 2 May 1800.
4. Ramos, p. 56: RS to JM, 2 May 1800.
5. BL Add MS 30927 f. 50: RS to TS, 23 March 1800.
6. *LC*, ii, 64: RS to STC, 1 May 1800.
7. Cabral, p. 117.
8. *LC*, ii, 121: RS to JR, Oct. 1800.

9. *LC*, ii, 77: RS to his mother, 23 May 1800.

10. *LC*, ii, 79: RS to TS, 30 May 1800.

11. Cabral, p. 99. Malcolm Jack points out that among 'those who may have qualified as Southey's "Goths" [was] the naturalist Heinrich Link, whose writing on flowers and plants was published at the time of Southey's first visit.' *Sintra: A Glorious Eden* (Manchester, 2002), p. 175 note.

12. *SL*, i, 113: RS to JM, 23 June 1800. It has been claimed that Southey met Mary Barker on his first visit to Lisbon. This is to identify her with the 'female friend' he described to Bedford in February 1796 as 'a charming girl' but whom he did not name. *NL*, i, 105–6. However, Mary was not in Portugal at the time, and he did not meet her until 1800. See David Bradbury, *Senhora Small Fry: Mary Barker and the Lake Poets* (Whitehaven, 2003), p. 3. Notes to this booklet can be found on the internet at www.trochos.supanet.com/barker/barkernotes5.htm. Unfortunately Bradbury did not have access to Robert Galloway Kirkpatrick Jr, 'The letters of Robert Southey to Mary Barker from 1800 to 1826' (Ph.D. Thesis, Harvard 1967), cited here by courtesy of the Harvard University Archives.

13. Joseph Cottle, *Reminiscences of Samuel Taylor Coleridge and Robert Southey* (London, 1847), p. 224.

14. Ramos, pp. 58–9: RS to JM, 1 Sept. 1800.

15. BL, Add MS 30928 f. 5: RS to CD, 25 July 1800. Cabral published this letter, reading 'genial' for 'jacobinical', p. 104.

16. *NL*, i, 236: RS to CD, 20 Jan. 1801.

17. Cabral, p. 109: RS to CD, [13 Sept. 1800].

18. Cabral, pp. 139–40.

19. *NL*, i, 233: RS to CD, Lisbon, 18 Dec. 1800.

20. *SL*, i, 132: RS to JM, 16 Dec. 1800; 140: RS to his mother, March 1800.

21. *NL*, i, 244: RS to JM, 27 March 1801.

22. Cabral, p. 168: RS to CD, 6 May 1801.

23. Cabral, p. 39.

24. Sidney George West, *Robert Southey, the Rev. Herbert Hill and the Bishop of Beja* (1945). Although the letter is dated 'Castro 11 April 1801', it must have been written on the 13th as Southey was in Beja on the 12th and in Castro Verde the next day. Cabral, p. 39.

25. Cabral, p. 163.

26. Ibid., p. 52.

27. *LC*, ii, 151: RS to STC, 11 July 1801.

28. Huntington Library, MS HM4829: RS to WT, 27 July 1801.

29. *NL*, i, 248: RS to Henry Southey, [Sept. 1801].

30. Bodleian Library, MSS Eng. Lett. c. 24 f.106v: RS to GB, 6 Sept. 1801. Cf. *LC*, ii, 162, where Cuthbert substituted 'vile' for 'damned', one of his many censorships of his father's letters.

31. *SL*, i, 168: RS to Edith Southey, Sept. 1801.

32. Kirkpatrick, p. 5: RS to Mary Barker, 10 Oct. 1801.

33. *LC*, ii, 169: RS to Edith Southey, 20 Nov. 1801.

34. *NL*, i, 264: RS to JR, 19 Dec. 1801.

35. *NL*, i, 267: RS to JR, [Jan. 1802].

36. Kirkpatrick, p. 20: RS to Mary Barker, [Dec. 1801].

37. Huntington Library, MS HM 4831: RS to WT, 11 Nov. 1801.

38. *SL*, i, 175: RS to GB, 20 Oct. 1801. Livery and seisin were feudal terms signifying legal possession.

39. *NL*, i, 381: RS to CW, 11 April 1805.

40. *NL*, i, 260: RS to CD, 2 Dec. 1801.

41. *LC*, ii, 180–1: RS to CW, 9 Jan. 1802.

42. *LC*, iii, 35: RS to GB, 6 March 1806.

43. *SL*, i, 294: RS to CW, 7 Dec. 1804.
44. *Annual Review* (1804), ii, 574; *NL*, i, 269–70: RS to JR, 6 Feb. 1802.
45. *LC*, ii, 191: RS to STC, 4 Aug. 1802.
46. Lynda Pratt, 'Coleridge's marriage in 1801–1802: an unpublished letter by Robert Southey' [to Charles Danvers], *Notes and Queries* (March 2002), 15–18.
47. *NL*, i, 272: RS to CD, 27 March 1802.
48. *NL*, i, 276: RS to CD, 10 May 1802.
49. Kirkpatrick, p. 37: RS to Mary Barker, 1 Sept. 1802.
50. *NL*, i, 298: RS to Charles Biddlecombe, 11 Dec. 1802.
51. Houghton Library, MS bMS Eng 265.1: RS to GB, n.d. [Dec. 1802].
52. *LC*, ii, 360: RS to TS, 7 Dec. 1805. For reviews of *Thalaba*, see Lionel Madden (ed.), *Robert Southey: The Critical Heritage* (London, 1972), pp. 63–8.
53. *NL*, i, 296: RS to CW, 5 Dec. 1802.
54. Francis Jeffrey, *On the Lake Poets* (Poole, 1998), p. 78.
55. Ibid., pp. 79–81.
56. Ibid., p. 83.
57. Ibid., pp. 65–6.
58. Houghton Library, MS bMS Eng 265.1: RS to GB, 21 Dec. 1802.
59. *SL*, i, 215: RS to JM, [1803].
60. NLW, MS 4811D: RS to CW, [Dec.] 1802.
61. Rochester University, MS A. S. 747: RS to John May, 9 March 1803.
62. Ramos, pp. 73–4: RS to JM, 19 April 1803.
63. *NL*, i, 284: RS to JR, 24 Aug. [1802].
64. NLW, MS 4811D: RS to CW, 30 Nov. 1802.
65. *NL*, i, 298–9: RS to CD, 11 Dec. 1802.
66. *Annual Review* (1803), p. 3.
67. Ibid., pp. 208, 216.
68. Huntington Library, MS HM 4839: RS to WT, 23 June 1803.
69. Cottle, *Reminiscences*, p. 228. Cottle seems to have been unaware of another reason for Southey's failure to rent Maes Gwyn – the landlord's discovery of his radical politics. C. Tilney, 'Robert Southey at Maes Gwyn, 1802', *National Library of Wales Journal* 15 (1967–8), 437–50.
70. Victoria University Library, Toronto: RS to STC, 12 Jan. 1803.
71. Huntington Library, MS HM 4837: RS to WT, 11 Jan. 1803; WT to RS, 17 Jan. 1803.
72. *SL*, i, 213: RS to JR, 20 Feb. 1803.
73. Rochester University Library, MS. A. S. 747: RS to JM, 20 July 1803.
74. *SL*, i, 219: RS to TS, 13 July 1803.
75. Kirkpatrick, pp. 44–5: RS to Mary Barker, 1 June 1803.
76. Kirkpatrick, p. 59: RS to Mary Barker, 19 Aug. 1803.
77. Pierpont Morgan Library: Sara Coleridge to RS, n.d. [stamp 25 Aug. 1803]. Sara added: 'my husband is a good man, his prejudices and his prepossessions sometimes give me pain but we have all a somewhat to encounter in this life. I should be a very, very happy woman if it were not for a few things – and my husband's health stands at the head of these evils!'
78. *SL*, i, 78: RS to JM, 19 Aug. 1803.
79. NYPL, Berg Collection: RS to WT, 24 Aug. 1803.
80. Kirkpatrick, p. 62: RS to Mary Barker, 25 Aug. 1803.
81. *LC*, ii, 226: RS to TS, 8 Sept. 1803.
82. *SL*, i, 270.
83. Huntington Library MS, RS to JR 24 Aug. 1803.
84. Bodleian Library, MS Don. 3. f. 13.
85. *SL*, i, 230: RS to Mary Barker, 8 Sept. 1803.
86. NLW, MS: RS to CW, Aug. 1802. His biographers observe such a change in him around

this time. See Mark Storey, 'Romantic Biography: The Case of Robert Southey', in Arthur Bradley and Alan Rawes (eds), *Romantic Biography* (Aldershot, 2003), p. 38.

87. *LC*, ii, 234: RS to GB, 10 Nov. 1803.

CHAPTER 6

1. Kirkpatrick, p. 68. *SL*, i, 231: RS to Mary Barker, 8 Sept. 1803.
2. *SL*, i, 232: RS to JM, 22 Sept. 1803; *LC*, ii, 239: RS to Richard Duppa, 14 Dec. 1803.
3. *NL*, i, 325: RS to CD, 8 Sept. 1803.
4. See the plans of the house in Harold W. Howe, *Greta Hall: Home of Coleridge and Southey* (Sevenoaks, 1977), with revisions by Robert Woof, pp. 114–16.
5. *SL*, i, 353: RS to Mary Barker, Nov. 1803.
6. A. C. Grayling, *The Quarrel of the Age: The Life and Times of William Hazlitt* (London, 2000), pp. 89–90. *LC*, i, 238; RS to Richard Duppa, 14 Dec. 1803.
7. *NL*, ii, 93: RS to JR, 11 Jan. 1814.
8. *PW*, v, 419–22.
9. BL, Add MS 30928 f. 39: RS to CD, 19 Nov. 1803. Cf. *NL*, i, 336.
10. Huntington Library, MS HM4848: RS to WT, 23 Nov. 1804.
11. *NL*, i, 341: RS to CD, 9 Dec. 1803.
12. *NL*, i, 333: RS to CD, 7 Nov. 1803.
13. See Kenneth Curry, 'Southey's Contributions to the *Annual Review*', *Bulletin of Bibliography* 16 (1939), 195–7.
14. *NL*, i, 327: RS to JR, 12 Sept. 1803.
15. *Annual Review* 2 (1804), 295, 296. RS held that Malthus was attacking William Godwin's notion of human perfectibility: 'Mr Godwin has been knocked down by the wind of the pop-gun, the pellet has missed him.'
16. *SL*, i, 245: RS to John Kenyon, 19 Nov. 1803.
17. *Annual Review* 2 (1804), 546–7.
18. *NL*, i, 418: RS to GB, 22 March 1806.
19. Kirkpatrick, p. 73: RS to Mary Barker, late Nov. 1803.
20. *Annual Review* 2 (1804), 552.
21. Kirkpatrick, p. 73: RS to Mary Barker, late Nov. 1803.
22. *Annual Review* 2 (1804), 212.
23. Ramos, p. 88: RS to JM, 12 Dec. 1803.
24. NYPL, Berg Collection: RS to Henry Southey, 23 Jan. 1804.
25. *LC*, ii, 229–31: RS to TS, 29 Oct. 1803.
26. NLW, MS4811: RS to CW, 28 Sept. 1803.
27. *Annual Review* 2 (1804), 20.
28. *SL*, i, 275: RS to Mary Barker, 1 May 1804.
29. *LC*, iii, 21: RS to Nicholas Lightfoot, 8 Feb. 1806.
30. *NL*, i, 363: RS to JR, 15 Oct. 1804.
31. Kirkpatrick, p. 117: RS to Mary Barker, 29 May 1804. RS had expressed his dislike of the day in 'May 29 – Ode', written in 1798. *PW*, v, 206–7.
32. Ibid., p. 119: RS to Mary Barker, 8 June 1804.
33. *SL*, i, 123: RS to Mary Barker, 5 Aug. 1804.
34. BL, Add MSS 30928 f. 42v: RS to CD, 1 March 1804.
35. *NL*, i, 359: RS to CD, 11 Oct. 1804.
36. *SL*, i, 282: RS to CW, 28 July 1804.
37. NYPL, Berg Collection: RS to Richard Duppa, 29 March 1805.
38. *LC*, ii, 312–13: RS to GB, 20 Jan. 1805.
39. Ibid., pp. 225–31.

40. BL, Add MS 47891 f. 13: RS to John King, 28 Feb. 1805. He 'borrowed [the motto] from Garibay, one of my predecessors in Spanish history.'

41. Murray Archive: RS to John Murray, 27 Nov. 1813.

42. Kirkpatrick, pp. 126–8: RS to Mary Barker, Oct. 1804. Edith opened this letter, ostensibly, as she wrote in it, 'to see if he had given you a most terrific scolding'. Letters to Mary Barker appear to have been the only correspondence of her husband's that Edith inspected and added comments to, which might indicate a particularly close friendship between the two women, or a suspicion on his wife's part about Robert's correspondence with Mary. She added to this 'behold my two sisters and myself when we are talking about your behaviour . . . three Furies' and signed herself 'yours in great rage, Edith Southey'.

43. *The Letters of William and Dorothy Wordsworth*, ed. Ernest de Sélincourt, vol. 1: *The Early Years*, second edition, revised by Chester L. Shaver (Oxford, 1967), p. 516: Dorothy Wordsworth to Mrs Thomas Clarkson, 9 Dec. 1804.

44. *SL*, i, 290: RS to CW, 27 Nov. 1804.

45. *NL*, i, 369: RS to GB, 16 Dec. 1804.

46. Alethea Hayter, *The Wreck of the Abergavenny* (London 2003).

47. NLW, MS 4812D: RS to CW, 13 Feb. 1805 (not 4 April as in *LC*, ii, 321).

48. *Letters of William and Dorothy Wordsworth*, pp. 542, 544, 577.

49. Huntington Library MS, HM4850: RS to WT, 9 March 1805.

50. *Annual Review* 2 (1804), 312: RS's review of James Burney, *A chronological history of the discoveries in the South Sea or Pacific Ocean* (London, 1803). The 'strong evidence' was rehearsed in John Williams, *An Enquiry into the truth of the tradition concerning the discovery of America by Prince Madog ab Owen Gwynned about the year 1170* (London, 1791).

51. *PW*, ii, 8.

52. *LC*, ii, 324–5: RS to CW, 6 April 1805.

53. *NL*, i, 379–80: RS to GB, 6 April 1805.

54. Lionel Madden (ed.), *Robert Southey: The Critical Heritage* (London, 1972), pp. 103–4.

55. *NL*, i, 408: RS to Richard Duppa, 22 Nov. 1805.

56. *NL*, i, 395: RS to Joseph Cottle, 25 Aug. 1805.

57. Boston Public Library, MS C.1.22.6: RS to JM, n.d., endorsed 'rec'd 11 . . . July' [1805].

58. There is a brief journal of their journey in John Wood Warter (ed.), *Southey's Common-place Book* (4th series, 1851), pp. 526–31.

59. *SL*, i, 342: RS to CW, 20 Oct. 1805. Southey, who was just under six feet tall, described Jeffrey as being five feet, two inches in a letter to John Rickman on 27 Oct. and five feet, one inch in a letter to Richard Duppa of 22 Nov. *NL*, i, 406–7.

60. *LC*, ii, 348–9: RS to Edith Southey, 14 Oct. 1805.

61. Kirkpatrick, p. 163. It is perhaps significant that Warter omitted to publish this letter, though he clearly had access to all those between RS and Mary Barker.

62. Ibid., p. 186: RS to Mary Barker, 22 Feb. 1806. This was another letter Warter chose not to publish.

63. *SL*, i, 350. My italics.

64. *NL*, i, 407: RS to Richard Duppa, 22 Nov. 1805.

65. *LC*, ii, 42: RS to GB, 27 May 1806.

66. *Annual Review* 3 (1805), 708, 709.

67. NLS, MS 3875: RS to Walter Scott, 4 Feb. 1806.

68. *SL*, i, 362: RS to TS, 5 March 1806.

69. Ibid., p. 363. Warter omitted Southey's comment on Pitt, 'God be praised that the fellow is underground.' BL, Add MSS 30927 f. 109v.

70. *SL*, i, 358: RS to CD, 3 Feb. 1806.

71. *NL*, i, 416: RS to Henry Southey, 11 Jan. 1806. For Bishop Hatto see above p. 80.

72. *LC*, iii, 22: RS to Nicholas Lightfoot, 8 Feb. 1806. He also made the same observation that he had done to Mary Barker in Dec. 1801: 'I look the same way in the afternoon that I did in the morning but sunset and sunrise make a different scene.'

73. Bodleian Library, MSS Eng. Lett. d. 110. f. 9: RS to Nicholas Lightfoot, 8 Feb. 1806. His son Cuthbert omitted the passage following the words 'at the door' from *LC*, iii, 22.

74. Huntington Library MS HM 4872: RS to WT, 23 April 1806.

75. *NL*, i, 424: RS to Edith, 5 April 1806.

76. NYPL, Berg Collection: RS to Richard Duppa, 15 Feb. 1805.

77. *LC*, iii, 46: RS to GB, 5 July 1806.

78. BL, Add MS30927 f. 118: RS to TS, 28 July 1806. Cf. *LC*, iii, 51.

79. Bodleian Library, MSS Eng. Lett. c. 24. f. 20: RS to GB, 7–17 Sept. 1806.

80. *SL*, i, 395: RS to CW, 1 Oct. 1806.

81. *NL*, i, 448: RS to JR, April 1807.

82. *Annual Review* 5 (1807), 156.

83. Robert Southey, *The Remains of Henry Kirke White* (2 vols, London, 1807), i, 57.

84. Houghton Library, MSS Eng. 265.1.25: RS to JM, 29 Dec. 1806.

85. *NL*, i, 438: RS to TS, 25 February 1807.

86. NYPL, Berg Collection: RS to Charles Biddlecombe, 25 March 1807.

87. NLW, MSS 4812D: RS to CW, 27 March 1807. Cf. *LC*, iii, 69: RS to Richard Duppa, 27 March 1807.

CHAPTER 7

1. *LC*, iii, 73: RS to JM, 30 March 1807.

2. *SL*, ii, 2–3: RS to Mary Barker, 10 April 1807.

3. Kirkpatrick, pp. 234–5: RS to Mary Barker, 12 May 1807, a letter not published by Warter.

4. *NL*, i, 442: RS to CW, 27 March 1807.

5. 'Except a solitary sonnet to Lord Percy upon the slave trade I have not written a poem these seven years'. NLW, MS 4812D: RS to CW, Dec. 1809. The sonnet, beginning 'Percy! "Of virtuous father virtuous son"', Southey sent to Daniel Stuart on 21 March 1807 for publication in *The Courier. Letters from the Lake Poets . . . to Daniel Stuart*, ed. Mary Stuart (1889), p. 391.

6. NLW, MS 4812D: RS to CW, April 1807.

7. Bodleian Library, MSS Eng. Lett. c. 24. ff. 32, 38v: RS to GB, 14 and 27 March 1807.

8. Robert Southey, *Specimens of the later English poets* (3 vols, London, 1807), i, v–vi, xxix–xxxii.

9. *NL*, i, 444: RS to JR, 10 April 1807.

10. They are apparently quite rare. Jack Simmons, who edited a one-volume edition in 1951, observed that the Bodleian Library does not have a copy. Robert Southey, *Letters from England*, edited with an introduction by Jack Simmons (Gloucester, 1984), p. xxvi. A copy owned by Southey himself, annotated in his own hand, is preserved in the Brotherton Library, Leeds University.

11. Southey, *Letters from England*, Letter 12 and RS's note.

12. NYPL, Pforzheimer Collection: RS to Anna Seward, 25 July 1807.

13. Ibid.

14. Southey, *Letters from England*, Letter 56.

15. Ibid., Letter 12.

16. Ibid., Letters 26 and 38.

17. Ibid., Letter 61.

18. Ibid., Letters 29, 50–4, 57, 62, 64 and 68–7.

19. *LC*, iii, 88: RS to GB, 5 May 1807.

20. *SL*, ii, 50: RS to CW, 14 Jan. 1808.

21. NLW, MS 4812D: RS to CW, 14 Jan. 1808.

22. *LC*, iii, 122–3: RS to Walter Scott, 6 Dec. 1807.

23. *LC*, iii, 125: RS to Walter Scott, 6 Dec. 1807.

24. Huntington Library, MS HM4856, RS to WT, July 1807.
25. *Annual Review* (1808), pp. 122, 479.
26. Harry Ransom Humanities Research Center, University of Texas, MS: RS to [Anna Seward], 13 Feb. 1808.
27. *SL*, iv, 335–6: RS to Mrs Bray, 21 March 1833.
28. Dr Williams Library, Crabb Robinson MSS: Henry Crabb Robinson to Thomas Robinson, March 1808.
29. Ramos, p. 115: RS to JM, 16 April 1808.
30. Kirkpatrick, p. 280: RS to Mary Barker, 14 June 1808.
31. *SL*, ii, 77, 78: RS to JM, 29 June 1808.
32. Cornell University Wordsworth Collection: RS to Thomas Southwood Smith, 15 Aug. 1808.
33. Boston Public Library, MSS 333 no. 9.
34. Kirkpatrick, p. 298: RS to Mary Barker, 27 Sept. 1808.
35. *NL*, i, 484: RS to Humphry Senhouse, 19 Oct. 1808.
36. Victoria and Albert Museum: RS to Walter Savage Landor, 26 Nov. 1808; LC, iii, 116: RS to TS, 30 Oct. 1808. Cuthbert Southey, for once, did not censor his father's letter, for a word, presumably 'arse', is erased in the original in BL, Add MSS 30927 f. 143.
37. *NL*, i, 475: RS to Anna Seward, 28 May 1808.
38. Bodleian Library, MSS Eng. Lett. c. 24. f. 82: RS to GB, 9 Nov. 1808. Cf. *LC*, iii, 183–4, where Cuthbert Southey omitted the passage in (my) italics without indicating the omission.
39. Bodleian Library, MSS Eng. Lett. c. 24. f. 86: RS to GB, 18 Nov. 1808.
40. Harry Ransom Humanities Research Center, University of Texas: RS to John Morgan, 6 Feb. 1809.
41. *LC*, iii, 189: RS to GB, 24 Nov. 1808 [misdated 17 Nov. by Cuthbert Southey].
42. *LC*, iii, 198: RS to Walter Savage Landor, 26 Nov. 1808.
43. *NL*, i, 490: RS to Herbert Hill, 11 Nov. 1808.
44. *LC*, iii, 219: RS to GB, 12 Feb. 1809.
45. *PW*, iv, 83.
46. *NL*, i, 501: RS to Walter Scott, 11 March 1809.
47. Huntington Library, MS RS 139: RS to JR, March 1809.
48. Keswick Museum: RS to Herbert Hill, 8 March 1809.
49. Keswick Museum: RS to Henry Southey, 28 Jan. 1809.
50. *SL*, ii, 278: RS to White, 11 March 1810 [?]; *Lord Byron: The Major Works*, ed. Jerome J. McGann (Oxford, 2000), p. 6.
51. Keswick Museum: RS to Henry Southey, 28 Jan. 1809.
52. *LC*, iii, 224: RS to TS, April [misdated 14 March] 1809.
53. Kirkpatrick, p. 313: RS to Mary Barker, 13 May 1809. Passage omitted in *SC*, ii, 137–9.
54. Keswick Museum: RS to Henry, 27 May 1809.
55. *SL*, ii, 143: RS to CD, 22 May 1809.
56. Bodleian Library, MSS Eng. Lett. c. 24. f. 112: RS to GB, 9 July 1809.
57. Cumbria Archives Service, Carlisle, MS D/Lons/L1/2/60: Sir George Beaumont to Lord Lonsdale, 22 July 1809.
58. *LC*, iii, 245–6: GB to RS.
59. Cumbria Archives Service, Carlisle, MS D/Lons/61/2/60: RS to Sir George Beaumont, n.d. Beaumont forwarded it to Lord Lonsdale on 25 Aug. 1809.
60. Bodleian Library, MSS Eng. Lett. c. 24. f. 115: RS to GB, 12 Aug. 1809.
61. *LC*, iii, 248: RS to Walter Scott, 6 Aug. 1809. Southey's comment was fair enough, for Dutens published no serious work of history, and had mainly pursued a diplomatic career.
62. Cumbria Archives Service, Carlisle, MS D/Lons/61/2/60: Sir George Beaumont to Lord Lonsdale, 25 Aug. 1809.
63. Keswick Museum: RS to Herbert Hill, 31 Aug. 1809.

CHAPTER 8

1. Ramos, p. 118: RS to JM, 6 Dec. 1809.
2. *SL*, ii, 169: RS to TS, 18 Oct. 1809.
3. *LC*, iii, 262–3: RS to STC, [Oct.] 1809. Southey was fond of this comparison, making it in letters to John Rickman (*LC*, iii, 274) and Mary Barker (*SL*, ii, 189).
4. NYPL, Berg Collection: RS to JM, 4 Dec. 1808, written on a large prospectus for the *Friend*.
5. *NL*, i, 511: RS to CD, 15 June 1809.
6. *QR* 13 (April 1815), 234.
7. Keswick Museum: RS to Henry Southey, 30 Dec. 1809.
8. *QR* 3 (Feb. 1810), 218–62.
9. Ramos, pp. 120–1: RS to JM, 9 March 1810.
10. *SL*, ii, 187: RS to TS, 9 Jan. 1810.
11. *Edinburgh Annual Register for 1808* (1810), p. 64.
12. Huntington Library, MS 4865: RS to WT, 1 April 1810.
13. *Edinburgh Annual Register for 1808* (1810), pp. 25, 27–8.
14. Keswick Museum: RS to Herbert Hill, Aug. and 10 Oct. 1810.
15. NLS, MS 1817, p. 19: RS to James Ballantyne, 19 Sept. 1810 (copy).
16. Dr Williams Library, Crabb Robinson MSS, RS to Don Manuel Abello, 7 Nov. 1810.
17. Bodleian Library, MSS Eng. Lett. c. 24. f. 123v: RS to GB, 8 Nov. 1809.
18. *Edinburgh Annual Register for 1811* (1813), p. 32.
19. 'Perceval it seems is perfectly taken with my remarks upon the Methodists and would probably give me a living if I were in a situation to take one.' Keswick Museum: RS to Herbert Hill, 9 June 1811.
20. *SL*, ii, 203: RS to Walter Savage Landor, 27 Sept. 1810.
21. Lionel Madden (ed.), *Robert Southey: The Critical Heritage* (London, 1972), p. 137.
22. Kirkpatrick, p. 350: RS to Mary Barker, 24 March 1811.
23. *NL*, ii, 3: RS to GB, 14 Jan. 1811.
24. Kirkpatrick, pp. 345–6: RS to Mary Barker, [January 1811].
25. Huntington Library, MS HM4868: RS to WT, 21 Jan. 1812.
26. *Edinburgh Annual Register for 1809* (1811), p. 288.
27. Bodleian Library, MSS Eng. Lett. d. 47. f. 23: RS to GB, 14 March 1817.
28. NYPL, Berg Collection: RS to Lord Ashley, 28 May 1832.
29. Keswick Museum: RS to Herbert Hill, 9 June 1811.
30. *Edinburgh Annual Register for 1809* (1811), pp. v–vi. The advertisement is dated 27 July 1811, presumably the date on which the *Register* appeared.
31. *LC*, iii, 311: RS to GB, 9 June 1811.
32. Keswick Museum: RS to Henry Southey, 15 May 1811.
33. NLS, MS 1676 f. 28: RS to Robert Lundie, 19 May 1811 (copy).
34. *SL*, ii, 227: RS to Edith May Southey, 8 July 1811.
35. *Henry Crabb Robinson on Books and their Writers*, ed. Edith J. Morley (3 vols, London, 1938), i, 39–41. The poem on a Quaker developed into *Oliver Newman*.
36. Keswick Museum: RS to Henry Southey, 5 Sept. 1811.
37. BL, Add MSS 47890 f. 244v: RS to CD, 10 Jan. 1811; *LC*, iii, 295: RS to Walter Savage Landor, 11 Jan. 1811.
38. Murray Archive: RS to John Murray, 2 Nov. 1811.
39. *QR* 6 (1811), 289.
40. *LC*, iii, 319: RS to JM, 2 Nov. 1811.
41. *The Letters of Percy Bysshe Shelley*, ed. Frederick L. Jones (2 vols, Oxford, 1964), i, 183.
42. Ibid., i, 208.
43. *NL*, ii, 33–4: RS to WW, [April 1812].
44. *Letters of Percy Bysshe Shelley*, i, 212.

45. Ibid., i, 219.
46. *LC*, iii, 325–6: RS to GB, 4 Jan. 1812.
47. Kirkpatrick, p. 374: RS to Mary Barker, 8 Jan. 1812.
48. *NL*, ii, 21: RS to CD, 13 Jan. 1812.
49. *Letters of Percy Bysshe Shelley*, i, 233, 249.
50. Ibid., i, 223.
51. Bodleian Library, MSS Eng. Lett. c. 24. f. 189: RS to GB, Jan. 1812.
52. Mirehouse MSS, RS to John Spedding, 27 March 1811. I wish to thank Mr John Spedding for allowing me to cite this letter.
53. Bodleian Library, MSS Eng. Lett. c. 24. f. 189: RS to GB, Jan. 1812.
54. *NL*, ii, 23: RS to J. Burney, 19 Jan. 1812.
55. *LC*, iii, 326–7: RS to GB, 17 Jan. 1812.
56. *Edinburgh Annual Register for 1809* (1811), p. 122.
57. Geoffrey Carnall, *Robert Southey and his Age: The Development of a Conservative Mind* (Oxford, 1960), p.122. Geoffrey Carnall was the first historian to point out that the *Register* documents Southey's shift from radical to conservative more than any other source.
58. *LC*, iii, 32: RS to JM, 2 Nov. 1811.
59. BL, Add MSS 47890 f. 101: RS to TS, 7 Dec. 1811.
60. Murray Archive: RS to John Murray, 13 Dec. 1811. RS also outlined it to Colonel Peachy, BL, Add MSS 28603 ff. 9–10, 26 Dec. 1811.
61. A copy of the contract is in Rochester University Library, MSS A. S. 727.
62. Bodleian Library, MS Don. d. 6. f. 4: RS to R. Gooch, 23 March 1812.
63. Bodleian Library, MSS Eng. Lett. c. 24. f. 203: RS to GB, 16 May 1812. Cf. *LC*, iii, 339, where Cuthbert Southey silently omitted the sentence on plenary inspiration of the Scriptures.
64. NLW, MS 4812D: RS to CW, 20 May 1812.
65. BL, Add MSS 47890 f. 106: RS to TS, 27 May 1811. Cf. *SC*, ii, 274.
66. *LC*, iii, 341: RS to GB, 17 May 1812.
67. *SL*, ii, 281: RS to TS, 17 June 1812.
68. *SL*, ii, 294: RS to Neville White, 27 Sept. 1812.
69. Yale University, Beinecke General MSS 298, box 1, folder 21: RS to James Montgomery, 2 Jan. 1812.
70. Kirkpatrick, p. 380: RS to Mary Barker, 28 Jan. 1812.
71. Ibid., p. 385: RS to Mary Barker, 13 Feb. 1812.
72. Ibid., p. 399: RS to Mary Barker, 20 May 1812.
73. NYPL, Berg Collection, Mary Barker to RS, 24 May [1812].
74. *SL*, ii, 280: RS to Mary Barker, 9 June 1812.
75. BL, Add MSS 30928 f. 127: RS to CD, 5 Jan. 1813.
76. *QR* 16 (1812), 337.
77. Duke University, John Freeman Milward Doraston Papers: John H. Reynolds to Doraston, 28 Dec. 1812.
78. Robert Southey, *Southey on Nelson: The Life of Nelson*, ed. Richard Holmes (London, 2004), p. xliii.
79. Ibid., p. 288.
80. Murray Archive: RS to John Murray, 2 Nov. 1811.
81. Southey, *Southey on Nelson*, pp. 50, 51.
82. Ibid., p. xxviii.
83. Keswick Museum: RS to Herbert Hill, 1 Feb. 1813.
84. *SL*, ii, 321–2: RS to CW, 24 April 1813.
85. *NL*, ii, 59: RS to Herbert Hill, 21 May 1813.
86. *SL*, iii, 324: RS to CW, 23 May 1813.
87. Keswick Museum: RS to Herbert Hill, 18 July 1813.

88. Murray Archive: RS to John Murray, 23 July 1813.
89. Ramos, p. 128: RS to JM, 29 Aug. 1813.
90. There was an attempt to revive the *Register* in 1814. John Murray, who had apparently discussed the possibility with Ballantyne, approached Southey about contributing to it. Southey replied, 'You lead me into temptation when you hint at a continuance of the Register. I threw it up because my payments were stopt in an unhandsome way.' Murray Archive: RS to John Murray, 12 Dec. 1814. 'If Murray were to offer me 500£ for a Register', he told Bedford on 22 Dec., 'I certainly should not for a moment hesitate.' He balked, however, at writing the history from 1812, and advised starting it with the peace. *LC*, iv, 92–3. On 23 Dec. RS wrote to Ballantyne, 'I do not think I could do better than renew a labour which was not laid down for want of inclination to continue it.' Rochester University MS A. S. 727. Nothing came of the proposal. It was not until Oct. 1818 that Southey received his final payment from Ballantyne. *SL*, iii, 104: RS to GB, 26 Oct. 1818.

CHAPTER 9

1. Robert Southey, *The Doctor*, ed. John Wood Warter (London, 1848), p. 1.
2. *NL*, ii, 67, 72: RS to Edith Southey, 5 and 16 Sept. 1813.
3. Pierpont Morgan Library, MS MA 1005: RS to John Wilson Croker, 25 Nov. 1812.
4. *LC*, iv, 42: RS to CW, 20 Sept. 1813. 'You will admire the reason', Southey told Wynn, 'and infer from it that I ought to have been made historiographer because I had written Madoc.'
5. *NL*, ii, 64: RS to Walter Scott, 31 Aug. 1813.
6. *NL*, ii, 66: RS to Edith Southey, 5 Sept. 1813.
7. *Henry Crabb Robinson on Books and their Writers*, ed. Edith J. Morley (3 vols, London, 1938), i, 132. WW in fact published *The Excursion* in 1814; he announced it as the second part of his projected *The Recluse*, which he never completed.
8. *NL*, ii, 77: RS to Edith Southey, 28 Sept. 1813.
9. BL, Add MSS 47887 f. 113: RS to Mary Barker, 9 Nov. 1813.
10. *NL*, ii, 91: RS to CD, 7 Jan. 1814.
11. Kirkpatrick, p. 427: RS to Mary Barker, 14 May 1814.
12. Southey, *The Doctor*, p. 10.
13. Murray Archive: RS to John Murray, 27 Nov. 1813.
14. *SL*, ii, 340: RS to Neville White, 12 Dec. 1813.
15. *LC*, iv, 52: RS to JR, 17 Dec. 1813.
16. *LC*, iv, 54: RS to Herbert Hill, 28 Dec. 1813.
17. Bodleian Library, MS Don d. 3 f. 76v: RS to Henry Southey, 2 March 1814.
18. *SL*, ii, 338: RS to Walter Savage Landor, 16 Nov. 1813.
19. Quoted in Storey, p. 229.
20. *NL*, ii, 93: RS to JR, 11 Jan. 1814.
21. Bodleian Library, MSS Eng. Lett. c. 25. f. 74v: RS to GB, 13 April 1814.
22. *LC*, iv, 73: RS to Neville White, 29 April 1814.
23. *The Diaries and Correspondence of James Losh*, ed. Edward Hughes (2 vols, London, 1962), i, 51.
24. *SL*, ii, 421: RS to GB, 8 Aug. 1815.
25. Robert Southey, *Roderick the last of the Goths* (London, 1814), pp. 116–34, Book Ten 'Roderick and Florinda'.
26. *Poems of Robert Southey*, ed. Maurice H. Fitzgerald (Oxford, 1909), p. vi.
27. Victoria and Albert Museum, Forster MS 48.G.31 f.19v: RS to Walter Savage Landor, 3 March 1813.
28. NLS, MS 2245: RS to James Hogg, 24 Dec. 1814.

29. *NL*, ii, 111: RS to John Wilson Croker, 6 Dec. 1814. Charlotte did get engaged again to Prince Leopold of Saxe-Coburg, whom she married in 1816 when Southey was able to recast the poem as *Carmen Nuptiale*.

30. *SL*, ii, 400: RS to JR, 12 Feb. 1815.

31. *QR* 13 (1815), 54.

32. *LC*, iv, 117: RS to GB, 24 June 1815.

33. *LC*, iv, 121: RS to Henry Southey, 23 Aug. 1815.

34. *LC*, iv, 121: RS to Henry Southey, 23 Aug. 1815. As Mark Storey observes, 'so much for the happy, sociable family man'. *Robert Southey: A Life* (Oxford, 1997), p. 241.

35. W. A. Speck, 'Robert Southey's Letters to Edward Hawke Locker', *Huntington Library Quarterly* 62 (2000), 154.

36. Robert Southey, *Journal of a Tour in the Netherlands in the Autumn of 1815* (London, 1903), p. 50.

37. *LC*, iv, 127–32: RS to JR, 2 Oct. 1815.

38. *LC*, iv, 135: RS to JM, 6 Oct. 1815.

39. *Diaries and Correspondence of James Losh*, i, 63. The text is quoted from *The Poetical Works of Robert Southey* (London, 1850), pp. 727–56.

40. *NL*, ii, 126: RS to CW, 15 Dec. 1815.

41. Murray Archive: RS to John Murray, 'Wednesday 3 o'clock' [Nov. 1815].

42. *The Poetical Works of Robert Southey*, p. 728.

43. Brotherton Library, Leeds University, MS. There is a slightly different version in *LC*, iv, 190.

44. Kirkpatrick, p. 408. Mary wrote this passage in red ink at the end of Southey's letter to her of 9 June 1812. Warter printed it as a footnote to the letter. *SL*, ii, 279–80.

45. NYPL, Berg Collection: RS to William Wilberforce, 25 July 1816.

46. *SL*, ii, 279–80: RS to Mary Barker, 9 June 1812.

47. Columbia University MSS: RS commonplace book.

48. *LC*, iv, 177: RS to C. H. Townshend, 16 May 1816.

49. *Minnow among Tritons: Mrs S. T. Coleridge's Letters to Thomas Poole, 1799–1834*, ed. Stephen Potter (London, 1934), pp. 42, 47.

50. *LC*, iv, 181: RS to Herbert Hill, 4 May 1816.

51. *QR* 15 (1816), 2.

52. Lionel Madden (ed.), *Robert Southey: The Critical Heritage* (London, 1972), pp. 221–2.

53. *QR* 15 (1816), 227.

54. *Henry Crabb Robinson*, i, 192, 193.

55. Houghton Library, fMS Eng. 948: RS to Josiah Conder, 10 Dec. 1816.

CHAPTER 10

1. BL, Add MS 28603 ff. 23v–24: RS to Colonel William Peachy, 6 Dec. 1816.

2. Pierpont Morgan Library: George Canning to RS, 4 April 1817.

3. See above p. 106.

4. *Correspondent* 1 (1817), letter 3 and *Correspondent* 2 (1817), letter 1.

5. *SL*, ii, 326: RS to CW, 6 July 1813.

6. *SL*, iii, 53: RS to GB, 20 Jan. 1817.

7. On the emergence of 'a more tolerant, broader based Evangelicalism' during the Napoleonic era, see K. Hylson-Smith, *Evangelicals in the Church of England, 1734–1984* (London, 1988), p. 68 Let seq.

8. *Correspondent* 2 (1817), p. 176.

9. *QR* 31 (1816), 248, 271.

10. Thomas Love Peacock, *Melincourt* (1896; 1st edition 1818), p. 290.

11. See above, pp. 51–2.

12. *SL*, iii, 62: RS to JR, [2 March] 1817.
13. *LC*, iv, 251 note. Eldon also warned Southey that he could not recover damages 'for a work which is in its nature calculated to do an injury to the public'. This is sometimes taken to be the basis on which he refused an injunction. However, the ruling makes it quite clear that it was because Southey's claim to the copyright had been disputed. What the abstruse legal point seems to have been is that, even if he established his claim to it, he would not be able to sue for the damage to his reputation.
14. *NL*, ii, 154: RS to Colonel William Peachy, 9 April 1817.
15. *SL*, iii, 69: RS to CW, 6 April 1817.
16. *NL*, ii, 149: RS to John Murray, 14 Jan. 1817.
17. Princeton University, MSS, RS to ?, 22 March 1817.
18. *LC*, iv, 242: RS to Messrs Longman, 15 Feb. 1817.
19. *A Letter to William Smith M. P. from Robert Southey Esq* (London, 1817), p. 44; *LC*, iv, 390.
20. McGill University, MS 563: RS to Robert Bloomfield, 8 May 1817.
21. *NL*, ii, 158: RS to Edith Southey, 11 May 1817.
22. NYPL, Berg Collection, Journal, p. 10. This manuscript ends with the party leaving Paris on 21 May. There are fragments from the later Journal published in *LC*, iv, 267–9, 273–4.
23. *NL*, ii, 165: RS to Edith Southey, 2 July 1817.
24. NYPL, Berg Collection: RS to Joseph Cottle, 2 Sept. 1817.
25. *LC*, iv, 276: RS to CW, 23 Aug. 1817. Cuthbert Southey characteristically cautioned his readers against assuming that his father was a heavy drinker of wine.
26. Liverpool University Library: RS to Blanco White, 19 Nov. 1817.
27. *QR* 19 (1818), 81, 86.
28. Newnham College Library, Cambridge: RS to Edward Nash, 29 March 1818.
29. Kirkpatrick, p. 448: RS to Mary Barker, Jan. 1818. 'Pray of what order may the nuns be?' he asked her.
30. NLW, MS 4813D: RS to CW, 8 March 1818.
31. Pierpont Morgan Library, MS MA 1005: RS to John Wilson Croker, 11 May 1818.
32. William Anthony Hay, 'Henry Brougham and the 1818 Westmorland Election', *Albion* 36, 1 (2004), 42. The lines are from 'Rob Roy's Grave'.
33. *NL*, ii, 187: RS to TS, 11 July 1818.
34. Bodleian Library, MSS Eng. Lett. d. 47. f. 108: RS to GB, 6 July 1818.
35. Keswick Museum: RS to Henry Southey, 7 July 1818.
36. Brotherton Library, MS 8439. Excerpts from it were published in 1821 as an appendix to 'Carmen Triumphale'.
37. Keswick Museum: RS to Herbert Hill, 10 July 1818.
38. Dowden, p. 10: RS to Caroline Bowles, 17 June 1818.
39. Murray Archive: RS to John Murray, 18 Dec. 1818.
40. Keswick Museum: RS to Henry Southey, n.d. [late 1819].
41. Murray Archive, RS to John Murray, 19 Oct. 1819; *Lord Byron: The Major Works*, ed. Jerome J. McGann (Oxford, 2000), p. 373. Southey always called himself Robert, never Bob.
42. Keswick Museum: RS to Henry Southey, 24 Feb. 1819.
43. *SL*, iii, 123: RS to GB, 27 Feb. 1819.
44. Keswick Museum: RS to Herbert Hill, 25 June 1819.
45. Robert Southey, *Journal of a Tour in Scotland in 1819*, with an introduction and notes by C. H. Herford (London 1929), pp. 2, 184–5, 227.
46. NYPL, Berg Collection: RS to TS, 7 Sept. 1819.
47. *The Poetical Works of Robert Southey* (London, 1850), pp. 180–1.
48. *Journal of a Tour in Scotland*, p. 263. Yahoos were the ape-like creatures governed entirely by their passions in the last book of Jonathan Swift's *Gulliver's Travels*. Southey's employment of the term is an instructive insight into his dread of the mob. His son Cuthbert

suppressed his use of it. On 22 Oct. 1825 RS wrote to Henry Taylor to 'speak of large towns and manufacturing districts where the Yahoo population has outgrown the churches'. Bodleian Library, MSS Eng. Lett. d. 6. f. 28. Cuthbert replaced 'Yahoo' with 'neglected' (*LC*, v, 237). On 10 April 1826 Southey wrote to John Rickman that 'in some neap tide the Yahoos will break loose, Radicalism, Rebellion and Ruin will rush in through the breach which hunger has made.' Huntington Library, MS RS471. Cuthbert omitted the phrase 'the Yahoos will break loose' (*LC*, v, 250).

49. Pierpont Morgan Library, MS MA 1005: RS to John Wilson Croker, 9 Jan. 1820.
50. *NL*, ii, 202 note, where the whole of Southey's draft is reproduced. It accompanied a letter to General William Peachy. RS sent it to others including Sir Humphry Senhouse and Lord Lonsdale. Rochester University Library, Senhouse MSS; Cumbria RO Carlisle, Lonsdale Papers, D/Lons/L1/2/60.
51. *The Cumberland Pacquet and Ware's Whitehaven Advertiser*, 26 Oct. 1819.
52. *Carlisle Journal*, 30 Oct. 1819.
53. Rochester University Library, Senhouse MSS: RS to Humphry Senhouse, 17 Nov. 1819.
54. *LC*, iv, 360: RS to Neville White, 20 Nov. 1819.
55. *QR* 23 (1820), 28–30.
56. Ibid., p. 554.
57. *SL*, iii, 178: RS to Mary Barker, 10 Feb. 1820.
58. *LC*, v, 34: RS to GB, 26 March 1820.
59. Murray Archive: RS to John Murray, 5 April 1820.
60. *Monthly Magazine*, June 1820, quoted in Lionel Madden (ed.), *Robert Southey: The Critical Heritage* (London, 1972), p. 272.
61. *SL*, iii, 234: RS to T. Longman, 7 Feb. 1821.
62. *The Poetical Works of Robert Southey* (1850), pp. 207–8, where the poem is misdated 1820.
63. *Henry Crabb Robinson on Books and their Writers*, ed. Edith J. Morley (3 vols, London, 1938), i, 239.
64. *LC*, v, 83: RS to Nicholas Lightfoot, 2 June 1821. He also recalled it as being, if not the most melancholy, then the loneliest day of his life. *LC*, v, 174: RS to GB, 27 April 1824.
65. *NL*, ii, 214–15: RS to Edith Southey, 16 June [1820], and note 4 citing J. T. Coleridge, *A Memoir of the Reverend John Keble* (Oxford, 1869), i, 93–4.
66. Dowden, pp. 357–66. There are facsimile copies of Southey's letters to Shelley in the Wordsworth Collection at Cornell University.
67. Ramos, p. 190: RS to JM, 18 Nov. 1820.
68. Keswick Museum: RS to Herbert Hill, 29 Nov. 1820.
69. *SL*, iii, 222: RS to GB, 26 Dec. 1820.
70. William Angus Knight (ed.), *Memorials of Coleorton* (2 vols, Edinburgh, 1887), ii, 202.
71. Byron, *The Vision of Judgement* (Paris, 1822), lines 720, 721.
72. W. Braekman (ed.), *Letters by Robert Southey to Sir John Taylor Coleridge* (1964), p. 118: RS to Coleridge, 18 Jan. 1821.
73. Robert Southey, *A Vision of Judgement*, Preface; cf. above, p. 117.
74. Keswick Museum: RS to Herbert Hill, 18 April 1821.
75. *SL*, ii, 262: RS to Herbert Hill, 2 July 1821.
76. *LC*, v, 98.
77. *QR* 25 (1821), 331, 347.
78. Madden, *Robert Southey*, pp. 290–2.
79. Cited in Peter Cochran, 'Why did Byron hate Southey?', pp. 6–7, paper posted on the website of the International Byron Society.
80. *LC*, v, 349–54.
81. Cited in Cochran, 'Why did Byron hate Southey?', p. 10.
82. Madden, *Robert Southey*, pp. 296, 299–300.

CHAPTER 11

1. Edinburgh University Library, MS La. IV. 3. 4: RS to David Laing, 20 Feb. 1822.
2. *NL*, ii, 249: RS to Joseph Cottle, 25 June 1823. He still had to complete *A Tale of Paraguay* and *All for Love*.
3. Robert Southey, *History of the Peninsular War* (1823), i, 2. Although it did not appear until 1823 the volume was sent to the press before the end of 1822.
4. *SL*, iii, 319–20: RS to Herbert Hill, 20 July 1822.
5. Princeton University, Taylor Collection: RS to Sarah Browne, 31 Jan. 1822.
6. Robert Southey, *The Book of the Church* (4th edition, 1837), pp. 169, 511, 545.
7. Sheridan Gilley, 'Nationality and Liberty, Protestant and Catholic: Robert Southey's Book of the Church', in Stuart Mews (ed.), *Religion and National Identity* (Oxford, 1982), p. 418.
8. *SL*, iii, 325–6. RS to Herbert Hill, 31 Aug. 1822. The 'History' was never published because, as Warter explained in a footnote to this letter, 'as a mercantile speculation Messrs Longman and Co did not consider that the publication would answer. IT BIDES ITS TIME.' Alas it no longer bides its time, since the manuscript, which Warter claimed he had in his possession, has since disappeared.
9. *SL*, iii, 340: RS to CW, 26 Oct. 1822.
10. *QR* 28 (1823), 510. January issue, published in July.
11. Pierpont Morgan Library, MS 4500: RS to Sir William Knighton, 25 Nov. 1822.
12. *LC*, v, 131: RS to GB, 20 Dec. 1822.
13. Lionel Madden (ed.), *Robert Southey: The Critical Heritage* (London, 1972), p. 303.
14. Huntington Library, MS RS427: RS to JR, 4 Jan. 1823.
15. Duke University Library, MSS, Sir William Napier to J. Colborn, *c.* 6 Jan. 1823.
16. Dr Williams Library: RS to Henry Crabb Robinson, 22 Feb. 1823.
17. *SL*, iii, 378: RS to JR, 1 Feb. 1823.
18. Keswick Museum: RS to Herbert Hill, 28 March 1823.
19. Murray Archive: RS to John Murray, 23 April 1823.
20. Keswick Museum: RS to Henry Southey, 5 May 1823.
21. *SL*, iii, 374–5: RS to CW, 25 Jan. 1823.
22. *LC*, vi, 288: RS to Edward Moxon, 2 Feb. 1836.
23. *SL*, iii, 383: RS to GB, 22 March 1823.
24. *NL*, ii, 245: RS to William Gifford. Curry gives the date as 'Spring 1823' though the original in the Murray Archive is endorsed 'April'.
25. *The Lancet*, 5 Oct. 1823.
26. Pierpont Morgan Library, Charles Lamb to RS, 10 May 1830.
27. Robert Southey and Caroline Bowles Southey, *Robin Hood: A Fragment* (Edinburgh, 1847), pp. viii, ix; RS to Caroline Bowles, 4 Nov. 1823.
28. Rochester University Library: RS to Cuthbert Southey, 14 Jan. 1824.
29. *NL*, ii, 262–3: RS to Edith May Southey, 1 Jan. 1824.
30. *SL*, iii, 416: RS to CW, 8 May 1824.
31. Dowden, p. 50: RS to Caroline Bowles, 9 Nov. 1823.
32. Ibid., p. 54: RS to Caroline Bowles, 28 Feb. 1824.
33. *LC*, v, 142: RS to George Ticknor, 16 July 1823.
34. Murray Archive: RS to John Murray, 6 Sept. [1823].
35. *LC*, v, 165: The bishop of London to RS, 25 Feb. 1824.
36. Murray Archive: RS to John Murray, 15 Dec. 1824.
37. Bodleian Library, MSS Eng. Lett. c. 26. f. 229: RS to GB, 23 Dec. 1824.
38. *SL*, iii, 464: RS to Henry Southey, 12 Jan. 1825.
39. *SL*, iii, 467: RS to Neville White, 17 Jan. 1825.
40. Victoria University Library, Toronto: RS to Charles Butler, 2 March 1818.
41. Huntington Library, MS LR327: RS to Edward Hawke Locker, 8 Jan. 1825.

42. Bodleian Library, MSS Eng. Lett. d. 6. f. 10v: RS to Henry Taylor, 24 Jan. 1825.
43. Keswick Museum: RS to Herbert Hill, 12 Feb. 1825.
44. Victoria and Albert Museum: RS to Walter Savage Landor, 28 May 1825.
45. *NL*, ii, 283–4: RS to Edith Southey, 9 June 1825.
46. *LC*, v, 232–3: RS to Kate Southey, 16 July 1825.
47. Dowden, p. 84: RS to Caroline Bowles, 27 July 1825.
48. Dowden, p. 88: RS to Caroline Bowles, 14 Oct. 1825.
49. Dowden, pp. 89, 92: RS to Caroline Bowles, 20 Nov. 1825; Caroline to RS, 8 Dec. 1825.
50. *SL*, iii, 504: RS to Herbert Hill, 4 Sept. 1825.
51. *QR* 33 (1826), p. 410.
52. *NL*, ii, 288–90: RS to Walter Scott, 25 Nov. 1825.
53. Harry Ransome Humanities Research Center, University of Texas: RS to John Coleridge, 11 Dec. 1825 (copy).
54. *SL*, iii, 514: RS to JR, 4 Dec. 1825.
55. NLW, MSS 4813D: RS to CW, 21 Jan. 1826.
56. Robert Southey, *Vindiciae Ecclesiae Anglicanae* (1826), p. xv.
57. *SL*, iii, 526: RS to Neville White, 11 Feb. 1826. Southey made a similar prediction to James Heraud. 'The steam engine cannot continue to go on half a century longer (probably not half that time) as it has during the last twenty years, without blowing up the whole fabric of society.' Huntington Library, MS HM6624: RS to James Abraham Heraud, 30 April 1826.
58. W. Brackman (ed.), *Letters by Robert Southey to Sir John Taylor Coleridge* (London, 1964), p. 173: RS to John Coleridge, 13 Feb. 1826.
59. *NL*, *i*, 305: RS to Edith Southey, 25 May 1826.
60. Kirkpatrick, p. 467: RS to Mary Barker, 21 July 1825.
61. *SL*, iii, 543: RS to Mary Barker, 30 April 1826.
62. Ramos, p. 217: RS to JM, 6 May 1826.
63. Kirkpatrick, pp. 477, 479: RS to Mary Barker, 'Christmas day' 1826 (not sent until 13 Jan. 1827).
64. *LC*, v, 262: RS to Richard White, 1 July 1826.
65. *SL*, iv, 7: RS to John Kenyon, 12 July 1826.
66. Keswick Museum: RS to Herbert Hill, 16 July 1826. See also *LC*, v, 255–9: RS to Edith May, Bertha and Kate Southey; *SL*, iv, 10–11: RS to Henry Southey; Kent Archives Office, MS U1590.359: RS to TS [copy].
67. *LC*, v, 252.
68. Yale University, Beinecke General MSS 298. 21: RS to Mary Brent Morgan, 30 Nov. 1826.
69. Ramos, p. 220: RS to JM, 15 Dec. 1826.
70. *LC*, v, 287: RS to Walter Savage Landor, 21 Feb. 1827.
71. *NL*, ii, 308: RS to GB, 14 Jan. 1827.
72. Library of Congress, Andrew Stevenson Papers, 1810–1859: RS to John Kenyon, 29 Jan. 1827.
73. *NL*, ii, 311 note.
74. Dowden, p. 122: RS to Caroline Bowles, 10 July 1827.
75. *SL*, iv, 61: RS to Mrs Hughes, 21 Sept. 1827.
76. *SL*, iii, 478: RS to Herbert Hill, 6 March 1825.
77. *QR* 36 (1827), 305.
78. *SL*, iv, 58: RS to Henry Southey, 26 April 1827. Southey's letter rejecting £50 is preserved in Newnham College Library, Cambridge: RS to R. P. Gillies, 2 April 1827.
79. *NL*, ii, 313: RS to John Murray, 16 June 1827.
80. Murray Archive: RS to John Murray, 28 July 1827.
81. Huntington Library, MS LR 331: RS to Edward Hawke Locker, 24 Sept. 1827.
82. BL, Add MSS 47890 f. 133: RS to TS, 24 July 1827.

83. Bodleian Library, MSS Eng. Lett. d. 148. f. 94: RS to GB, 24 Oct. 1827.
84. Murray Archive: RS to John Murray, 17 Dec. 1827.
85. *QR* 37 (1828), 260.
86. *NL*, ii, 328: RS to Henry Taylor, 29 Oct. 1828.
87. *NL*. ii, 124: RS to Caroline Bowles, 24 Feb. 1828.
88. *LC*, v, 323: RS to Allan Cunningham, 24 Feb. 1828.
89. Fitzwilliam Museum, Cambridge, Ashcombe Collection, II 28 (b): RS to [Longman], 'Harley street Saturday noon', [?31] May 1828.
90. *Henry Crabb Robinson on Books and their Writers*, ed. Edith J. Morley (3 vols, London, 1938), i, 357.
91. Keswick Museum: RS to Bertha, 1 June 1828.
92. *NL*, ii, 323: RS to Caroline Bowles, 24 Feb. 1828.
93. *SL*, iv, 81: RS to Mrs Hughes, 30 Dec. 1827.
94. Rochester University Library, Senhouse MSS: RS to Humphry Senhouse, 31 Oct. 1825.
95. Keswick Museum: RS to TS, 1 Oct. 1828.
96. Robert Southey, *Sir Thomas More, or Colloquies on the Progress and Prospects of Society* (2 vols, London, 1829), i, 38.
97. Cumbria Record Office, Carlisle, Lonsdale Papers D Lons/L/2/69/90, draft of Viscount Lowther to 'Sir George' [Murray, secretary of state for the colonies, May 1828–Nov. 1830] n.d. [1828]. 'I write at the request of Lord Lonsdale to ask an appointment which is shortly to become vacant for a brother of the Laureate, who as the most powerful literary supporter of the Tories in the present day is doubtless intitled to some consideration.' The post was that of auditor and clerk of the Council at the Cape of Good Hope. On 27 October 1828 RS recommended the Cape to his brother Tom. *SL*, iv, 120.

CHAPTER 12

1. Robert Southey, *Sir Thomas More, or Colloquies on the Progress and Prospects of Society* (2 vols, London, 1829), i, xiii–xiv.
2. *Henry Crabb Robinson on Books and their Writers*, ed. Edith J. Morley (3 vols, London, 1938), i, 359–60.
3. Bodleian Library, MSS Eng. Lett. d. 6. f. 255: RS to Henry Taylor, 12 Feb. 1829.
4. *LC*, vi, 24: RS to Mrs Hodson, 10 Feb. 1829.
5. *Cumberland Pacquet*, 10 March 1829. RS sent letters to the *Westmorland Gazette*, but a search through the issues for Jan.–April 1829 failed to identify them.
6. Bodleian Library, MSS Eng. Lett. d. 6. f. 263: RS to Henry Taylor, 5 March 1829.
7. NYPL, Berg Collection: RS to the bishop of Bath and Wells, 21 March 1829. The bishop presented the petition to the House of Lords on 23 March.
8. Bodleian Library, MSS Eng. Lett. 6, f. 291: RS to Henry Taylor, 9 June 1829.
9. Brotherton Library, MS: RS to Mrs Opie, 30 Aug. 1829 [draft].
10. *LC*, vi, 147: RS to Walter Savage Landor, 22 Aug. 1829.
11. *SL*, iv, 169: RS to GB, 3 March 1830.
12. Bodleian Library, MS Don. d.s. f. 305: RS to Henry Southey, 4 Jan. 1830.
13. *LC*, vi, 85: RS to Mrs Hodson, 20 Jan. 1830; *The Pilgrim's Progress with a Life of John Bunyan by Robert Southey* (London, 1830).
14. *Attempts in Verse by John Jones . . . with . . . an introductory essay on the lives and works of our uneducated poets by Robert Southey* (London, 1831), p. 7.
15. Ibid., p. 8.
16. Bodleian Library, MSS Eng. Lett. d. 48. f. 174: RS to GB, 21 July 1830.
17. *SL*, iv, 191: RS to John Wood Warter, 28 July 1830.
18. *LC*, vi, 118: RS to JR, 11 Sept. 1830.
19. Rochester University, MSS: RS to Andrew Bell, 16 Nov. 1830.

20. *The Greville Memoirs, 1814–1860*, ed. Lytton Strachey and Roger Fulford (8 vols, London, 1938), ii, 58. Cited in Simmons, p. 184.
21. *The Letters of John Stuart Mill*, ed. Hugh S. R. Elliot (2 vols, London, 1910), i, 13. Cited in Simmons, p. 184.
22. Mary Stuart, *Letters from the Lake Poets* (London, 1889), p. 424: RS to Daniel Stuart, 6 Dec. 1830.
23. Keswick Museum: RS to Bertha Southey, 12 Jan. 1831.
24. *LC*, vi, 140: RS to Mrs Hodson, 7 Feb. 1831.
25. Murray Archive: RS to John Murray, 26 Dec. 1830.
26. *NL*, ii, 361: RS to GB, 29 Jan. 1831.
27. *QR* 44 (1831), 265.
28. Ibid., p. 314.
29. Ibid., p. 315.
30. Victoria University Library, Coleridge Collection: RS to Derwent Coleridge, 17 Dec. 1830.
31. NYPL, Berg Collection: RS to Edith Southey, 18 Jan. 1831.
32. Victoria University Library, Coleridge Collection: RS to Bertha Southey, 21 Jan. 1831.
33. Rochester University, MS S727: RS to Miss Fletcher, 31 Jan. 1831.
34. *LC*, vi, 130: Lord Brougham to RS, Jan. 1831.
35. *SL*, iv, 209: RS to CW, 3 March 1831.
36. *SL*, iv, 206: RS to JR, 12 Jan. 1831.
37. *LC*, vi, 136: RS to Lord Brougham, 1 Feb. 1831. Guelphs and Ghibellines were rival factions in medieval Italy.
38. NYPL, Berg Collection: RS to Lord Ashley, 12 Feb. 1831.
39. Rochester University, MS S727: RS to Lord Ashley, 3 April 1831.
40. *SL*, iv, 210: RS to CW, 3 March 1831.
41. Bodleian Library, MSS Eng. Lett. d. 7. f. 14v: RS to Henry Taylor, 19 March 1831. Cf. *LC*, vi, 146 note.
42. Bodleian Library, MS Don. d. 3. f. 324v: RS to Henry Southey, 9 April 1831.
43. NYPL, Berg Collection: RS to Philip Henry Stanhope, 3 April 1831. Mahon was to publish his *History of the War of Succession in Spain 1702–14* in 1832.
44. Bodleian Library, MSS Eng. Lett. d. 6. f. 70: RS to Henry Taylor, 20 April 1831.
45. Yale University, Beinecke Library, Osborn MS 14114: RS to Alan Cunningham, April 1831 (copy).
46. Yale University, Beinecke Library, Osborn MS 14128: RS to Mrs Hodson, 30 July 1831.
47. *SL*, iv, 221: RS to CW, 6 June 1831.
48. Ramos, p. 247: RS to JM, 1 Oct. 1831.
49. *SL*, iv, 247: RS to Edith May Southey, 8 Nov. 1831.
50. Yale University, Beinecke Library, Osborn MS 14128: RS to Mrs Hodson, 30 July 1831.
51. *LC*, vi, 153: RS to Neville White, 15 July 1831. In the event, when Bell died in January 1832, Southey did get a legacy of £1,000.
52. *NL*, ii, 371: RS to Henry Southey, 15 Oct. 1831.
53. *SL*, iv, 242: RS to John Wood Warter, 19 Oct. 1831.
54. Ramos, p. 249: RS to JM, 30 Nov. 1831.
55. NYPL, Berg Collection: RS to Andrew Bell, 8 Nov. 1831.
56. *SL*, iv, 249–50: RS to Mrs Bray, 24 Nov. 1831.
57. Keswick Museum: RS to Edward Hill, 15 Dec. 1831.
58. *LC*, vi, 175: RS to Neville White, 10 Jan. 1832 (misdated June).
59. NYPL, Berg Collection: RS to Lord Ashley, 16 Jan. 1832.
60. Keswick Museum: RS to Henry Southey, 31 March 1832. RS was overjoyed at completing the last volume of his *History of the Peninsular War*, telling Bedford that had he been within reach 'I should have taken my hat and my walking-stick, and set out for the satisfaction of singing "O be joyful" in your presence, and with your aid.' *LC*, vi, 186: RS to GB, 1 April 1832.

61. *SL*, iv, 271: RS to John Wood Warter, 18 April 1832.
62. *SL*, iv, 277: RS to John White, 13 May 1832.
63. *SL*, iv, 282: RS to Mrs Bray, 12 June 1832.
64. Yale University, Beinecke Library, Osborn MSS file 5: 14109: RS to Caroline Bowles, 2 July 1832.
65. Manchester Public Library, Crossley Papers 24. 091.524: RS to Charles Swain, 25 July 1832. In fact problems with a business partner had led Swain to abandon the proposed visit.
66. *SL*, iv, 294: RS to Mrs Bray, 9 Aug. 1832.
67. *QR* 47 (1832), 458, 496, 500.
68. *NL*, ii, 385–6: RS to Mrs Hodson, 24 Oct. 1832. Sir Robert Inglis expressed his surprise 'that a gentleman should use such language in a letter to a lady'. Duke University Library: Sir Robert Inglis to Mrs Hodson, 28 Jan. 1848.
69. *QR* 47 (1832), 516.
70. Harry Ransome Humanities Research Center, University of Texas at Austin MSS: RS to [?John Murray], 31 Oct. 1832.
71. *SL*, iv, 318: RS to Mrs Hughes, 27 Dec. 1832.
72. *NL*, ii, 383: RS to JR, 23 Oct. 1832.
73. Huntington Library, MS RS621: RS to JR, 20 Feb. 1832.
74. Princeton University, Taylor MSS: RS to Mrs Brook, 13 Oct. 1832.
75. Keswick Museum: RS to Henry Southey, 27 Nov. 1832.
76. Harry Ransome Humanities Research Center, University of Texas at Austin MSS: RS to Derwent Coleridge, 30 Dec. 1832.
77. *NL*, ii, 392: RS to Mrs Hodson, 12 Feb. 1833.
78. *NL*, ii, 391: RS to John Wood Warter, 23 Jan. 1833.
79. NYPL, Berg Collection: RS to Lord Ashley, 6 Feb. 1833.
80. Bodleian Library, MSS Eng. Lett. d. 49. f. 37: RS to GB, 24 April 1834.
81. Bodleian Library, MSS Eng. Lett. d. 9. ff. 32–3: RS to Henry Taylor, 27 May 1837.
82. *NL*, ii, 396: RS to GB, 23 March 1833.
83. *LC*, vi, 212: RS to JM, 20 May 1833.
84. Rochester University, MSS: RS to Mrs Bray, 7 Aug. 1833.
85. *Henry Crabb Robinson*, i, 431.
86. *LC*, vi, 229: RS to GB, 10 Jan. 1834.
87. Yale University, Beinecke General MSS 298/47: RS to 'Madam', 'Somewhere', 29 Aug. 1837.
88. *QR* 51 (1834), 69. Lockhart's review.
89. *SL*, iv, 369: RS to Mrs Bray, 30 Jan. 1834.
90. *NL*, ii, 404: RS to Lockhart, 3 Feb. 1834.
91. *QR* 51 (1834), 69, 95.
92. *LC*, vi, 229: RS to GB, 10 Jan. 1834.
93. Dowden, p. 325: RS to Caroline Bowles, 22 June 1835.
94. *NL*, ii, 396: RS to GB, 23 March 1833.
95. Keswick Museum: RS to Henry Southey, 19 May 1834.
96. *SL*, iv, 381: RS to Mrs Hughes, 14 Aug. 1834.
97. Ramos, p. 266: RS to JM, 29 Aug. 1834.
98. Manchester Public Library, Crossley Papers 24. 091.524: RS to Charles Swain, 9 March 1838.
99. Keswick Museum: RS to Henry Southey, 11 Sept. 1834.
100. Keswick Museum: RS to Henry Southey, 25 Sept. 1834.
101. *The Journal of William Charles Macready, 1832–1851* ed. J. C. Trewin (London, 1967), p. 33.
102. NLW, MSS 4813D: RS to CW, 17 Dec. 1834.
103. Keswick Museum: RS to Henry Southey, 25 Sept. 1834.

CHAPTER 13

1. *LC*, vi, 244: RS to GB, 2 Oct. 1834.
2. Keswick Museum: RS to Bertha and Kate Southey, 2 Oct. 1834. RS repeated the expression in a letter to GB, 20 April 1835. 'Natural want of chearfulness is the great drawback upon the tendency to recovery.' Bodleian Library, MS Eng. Lett. d. 49. f. 81.
3. Cumbria Record Office, Carlisle, MS QRP3/43–51. Cumberland Poll Book, 1835. Colonel William Peachy also voted for Irton and Stanley. John Spedding of Mirehouse cast a single vote for Aglionby.
4. *NL*, ii, 406: RS to Edith May, 3 April 1834. See above p. 220.
5. The complicated story is told in Norma Russell, *A Bibliography of William Cowper* (Oxford, 1963), pp. 227–39. Southey eventually outmanoeuvred Grimshawe by obtaining the permission of Mrs Anne Bodham, the administratrix of Cowper's estate, to publish the letters in his edition. Four volumes of Southey's correspondence with Baldwin and Cradock are deposited in the Fitzwilliam Museum, Cambridge, and a box of his letters to Baldwin and others, including Mrs Gaskell, relating to his edition of Cowper is in Princeton University Library, MSS C0134/6.
6. Keswick Museum: RS to Henry Southey, 2 Oct. 1834.
7. *NL*, ii, 438: RS to Mrs Hodson, 26 Jan. 1836. RS referred her to his *Life of Cowper*, ii, 257. 'All that is said in that page about a system of excitement and spiritual directors will be felt by Mr Whiteside like a thrust under his fifth rib.'
8. Keswick Museum: RS to Bertha, 8 March 1835. It is therefore hard to explain why he arranged to have copies of his *History of Brazil* and *Colloquies on Society* 'in handsome binding' sent to Whiteside in Ripon on 15 July 1835. Huntington Library, MS MA 1632: RS to [Longman].
9. *LC*, vi, 295: RS to JM, 13 June 1836.
10. Lionel Madden (ed.), *Robert Southey: The Critical Heritage* (London, 1972), p. 461. It was in a conversation with Carlyle at this time that RS vented his anger on the subject of De Quincey. See above p. xii.
11. Keswick Museum: RS to Henry Southey, York, 20 March 1835.
12. Keswick Museum: RS to Bertha Southey, 20 March 1835.
13. Keswick Museum: RS to Bertha Southey, Scarborough, 24 March 1835.
14. Keswick Museum: RS to Bertha Southey, Scarborough, 29 March 1835.
15. Keswick Museum: RS to Bertha Southey, 20 March 1835. Isabella Fenwick was a friend of Henry Taylor.
16. *LC*, vi, 261–2: RS to Cuthbert Southey, 27 March; and RS to Henry Taylor, 2 April 1835.
17. Keswick Museum: RS to Bertha Southey, 20 March 1835.
18. *LC*, vi, 264: RS to Sir Robert Peel, 7 April 1835. Anticipating the imminent collapse of Peel's ministry, he added 'if you now retire from power it cannot be long before you will be borne in again upon the spring-tide of public opinion. Nothing in the course of public affairs has ever appeared to me more certain than this.'
19. *NL*, ii, 420: RS to CW, 8 Feb. 1835.
20. Yale University, Beinecke General MS 298 box 1/30: RS to John Sheppard, 16 Nov. 1835.
21. Murray Archive: RS to John Murray, 17 June 1835.
22. *NL*, ii, 426: RS to CW, [June] 1835.
23. *SL*, iv, 407: RS to Mrs Hughes, 1 July 1835.
24. *NL*, ii, 440: RS to CW, 21 Feb. 1836.
25. Keswick Museum: RS to Henry Southey, 29 Dec. 1835.
26. *LC*, vi, 278: RS to the dean of Westminster, 12 Nov. 1835.
27. *NL*, ii, 440: RS to CW, 21 Feb. 1836.
28. *SL*, iv, 446: RS to CW, 9 April 1836.
29. Keswick Museum: RS to Henry Southey, 19 June 1836. It did no good, for the following

March Edward was in another scrape, which entailed the risk of his going to jail. RS to Henry Southey, 23 March 1837.

30. Keswick Museum: RS to Henry Southey, 24 March 1836.
31. Hampshire Record Office, May MS 2m69/90: Henry Southey to JM, 23 Sept. 1836.
32. Keswick Museum: RS to Henry Southey, 4 Oct. 1836.
33. *NL*, ii, 456: RS to Joseph Cottle, 30 Sept. 1836.
34. Harry Ransome Humanities Research Center, University of Texas at Austin: RS to Sir John Coleridge, 10 Oct. 1836. See also RS's letters to Joseph Cottle of 26 Feb., 5 March, 14 April and 30 Sept. 1836 in *NL*, ii, 441–57. Kenneth Curry demonstrates how Cottle misused them to vindicate his own role in his *Early Recollections chiefly relating to the late Samuel Taylor Coleridge during his long residence in Bristol* (1837). See also Lynda Pratt, 'The Media of Friends or Foes? Unpublished Letters from Joseph Cottle to Robert Southey, 1834–7', *The Modern Language Review* 98 (2003), 545–62.
35. John Wood Warter (ed.), *Southey's Common-place Book* (4th series, 1851), p. 539.
36. *SL*, iv, 473: RS to Mrs Bray, 6 Nov. 1836.
37. *LC*, vi, 311.
38. Harry Ransome Humanities Research Center, University of Texas at Austin: RS to Derwent Coleridge, 4 Nov. 1836.
39. *SL*, iv, 487: RS to Kate Southey, 17 Dec. 1836.
40. University of Rochester, MSS: RS to Mrs Bray, 21 Dec. 1836.
41. *SL*, iv, 491: RS to Mrs Bray, 3 Jan. 1837.
42. *SL*, iv, 509: RS to Mrs Hughes, 20 May 1837.
43. *NL*, ii, 468: RS to Joseph Cottle, 9 May 1837.
44. *LC*, vi, 327–30: RS to [Charlotte Brontë], [March] and 22 March 1837.
45. *LC*, vi, 331: RS to Henry Taylor, 30 March 1837. Cuthbert omitted from this letter the passage dealing with the dispute between himself and Warter. See Bodleian Library, MSS Eng. Lett. d. 9. f. 8.
46. University of Rochester, MSS: RS to Mrs Bray, 15 May 1837.
47. University of Rochester, MSS: RS to Mrs Bray, 2 Aug. 1837.
48. Keswick Museum: RS to Henry Southey, 22 Oct. 1837.
49. *SL*, iv, 533: RS to GB, 10 Oct. 1837.
50. Bodleian Library, MSS Eng. Lett. c. 290: John Wood Warter to JM, 23 Oct. 1837. The same observation was made of Queen's students by Christ Church undergraduates when the present author was a scholar at Queen's College in the 1950s.
51. *SL*, iv, 531: RS to CW, 3 Oct. 1837.
52. *LC*, vi, 346. RS to ?, 3 Nov. 1837.
53. Keswick Museum: RS to Henry Southey, 16 Nov. 1837.
54. *LC*, vi, 347: RS to Joseph Cottle, 16 Nov. 1837.
55. Bristol Reference Library, MSS G1375/28: Joseph Cottle to RS, 19 Nov. 1837.

CHAPTER 14

1. Bodleian Library, MS Don. d. s. f. 353: RS to Henry Southey, 28 Dec. 1837.
2. Bodleian Library MS, Eng. Lett. d. 9. f. 85: RS to Henry Taylor, 20 Nov. 1837; *NL*, ii, 473: RS to WW, 29 April 1838.
3. Rochester University, MS: RS to Mrs Bray, 21 Jan. 1838.
4. Yale University, Beinecke Library, Osborn MSS file S. 14138: RS to G. F. Mathison, 8 March 1838.
5. *LC*, vi, 140: RS to Mrs Hodson, 7 Feb. 1831.
6. *LC*, vi, 358: RS to GB, 29 Dec. 1837.
7. Bodleian Library, MS Don d. s. f. 357: RS to Henry Southey, 14 Jan. 1838.
8. *NL*, ii, 470: RS to John Kenyon, 14 March 1838.

9. Rochester University, MSS: RS to Mrs Bray, 11 April 1838.

10. Ibid.

11. Lionel Madden (ed.), *Robert Southey: The Critical Heritage* (London, 1972), pp. 464–6.

12. Manchester Public Library, Crossley MS, 091.524: RS to Charles Swain, 1 May 1838.

13. Ramos, p. 288: RS to JM, 22 May 1838.

14. Bodleian Library, MS Don. d. s. f. 359: RS to Henry Southey, 4 June 1838.

15. *LC*, vi, 368: RS to Miss Charter, 11 April 1838; ibid., 370: RS to Henry Taylor, 10 June 1838.

16. West Sussex Record Office, Chichester, Papers of Anna Eliza Bray, Box 3, 'Copy of Mrs Southey's narrative'. I am indebted to Lynda Pratt for a photocopy of this manuscript, and to Mr E. M. Kempe for permission to quote from it. Unless other citations are provided, all quotations in this chapter are from it.

17. Bodleian Library MS, Eng. Lett. d. 9. f. 134: RS to Henry Taylor, 28 May 1838. RS's letters to Caroline in 1838 were apparently destroyed. Simmons, p. 247 note 345. She quotes several in her narrative, but does not date them.

18. Cornell University, Wordsworth Collection: RS to Henry Taylor, 22 July 1838.

19. *SL*, iv, 549: RS to Neville White, 26 Aug. 1838. RS had stayed with White in Norwich on his way south.

20. Keswick Museum, RS to Henry Southey, 26 Aug [1838]. The commission was to pay Longman 14/6d for a book for Caroline.

21. *Henry Crabb Robinson on Books and their Writers*, ed. Edith J. Morley (3 vols, London, 1938), ii, 554, 556.

22. *LC*, vi, 373–4.

23. Cuthbert claimed to observe a deterioration in RS's handwriting in the journal, though Adolfo Cabral, who edited it for publication, noted 'I doubt this, at least to any significant extent'. Cabral, p. 233. Cabral published a facsimile of the last page of the journal, which bears out his observation (p. 230). The journal breaks off on 25 Sept., though RS did not return to England until 11 Oct. Cuthbert thought this was further evidence of his worsening mental state, but Cabral gives cogent reasons for rejecting this view. Ibid., p. 230. He also published letters from RS written in France pp. 232–48.

24. Cabral, pp. 228–9.

25. *Henry Crabb Robinson*, ii, 554.

26. Cabral, p. 248: RS to GB, 7 Oct. 1838.

27. *NL*, ii, 479–80: RS to Bertha Southey, 15 Oct. 1838. The letter was presumably intended to inform Kate as well.

28. *SL*, iv, 556: RS to Edith May Southey, 20 Oct. 1838.

29. Keswick Museum: RS to Bertha Southey, 26 Oct. 1838.

30. Keswick Museum: RS to Henry Southey, 17 Dec. 1838.

31. NYPL, Berg Collection: RS to [Anon.], 4 Jan. 1839. The letter shows no sign of the deterioration in his handwriting that Cuthbert claimed to have detected in RS's journal of the holiday in France.

32. Robert and Charles Cuthbert Southey, *The Life of the Rev. Andrew Bell* (3 vols, London, 1844), p. vi.

33. Newnham College Library, Cambridge: RS to John Hookham Frere, 23 Jan. 1839.

34. *LC*, vi, 383: RS to Mrs Hodson, 18 Feb. 1839.

35. Fitzwilliam Museum, Cambridge, MS 169–1947: RS to William Davies, 24 April 1839.

36. Brotherton Library, Leeds MS Genq Sou B23021. Lynda Pratt, in a discussion of these verses, shows that Southey's were not composed for the occasion, but were taken from his unpublished poem *Oliver Newman*, while the last four stanzas of Caroline's had also been composed earlier. 'The "Marriage" Poems of Robert Southey and Caroline Bowles', *Notes and Queries* 50, no. 3 (new series, 2003), 282–7.

37. Hampshire Record Office, MS 2m69/91: Henry Southey to JM, 21 June 1839.

38. Bodleian Library MS, Eng. Lett. d. 9. f. 206: RS to Henry Taylor, 27 July 1839.

39. *LC*, vi, 387–8.
40. Hampshire Record Office, MS 2m69/92: Henry Southey to JM, 30 Aug. 1839.
41. Victoria University Library, MSS: 'Statement of Kate Southey about the affairs connected with her father's second marriage.'
42. Cornell University, Wordsworth Collection: RS to Henry Taylor, 13 Aug. 1839.
43. *SL*, vi, 575: RS to CW 6 Sept. [dated 5 Sept. by Warter. RS began it on the 5th but postponed completing it until the 6th]1839.
44. NLW, MS4813D: Caroline Southey to CW, 6 Sept. 1839. The letter concludes 'Forgive this hurried scrap, written as I am close to his elbow.'

EPILOGUE

1. Hampshire Record Office, MSS 2m69/93: Henry Southey to JM, 7 Oct. 1839.
2. Hampshire Record Office, MSS 2m69/96: Caroline Southey to JM, 4 Nov. 1839.
3. NYPL, Berg Collection MSS: Caroline Southey to Lord Ashley, 20 June 1840.
4. Cornell University, Wordsworth Collection: Caroline Southey to Bernard Barton, 20 June 1840.
5. Duke University Library, MS: Caroline Southey to L. T. Pilgrim, 17 Dec. 1840.
6. Dr Williams Library, Crabb Robinson MSS Letters 1841: Henry Crabb Robinson to James Masquerier, 18 Jan. 1841.
7. Boston Public Library, MSS ch.H.6.43: Caroline Southey to 'Sir', 29 July 1841.
8. Robert Southey and Caroline Bowles Southey, *Robin Hood: A Fragment* (Edinburgh, 1847), p. 248.
9. Hampshire Record Office, MSS 2m69/94: Henry Southey to JM, 18 Oct. 1841.
10. Hampshire Record Office, MS 2m69/102: Henry Southey to JM, 10 Nov. 1842.
11. Hampshire Record Office, MS 2m69/102: Caroline Southey to JM, 18 Nov. 1842.
12. Victoria University Library, MSS: 'Statement of Kate Southey about the affairs connected with her father's second marriage.'
13. Hampshire Record Office, MS 2m69/100: Caroline Southey to JM, 3 July 1842.
14. Hampshire Record Office, MS 2m69/103: Caroline Southey to JM, 9 Feb. 1843.
15. Rochester University, MSS: Caroline Southey to Mrs Bray, 22 March 1843.
16. Manchester Central Library, Swain MSS: Cuthbert Southey to Charles Swain, 17 April 1843.
17. Edward Quillinan, *Poems* (Ambleside, 1891), p. 91, 'Funeral of Robert Southey'.
18. Lionel Madden (ed.), *Robert Southey: The Critical Heritage* (1972), p. 416.
19. Houghton Library, Caroline Southey to Mrs Hughes, 18 Dec. 1843.
20. *LC*, vi, 365: RS to Cuthbert Southey, 7 Feb. 1838.
21. W. M. Thackeray, *The Four Georges*, quoted in Madden, *Robert Southey*, p. 434.
22. Simmons, p. 223.
23. Robert Woof, Introductory Essay to William Hazlitt, *The Spirit of the Age* (Grasmere, 2004), p. 25.
24. *NL*, i, 392: RS to TS, 22 Aug. 1805.
25. Kenneth Curry, *Southey* (London, 1975), p. 108.
26. *NL*, ii, 387: RS to GB, 28 Dec. 1832.
27. John Forster, *Walter Savage Landor: A Biography* (2 vols, London, 1869), ii, 406.

Bibliographical Note

Primary sources for Robert Southey's writings are voluminous. His manuscripts are held in repositories in Britain and North America. Most are listed by the National Registry of Archives, and the list can be accessed on their website at www.nra.nationalarchives.gov.uk. Not all of his extant papers are recorded by the NRA, however. His letters to John Murray, for instance, were not listed when I consulted them in Albermarle Street, London. They have since migrated to the National Library of Scotland in Edinburgh. It is necessary to consult the originals of Southey's letters since most of them remain unpublished, while many were poorly edited by his son Cuthbert Southey, in *The Life and Correspondence of Robert Southey* (6 vols, London, 1849–50), and son-in-law John Wood Warter, *Selections from the Letters of Robert Southey* (4 vols, London, 1856). Those edited by Kenneth Curry, *New Letters of Robert Southey* (2 vols, Columbia, 1965), and Charles Ramos, *The Letters of Robert Southey to John May 1797 to 1838* (1976), can be relied upon as accurate transcriptions. The title of the latter, however, is slightly misleading, as it only publishes those letters held in the Harry Ransom Humanities Research Center at the University of Texas, Austin. There are many more letters from Southey to May in other archives. A comprehensive scholarly edition of Southey's correspondence is indeed badly needed.

If all Southey's published works were to appear in a single edition they would take up many volumes. In addition to his biographies, histories, novel and poems there is a vast number of essays and reviews, scattered through various contemporary journals. *The Contributions of Robert Southey to the Morning Post* were edited by Kenneth Curry (1984). Lynda Pratt added to them poems he published there and elsewhere in the fifth volume, *Selected Shorter Poems c. 1793–1810*, of her magnificent five-volume edition *Robert Southey: Poetical Works, 1793–1810* (London, 2004). Apart from its publication of *Joan of Arc*, *Madoc*, *Thalaba the Destroyer* and *The Curse of Kehama*, his major poems are available to modern readers only in nineteenth-century editions such as *The Poetical Works of Robert Southey. Complete in One Volume* (London, 1850); or selections, for example *Poems of Robert Southey*, ed. Maurice H. Fitzgerald (Oxford, 1909), and Geoffrey Grigson, *A Choice of Southey's Verse* (London, 1970). *A Vision of Judgement*, however, was published along with Byron's *The Vision of Judgement* by E. M. Earl and James Hogg at Salzburg University in 1998.

With the exception of a small number of works, Southey's prose has suffered a similar fate. Southey's *Life of Nelson* has rarely been out of print since it first appeared in 1813. The most recent edition is by Richard Holmes, *Southey on Nelson: The Life of Nelson* (London, 2004). Southey's *Life of Wesley and the Rise and Progress of Methodism* was edited by Maurice H. Fitzgerald (2 vols, Oxford, 1925). But there is no modern edition of other biographies he wrote, for example of Andrew Bell, John Bunyan, William Cowper, Oliver Cromwell and the duke of Marlborough, or of his histories, *The History of Brazil* (3 vols, London, 1810–19) and *The History of the Peninsular War* (3 vols, London, 1823–32). Similarly his novel *The Doctor* in seven volumes, two of them published posthumously, has been neglected since its publication in one volume in 1848. *Omniana, or Horae otiosiores* by Southey and S. T. Coleridge, edited by Robert Gittings, was published by the Centaur Press in 1969. Jack Simmons edited Southey's *Letters from England: By Don Manuel Alvarez Espirella* (Alan Sutton, 1984). His translation of *The Chronicle of the Cid* appeared recently in a paperback edition published by Dolphin Books, as did an abridged edition of *Colloquies on Society* by IndyPublish.com, both without a date of publication. His essays and reviews, however, have still to be consulted in the originals. Jacob Zeitlin listed 'Southey's Contributions to "The Critical Review"' in *Notes and Queries* 4, (12th series, 1918), 35–6, 66–7, 94–6, 122–5. R. D. Havens recorded 'Southey's Contributions to the "Foreign Review"' in The *Review of English Studies* 8 (1932), 210–11. Kenneth Curry provided invaluable guides to his contributions to the *Annual Review* in the *Bulletin of Bibliography* 16 (1941), 196–7; with Robert Dedmon he listed those in the *Quarterly Review* in the *Wordsworth Circle* 6 (1975), 261–72; and he identified 'Robert Southey's Contributions to the *Monthly Magazine* and the *Athenaeum*' in the *Wordsworth Circle* 11 (1980), 215–18.

Kenneth Curry was one of a handful of scholars who kept an interest in Southey alive through the third quarter of the twentieth century. His *Southey* in Routledge's Author Guides (London, 1975) is an excellent brief introduction to his life and works. Its short bibliography attests to the paucity of secondary works available to students at that time. Among the few he listed, three are still required reading: Jack Simmons, *Southey* (1945); Geoffrey Carnall, *Robert Southey and his Age: The Development of a Conservative*

Mind (Oxford, 1960); and Lionel Madden (ed.), *Robert Southey: The Critical Heritage* (London, 1972).

Since 1975 there has been a revival of interest in Southey's creative writings. It is generally attributed by students of literature to Marilyn Butler's inaugural lecture at Cambridge University delivered on 10 November 1987, published as 'Repossessing the Past: The Case for an Open Literary History', in Marjorie Levinson, Marilyn Butler, Jerome McGann and Paul Hamilton (eds), *Rethinking Historicism: Critical Readings in Romantic History* (Oxford, 1989). Professor Butler sought to put Southey back on the canonical map. Her example has been followed by other literary scholars. Mark Storey's *Robert Southey: A Life* (Oxford, 1997) was the first major biography since Simmons's. Christopher J. P. Smith, *A Quest for Home: Reading Robert Southey* (Liverpool, 1997), explored his poetry of the years 1793 to 1805. Lynda Pratt investigated 'The Literary Career of Robert Southey 1794–1800' in her Oxford D.Phil. thesis of 1998. Dr Pratt has subsequently published several articles, outstanding among which is 'Patriot Poetics and the Romantic National Epic: Placing and Displacing Southey's *Joan of Arc*', in P. J. Kitson (ed.), *Placing and Displacing Romanticism* (Aldershot, 2001). When she came to prepare the edition of his poems mentioned above, thanks to the revived interest in his verse she was able to bring together an editorial team of Southey scholars. Carol Bolton and Paul Jarman helped her edit the second volume. Tim Fulford edited the third volume with the assistance of Carol Bolton again and Daniel E. White. The fourth volume was edited by Daniel Sanjiv Roberts. Southey's rehabilitation among Romantic poets can be discerned by his inclusion in recent studies of the period's literature. Among them, Simon Bainbridge, *British Poetry and the Revolutionary and Napoleonic Wars* (Oxford, 2003), is particularly relevant.

Historians and political scientists have marched to a different drum. Jonathan Mendilow, *The Romantic Tradition in British Political Thought* (London, 1986), has a chapter on 'Robert Southey and the Communal Values of Politics'. David Eastwood has written a number of seminal articles on Southey, including 'Robert Southey and the Meanings of Patriotism', *Journal of British Studies* 31 (1992), 265–87. David M. Craig's Cambridge Ph.D. thesis 'Republicanism Becoming Conservative: Robert Southey and Political Argument in Britain 1787–1817' (2000) is the most substantial investigation of Southey's political development since Geoffrey Carnall's.

Index

Abello, Manuel, Don, 139
Acta Sanctorum, 164, 177
Addington, Henry, 89, 95, 109, 111, 122
Aikin, Arthur, 95, 107, 109, 124, 125, *see also Annual Review*
Aikin, John, reviews *Joan of Arc,* 64
Allen, Robert, 39–40; introduced Coleridge and Southey, 42, 43
America, United States of, and 'Madoc', 17, 107, 111
    Edmund Burke on, 21
    Southey on, 37–8
    Pantisocratic commune 45–57
    Oliver Newman and, 187
Anniversary, 205
Annual Anthology, 12, 77, 83
Annual Review, 95, 104, 106, 109, 111, 114, 117, 123–4, 132–3, 137, 144, 186, *see also* Aikin, John
Anti-Jacobin, 54, 82, 85, 128
    attacks by, 81
    Southey on, 75, 94
    Southey's *Poems* censured by, 69–71, 73
    as *Anti-Jacobin Review and Magazine*, 74–5, *see also* Canning, George
Arch, J. and A. (publisher), 84
Ashley, Lord (*later* seventh earl of Shaftesbury), 142, 209, 214, 218, 220–1
'Aspheterism', 43, 48, 50
Athenaeum, 117, 150
Australia, 40, 44
Austria, 26, 127, 158

Babeuf, François Noël, 44, 67
Bacon, Roger, 96
Baldwin and Cradock (publishers), 222, 230, 233, 238

Ballantyne, James, 135, 136–9, 142, 147, 149, 152–3
Ballantynes (James and John, publishers), 132, 136, 137, 138, 152–3
Balliol College, *see* Oxford
Barker, Mary, 96, 101, 108, 110, 124, 125, 126, 141, 144, 154, 163, 166, 174, 197, 201
    first meets Southey, 85
    introduces Southey to Charlotte Smith, 91
    sketch for *Madoc,* 106–7
    Southey's relationship with, 112–13, 149–50, 152, 161
    argument with Fricker sisters, 157
    wrongly credited with coining phrase, 'the Satanic school', 180
    her marriage, 213–4
Bath and Wells, bishop of, 209
Bath, 45, 49, 52, 53, 72, 236
    Southey's childhood in, 5, 6, 7, 8, 9, 11, 14, 26
    Fricker family in, 35
    Southey's mother's boarding house, 28, 34, 50–1, 59, 69, 74
Bayley, Peter, reviewed by Southey, 105
Bean, William, 15–16
Beaumont, Sir George, 134–5, 194
Beddoes, Thomas, 66, 77–8
    Southey treated by, 76, 81
Bedford, Grosvenor Charles, 16–17, 33, 35, 36, 37, 40, 44, 45, 61, 134–5, 138, 154–5, 167, 182, 211, 221, 234, 255
    and *The Flagellant*, 19–20, 22
    contribution to first *Annual Anthology*, 77
    and *Specimens of the later English poets*, 107, 116, 120–1, 124

Bedford, Grosvenor Charles (*cont.*)
    Southey rebukes for pamphlet on Pitt,
        111–12
    as go-between with Gifford, 129
    godfather to Charles Cuthbert Southey,
        176
Bedford, Horace, 17, 33, 45, 46, 49, 66
Bedminster, 4, 6, 7, 8, 10, 213, 235
Bell, Dr Andrew, 133, 144–5, 147, 149,
    168, 190, 216–17, 220, *see also*
    Southey, Robert, *Life of the Reverend
    Andrew Bell*
Bellingham, James, 148
Betham, Mary, 183
Biddlecombe, Charles, 68, 71, 78, 80, 110
Bilderdijk, Willem, 198
Birmingham, 69, 108, 236, 241
Blake, William, 143
Bonaparte, Napoleon, Southey on, 82,
    94–5, 109, 114, 132, 136, 138, 139,
    158
Boswell, James, 163
Botany Bay, 44, 172, *see also* Southey,
    Robert, 'Botany Bay Eclogues'
Bowles, Caroline (Southey's second wife),
    175, 193–4, 195, 198–9, 201, 206,
    210, 212, 221, 231, 236
    meets Southey for the first time, 182
    visits Keswick for the first time, 193–4
    Southey's engagement and marriage to,
        242–55, *see also* Buckland
Bowles, William Lisle, 91, 236
    Fourteen Sonnets, 49
Bradford, William (Southey's great uncle), 6
Braxfield, Judge, 44
Brissot, Jacques, 37, 64,
Bristol, 3–12, 26, 34–6, 39–40, 46, 53–6,
    59–60, 65, 79, 80, 81, 83, 88, 91,
    95–6, 101, 125, 126, 213, 217, 236
Bristol library, 37–8, 55
Bristol Pneumatic Institute, 77–8
British Critic, 92, 195
Brixton, 36, 37, 59, 98
Brontë, Charlotte, 237
Brougham, James, 179
Brougham, Lord Henry, 147, 174–5, 214
Brown, Wade, 144
Bruges, 163
Brussels, 164, 173, 177, 197, 198, 201
Bryant, John Frederick, 11
Buckland, Hampshire, 213, 242, 243, 245,
    246, 247, *see also* Bowles, Caroline
Bunyan, John, 14, 210

Burdett, Sir Francis, 141, 146
Burke, Edmund, 21, 33, 170
Burnett, George, 28, 32, 39, 43, 44–5, 46,
    47, 48, 54, 57, 73, 140
Burney, Captain, 96
Burrard, Reverend George, 248
Butler, Charles, 196–7; 203
Byron, George Gordon, Lord, 35, 65, 66,
    117, 155–6, 175–6, 180, 184, 185–8,
    writings: *English Bards and Scotch
        Reviewers*, 132
    Ode to Napoleon Bonaparte, 159
    Don Juan, 186, 187–8
    Two Foscari, 187
    The Vision of Judgement, 188, 190, 206

Caius Gracchus, 44
Cadell and Davies (publishers), 66
Calvert, William, 179
Cambridge, 31, 42, 48–9, 66, 182
Cambridge University, 16, 19, 32, 35, 50,
    117, 134
Campbell, George, Reverend, 60
Campbell, Thomas, 91, 140
Canning, George, 69–70, 128–9, 134, 135,
    147, 169, 182, 196, 204, 212, *see also*
    Anti-Jacobin
Carlisle Journal, 179
Carlisle, 113, 147, 181, 217, 218
Carlisle, Sir Anthony, 68, 96
Carlyle, Thomas, 231, 241
Carnall, Geoffrey, 147
Caroline, Queen, 184–5
Carroll, Lewis (Charles Dodgson), 77
Carter, Elizabeth, *All the works of Epictetus*,
    29, 30
Cartwright, Major John, 78
Catholicism, and Catholic Emancipation,
    114, 149, 169, 190, 212
    Southey's attitude towards, 63, 86, 89,
        106, 108, 120, 124, 129, 145,
        196–7, 200, 204, 206, 208–9
Chamonix, 173
Charles I, 187
Charles II, 208
Chatterton, Thomas, Southey's edition of
    his poems, 68, 83, 90, 91, 92
Christ Church, *see* Oxford
Christal, Ann, 67
Cintra, 65, 85, 87, 88, *see also* Sintra
Clarke, James Stanier, *The progress of
    maritime discovery*, 106
    Life of Nelson, 137
    becomes historiographer royal, 149

Clarkson, Thomas, *History of the Slave Trade*, 170
Cobbett, William, 172, 186
Coleridge, Berkeley, death of, 77
Coleridge, Derwent, 102, 213, 220, 236
Coleridge, Hartley, 77, 78, 102, 156–7, 183
Coleridge, Henry Nelson, 210, 223
Coleridge, Sir John Taylor, 191, 196, 199–200, 204, 235
Coleridge, Samuel Taylor, 32, 65–6, 83, 88, 91–2, 95–6, 102, 104, 117, 118, 128, 138, 140–1, 150, 156–7, 208, 221, 235
 first meeting with Southey, 42
 meets the Fricker sisters, 46
 and the Pantisocratic scheme 43–51, 53–60;
 marriage to Sara Fricker, 60
 collaborates with Southey, 44, 45 6, 48–9 (*Fall of Robespierre*), 54–5, 57 (*Joan of Arc*), 79–80 ('Kubla Khan'), 117, 150 (*Omniana*)
 compared to Southey by Poole, 47–8
 as 'Nehemiah Higginbottom', 71
 Southey on, 69, 75–6, 79, 93 4, 119–20, 136–7
 The Friend, 136–7;
 death of, 224
 writings: 'To Simplicity', 71
 'Kubla Khan', 79–80
 'Ode Upon France', 81
 Osorio, 69, *see also Lyrical Ballads*
Coleridge, Sara (née Fricker, STC's wife), 35, 46, 53, 60, 77, 79, 88, 91, 97, 102, 145–6, 150, 156, 167, 180, 210
Coleridge, Sara (STC's daughter), 102, 180, 195, 210
Collins, Charles, 16, 19, 30, 33, 38
Cooper, 'Caliban', 13
Copeland, Thomas, 206, 241
Correspondent, 170, 181
Corry, Isaac, 89–90, 91
Corston (Somerset), 9, 10, 49
Cottle, Amos, 68; translation of *Edda*, 69
Cottle, Joseph (publisher), 52–3, 54, 60, 68, 71, 77, 84, 92, 95, 126, 156, 213, 238–9, 255–6:
 Early Recollections Chiefly Relating to the Late Samuel Taylor Coleridge, 235–6
Courier, 158, 188
Cowley, Abraham, 37, 38

Cowper, William, 15, 222, 235, *see also* Southey, Robert, *Life and Works of William Cowper*
Coxe, William, *Life of Marlborough*, 179
Critical Review, 71, 75, 83, 105
Croft, Sir Herbert, 92
Croker, John Wilson, 143–4, 155, 158, 165, 175, 196
Cromwell, Oliver, 185, 187
Cruttwell, Richard (publisher), 45
Cunningham, Allan, 205
Curry, Kenneth, 255

Dalrymple, Sir Hew, 127–8
Danvers, Charles, 76, 79, 83, 86, 110, 112, 126, 149, 159
Davies, William, 222, 230, 235, 237, 246, 247, 252
Davy, Sir Humphry, 77, 80, 81, 83, 86
de Staël, Madame, 155
Despard, Edward, 95, 103
Devon, 28, 79, 236
Devon, Lord, 236
D'Israeli, Isaac, 91, 223
Dobrizhoffer, Louis, 195
Dolignon, John, 15, 16
Dolignon, Mrs, 11, 12, 16, 21, 25
Dryden, John, 105, 121
Dublin, 89, 90, 103
Duppa, Richard, 96, 103, 108–9
Durham, 133, 138, 149, 182
Durham, bishop of, 182
Durham, University of, 220
Dutens, Louis, 135
Dyer, George, 67

Edinburgh, 44, 104, 110, 112–13, 116, 145, 174, 177
Edinburgh Annual Register, 132, 135, 136–7, 139, 140, 141, 142–3, 144, 146, 147, 149, 152–3, 156, 171, 192
Edinburgh Review, 123–4, 128, 129, 131, 132, 136, 139, 140, 144, 147, 161, 204, *see also* Jeffrey, Francis, *and* Scott, Sir Walter
Edward the Confessor, 78
Eldon, Lord, 171
Elliott, Ebenezer, 175, 194, 230
Elmsley, Peter, 16, 17, 83, 112, 113
Emmet, Robert, 103
Enfield, William, *History of Philosophy*, 38
Epictetus, 29–30, 38
Estlin, John Prior, 55

Evangelical Magazine, 181, 233
Evangelicalism, Southey's view of, 89, 106,
    108, 114, 117, 139, 170, 230–1, 238
Evans, Mary, 46, 53
Examiner, 167, 171
Exeter, 79, 104

Falmouth, 60, 62, 83, 122
Farren, Mrs (boarding house at
    Westminster), 14
Fenwick, Isabella, 231, 241
Ferdinand, King of Naples, 151
Fernando VII, 126–7, *see also* Spain
Fielding, Henry, 20
Fitzgerald, Maurice, 161
Flagellant, The (Westminster School
    magazine), 19–23, 26, 30
Flower, Benjamin, 48, 78
Flower, Thomas, 9, 10
Foot, Mr (schoolmaster), 8
Foreign Quarterly Review, 203, 205
Foreign Review and Continental Miscellany,
    205, 210
Fox, Charles James, 112, 114, 116, 185
Fox, George, 183
Fox, John, 206
France, 27, 33, 36, 37, 46, 64, 87, 89, 96,
    124, 126, 127, 136, 138, 151–2, 158,
    158–9, 240
    Southey visits, 172–3, 242, 243–4
French Revolution, 26, 27, 32, 33, 64, 66,
    81, 127, 137, 145, 151, 167, 189, 207
Frend, William, 31–2, 35, 36
Frere, John Hookham, 69, 70, 85, 223
Fricker family/sisters, 35, 36, 46, 51, 53,
    54, 102, 118, 157
Fricker, Edith, *see* Southey, Edith
Fricker, Eliza, 35, 232
Fricker, George, death of, 154
Fricker, Martha, 232
Fricker, Mary, *see* Lovell, Mary
Fricker, Sara, *see* Coleridge, Sara

George III, 89, 105, 120, 149, 167, 180,
    185
George, Prince Regent, *later* George IV,
    149, 155, 156, 167, 179, 181, 185,
    189, 209
    death of, 211
Gerrald, Joseph, 44, 51
Gibbon, Edward, 16, 30, 86, 191
Gifford, William, 82, 128–30, 132, 137,
    144, 165, 190, 193, 210, 212

poor health, 191
resigns editorship of *Quarterly Review*,
    196
see also Quarterly Review
Gilley, Sheridan, 190
Gillray, James, 74
Godwin, William, 38, 43, 48, 51, 58
Gooch, Robert, 210
Gray's Inn, 66, 67, 68, 72, 78
Gregoire, Henri, Southey reviews, 190
Grenville, Lord, 17, 114, 118, 120, 124,
    229
Greta Hall, Keswick, 91, 96, 97
    the Southeys temporarily move to,
        101–2, 108, 109–10, 115, 117,
        118
    becomes the Southeys' permanent home,
        119, 126, 136, 138, 167, 174, 210
        217, 220, 221–2, 240, 245–6, 250,
        253, 254
Grey, Charles, Earl, 211, 214, 215, 218

Hallam, Henry, *Constitutional History of
    England*, 205, 219
Hamilton, Lady Emma, 151, 152
Hamilton, Sir William, 151
Hardy, Thomas, 52
Harrogate, 190, 203, 204, 210
Hartley, David, 43
Hayes, Samuel ('Botch Hayes',
    schoolmaster), 15
Hays, Mary, 67, 81
Hazlitt, William, 102–3, 158, 167, 171,
    255
Heber, Reginald, 181
Henry V, 63
Hill, Edward, 4, 238
Hill, Herbert (Jnr.), 245, 246
Hill, Herbert (Southey's uncle), 4, 6, 13, 26,
    34
Hill, Joseph, 235
Hill, Lord, 182
Hill, Margaret, *see* Southey, Margaret
Hodson, Mrs Margaret, 220, 236
Hogg, James, 161–2
Hogg, Thomas Jefferson, 145
Holcroft, Thomas, 51
Holland House, 155, 159
Holland, Lord, 138
Holmes, Richard, 152
Homer, 233
Hone, William, 212
Hoole, John, *Jerusalem Delivered*, 12

Horne Tooke, John, 52, 115
Howe, Thomas, 30
Hucks, Joseph, 42, 44
Hughes, Mrs Anne Watts, 211, 224
Hume, David, 30, 191
Hunt, John Henry ('Orator'), 172, 178–9
Hunt, Leigh, *Foliage*, 183
Huntington, Reverend William, 183
Hutchinson, Sara, 203, 210, 221, 223

Imlay, Gilbert, 48
Inchbald, Elizabeth, 91
Iris, 96, 103
Italy, 88, 151, 169, 173, 184

Jackson, Cyril, 26
Jackson, Dr, 246
Jackson, William, 102, 110, 118, 136, 138
James II, 8, 209
Jardine, Alexander, 62
Jeffrey, Francis, 92–5, 112, 113, 123, 147, 161, 162, *see also Edinburgh Review*
Jesus College, Cambridge, 49
Johnson, Joseph (publisher), 49
Jones, Captain William, 243, 244
Jones, John, *Attempts in Verse*, 210–11
Junot, Marshal, 127, 128

Keats, John, 175
Keepsake, 205
Kenyon, John, 182, 202, 241, 242, 244
Kenyon, Lord, 235
Klopstock, Friedrich Gottlieb, 73
Knighton, Sir William, 191
Koster, Henry, 144, 163, 170
Koster, John Theodor, 86

Lamb, Charles, 68, 71, 81, 107, 143, 183, 193, 222, 255
Lamb, Thomas Davis, 16, 17, 22, 25, 27
Lamb, Thomas Philips, 16, 24, 25, 26, 27, 31
Lancaster, Joseph, 144
Lancet, 193
Landor, Walter Savage, 126, 130, 140, 144, 159, 161, 173, 235, 253
memorial poem to Southey ('In maintaining the institutions of his Country') 256
Gebir, 80, 84, 126
Lardner, Dionysius, 225
Lawrence, Sir Thomas, 91
Leavis, F. R., 25

Lewis, Matthew ('Monk Lewis'), 17
Lewis, Reverend Mr (tutor), 13–14
Liberal, 188, 190
Lightfoot, Nicholas, 28, 39, 50, 76, 115, 190, 213, 236
Lisbon, 58, 62, 64–5, 83, 84, 85, 86, 87, 115, 117, *see also* Portugal
Literary Gazette, 181, 191
Littleton, Sir Edward, 124, 126, 141, 149, 150
Liverpool, 88, 144, 148, 235
Liverpool, Lord, 149, 155, 168, 182, 203
Lloyd, Charles, 66, 68, 69, 71
Locker, Edward Hawke, 163
Lockhart, John Gibson, 199–200, 203, 204, 223, 230
London Magazine, 193
London, 48, 76, 140, 163, 168, 186, 195, 197, 213, 224, 240
Southey's dislike of, 30
Southey visits, 14, 53–4, 65–8, 78, 90–1, 96, 107–8, 115–16, 124–5, 143–4, 153–6, 164–5, 172, 182–3, 193–4, 206, 211–12, 214, 231, 236, 241, 243, 245, 247
Longman (publisher), 84, 107, 117, 121, 132, 181, 183, 210, 220, 221, 237
Lonsdale, Lord, 128, 134–5, 137, 174, 209, 216, 219
Losh, James, 66, 72, 133, 159, 164
Louis XIV, 159
Louis XVI, 23, 27
Lovell, Mary (née Fricker), 90, 102, 180, 210, 232, 240, 245, 253, 254
Lovell, Robert, 36
Poems 44, 49, 51, 52–3
The Fall of Robespierre, 45–6
death of, 65
Lowther Castle, 135, 137, 186, 209, 219
Lowther, Henry Cecil, 174
Lowther, William, 174
Lyrical Ballads, 60, 84, 88, 93
Southey's review of, 75–6, 79, 105, 110

Madrid, 62, 63, 126–7
Mahon, Lord, (Philip Henry Stanhope), 215, 219, 220
Malet, Arthur, 197–8
Malory's *Le Morte D'Arthur*, 18
Malthus, Thomas, *Essay on the Principle of Population*, 104–5, 150
Margarot, Maurice, 44
Marten, Henry, 70

Martin Hall, Westbury on Trim, 74
May, John, 4, 6, 14, 24, 83, 96, 136, 156,
        183, 190, 249, 255–6
Medwin, Thomas, 188
Methodism, 140, 197
    Southey on, 89, 95, 106, 120, 148,
        169–70, see also Southey, Robert,
        Life of Wesley
Microcosm, The (Eton magazine), 19
Mill, John Stuart, 212
Miller, Reverend, 31
Milton, John, 12, 70, 86, 121
Montagu, Basil, 157
Monthly Magazine, 71, 181
Monthly Review, 64, 92, 105, 112, 137
Moore, Sir John, 128, 191–2
Moore, Thomas, Epistles, Odes and Other
        Poems, 117, 186
More, Hannah, 89, 114
More, Sir Thomas, 173, 207
Morgan, John, 156
Morning Chronicle, 49, 158, 171, 196
Morning Post, 71, 73, 76, 77, 78, 80, 83,
        103
Muir, Thomas, 44
Murray, John (publisher), 137, 144, 147–8,
        151, 152, 153, 157–8, 183, 187, 188,
        192, 197, 207, 210
    Southey's disaffection with, 219–20, see
        also Quarterly Review
Myles, William, A Chronological History of
        the People called Methodists, 106

Napier, Sir William, 191–2
Naples, 151
Nash, Edward, 163, 172, 182, 183, 186
Necker, Jacques, On the French Revolution,
        66
Nelson, Horatio, Lord, 114, 137, 142,
        151–2, 175, see also Southey, Robert
        Life of Nelson
Nether Stowey, 47, 48, 69, 78, 79, 236
Netherlands, 244
    Southey visits, 197–8, 201
Newberry, Francis (publisher), 7, 11
Newton, Mrs (Chatterton's sister), 68
Nicol, William, 45, 221
Norwich, 73–4, 96, 104, 115
Nugent, Lord, 219

Observer (Bristol), 56
Opie, Mrs Amelia, 209

Owen, Robert, 178
Oxford, 6, 19, 31–6, 40, 42–5, 49, 107,
        115, 134, 145–6, 157, 181, 183, 225,
        237, 240, 241, 244
    Balliol College, 24, 26–31, 38, 39, 42,
        44, 52, 182
    Christ Church, 13, 16, 22, 24, 25, 26,
        28, 30, 38, 182, 211, 238

Paine, Thomas, 23, 27, 55
Palmer, Miss, 7, 10
Palmer, Thomas Fyshe, 44
Pantisocracy, 23, 38, 41, 43–54, 56–59, 79,
        111, 171, 172, 178
Paris, 27, 64, 158, 162, 172, 244, 254
Pasley, Colonel Charles, 144, 172
Peachy, Colonel William, 150, 169, 175
Peacock, Thomas Love, satirises Southey in
        Melincourt, 170–1
Peel, Sir Robert, 204, 206, 208, 211–13,
        218, 229, 232
Pemberton, Miss Sophia, 69
Perceval, Spencer, 139, 143, 147 185, 189
    assassination of, 148–9
Percy, Lord, 120
Peterloo massacre, 178–9
Picart, Bernard, Religious Ceremonies, 16–17
Pitt, William, 'the Younger', 29, 33, 78, 89,
        94–5, 111–12
    death of, 114, 116, 122, 138, 155, 170,
        185
Poole, Thomas, 47–8, 236
Pope, Alexander, 105, 121
Portland, duke of, 33–4, 139
Portugal, 6, 26, 59, 71, 82, 89, 90, 96,
        101, 110, 113, 114, 118, 119, 124,
        127, 130, 192, 216, 256
    Southey's trips to Portugal, 60, 62–5,
        (with Edith) 83–7, see also Lisbon,
        and Southey, Robert, History of
        Portugal
Powell, Madam, 4
Priestley, Joseph, 32, 48, 95
Provincial Magazine, 54
Pye, Henry James, 154, 155

Quarterly Review, 128, 129, 131–2, 140,
        144, 164–5, 167, 170, 171–2 173–4,
        175–6, 177, 179–80, 183, 187, 193,
        194, 195, 196, 199–200, 203,
        204–5, 212, 216, 219, 223, 230, see
        also Gifford, William, and Murray,
        John

Quillinan, Edward, 206, 253
'Funeral of Robert Southey', 254

Radnor, Lord, 201
Rickman, John, 68, 84, 89, 96, 104, 109,
    110, 124, 131–2, 138, 139, 158,
    163–4, 177, 182, 201, 214, 216,
    256
  collaboration with Southey, 219–20,
    221
Rickman, Mrs, 211
Ridgeway, James (publisher), 51, 171
Roberts, Augusta, 36
Roberts, William Hayward, *Judah Restored*,
    12
Robertson, William, 191
Robespierre, Maximilien, 37, 45–6, 64, *see
    also* Southey, Robert, *The Fall of
    Robespierre*
Robin Hood, 18, 175, 194, 206
Robinson, Henry Crabb, 66, 125, 139, 143,
    155, 168, 182, 192, 206, 222, 242,
    244, 251–2
Rousseau, Jean-Jacques, 16, 29, 30, 38
Rowe, Elizabeth, *Letters Moral and
    Entertaining*, 12

Sadler, Michael Thomas, 209, 221
Sayers, Frank, 54
Scarborough, 231, 232
Scott, Sir Walter, 12, 112, 115, 131–2, 134,
    140, 143, 153, 155, 159, 199–200,
    204, *see also Edinburgh Review*
Sealy, Mary, 133
Senhouse, Humphrey, 171, 172, 211, 243,
    244
Seton, Miss, 86
Seward, Anna, 29, 124–5, 128
Seward, Edmund, 28–30, 31, 32–3, 36, 45,
    50
  death of, 58
Shakespeare, William, 8, 121
Shelley, Percy Bysshe, 145–6, 147, 173,
    183–4, 186, 187, 241
  Revolt of Islam, 183
  Swellfoot the Tyrant, 184
Shenstone, William, 25
Sidney, Algernon, 185
Simmons, Jack, 255
Sintra, 65, 79, 84, 85, 87, 88, 127–8, 134,
    see also Cintra
Skiddaw, 95, 101, 102, 162, 163, 188
Smedley, Edward, 15

Smith, Adam, 47, 87, 151, 169, 178
Smith, Charlotte, 91
Smith, Mrs Mary Slade (Mary Barker),
    213–4
Smith, William, 171, 172
Somerville, Lord, 180, 255
Southampton, 67, 244, 247
Southcott, Joanna, 108, 199
Southey, Bertha (daughter), 133, 138, 143,
    198, 212, 218, 231, 233, 238, 240,
    242, 245–6, 252, 253
Southey, Caroline (Southey's second wife),
    see Bowles, Caroline
Southey, Charles Cuthbert (son), 176–7,
    194, 202, 220, 222, 223, 225, 231,
    232, 233, 237–8, 240, 241, 242,
    244–6, 249, 252, 253
  tours West Country with his father, 234,
    235–6
  *Life and Correspondence of the late Robert
    Southey*, 236, 254–5
Southey, Edith (née Fricker, Southey's first
    wife), 35–6, 42, 50, 53, 54, 62–3, 65,
    67, 68, 69, 71–2, 78, 79, 80, 88, 90,
    91, 92, 96, 97, 101, 102, 107,
    112–13, 114, 115, 116, 118, 124,
    130, 131, 143, 144, 145–6, 152, 155,
    157, 163, 175, 176, 183, 194, 199,
    240, 242, 243, 251
  Southey proposes to, 40
  marriage to Southey, 60–1
  Southey's verse letter to, 74
  visits Portugal with Southey, 83–7
  decline in health, 201, 202, 203, 206,
    210, 213, 217, 224–5, 229, 230–3,
    234, 235, 236, 237
  death of, 238–9, *see also* Fricker
    family/sisters
Southey, Edith May (daughter), 107, 113,
    130, 143, 163, 190, 194, 211, 217,
    222, 224, 236, 245, 253
Southey, Edward (brother), 103–4, 110,
    156, 202, 234
Southey, Eliza (sister), 5
Southey, Emma (daughter), 124, 130
  death of, 133
Southey, Henry (brother), 5, 86, 88, 104,
    110, 113, 114, 116, 124, 133, 138,
    149, 163, 182, 183, 186, 190, 191,
    192, 198, 211, 217, 219, 221, 224,
    234, 243
  attends Southey in final illness, 248–50,
    251–2

Southey, Herbert (son), 98, 114, 118, 130, 133, 143, 150, 163, 175, 223
  death of, 166–7, 168, 172
Southey, Isabel (daughter), 149
  death of, 202, 206
Southey, John Cannon (brother), 4
Southey, John Cannon (uncle), 28, 40, 112, 180
Southey, Katherine ('Kate', daughter), 138, 233, 234, 238, 240, 241, 242, 245, 249, 250, 252–3, 254
Southey, Louisa (sister), 5
Southey, Margaret (née Hill, Southey's mother), 3, 4, 9, 12, 34, 49, 69, 71, 98
  death of, 90–1
Southey, Margaret ('Peggy', cousin), 74, 90
Southey, Margaret (daughter), 92
  illness and death of, 96–7, 98, 102
Southey, Margaretta (sister), 5, 19
Southey, Mary (aunt), 183, 213, 236
Southey, Robert (father), 3–4, 5, 7, 8, 9, 10, 11, 12, 14
  bankruptcy and death, 27–8, 104
Southey, Robert, expulsion from Westminster School, 21–3
  considers a medical career, 39
  first meeting with Coleridge, 42
  gives series of public lectures, 55–6
  his legal studies, 59, 65–9, 78, 81
  first meeting with Wordsworth, 59–60
  marries Edith Fricker, 60
  trips to Portugal, 60, 62–5, (with Edith) 83–7
  financial problems, 71, 78, 83, 121, 167, 193, 203
  first encounter with Mary Barker, 85
  works in Dublin, 89–90
  death of his mother, 90
  moves to Keswick, 101
  beginning of friendship with Wordsworth, 111
  compared to Wordsworth and Coleridge, 93–4, 111, 159
  stewardship of Derwentwater estates, 134–5
  first encounter with Shelley, 145–6
  offered laureatship 155
  appointed member of the Royal Spanish Academy, 161
  awarded honorary degree at Oxford, 181–2
  first meeting with Caroline Bowles, 182
  financial independence, 229–30
  death of Edith, 238–9
  final trip to France, 243–4
  marries Caroline Bowles, 248
  illness, 76–7, 80–1, 92, 127, 131, 206, 241
  descent into senility, 243–50
  death, 253
  writings: *All for Love or the sinner well saved*, 205
Amadis of Gaul, 92
'The Battle of Blenheim', 74, 164, 180
Bibliotheca Britannica, 96
The Book of the Church, 16, 147–8, 183, 189, 190, 192, 193, 198, 201
  reviewed, 195–7
'Botany Bay Eclogues', 39, 44, 48–9
Carmen Triumphale, 158
'The Cataract of Lodore', 189
  The Chronicle of the Cid, 116, 127, 132
'To a College Cat', 33, 34
'Consolation', 165–6
The Curse of Kehama, 13, 17, 92, 116, 126, 130–1, 143, 195, 256
  reviewed, 140
'The Destruction of Dom Daniel', *see Thalaba*
'The Devil's Thoughts'/'The Devil's Walk', 79
The Doctor, 25, 112, 127, 154, 157, 194, 211, 216, 221, 222–3, 237
'Elinor', 40, 49
Essays Moral and Political, 210
'To the Exiled Patriots', 44
The Fall of Robespierre, 44, 45–6, 48
'God's Judgement on a Bishop', 80
Harold, or the Castle of Morford, 18–19
'History', 73
History of Brazil, 86, 118, 126, 130, 138, 167, 173, 177, 187
History of the Monastic Orders, 177, 210, 232, 246
History of the Peninsular War, 153, 158, 165, 187, 189, 190, 194, 205, 210, 216
  reviewed, 191–2

History of Portugal, 81, 84, 86, 87, 91, 96, 106, 110, 116, 117, 149, 190, 232, 246
'To Horror', 17–18
'Hymn to the Penates', 9
'Inscription for . . . Henry Marten, the regicide . . .', 70
'Inscriptions for the Caledonian Canal', 177–8
Joan of Arc, 36–7, 44, 45, 46, 52, 54, 59, 60, 63–4, 69, 71, 72–3, 80, 84, 111, 167, 237, 244
  reviewed and attacked by the *Anti-Jacobin Review and Magazine*, 74–5
'A Lamentation', 103
The Lay of the Laureate, 167
Letter to William Smith, 172
Letters from England by Don Manuel Alvarez Espriella, 108–9, 112, 116, 121–3
Letters written during a short residence in Spain and Portugal, 62, 65, 127
Life of the Reverend Andrew Bell, 221–2, 230, 237, 246
Life of John Bunyan, 210
Life and Works of William Cowper, 230, 233
Life of Nelson, 137, 142, 144, 149, 151–2, 233
'Life of Wellington', 164–5
Life of Wesley, 169–70, 173, 179, 180–1, 182, 183, 232, 233, 234
'Lines upon Christmas Day 1795', 62
Lives of the British Admirals, 210, 220, 221, 225, 237, 242
Madoc, 17, 53, 57, 66, 69, 74, 76, 79, 84, 88, 90, 104, 106–7, 108, 109, 111, 115, 123, 126, 132, 137, 195
  reviewed, 112
'Marriage' poems, 247–8
'Mary the Maid of the Inn', 76
Metrical Tales, 109
Sir Thomas More: or, Colloquies on the Progress and Prospects of Society, 173, 183, 190, 194, 205, 207, 208, 209, 216, 219, 221
'Ode on the portrait of Bishop Heber', 181
'The old man's comforts and how he procured them', 76–7

'The Old Woman of Berkeley', 83
Oliver Newman, 175, 183, 187, 195
Omniana, 117, 150
'On the Means of Improving the People', 174
Palmerin of England, 116, 121
'Pelayo, the Restorer of Spain', *see* *Roderick, The Last of the Goths*
Poems, 52, 69, 74, 77
'The Poet's Pilgrimage to Waterloo', 164, 165
The Remains of Henry Kirke White, 117, 121
'The Retrospect', 9, 28, 49–50
Robin Hood: A Fragment, 252
Roderick, The Last of the Goths, 126, 150, 159–62, 195, 198, 256
'The Soldier's Wife', 54
  parodied, 70–1
'Sonnet for a friend', 15
Specimens of the later English poets, 107, 116, 120–1, 124
A Tale of Paraguay, 173, 194–5
Thalaba the Destroyer, 17, 79. 80, 83, 84–5, 86, 95, 111, 123, 126, 143, 195, 256
  reviewed, 92–4
'The Triumph of Woman', 66
'The Widow', parodied, 69–70
Vindiciae Ecclesiae Anglicanae, 197, 199, 200
A Vision of Judgement, 117, 174, 180, 182, 185–6, 187–8
'The Vision of the Maid of Orleans', 72
Wat Tyler, 44, 51–2, 171, 172
Southey, Thomas ('Tom', brother), 11, 45, 69, 83, 84, 85, 92, 96, 104, 107, 109, 110, 116, 125, 126, 143, 149, 151, 183, 192–3, 220, 234, 238
  death of, 241
  Chronological History of the West Indies, 195
Southey, Thomas (uncle), 3, 5, 10, 12, 112
Spain, 62, 63, 87, 126–7, 129, 132, 138, 144, 145, 158, 159, 192, 216, 234
Sparrow, Robert, 14–15
Spectator, 11
Spedding, John, 146–7
Spenser, Edmund, 12, 18, 25, 27, 121
Sterne, Laurence, *Tristram Shandy*, 25, 223

Strachey, George, 15, 19, 20
Stuart, Daniel, 71, 73
Susquehanna River, 46, 48
Swain, Charles, 218, 224, 241
Switzerland, 173, 187

Tasso, Torquato, *Gerusalemme Liberata*, 12
Taunton, 213, 236, 241
Taylor, Henry, 73, 197, 198, 201, 202, 212, 221, 232, 233, 237, 242, 249
Taylor, William, 73, 76, 77, 88, 95, 96, 97, 103, 115, 124, 141
Telford, Thomas, 177, 229
Thackeray, William Makepeace, 255
Thelwall, John, 52, 66, 103
Ticknor, George, 127, 195
Tintern Abbey, 56, 57, 75, 105
Town and Country Magazine, 12
Trifler, The (Westminster School magazine), 19–20
Turner, Sharon, 96, 124, 180
Tyler, Elizabeth (aunt), 4, 5–8, 10, 11, 12, 13, 14, 16, 28, 34, 104
   cuts Southey out of her life, 50, 58
Tyler, John, 4
Tyler, William (uncle), 12–13

Universal Review, 195

Victoria, Queen, 223
Vincent, Dr William, 20–2, 26, 233
Voltaire, 16, 30

Wakefield, Gilbert, 78
Wales, 42, 46
   Pantisocratic commune in, 53–4, 57
   Southey visits, 44–5, 76, 88–9, 92, 144, 181–2
   and 'Madoc', 107, 111
Walpole, Horace, 124
Warter, John Wood, 211, 213, 222, 223, 224, 235, 237, 238, 253
   Selections from the Letters of Robert Southey, 255
Waterhouse, Samuel, 86, 87
Waterloo, 162
   Southey visits battlefield of, 163–4
Watson, Richard, *Chemical Essays*, 25
Watts, Isaac, 25
Weeks, Shadrach, 14, 51

Wellesley, Lord, 149
Wellington, Sir Arthur Wellesley, duke of, 120, 127–8, 158, 204, 206, 211, 212–13, 218
   Southey on, 163, 164–5, 175, 208
Wesley, John, *see* Methodism; *and* Southey, Robert, *Life of Wesley*
Westall, William, *View of the Lakes*, 183
Westminster Abbey, 21, 184
Westminster School, 8, 13, 14–17, 19, 20, 25, 30, 53, 106, 146, 210, 233, 255
   Southey's expulsion from, 21–3, 24, *see also The Flagellant*
Whitbread, Samuel, 138, 139
White, Henry Kirke, 105, 117, 175, *see also* Southey, Robert, *Remains of Henry Kirke White*
White, Reverend James, 222
White, Neville, 182, 183, 197, 198
Wilberforce, William, 117, 170, 175
Wilkes, John, 185
William IV, 211, 218
Williams, William, 10–11, 13, 71
Wilson, Mrs, 118, 136, 143, 180
Winterbottom, William, 171
Wollstonecraft, Mary, 48, 63, 66–7, 85, 187
Women, Southey's attitude towards, 62–3, 67, 85, 190
Woof, Robert, 255
Worcester, 31
Wordsworth, Caroline (WW's daughter by Annette Vallon), 172
Wordsworth, Dorothy, 71, 110, 111
Wordsworth family, 218, 221
Wordsworth, John, 110
Wordsworth, William, 59–60, 71, 88, 104, 105, 115, 126, 128, 140, 143, 155, 163, 174–5, 187, 203, 211, 216–17, 222, 234, 237, 241, 251, 253
   beginning of friendship with Southey, 110–11
   compared to Southey, 93–4, 111, 159
   writings: *The Borderers*, 69
   Excursion, 162
   Inscription for St Herbert's Island, 176
   Poems in two volumes, 123
   'Ye vales and hills, whose beauty hither drew', 254, *see also Lyrical Ballads*
Wraxall, Mrs, 12

Wynn, Charles Watkin Williams, 16, 17,
    30, 33, 40, 78, 111, 114, 120, 144,
    171, 176, 181, 192–3, 200, 215, 255
  and *The Flagellant*, 19–20
  and financial support of Southey, 57, 68,
    83, 121
  tries to help Southey gain employment,
    87–9, 115, 118, 119
  godfather to Cuthbert, 175
  Southey's last letter to, 250

York, 145, 225, 229, 230, 231, 232
York, Duke of, 129, 139, 143
Yorkshire, 210

Zouch, Thomas, *Memoirs of Sir Philip
    Sidney*, 133